Ehud Ben Zvi
A Historical-Critical Study
of the Book of Zephaniah

Beihefte zur Zeitschrift für die alttestamentliche Wissenschaft

Herausgegeben von
Otto Kaiser

Band 198

Walter de Gruyter · Berlin · New York
1991

Ehud Ben Zvi

A Historical-Critical Study
of the Book of Zephaniah

Walter de Gruyter · Berlin · New York
1991

∞ Printed on acid-free paper which falls
within the guidelines of the ANSI to ensure
permanence and durability.

Library of Congress Cataloging-in-Publication Data

Ben Zvi, Ehud, 1951—
    A historical-critical study of the book of Zephaniah / Ehud
Ben Zvi.
        p.   cm. — (Beihefte zur Zeitschrift für die alttestament-
    liche Wissenschaft ; 198)
        Revision of the author's thesis (Ph. D.) — Emory Univer-
    sity, 1990.
        Includes bibliographical references.
        ISBN 0-89925-814-X (alk. paper)
        1. Bible.   O. T.   Zephaniah — Commentaries,   I. Title,
    II. Series.
    BS410.Z5 vol. 198
    [BS1645.3]
    221.6 s—dc20
    [224'.9607]
                                                    91-24722
                                                    CIP

Die Deutsche Bibliothek — Cataloging in Publication Data

Ben Zvi, Ehud:
A historical-critical study of the book of Zephaniah / Ehud Ben
Zvi. — Berlin ; New York : de Gruyter, 1991
    (Beihefte zur Zeitschrift für die alttestamentliche Wissenschaft ;
    Bd. 198)
    Zugl.: Atlanta, Univ., Diss., 1990
    ISBN 3-11-012837-3
NE: Zeitschrift für die alttestamentliche Wissenschaft / Beihefte

ISSN: 0934-2575

Printed in Germany
Printing: Werner Hildebrand, Berlin 65
Binding: Lüderitz und Bauer, Berlin 61

To my wife, Perla Mónica

Acknowledgments

This work is a revised version of a Ph.D. dissertation completed at Emory University in 1990. I wish to express my gratitude to the staff and the students of the Department of Old Testament at Emory University for their individual and collective contributions to the existence of the intellectually challenging and emotionally supportive environment that nurtured my mind—and my soul—during my years in the graduate program.

I owe a special debt to a friend who has always been present when needed; a friend whose sound advice has been a constant assistance for reaching informed decisions, both on academic and other issues; to my teacher and advisor, Prof. Gene M. Tucker. I am also especially grateful to Prof. John H. Hayes for his continuous encouragement, for his friendship, and for the innumerable stimulating conversations that we have had in these years, almost any time I walked in his office. My thanks are also due to Prof. Martin J. Buss for his detailed and helpful comments at every stage of my writing, to Prof. J. Maxwell Miller and Prof. Hava T. Rotschild for their thoughtful comments on the penultimate form of this book, and to Prof. Carol Newsom, Prof. Hendrikus Boers and Prof. Vernon K. Robbins for their assistance on specific issues.

I wish to express my appreciation to Prof. Dr. Otto Kaiser for accepting this work for publication in *BZAW*, and above all, for his contribution to the study of the Latter Prophets. His work has influenced mine on many aspects, and for that I am very thankful.

Finally, an honest statement of acknowledgments must reflect the background against which the study was prepared. My children, Amos, Naamah and Micha, have had a very important role in shaping this background. They deserve special thanks for their patience and supportive understanding. The central figure of this background is certainly my wife and best friend, Perla Mónica. Without her loving support and her sacrifices, this work would have never been written. This book is dedicated to her.

Edmonton, Alberta, winter 1991   Ehud Ben Zvi

Contents

1. Introduction

1.1 General Issues

1.1.1. Concerning the Historical-Critical Methods in Biblical Studies

In the introduction to his recent book on Zephaniah, House wrote:

> Thus, one must build on historical studies and move on to other problems instead of dealing continually with old questions. If historical criticism is no longer used, then some new method of approaching Zephaniah must be sought. In recent years many scholars have turned to various forms of literary criticism to explicate the Old Testament.[1]

House rightly points to a growing tendency in modern biblical research. The distinctive character of this tendency is better expressed by the protasis of his second sentence than by its apodosis. The relevance of various forms of literary criticism for the understanding of the biblical texts is self-evident. The moot point is whether the historical-critical methods should be "no longer used."

In general terms, one may discern two different claims against reliance on historical-critical methods. The first claim is that historical (including socio-historical) knowledge is unnecessary for the understanding of biblical texts and therefore historical-critical methods are useless. The

---

[1] House: 14-15.

second claim is that the *methods* are *unreliable*, that they lead to equivocal conclusions, and that they are dependent on the subjectivity of the scholar.

The implications of the first claim are far-reaching. Words, sentences, described attitudes, and literary works have their meaning because they represent the value given to a certain variable in a certain systemic universe of meaning. For example, the superscription in Zeph 1:1:

> The 'word' of YHWH that came to Zephaniah . . . in the
> days of Josiah son of Amon, king of Judah.

is meaningful because in the universe of the author: (a) the word of YHWH could come to human beings, in the days of Josiah, and (b) not every Judean living in those days received the word of YHWH. Had the word of YHWH been a universal phenomenon or, alternatively, an unthinkable possibility, this superscription would be meaningless and therefore never written. Only the existence of different potential values for a specific variable makes it possible to convey meaning by assigning values to such a variable. In other words, in a world where all its creatures are sitting forever, and none have even thought about any alternative situation, there is no meaning to a sentence like: "we are sitting." But in our world, "we are sitting" may stand against "we are standing/ walking/ running" and the like, or against "we had been sitting" and the like, or both, and consequently "we are sitting" may be meaningful. How do we discriminate—as we all do—among all these possible meanings? Clearly, because our understanding of any specific "we are sitting" is dependent on our conscious or unconscious presupposition concerning the *probable* alternatives to "we are sitting," among all of the theoretically possible alternatives. Therefore, only the *difference between any specific "we are sitting" to its possible alternatives conveys meaning*. This conclusion leads to a central question concerning our competence to understand messages: How do we discern the possible alternatives to particular expressions?

We discern such alternatives because we envisage the general universe in which the act or message takes place. We can read and understand the biblical books because we build a mental image of the universe in relation to which every saying, story, figure and the like, in the book can be understood.

The text itself sometimes provides considerable help for building this necessary mental image. For instance, according to Gen 38:14-15, Judah thought that Tamar was a harlot because she covered her face with a veil. But obviously this was not Rebekah's intention when she covered her face with a veil before meeting Isaac (Gen 24:64-65). Clearly, the text in Genesis 24 does not allow such a reading. In a similar way, no reader will fail to understand that אָסֵף אֹסֵף in Zeph 1:2 means quite the opposite of אֲסֹף אָסֹף in Mic 2:12.[2] However, in most cases, the text by itself does not provide all the elements necessary to build our image of the universe that stands in the background of the text. For instance, it is the contention of the author of Zeph 1:1 that the 'Word of YHWH' came to Zephaniah at a certain historical time, in the days of Josiah. Either consciously or unconsciously, any reader of the text develops an image of the days of Josiah and sets it as a background against which the text is read. How does a reader develop a certain image of Josiah's days without using the historical-critical method? Plastic arts provide a clear answer: biblical figures have been pictured as Romans, Medievals (Christians or Jews), Bedouins, etc. A particular reader's present understanding of reality tends to fill the gaps of actual knowledge of the past. The well known descriptions of the prophets as philosophers, social revolutionaries, pious Jews keeping all the commands of the rabbinic halakah, romantic poets, etc., also reflect the same tendency.

---

[2] אָסֵף אֹסֵף (Zeph 1:2) occurs in an announcement of judgment and means "I will sweep away (everything)." אֲסֹף אָסֹף (Mic 2:12) occurs in an announcement of salvation and means "I will gather (Jacob, all of you)."

The result is: a *reader-centered* understanding of the biblical texts, constrained only by certain clear contextual demands of the texts and only insofar as the text is understood in its "literal sense."[3] This type of reading has been attested for more than two millennia in communities based on or influenced by biblical traditions. This does not mean, however, that such reading has no perils. The main interpretative key in a reader-centered understanding is the reader, either the "I" or the communal "we." In either case it is a self-centered reading. The text turns out to be "near" and intelligible, but the price is that religious and cultural ideas, social, political and religious institutions and movements, and of course prophecy and prophets, are deprived of their original background and meaning in order to fit *one standard: "mine" or "ours."*

During most of the last two millennia there was either a relatively limited awareness of the distance between the reader's society and the biblical societies or an acceptance of the surface (and sometimes polemical) claims of the biblical texts that blurred the actual situation faced by the author and his or her community or both. Consequently, there was only a relatively limited awareness that the given 'literal' interpretation implies a refusal to deal with the message developed in the biblical societies in their own terms. The situation today is completely different. The refusal to consider the world of biblical societies in their own terms, in so far as possible, and the conscious decision to understand *their* world *only* in self-centered terms, either personal or communal, clearly does not result from ignorance of the differences between the reader's world and the biblical worlds, but from the decision to obliterate these differences. This decision thus negates the relevancy of any human culture that differs from the culture of the reader.

---

3 As is well known, the literal interpretation was only one of the "levels" of interpretation in classical biblical interpretation, either Jewish or Christian.

The historical-critical understanding of the biblical text intends to provide a necessary balance to the unilateral aspects of any self-centered approach. It is aimed at sharpening the awareness that the biblical texts were written in societies that are strange to us, the modern readers. Its goal is to provide the basic elements for the understanding of the social and conceptual background against which the different biblical texts were written.

The second claim against the use of historical-critical methods (i.e., that the *methods* are *unreliable*) acknowledges the importance of the goals of these methods but claims that they lead to equivocal conclusions, and that they are dependent on the subjectivity of the scholar.

To be sure, scholars guided by similar critical-historical methods have reached no unanimity on a vast range of critical questions. Moreover, any glimpse of the history of biblical research shows that even when scholarly consensus is finally reached it does not hold for more than one generation or two. Furthermore, there is no doubt that the subjectivity of the scholar has an important role in his or her research.

Granted that all the above is true, the main question concerns the meaning of these facts. Critical methods are not supposed to provide an ultimate truth in the natural sciences, in the humanities, or anywhere. They can only provide hypotheses that could be, but have not yet been falsified. These hypotheses are never eternal truths but only falsifiable hypotheses whose acceptance is always provisional.

Moreover, in addition to the limitations inherent in any critical method, the critical historian must cope with a situation in which he or she can never devise experiments in order to falsify alternative interpretations of a certain set of historical data. Instead, he or she must test the degree of correspondence between a certain historical hypothesis (interpretation) and the known data without recurring to *ad hoc* reinterpretation of the data (circular thinking). If the main elements of the hypothesis or its logical inferences do not correspond with the known data (unless *ad hoc* interpretations are introduced), then the critical historian should reject the hypothesis.

The historical-critical method in biblical studies can be schematized as follows: (a) the relevant biblical data is to be inferred from the text according to several procedures (textual and linguistic analysis, considerations about the existence of a composite unit, identification of different units, determination of genre, etc.); (b) the data are classified and compared with other sets of biblical data established by similar methods; (c) a working hypothesis is developed on the basis of such comparisons; the working hypothesis must be potentially falsifiable; and (d) if the working hypothesis is not falsified by biblical or extra-biblical data (e.g., historical data, archaeological data, etc.) and if it does not lead by logical deduction to inferences that are falsified by some existent data, then the working hypothesis is not to be rejected. In other words, it is confirmed so long as the conditions expressed in the protasis of point (d) remain unchanged. Sociological or anthropological models may be used in biblical studies for heuristic purposes. They are introduced in stage (c) of the present schema as a working hypothesis to be tested against the available data. Obviously, for practical reasons related to the nature of biblical research, a hypothesis is considered not-falsified by the data if there is a relatively high degree of probability for the correspondence between the hypothesis and the data; total certainty, which is impossible to achieve, is not required for such purpose.

Does this method eliminate the influence of the subjectivity of the scholar in his or her research? By no means. The kind of questions that a certain scholar asks the text and to a certain extent the kind of models that he or she is inclined to test against the available data are likely to be related to his or her personality, his or her conceptual world, and his or her experiences and needs. Thus, it is likely that a feminist, a marxist, a conservative capitalist, or a liberal, would ask different questions. This subjectivity provides the multiplicity of points view that is necessary for a better understanding of biblical societies and their religio-cultural works. Obviously, this subjectivity does not mean that all the imaginable hypotheses have the same validity, but that any personal point of view is a legitimate starting point for the development of an hypothesis that (a) should be potentially falsifiable, and (b) that should be tested according to a set of known criteria (i.e., correspondence with data, without positing *ad hoc* explanations). The results of such testing should be considered compelling.

To be sure, there are cases in biblical studies (but obviously not only in biblical studies) in which two alternative theories have not been falsified. In such cases, subjectivity has a role in the crystallization of personal preferences but the method compels both sides to accept that the other holds also a possible answer.

Finally, it is worth stressing that biblical scholars, as any other persons who work on research, are human beings and tend to err, individually and sometimes collectively. In such cases, the fact that the criteria of the historical-critical method are publicly known provides the best and probably only warrant that erroneous hypothesis eventually would be rejected.

The longing for "solid" truth from historical-critical methods in biblical studies may be understandable in psychological terms, but historical-critical methods (or any critical method) cannot satiate that longing. The historical-critical methods in biblical studies at their best may provide only probable (i.e., not yet falsified) hypotheses concerning biblical societies, their literature, and their religious thought. The alternative to the historical-critical methods is either a plethora of hypotheses without any publicly-known and critical criteria on which to assign validity, or a self-centered reading of the text, in which there is one standard: the conceptual world of the reader, be it individual or communal.

1.1.2. Concerning the Study of the Prophets and Prophecy

About a hundred years ago there was a widespread consensus that the prophets were religious geniuses.[4] The Hebrew prophets were the great "theologians" who developed the idea of "ethical monotheism" (e.g., Wellhausen, Duhm). During the first decades of the present century there was a clear tendency to consider the prophets as poets and to emphasize the psychological aspects of the prophetic experience (e.g., Gunkel, Höschler). Scholars who stressed the role of cult or kingship or both tended to attach the figure of the prophet to cultic institutions or to the monarchy (e.g., Mowinckel, Johnson, Cross), whereas others emphasized the "covenantal" function of the prophets (e.g., Kraus), or their roots in wisdom (e.g., Terrien). On the basis of sociological or anthropological models, the prophets have been considered "charismatic" figures (Weber), or "mediators." In recent years socio-anthropological methods have been used in order to define the social loci of the prophets and their roles in society (e.g., Wilson, Petersen), or the feedback mechanisms involved in the performance of the prophetic role (e.g., Overholt).

Although clearly different and in many aspects contradictory, all these approaches converge on one point: *the figure of the prophet is at the center*.

If there is a close link between either the prophetic book or the individual traditions that composed it, or both, and the prophet (see, Hayes, 1988), then studies of the prophet tend to overlap, at least partially, studies of the prophetic book and the individual traditions in it. If, on the contrary, considerable parts of a prophetic book, or even most

---

4 For history of modern research over the last hundred years, see Clements,1983: 61-94. For the developments in the study on prophecy and prophets in the last four decades, see Tucker, 1985.

of it, are not considered the "word of the prophet,"[5] but the work of
"tradents" (i.e., theologians who reflected on their given traditions, reac-
tualized them and eventually shaped or reshaped them), then there is
clear break between the prophet and the prophetic book and its traditions.
In the past, this break led to an effort to discover the *ipsissima verba* of
the prophet and to the scorn of the remaining "dross," that is, the so
called "unauthentic" passages.[6] Today, although this tendency has been
largely abandoned, a full development of the awareness of the
implications of this position is still a desideratum. Clearly, this position
implies that not the "classical" prophet but a different type of "prophet"
(namely, the tradent) is responsible for the structure and overall message
of many prophetic books, as well as, of many (or even most) of the
individual units in these books.[7]

---

5 For instance, Hölscher and Garscha on Ezekiel; Duhm, Mowinckel, Mc Kane, Carroll and most
  scholars on Jeremiah; Vermeylen, Barth, and Clements on Isaiah 1-39.

6 This tendency was based on a clear conviction that the ipsissima verba contain or refer to the
  Word of God as it was given to the prophet, and consequently they are of considerable religious
  and theological importance. Leaving aside religious value-judgments, it is noteworthy that the
  biblical text claims for the divine character of the prophetic book as whole (see the
  superscriptions) and that many of the "unauthentic" passages occur in the form of divine
  speech, like the "authentic" passages. In such cases, the biblical text clearly claims that both
  the "authentic" and the "unauthentic" passage are the " word" of God. It is only the contention
  of some modern scholars that they know that the former were actually the words of God, or
  bear testimony to them, and the latter only a fake.

7 Whether these "prophets" should be called prophets or not depends on the definition of the term
  "prophet." The term prophet is generally used for (a) the so-called pre-classical prophets like
  Micaiah son of Imlah (1 Kgs 22), Elijah, and Elisha; (b) several prophets mentioned in the
  sources of the dtr. history (e.g., Hulda, see 2 Kgs 22:14-20*); (c) prophets mentioned in the dtr-
  P redactional tradition (e.g., Jehu son of Hanani, see 1 Kgs 16:1-4); (d) warning prophets
  calling for the observation of YHWH's commands and repentance, as those mentioned in the
  dtr-N redactional tradition (e.g., 2 Kgs 17:13), in Chronicles (e.g., 2 Chr 12:5-8) and cf. Zech
  1:1-6; (e) clearly ecstatic prophets (see, for instance, 1 Sam 10:9-12; 2 Kgs 3:15; Zech 13:2-6);
  and (f) non-Yhwistic prophets (see 1 Kgs 18:19-40). Consequently, the term 'prophet' as used
  in the Hebrew Bible and in modern scholarship does not fit a narrow definition. The "prophets"
  mentioned above may have been responsible for a large amount of prophetic literature and tend
  to express themselves in prophetic forms. However, they did not call themselves nor were
  called "prophets" by someone else in the OT, unlike all the mentioned above. To a certain
  extent they may be compared with the apocalypticists (e.g., the authors of Ezra IV, 2 Baruch or
  the different units of Enoch) who did not claim that they received the divine instruction but
  someone else did. However, it is likely that these "prophets" were more directly attached to a
  certain reservoir of traditions about the prophet than the apocalypticists were (see, for instance,
  Mc Kane's idea of "rolling corpus," Mowinckel's idea of disciples, and the concept of a
  "kernel" of the prophetic book).

The inner logic of this line of interpretation demands that the study of prophetic books and their traditions should not be centered only (or even mainly) in the figure of the classical prophet, his or her conceptual world, political and social environment, social role, or public, but on the conceptual world, political and social environment, social role and public of these tradents. In plain words, the tendency to consider more and more elements in a prophetic book posterior to the historical prophet mentioned in the superscription demands a *tradents centered interpretation*, at the very least on equal footing with interpretation focused on the prophetic figures.

Thus, the main critical point in modern research on the Latter Prophets is whether a specific book is closely connected with the prophet mentioned in the superscription, or at least whether the vast majority of its units go back to the prophet or his period, or, alternatively, whether the book and the vast majority of its units are the result of the work of authors, redactors, or tradents who lived one or more generations later than the prophet.

There is no general answer for such a question; every prophetic book should be considered separately. This work, with its emphasis on the compositional and redactional history of the book of Zephaniah, is an attempt to contribute to this ongoing discussion, but only from the standpoint of the book of Zephaniah. Thus any possible conclusions would hold only insofar as they refer to the book of Zephaniah.

The main methodological lines for this endeavor, however, cannot be *ad hoc*, i.e., "Zephanianic." In general terms, it is obvious that if the testimony of the superscriptions had been clearly authoritative, then the question of authorship would never arise. But the results of biblical research concerning Jeremiah and Isaiah 34-35, Deutero-Isaiah and Trito-Isaiah, for instance, showed that the texts subsequent to the superscription could not always be assigned to the mentioned historical prophet. Moreover, since the superscription is written in the third person, it never claims to be the word of the prophet but the word of its author. The superscription represents its author's point of view about "authorship" and about the way in which the subsequent prophecy should be understood, that is, as given to a certain person at a certain time and place. Since the superscription represents its author's point of view, it is important to consider his or her notions of authorship. Are these notions close to ours based on copyright, or does the author of the superscription claim that the subsequent text conveys the *meaning* of what—according to his or her knowledge—a certain prophet prophesied, but not the prophet's own words or acts, or did he or she write the superscription in order to provide the literary hero who holds together otherwise diverse traditions, or both, at the same time? There is no doubt that any choice among these possibilities leads to important exegetical conclusions. It seems that only on the grounds of a specific superscription, one cannot reach a critical decision. Moreover, an analysis of the superscriptions themselves shows that they were not written by a single hand; therefore different approaches cannot be ruled out. In other words, one cannot automatically apply the proposed meaning of one superscription to the other. It seems reasonable, therefore, to restrain ourselves from accepting beforehand *any* of the proposed interpretations of the superscription.[8]

To be sure, no one doubts that there were prophets in ancient Israel and Judah, and that prophets spoke. Also they were not "some kind of maniac, appearing on the temple square or the market place more or less in ecstasy, crying out a few words and then disappearing again" (from Kapelrud's criticism of Gunkel's approach, Kapelrud,1975:29). But, on the other hand, the assumption that the biblical books consist mainly of direct records of the prophetic preaching remains at the very least unproved. Moreover, it should be noticed that even the relatively large units of the prophetic books contain only a few minutes of speech. The

---

8 I wrote elsewhere (Ben Zvi, 1991: 108-10) on the general issue of the superscriptions of the prophetic books and on Isa 1:1 in particular.

reading of Zeph 1:2-2:3 takes about three or four minutes (the reading of the entire book of Zephaniah takes about ten minutes); the reading of the Book of Obadiah takes less time but not less than most individual prophetic speeches, oracles, or sayings. If the idea that prophets appeared "on the temple square or the market place more or less in ecstasy, crying out a few words and then disappearing again" is quite ridiculous, so is the idea that the prophet gathered the people in order to give a speech whose length was somehow between a few seconds and a very few minutes and then disappeared, sometimes forever, and sometimes only in order to appear again for a few minutes or seconds. Even much more difficult to believe is that a significant social group found these fugacious speeches so important that they should be passed on from generation to generation according to the exact words of the prophet.

The point of departure for any discussion of this topic has to be the only sure fact that they were written books, that were transmitted generation after generation because they were meaningful to their readers, i.e., their readers considered themselves as the addressees of a message that was originally addressed to someone else, at a different time. Accordingly, one should conclude that these books have been reinterpreted by each generation. In addition, since it is generally accepted that at least in several cases the reinterpretation has influenced the text, one should conclude that the sacredness of the received text was not a feature of a "new born text" but an approach that has been developed during time and for each text independently. Eventually, this approach froze the MT, first the Torah and later the Former and Latter Prophets. Significantly, the text of the Torah was not frozen in the monarchic period or even soon thereafter.

In some cases, thematic aspects and more often linguistic aspects may be helpful for the discernment of interpretative additions. The existence of large numbers of parallels in the OT, sometimes a verse and sometimes large units, points clearly to the use of previous written sources in the process of composition of new written literary pieces. It is noteworthy that this evidence of parallels exists despite the relatively small corpus of written works in our hands. However, since it is highly improbable that the entire literary output of the monarchic period was about a dozen books and that of the entire biblical period little more than twenty, it has to be admitted that our attested parallels are only a fraction, and probably a small one, of the real parallels. The probable number of related ideas and expressions was even greater than the word for word parallels. These parallels point to the nature of the process of writing: it was not plagiarism, but the use of existent building blocks in order to build new buildings. Considering the above mentioned features, and even the relationship between the spoken word and the written account of it (cf. Thucydides' saying about the accuracy of the speeches,[9] even if it refers to a different literary genre) it seems obvious that the view that a prophetic book as a whole carries the "tapes" of the prophet's utterances or even an accurate picture of them cannot be sustained. This does not rule out the possibility that the prophetic book includes traditions reflecting deeds and sayings of the prophet, and the possibility that they were written during his lifetime or close to it. Instead, this analysis points to the necessity of a critical discussion of every unit in the book, without taking an early date for granted because of the poetic character of the unit or simply because the evidence pointing to a late date is "suggestive" but not compelling. On the other hand, a late date cannot be taken for granted only because the text contains a prophecy of salvation, or because of single Hebrew word that occurs nowhere else but in a relatively late biblical book.

---

[9] "So my habit has been to make the speakers say what was in my opinion demanded of them by the various occasions, of course adhering as possible to the general sense of what they really said" (Thucydides, *The Peloponnesian War*, Book I, 22; ET T. Crawley, revised by R. Feetham).

The fundamental goal of this work is to determine, insofar as possible, the relationship of the book of Zephaniah and its individual units to their historical—in its comprehensive meaning— circumstances.

1.2 Methodological Guidelines

The issues discussed above clearly emphasize the importance of methodological considerations. In general terms, the following methodological guidelines are proposed for this study on the book of Zephaniah:

(a) Analysis of the text at the level of the individual words and expressions, including textual criticism and a comparative analysis of the occurrence of words and expressions in Zephaniah and elsewhere in the Hebrew Bible. Special attention would be given to words and expressions occurring with different meanings in different biblical corpora, and to those having a clear tendency to occur in a specific biblical corpus but tending to be "replaced" by alternative words and expressions in other biblical corpora.

(b) Division of the text to its small literary units by form-critical criteria (e.g., openings, concluding words, changes in genre, changes of speaker, etc.).

(c) Comparative analysis of the small units discerned in stage (b) with discontinuities in the distribution of linguistic affinities (stage a). The aim of this stage is to test the possibility that different form-critical units have different affinities, and therefore may have different origins.

(d) Study of the contents of these small units, including recognition of genre and probable historical references. If stage (c) suggests affinities between a certain unit and a certain biblical corpus, these suggested affinities are to be tested by a comparative analysis of contents. If stage (a) suggests the existence of possible additions to the text, then a discussion of the content of the proposed texts (with and without the additions) is to be carried out.

(e) Analysis, and comparative analysis, of specific topoi and issues occurring in Zephaniah and elsewhere in the Hebrew Bible (e.g., the people who believe that God will do nothing good or bad [see Zeph 1:12, cf. Mal 3:13-18; Ps 10:11-13, and see also Ps 14:1=53:2], the Day of YHWH, and others; see section 1.3). The analysis of the ideas expressed in topoi and issues may suggest a profile of the sociological self-understanding of the author responsible for such ideas, at least in several cases.

(f) The results of stages (c), (d) and (e) may suggest the existence of a network of references among different biblical texts, a network based on similar language conveying similar ideas. If that is the case, then the existence of such a network suggests the existence of some degree of social affinity between the authors and the society that they reflect. This point should be addressed from a social and historical perspective.

(g) Study of the structure of the entire book and the message conveyed by that structure. This analysis should take into account that neither the text nor its structure was composed in an a-temporal context. Communicative messages are not a-temporal and do not exist outside social reality. Accordingly, the meaning of the structure of the book to the community, from which and for which the book was written, cannot be disassociated from the proper historical, social, cultural, and religious context in which the community (or communities) lived.[10] This analysis should also take into account that the written text was read (and learned) by the community as a dynamic and structured sequence of literary sub-

---

[10] Cf. Gerstenberger's general approach to the question of meaning as expressed in E. S. Gerstenberg, "Canon Criticism and the Meaning of *Sitz im Leben*," pp. 20-31 in G. M. Tucker, D. L. Petersen, and R. R. Wilson (ed.), *Canon, Theology, and Old Testament Interpretation. Essays in honor of Brevard S. Childs* (Philadelphia: Fortress, 1988).

units.[11] Accordingly, the dynamic aspects of the structure should come to the forefront in a historical-critical analysis of the communicative message of the structure of the book. [12]

(h) Comparative study of the structure of the entire work and its message. If the results of this analysis suggest structural similarities with a given biblical corpus, then sociologico/anthropological heuristic models (e.g., dissonance theory) and historical data may be helpful describing the type of historical society in which such a message may have been arisen.

(i) Analysis of the possible redactional or compositional order/s that precede the present structure of the work. This stage is of critical interpretative importance because before the compositional stage there is no real text but only separate traditions. However, it should be noticed that compositional devices and compositional structure are not always self-evident (e.g., the Book of Hosea).

(j) Conclusions concerning the compositional and redactional history of the Book of Zephaniah, on the basis of the most probable conclusions reached in the stages a-h.

---

[11] That is, verse follows verse and unit follows unit. The fact that verse *follows* verse is stressed by numerous cases of ongoing heightening. The fact that unit *follows* unit is underscored by many cases in which the ambiguity brought about by a certain unit is resolved by the next one. If the minor units were read as sequential, it is most likely that also the large unit (i.e., the entire book) was understood sequentially, though not necessarily in a consistent linear way (see chapter 4.5 in this book).

[12] I largely agree with M. V. Fox's critique of the methodological approach known as "Rhetorical Criticism." See, M. V. Fox, "The Rhetoric of Ezekiel's Vision of the Valley of the Bones," *HUCA* 51 (1980) 1-15, esp. 1-4.

1.3 Special Issues in the Book of Zephaniah

Although the book of Zephaniah is a relatively small book, it contains a rare concentration of references to central issues in the history of ancient Israel and especially in the history of the ideas of ancient Israel. Among the issues and questions that deserve special attention one may note:

(a) In addition to the issues concerning the actual meaning of the superscription mentioned above, it is clear that Zeph 1:1 claims that the subsequent text should be read against the background of Josiah's reign. But what did this mean for the author of the superscription? The underlying image of the kingdom of Josiah that corresponds to the different layers of the text is worthy of analysis. Especially interesting is the question: How does this image—or images—relate to other images of Josiah's kingdom in the OT?

(b) The literal meaning of Zeph 1:2-3 depends on the meaning of אדמה, "adamah." Does the author refer literally to a "world destruction," or to the "destruction of the land," or is he or she intentionally ambiguous? If the reference to a "world destruction" is preferred, can Zeph 1:2-3 be considered a conscious reversal of the creation? To be sure, if this is the case, and if the text in Zeph 1:2-3 is dependent on—and rejects—the main message of Genesis 1-9, then this "fact" would have significant consequences in both pentateuchal and Zephaniah's studies. But is this the case?

(c) The Day of YHWH in the book of Zephaniah, or in its different redactional levels, and its relation to other images of the Day of YHWH in prophetic literature is obviously an issue worthy of careful study. In this respect the probable influence of so-called wisdom expressions in Zeph 1:15 (e.g., יום עברה [cf. Prov 11:4, Job 21:30], the pair משואה and שאה [cf. Job 30:3, 38:27]) is of particular interest.

(d) Zeph 1:4-5 contains what seems to be a clear reference to "foreign cults." Were they foreign cults or was the reference an expression of a polemic stance? What is the probable historical situation to which this note refers?

(e) What is the probable social, economic and urban situation to which Zeph 1:8-10* refers? If this situation corresponds to that of the late monarchy, to what redactional and historical conclusions does this correspondence lead?

(f) Zeph 1:13 refers to those who believe that God will do nothing, either good or bad. This topos occurs elsewhere in the OT (see Mal 3:13-18; Ps 10:11-13, cf. Ps 14:1=53:2). Taking into consideration that the quotations of the thoughts of the opponents (e.g., Ezek 25:8) are more likely to be a statement aimed to the author's group than a real citation, and taking into account that the people who did not expect any action of God are described as wealthy (cf. Zeph 1:18, see also Zeph 3:11-12), may this topos suggest the existence of a community that feels deprived? If that is the case then the idea of cognitive dissonance may provide a helpful heuristic model for the understanding of this topos.

(g) Zeph 2:1-3* is a call for repentance. Such a call is supposed to preempt the disaster (pace Hunter). Zeph 2:3 includes, however, an אולי clause of salvation (cf. Am 5:15). This אולי ("perhaps") is highly significant for the understanding of the theology of the author. This אולי is the only way in which the freedom of God can be preserved in such circumstances. Obviously, this theological position is also an attempt to cope with the fact that reality may contradict any inflexible theory of divine retribution. The freedom of God in calls for repentance is an issue worthy of further study.

(h) The reference to כל ענוי הארץ in Zeph 2:3 should be studied in relation to the other references to ענוים in the OT, and especially in relation to those in which the people who will be saved in the day of judgment are described as ענוים (e.g., Ps 10:11-13 [see above], 37:10-11, 76:10 [כל ענוי הארץ], 147:7).

(i) Zeph 2:4-15 is the oracles against the nations (OAN) section of the book of Zephaniah. Since prophecies against the nations occur as the second element in a tripartite structure (prophecies of judgment against

Judah/Israel, OAN, announcements of salvation) in the books of Zephaniah, Isaiah, Jeremiah (LXX) and Ezekiel, one can hardly consider this structure to be the result of the personal idiosyncrasy of these prophets, or the authors and redactors of these books. This tripartite structure was popular because it expressed a certain meaning that was relevant to particular communities. The analysis of this meaning merits careful study.

The OAN section is composed of different prophecies. Although there are some features common to several OAN sections, each prophetic book has its own list of nations, and its own emphasis on some of them. Theoretically, this fact may be explained: (a) in terms of the historical situation, i.e., the historical situation in the days of Josiah, or (b) in terms of the author's/ redactor's image of the days of Josiah. Therefore, the extent of correspondence (or discrepancy) between these prophecies and the historical situation in the days of Josiah should be analyzed. If the historical situation does not fit the one described in the prophecies then it probably reflects an "historical" image. This image should be compared with other images of the days of Josiah occurring elsewhere in the OT. If this image stands at odds with other images, one may consider the possibility that this list creates an historical image. If after a critical analysis the latter option is preferred, this can only point to temporal detachment between Josiah's days and the present form of the unit.

In addition to this analysis, each prophecy has to be studied as a unit by itself. Specific political and geographical traditions may be reflected in these prophecies (e.g., Zeph 2:4-6).

(j) Zeph 2:11 is another note in a series of notes in the OT (e.g., Ex 15:11, Deut 32:8 [see LXX, BHS note]; Ps 82) pointing to the belief that (a) there are other gods besides YHWH, (b) that these gods are related to foreign peoples while YHWH is related to Israel, (c) that YHWH is supreme over all these gods, and (d) that YHWH will destroy or depose or diminish their power. The importance of these notes for the understanding of at least one stream in Israel's theological thinking is evident.

(k) Zeph 3:3-4 refers to the elite of the people. Significantly, a comparison between this note and Zeph 1:4-9 shows a clear difference in language, in the composition of the list and in the described offenses (i.e., in the explanation of what may cause or has caused the divine judgment). Such differences may reflect different streams of thought, and perhaps different historical situations. Affinities between each of these two units and different biblical corpora may be helpful in the analysis of these two notes.

(l) From a socio-political point of view, the mention of שפטיה and שׂריה in Zeph 2:3, as two different entities suggests the existence of a judicial organization in which the "officers" have no judicial power. This issue deserves careful study.

(m) Zeph 3:9-20 contains different units referring to the ideal situation, after the divine judgment. Since these units tend to mention what their author considered more characteristic of the ideal system, or of the situation in which the ideal system comes into being, an analysis of these units is likely to shed light on the ideological world of the author, and indirectly on the author's society.

(n) A special case of the image of the ideal future is the topos concerning the "peoples" recognizing YHWH (see Zeph 3:9-10, cf. Isa 2:2-4; Mic 4:1-4/5; Zech 14:16). As in the other units, the *specific* characteristics ascribed to the ideal situation of the people reflects the ideological and theological world of the writer of the unit.

(o) There is a tendency in modern biblical research to find deuteronomistic influences in Genesis-Malachi (according to the order of the Hebrew Bible). An evaluation of the testimony of the Book of Zephaniah in this respect is a worthy endeavor.

2. Zephaniah through the Ages' Mirror: History of Interpretation

At the beginning of the second century BCE, Ben Sira[1] wrote:

> may the bones of the Twelve Prophets revive out of their place
> for they comforted Jacob and delivered them with their
> confident hope (Sir 49:10).[2]

Even the most cursory reading of the prophetic books shows that these books contain not only words of comfort and hope but also many words of despair, and undoubtedly unfulfilled prophecies as well (e.g., Hag 2:21-23). Clearly, Ben Sira's words are dependent on and reflect the traditio of his time (i.e., the reinterpretation of the given text (traditum) in order to maintain its relevancy for the living community).[3] One may assume that Ben Sira's words point to a central aspect of the development of the traditio, namely, that the prophetic books were not transmitted because of the "fulfilled" or "unfulfilled" prophecies they contain, but because of the hope that they conveyed to their readers. One should assume that it is not by blind chance that all the books included in The Twelve conclude with a notice of salvation, or hope.[4] Such concluding

---

[1] Ben Sira lived at the beginning of the second century BCE; see Nickelsburg, 55-56.

[2] Trans. E. J. Goodspeed, The Apocrypha (New York: Random House, 1959). Cf. P.W. Skehan and A. A. Di Lella, *The Wisdom of Ben Sira* (AB 39, New York: Doubleday, 1987) 540. The NJB translates: "As for the twelve prophets may their bones flower again from the tomb, since they have comforted Jacob and redeemed him in faith and hope."
The Hebrew text from Cairo Geniza reads: וגם שנים עשר הנביאים תהי עצמתם
פר]חת מתח[תם אשר החלימו את יעקב וי ש]בהוהו באמנת תקוה]

[3] For traditio and traditum, in general, see Fishbane: 6-19 and Knight: 5-20. Traditum refers to the material that is transmitted; *traditio* refers to the entire process of transmission. See, Knight: 5; Fishbane: 6.

[4] Notices of salvation explicitly refer to a future "well-being" that will be brought by YHWH, by YHWH's actions (cf. Tucker,1971: 61). Notices of hope, which is a broader category, are those that convey hope to their readers or hearers, even if they do not refer

notes clearly stress the element of hope and provide an interpretative key for subsequent communities of readers.[5]

Obviously, a future-centered interpretation may lead—and indeed has often led—to an understanding of the prophetic book as a complex system of cryptograms referring to the living situation of the interpreting community. Thus, the future mentioned by the prophet may become or may be becoming present (e.g., Qumran pesharim[6]), or may turn into an apocalyptic future, or may be interpreted eschatologically, or any combination of the three. Qumranic commentaries (pesharim) on Zephaniah have been found in caves 1 and 4.[7] The existence of an apocalyptic image of Zephaniah is attested by the extant fragments of the Apocalypse of Zephaniah and by later references to this work.[8] In addition, one may mention that according to an interpretation to Mic 5:4[9] that appears in b. Sukk. 52b, the eight princes of human beings (אדם נסיכי) are Jesse, Saul, Samuel, Amos, Zephaniah, Hezekiah, Elijah and Messiah.[10] According to this interpretation, the future acts of these princes are the first step into the Messianic period. The origin and date of the tradition reflected in this tractate are uncertain.[11]

---

to a specific future, or to specific acts of YHWH in the future. For instance, Hos 14:10; Jon 4:10-11; Mic 7:18-20; and Hab 3:17-19 can hardly be considered notices of salvation but they undoubtedly express and convey a sense of hope which is based on the attributes of YHWH.

[5] Cf. Abrabanel on Zephaniah.

[6] For Pesharim see Horgan,1979 and Horgan,1986: 247-58 and the bibliography cited there.

[7] See Horgan, 1979: 63-64,191-92.

[8] The Apocalypse of Zephaniah, or its kernel, was probably written in a Hellenistic Jewish milieu sometime between 100 BCE and 100 CE. See Wintermute, Kuhn and Schürer, III: 803-04, and the bibliography cited in these works. It is noteworthy that when Clement of Alexandria quotes "the prophet Zephaniah" in Stromata V.77 he quotes ApZeph and not the Book of Zephaniah.

[9] "We will set over it [Assyria] seven shepherds, eight princes of men" (NJPSV).

[10] According to the text in the MSS and to Saadia Gaon's quotation of b. Sukk. 52b; the printed text reads: "Zedekiah, Messiah and Elijah" after Zephaniah. See Saadia Gaon, The Book of Beliefs and Opinions (ET S. Rosenblat, Yale Judaica Series 1, New Haven: Yale University Press, 1948) 276, 286 n.22, 429. Saadia refers to Mic 5:4 (and its interpretation) as textual evidence for the doctrine of the resurrection of the dead at the time of the redemption. According to Rashi there are no grounds for the proposed identification of the eight princes (see Rashi on b. Sukk. 52b).

[11] Cf. L. Ginzberg, V: 142.

However, most of the Jewish traditions concerning Zephaniah seem to be "historically" or "biographically" oriented; i.e., their goal was to explain certain aspects of Zephaniah's life, preaching, and his place in the transmission of the divine instruction. For instance, according to Pesiq. R. 26, 129b, Jeremiah, Huldah and Zephaniah prophesied to the same generation, but in different social environments: Huldah prophesied among the women, Jeremiah in the streets (שוקים), and Zephaniah in the synagogues (בתי כנסיות); [12] according to b. Meg. 15a, Zephaniah was a Jerusalemite,[13] and the son of a prophet (Cushi son of Gedaliah). Another tradition states that the Book of the Twelve was "written" (כתבו) by the Men of the Great Assembly (אנשי הכנסת הגדולה),[14] i.e., in the Persian period. Whether this כתבו means "written" or "interpreted" was a debated point already in ancient times.[15] In addition, the saying of R. Hanana in Pesiq. Rab Kah. section Nahamu (נחמו)10, may be understood as claiming that Zephaniah (also?)[16] prophesied after the destruction of the Temple.[17]

---

[12] This midrash was probably written c. 9th century. Radak mentioned this tradition in his commentary on Zephaniah and so did Abrabanel, and the latter also mentioned his source, i.e., Pesikta Rabati. There is also a tradition that Jeremiah received (the oral) Torah from Zephaniah and his court (See, Moses Ben Maimon, *Mishne Torah* I [S. Liberman (ed.), Jerusalem: Mosad HaRav Kuk] Introduction, 1. 20-21), according to the same tradition Zephaniah received Torah from Habakkuk and his court (ובית דינו וירמיה קבל מצפניה ובית דינו צפניה קבל מחבקוק). The references to ובית דינו are based on the concept that the transmission of the (oral) Torah should not be from the individual to the individual.

[13] Cf. *The Lives of the Prophets*, Zeph 1 (Torrey: 29, 44), according to which Zephaniah was a Simeonite, from the city of Sarabatha. For questions of date and origin of *The Lives of the Prophets*, see Torrey: 6-13, Hare, and Schürer, III: 783-86 and the bibliography cited there.

[14] See b. B. Bat. 15a.

[15] Rashi understands כתבו as "written'" but according to the position expressed in Abot R. Nat. 1, 2-3 כתבו means "interpreted."

[16] The New Oxford Ms. reads, בחורבנה של ירושלים קדם חורבנה ואחר חורבנה.

[17] So Ginzberg, VI: 314. The text reads,... צפניה ... הן ואילו המקדש בית לאחר שנתבאו נביאים שמונה. One is tempted to understand, eight prophets who prophesied (about events) after the exile. This reading would be in accordance with Medieval and midrashic interpretations of Zephaniah, but the same holds true for other prophets who are not mentioned in the list of eight (e.g., Isaiah). Different versions of the list itself exist in different MSS, Zephaniah, Haggai, Zechariah, Malachi, and Ezekiel occur in all of them; Jeremiah, Joel and Amos in most of them. Whenever one of the latter is not mentioned, the names of either Nahum, Micah or Habakkuk occur.

Generally speaking, in Jewish communities of the "rabbinical" period, Zephaniah, and the other prophets as well, were considered preachers of the Torah.[18] They were preachers of repentance who called for the observance of the Torah, and heralds of a "Messianic" salvation yet to come as well. At the same time, Christian communities saw Zephaniah, and the other prophets as well, mainly as prophets of the Christ who had come.

In any case, both communities agreed that all the prophets spoke, to a large extent, in one voice and in accordance with their entire corpus of sacred literature, be it the Hebrew Bible and the Oral Law or be it a Christologically oriented Old Testament, the New Testament and the traditions of the Church. Since the sayings of the prophet were considered inspired and in harmony with the entire sacred literature, then there was a tendency to focus on the text rather than on the prophet, and even more on individual verses, in order to use them as prooftexts supporting either Christian positions[19] or the halachic or aggadic positions of a sage or "the sages."[20]

A variant of the prooftext pattern is the communal reading of certain passages of the book. According to the triennial cycle of Torah readings, the Haftarah to Gen 11:1 ויהי כל הארץ שפה אחת ודברים אחדים ("the whole world had one language and the same words") was Zeph 3:9-17,20, that begins with לקרא כלם בשם ה' לעבדו שכם אחד כי אז אהפך אל עמים שפה ברורה, which in its context means, "certainly, I will change the speech of the peoples to a pure speech, so all of them may invoke the name YWHW and serve YHWH with one accord," but whose reading immediately after Gen 1:11 suggests to the

---

[18] Cf. B. J. Bamberger, "The Changing Image of the Prophet in Jewish Thought;" pp. 303-23 in *Interpreting the Prophetic Tradition. The Goldenson Lectures 1955-1966.* (Cincinnati: HUC Press/ New York: Ktav, 1969); esp. pp. 306-7.

[19] E.g., Saint Agustine, *City of God* (LCB, Cambridge: Harvard University Press, 1965) 493-97, i.e., book 18.23. Note the non-Vulgate, quite different from MT, and clearly exegetical Latin translation of Zeph 3:9-12 at the end of the section, p. 496. Cf., for instance, Cyprian's (d. 258 CE) use of the Minor Prophets, see M.A. Fahey, *Cyprian and the Bible: a Study in Third-Century Exegesis* (Tübingen: J.C.B. Mohr, 1971) 240-258.

[20] E.g., b. Berak. 57b, b. Pesah. 7b, Gen R. 88.7.

community a paratextual meaning[21] of one universal language and of a reversal to the ideal situation that existed before the building of the "Tower" (Gen 11:2 ff.). Thus it was a "textual" confirmation of the hopes of the people responsible for this arrangement of readings.[22]

Significantly, there are relatively few quotations of the Book of Zephaniah in the Christian and Jewish literature of the first centuries CE. Zephaniah is not directly quoted in the New Testament, though there are passages in the New Testament that may recall passages in the Book of Zephaniah.[23] *Biblia Patristica*[24] counts only twenty references to Zephaniah in the patristic literature until the third century (excluding Origen) and six of them are to Zeph 1:1, and one even to ApZeph.[25] Similarly, John Chrysostom (c.341-407 CE) refers only to four verses of Zephaniah in his entire work (Zeph 2:11; 3:3, 9, 10).[26] But the index of verses, or specific biblical contents, to which there is at least one reference in Chrysostom's work, contains thirty-four entries for Hosea and Amos,

---

[21] That is, a meaning that evolved out of the reading of these two different texts, one after the other, in one communal service and as a liturgical unit.

[22] For the triennial cycle, see J. Mann, *The Bible as read and preached in the Old Synagogue*. 2 vol. (Cincinatti: HUC, 1966). For the Book of Zephaniah in the triennial cycle, see Mann, I: 91, II: 201.

[23] For instance, one may compare Matt. 13:41 with Zeph 1:3; Rom 15:6 with Zeph 3:9; Rev 6:17 with Zeph 1:14; Rev 14:5 with Zeph 3:13 and Rev 16:1 with Zeph 3:8.
Butcher has proposed that the sequence of events in Acts 1-15 is based on Zeph 3:8-13, and that the author of Acts 1-15 (Luke) may have appropriate concerns and motifs from Zephaniah. See Butcher, 1972.

[24] Université des sciences humaines de Strasbourg. Centre d'analyse et de documentation patristiques/ Allenbach J., Benoit A. et al, *Biblia Patristica: index des citations et allusions bibliques dans la littérature patristique. Vol. 1, Des origines à Clément d'Alexandrie et Tertullian. Vol. 2, Le troisième siècle (Origène excepté)* (Paris: Editions du Centre national de la recherche scientifique, 1975).

[25] This number of references to Zephaniah is in sharp contrast with the 183 references to Zechariah in the same corpus, the 140 to Hosea, 114 to Malachi, 85 to Amos, 76 to Jonah, 70 to Joel, 60 to Micah, 52 to Habakkuk. On the other hand there are only 16 references to Haggai, 11 to Nahum and 3 to Obadiah. Obviously, the length of the book may have been a factor in the number of quotations or references to each of the prophetic books mentioned above. The number of references per verse in *Biblia Patristica* for The Twelve is as follows: Hos 0.71, Joel 0.96, Am 0.58, Obad 0.14, Jonah 1.58, Mic 0.57, Nah 0.23, Hab 0.93, Zeph 0.38, Hag 0.42, Zech 0.87, Mal 2.08. These numbers point to a clear tendency, namely, Zephaniah is not among the most quoted and referred books. The only writer in this period who shows a certain tendency to refer to the Book of Zephaniah is Cyprian of Carthage. See M.A. Fahey, *Cyprian and the Bible*, 240-258.

[26] R.A. Krupp, *Saint John Chrysostom: A Scripture Index* (Lanham, NY/ London: University Press of America, 1984).

twenty-five for Malachi, twenty-one for Micah, nineteen for Zechariah, thirteen for Jonah, and eight for Habakkuk. Only Nahum (two references) and Obadiah (zero references) were less mentioned than Zephaniah.[27] These figures suggest that neither Zephaniah nor the Book of Zephaniah played a main referential role among the Minor Prophets in the Christian communities of the first centuries.[28]

To a large extent, the same holds for Jewish communities. There is no reference to Zephaniah in the Mishnah, and there is only one reference to the Book of Zephaniah in Leviticus Rabbah (ca. 400-450 CE).[29] Furthermore, in the entire Midrash Rabbah, Zephaniah is the least mentioned book among The Twelve.[30] The pattern of biblical references to The Twelve is somewhat different in the Babylonian Talmud. However, even in the Babylonian Talmud there are references to only fourteen verses of Zephaniah (i.e., 0.26 references per verse) and this is

---

[27] The number of references per verse of the Twelve is as follows: Hos 0.17, Joel 0.16, Am 0.23, Obad 0, Jonah 0.27, Mic 0.20, Nah 0.04, Hab 0.14, Zeph 0.08, Hag 0.13, Zech 0.09, Mal 0.45. One may conclude that the general trends observed in Biblia Patristica occur also in John Chrysostom's work.

[28] The figures mentioned above clearly show that the centrality of the prophetic book is not necessarily related to the length of the book (cf. Jonah and Joel, for instance).

[29] There are 23 references to Hosea (0.12 per biblical verse), Joel 5 (0.07), Am 30 (0.21), Obad 5 (0.24), Jonah 2 (0.04), Mic 12 (0.11), Nah 5 (0.11), Hab 12 (0.21- half of references to to Hab 3:6-), Zeph 1 (0.02), Hag 2 (0.05), Zech 22 (0.10), Mal 17 (0.31). See J. Neusner, *Judaism and Scripture. The Evidence of Leviticus Rabbah.* (Chicago and London: University of Chicago Press,1986) 611 ff.

[30] This collection of Jewish midrashim of whom the earlier are from the fifth century and later from the eleventh century can only point to general trend in Jewish communities. In the entire collection there are 204 references to Hosea (1.04 per biblical verse), Joel 55 (0.75), Am 122 (0.84), Obad 36 (1.71), Jonah 28 (0.58), Mic 94 (0.90), Nah 31 (0.66), Hab 47 (0.84), Zeph 17 (0.32), Hag 18 (0.47), Zech 155 (0.73), Mal 110 (2.0). See Slotki's index in H. Freedman and M. Simon (ed) *Midrash Rabbah* (London: Soncino Press, 1939), vol X. Obviously, such numbers do not imply that the content of certain verses of Zephaniah may have been influential and highly regarded. For instance, the climax in the list of wondrous divine deeds in Gen. R. 88.7 is the making of the entire world one band and the corresponding biblical quotation is Zeph 3:9. Cf. Abrabanel's commentary on this verse.

It is worth noting that there are differences between the patterns of references to The Twelve of Jewish and Christian communities, commentators. These differences may be explained partially by different theological approaches, and partially by the different social and political circumstances in which these communities lived. Accordingly, an analysis of the differential patterns of biblical quotations should take into account dyachronical and geographical considerations. Such analysis, according to biblical texts, as well as biblical themes, is a worthy endeavor but it stands beyond the limits of this work.

slightly less than the average of the b. Talmud (around 0.33 references per verse of The Twelve).[31]

The reasons for the relatively low number of references to the Book of Zephaniah in the writings of Christian and Jewish communities may have been different and may have changed from time to time. Perhaps the fact that the Book of Zephaniah contains a "messianic" or "eschatological" image but one without a "human" Messiah has contributed to the relative low number of references to the book. In any case, the reasons for this feature are worthy of study. That issue, however, is beyond the limits of this work.

Whatever the reasons, Zephaniah did not turn into a relatively popular prophet except—and perhaps—in the last two decades.[32] For instance, although Luther wrote in his commentary on Zephaniah: "Among the minor prophets, he makes the clearest prophecies about the kingdom of Christ,"[33] he did not tend to refer to Zephaniah in his sermons;[34]

---

[31] The distribution of the number of verses of The Twelve mentioned of quoted in the b. Talmud among the different books is as follows: Hos 77 (0.40 per verse), Joel 15 (0.21), Am 49 (0.34), Obad 7 (0.33), Jonah 13 (0.27), Mic 33 (0.31), Nah 8 (0.18), Hab 18 (0.32), Zeph 14 (0.26), Hag 8 (0.21), Zech 75 (0.36), Mal 32 (0.58). Again, the reader is cautioned against "instant" conclusions from these data. The importance or centrality of specific themes occurring in these prophetic books may be bypassed by these figures. E.g., at least from the Talmudic times, the haftarah of the Minhah service in Yom haKippurim has been from Jonah, see b. Meg. 31a. The differences between the pattern of quotations of the b. Talmud and that of Midrash Rabbah are worthy of study, but they stand beyond the scope of this work.

[32] In the Middle Ages, Zephaniah's name evoked the image of the "search with the lamp" (cf. Zeph 1:12), the image of the total destruction (cf. Zeph 1:2-3). See, for instance Zephaniah's characterization in the Cathedral of Reims, and in the Cathedral of Amiens. For plastic arts as a testimony for the perceptions of the prophets in the Middle Ages, see, for instance, E. Mâle, *Religious Art in France. The Thirteen Century* (ET M. Mathews, Princeton: Princeton University Press, 1958) 165 ff.

Clearly, this is the overall picture but one may find exceptions. For instance, the pattern of biblical references on The Twelve in Saadia Gaon's *The Book of Beliefs and Opinions*, is different. Saadia chose Zeph 1:14, 15,17,18; 2:1,2 as the biblical proof-texts "concerning a day reserved by God for retribution (Saadia, 332-33). He describes the day of judgment and redemption first with references to Ezek 38:11,15 (Gog and Magog), and then he writes: "Now the folk that will be assembled about him will be divided in two categories, one consisting of notorious sinners marked out for perdition, the other of people who have mended their ways in order to enter the faith." The biblical quotation concerning the former is from Joel 4:9-14, and concerning the latter from Zeph 3:9 (See Saadia: 305-06). Cf. also note 9. The well-known hymn "Dies Irae" (written c.12th-13th century) is based, partially, on Zeph 1:14-16.

[33] Luther: 319

moreover, the *Bibliotheca disputationum theologico-philologico exegeticarum in V & N Testamentum* (published in Hamburg in 1736), an index of main biblical studies written during the fifteenth century and the first third of the sixteenth century, contains only fifteen entries for Zephaniah, the second lowest number for one of The Twelve.[35] Relatively few studies on Zephaniah have been published; furthermore, the index of German dissertations published a century later showed only five dissertations on Zephanic issues.[36]

Zephaniah continued to be relatively scarcely quoted in modern sermons and in modern OT theologies.[37] Furthermore, some scholars tend to give low value to Zephaniah, and to the Book of Zephaniah. For instance, according to J. M. P. Smith, "Zephaniah can hardly be considered great as a poet."[38] Sixty years later, Sandmel wrote, "Zephaniah seems not to rise to the stature of Micah or Isaiah."[39] For other modern scholars, the Book

---

[34] Cf. the biblical references to the prophets in Martin Luther, *Sermons* (*Luther's Works* vol. 51-52, ET J. Doberstein, Philadelphia: Muhlenberg Press, 1959), there are none to Zephaniah, but four to Hosea and Micah; two to Habakkuk, one to Zechariah and to Malachi; and no less than forty-seven to Isaiah.

[35] Cf. Hosea seventy-six entries, Joel forty-three, Amos thirty-two, Obadiah twenty-three, Jonah fifty-nine, Micah forty-five, Nahum thirteen, Habakkuk twenty-six, Haggai thirty-three, Zechariah seventy-five, Malachi fifty-eight. See *Bibliotheca disputationum theologico-philogico-exegeticarum in V & N Testamentum* (Hamburgi: Literis Saalicathianis, 1736) 329-66. Cf. these trends of references with those in *Biblia Patristica*.

[36] Cf. Hosea thirty-six, Joel four, Amos thirteen, Jonah three, Micah thirteen, Habakkuk thirteen, Haggai nine, Zechariah thirty-seven, Malachi twenty-five. See O. Fiebig, *Corpus Dissertationum Theologicarum* (Lipsiae: T. O. Weigel, 1847, rep. Amsterdam: B.R. Grüner, 1971) 269-70. The five dissertations are: Beye H., consider. vatic. Zephan II,8-11 de ruina Moabit etc., Gryph 1705; Iken C., de Cemarim 2 Reg XXVII,5. Hos X,5. Zeph I,4, Brem. 1729; Burschen J.F., de Gaza derel. futura. Zeph II,4, Lips. 1768; Friederici E.L., de animal. quor. fit mentio Zeph 2,14, Goett 1769; Anton C.T. Cap III Zephaniae versio et nova ejusd. versum 18 expon. ratio, Gorlic 1811. One may add that in 1818 D.A. Coelnn published his study on the entire Book of Zephaniah (*Spicilegium Observationum Exegetico-Criticarum ad Zephaniah Vaticinia* [Vratislaviae: Barthii Academics, 1818]).

[37] See the index of biblical references in the modern Old Testament theologies written by Eichrodt, Köhler, Zimmerli, Westermann, etc.

[38] J. M. P. Smith: 176.

[39] S. Sandmel, *The Enjoyment of Scripture: the Law, the Prophets and the Writings* (NY: Oxford University Press, 1972), 257. To be sure, he has even harsher words for Ezekiel, see p. 226.

of Zephaniah, or Zephaniah, shows few "new ideas," i.e., the book, or the prophet echoes ideas found elsewhere in the prophetic literature.[40]

Against this background, signs of change are already perceptible. Theological streams that have become more and more important in recent years tend to find the Book of Zephaniah, or the prophet, relevant for the development of a biblical theological stance concerning poverty.[41] Also the supposedly African origin of Zephaniah has evoked special interest in the United States.[42] In addition, an unparalleled number comprehensive studies on Zephaniah has been published during the last two decades, especially in Europe.[43] This trend suggests that the days of relative oblivion have just passed for the Book of Zephaniah. This work is another contribution to this trend.

Although in both Christian and Jewish traditions, the Book of Zephaniah has been less quoted and less influential than other books in the Latter Prophets, it has always been considered a sacred book, and accordingly it has been studied and interpreted generation after generation.

A complete survey of the history of interpretation of the Book of Zephaniah would begin with inner biblical interpretations.[44] It would include the Qumranic material (1QpZeph, 4QpZeph) and interpretative notes in material from the Second Temple Period and thereafter (e.g., Ben Sira, ApZeph, Life of the Prophets, midrashim, New Testament and early

---

[40] E.g., "Zephaniah, in his denunciation of religious syncretism and political corruption, applies the teaching of Isaiah to his own day and derives from Amos the dismal conception of 'the Day of the Lord'" (Pfeiffer: 601); cf. Taylor: 1114-15. Contrast it with the appreciation of Kapelrud (87), several years later, see below.
For a similar analysis of modern scholarship on Zephaniah, see House: 10. However, House does not mention several developments in the last few years, and see below. Also cf. Butcher.

[41] E.g., N. Lohfink, 1984; 1987, esp. 59-63; cf. Stuhlmacher.

[42] E.g., Rice.

[43] E.g., Sabottka, 1972; Kapelrud, 1975; Irsigler, 1977; Krinetzki, 1977; Edler, 1984; Martin, 1985; Seybold, 1985; House 1988. One may consider as well the articles of Langhor 1976; Ribera Florit, 1982; and Renaud, 1986, and Ball's dissertation, 1972, published only in 1988. It is noteworthy that some of these scholars praise the book, or sections of it, or the prophet, in a quite unqualified way (see, Martin, II: 20, Edler: 257-58, Boadt: 229).

[44] From simple quotations like 2 Chr 15:7, which is a combination of Zeph 3:16b and Jer 31:16 (see Willi:226), to interpretations of a certain passage as suggested by Fishbane (461-64).

patristic literature). One would also need to consider the division of the MT Zephaniah into paragraphs,[45] and obviously the Targum[46] as well as interpretative trends in other ancient translations. The commentaries on The Twelve written by the fifth century Church Fathers would require special consideration.[47]

Such a thorough history of interpretation would be neither brief nor especially helpful as an introduction to a modern historical-critical analysis of the book. This is especially true because modern critical methods of research are based on different presuppositions and guidelines than those of the early commentators.[48] Since there is no common methodological basis, one cannot compare their "historical-critical" analysis of the Book of Zephaniah with a modern historical-critical analysis of the book. The same holds true for the commentaries on Zephaniah written by Jewish Medieval exegetes such as Rashi (d. 1105), Ibn Ezra (d.1164), and Radak

---

[45] Such a division is already attested in the text of Wadi Murabba'at and the division, as well as the text, are very close to MT, except for some interchange between open and closed paragraphs (See *DJD* II, 200-02). Exegetically, this division of the text does mean that Palestinian Jewish communities, in the 2nd century CE, interpreted Zeph 2:1-3 along with the following verses and not with the precedent verses (i.e., according to the massoretic tradition); and that Zeph 3:1 and Zeph 3:14 were understood by these communities as the opening passage of new units.

[46] The exegetical features of Targum Jonathan to the Prophets (Tg. Neb.) are well-known. Turning to Zephaniah, the tendency to stress transcendence over possible anthropomorphisms and immanence is clear (cf. Tg. Zeph 1:1, 12, 3:5, 15, 17; on the general issue of anthropomorphisms and immanence in Targum Jonathan for the Minor Prophets, see, for instance, J. E. Petersen, especially 80-108; cf. Ribera Florit: 130-31). There is also a clear attempt in the Tg. Neb. to describe those who are to be destroyed in unequivocally negative terms, and accordingly to provide an answer to the general problem of theodicy, as triggered by the wholesale destruction mentioned in Zephaniah (e.g., Tg. Zeph 1:7, 18; 2:5; see Ribera Florit: 131). Also the rendering of the MT expression עם עני דל in Zeph 3:12 (i.e., the faithful remnant) as עם ענותן ומקביל עלבן in Tg Zeph 3:12 is worth noting, both from a sociological point of view and from the point of view of the Ebed-YHWH traditions. Both the date of Targum Jonathan and the date of the traditions included in it are moot points in modern research.

[47] E.g., the commentaries on the Twelve, written by Jerome (d.419/20), Cyril of Alexandria (d. 444 CE), and Theodore of Mopsuestia (d.428). That is, three representatives of different schools and lines of thought in the early Church. For the commentaries on Zephaniah, see P.E. Pusey (ed.), *Cyrilli Archiepiscopi Alexandrini, In XII Prophetas* (Bruxelles: Culture et Civilisation, 1965), II 167-240; H. N. Sprenger (Einl u. Ausg), *Theodori Mopsuesteni Commentarius in XII Prophetas* (Wiesbaden, Otto Harrassowitz, 1977), 280-301; S. Hieronymi, *Commentarii in Prophetas Minores* (Corpus Christianorum, Series Latina LXXVI a, Turnholti: Typography Brepols Editores Pontifici, 1970), 655-711.

[48] Cf. J. M. Miller: 12-14.

(i.e., David Kimchi, d.1235), even though they may be considered precursors of modern philological and comparative textual methods,[49] and those written by Luther (d. 1546) and Calvin (d.1564),[50] even though, from a modern point of view, they may be considered precursors of the historical-critical method.[51]

The main purpose of a review of the history of interpretation in a modern historical-critical analysis to provide the essential background against which the thesis of the work is to be understood. Accordingly, it seems appropriate to present a short survey of the main questions asked in modern historical-critical research on the Book of Zephaniah, and of the main answers given to them.[52]

The main question in Zephanic studies in this century has concerned the message of the prophet. But, obviously, one cannot know what the message of the prophet was if one does not know what the prophet said or wrote. Therefore, a second question has come to the forefront: *What* did the prophet say or write? Or in other words, which parts of the Book of Zephaniah are "authentic"? Moreover, the message of the prophet cannot be understood only on the basis of what he said (or wrote) but also *when* and to *whom*.. Finally, there is also the *who* question. That is, what was the social location of the prophet? No one will doubt that at least some facets of Zephaniah's message would have a different sound if the prophet

---

[49] For the commentaries of Rashi, Ibn Ezra and Radak on Zephaniah, see Miqraot Gedolot. The Twelve (NY: Tanach Publishing Co., 1959) 281-89 (Hebrew). It is worth noting that Radak also explicitly stressed the existence of paronomasia. Cf. Radak on Zeph 2:4, and see Melamed, 1978: 849-51.

[50] See M. Luther, *Lectures on the Minor Prophets* (ET R.J. Dinda; Luther's Works vol. 18, St. Louis: Concordia, 1975) and J. Calvin, *Commentaries on the Twelve Minor Prophets*, vol. 4 (ET J. Owen, Grand Rapid: Eerdmans, 1950) 183-312.

[51] Obviously, these considerations are valid insofar as one deals with the non-critical commentaries *as commentaries*; insofar as one approaches them on specific issues, such as the meaning of words, expressions, etc., they are of undisputable value for biblical studies, and accordingly, there are numerous references to these works in the notes section of this work.

[52] The rapid development of literary criticism in biblical studies during the last years has also an impact in Zephanic studies (e.g., House). However, literary criticism does not ask the same kind of questions that the historical-critical methods ask, nor does it use the same methodology.

came from a temple-slave family[53] rather than from the royal house, as sometimes proposed.[54]

To conclude, the questions of what, when, to whom and who have been the main focus in modern historical-critical research.[55]

Although there is general agreement about the existence of small glosses in the text (e.g., עם הכהנים, Zeph 1:4),[56] there is no scholarly consensus over which parts of the Book of Zephaniah are Zephanic and which are not. Nevertheless, there is a widespread assumption that any part of the Book of Zephaniah is Zephanic unless the opposite is proved.[57] That is, the claim of the superscription is accepted on its face value, at least for a considerable part of the book.

An overall view of the issue shows that the Zephanic character of three blocks of material has been at the center of the scholarly discussion concerning the scope of the "authentic" (i.e., Zephanic) material in the Book of Zephaniah: (a) Zeph 1:2-3; (b) Zeph 2:7-11; and (c) Zeph 3:8(14)-20.

The unit consisting of Zeph 1:2-3, or certain part of it, has been considered late, and non-Zephanic, mainly because of its "eschatological"

---

[53] So Bentzen, II: 153.

[54] See J. M. P. Smith: 182-3. This idea had already been proposed by Ibn Ezra, questioned by Radak ("this is possible but there is no proof"), and totally rejected by Abrabanel.

[55] Neither a reader-oriented approach nor a book-as-object approach would ask these questions. The field of Zephanic studies has been dominated by the historical-critical approaches, provided that the term historical-critical is understood in its comprehensive meaning.

[56] For a helpful table of the "authentic" passages according to Rudolph, Elliger, Horst, Keller, Deissler, Gerleman, Krinetzki, Kapelrud, Sellin, Ramir, Bic, Deden, George, Taylor, Langhor, Marti, Irsigler and Edler, see Edler: 261-63. All the scholars mentioned above agree that the expression עם הכהנים is an addition, to them one may add J. M. P. Smith (187-88), Seybold (1985: 13-14, 109), who considers the vv. 3-6 an addition, and others. But see Ball,1972/1988: 25, and cf. House: 118,126.

[57] See, the characteristic expression: "Man hat keinen Anlass Zephanja diese Worte (Zeph 2:8-9) abzusprechen" (Gerleman, 1942: 40). Gerleman did not ask whether there are reasons for attributing these verses to the prophet Zephaniah, who lived in the days of Josiah, except for a possible understanding of the superscription. Cf. with "So there is no *overwhelming* reason to assume that most of this material has been added at a later date (the emphasis is mine)" (Boadt, 1982: 222) and see the short review of the discussion about Zeph 1:2-3 in Langhor, 1976: 4-5.

or universal outlook.[58] Accordingly, this exegetical approach restricts the scope of the message of the prophet Zephaniah. Most scholars, including the vast majority of those who consider most of Zeph 1:2-3 Zephanic, consider והמכשלות את הרשעים in v. 3 an explanatory gloss.[59] The addition of this phrase in v. 3 introduces an ethical reason for the punishment. If the piece is removed from the "original" Zephanic message, then the proposed meaning of the unit would change accordingly.

The main arguments for the lateness of Zeph 2:8-11, or most of its verses, involve: (a) stylistic differences from the announcement of judgment against Philistia, (b) the mention of שארית and יתר pointing to the remnant (if they are not understood as later additions[60]), (c) the "eschatological" contents of v. 11 (if this verse was an original element of the unit at all),[61] and (d) historical improbability, i.e., the described situation of Moab and Ammon scorning Judah and taking advantage of its disgrace does not fit the historical data concerning the days of Josiah but those of the first decades of the sixth century.[62] Those who accept the Zephanic origin for most or all of these verses answer these objections by pointing to rhetorical and literary devices that unify the text;[63] by asserting

---

[58] Cf. Gerleman,1942: 5; Taylor: 1010; Edler: 74-78; Pfeiffer: 600. Those who supported the Zephanic origin of these verses also focused their contra-arguments in the contents of the verses, e.g., J. M. P. Smith: 185-86; Kapelrud: 15-20. But Langhor's suggestion is based on stylistic grounds, Langhor,1976: 5.

[59] Cf. Irsigler,1977: 11-14; Rudolph,1975: 261; Krinetzki 254, Kapelrud,1975: 22. It is noteworthy that in both cases, והמכשלות את הרשעים and עם הכהנים, the almost general agreement concerning their non-Zephanic origin co-exists with a "failure" to occur in G*.

[60] So, for instance, Renaud,1986: 15.

[61] For instance, according to Gerleman, neither for v. 10 nor v. 11 are original elements of the unit. See Gerleman, 1942: 40; cf. Boadt,1982: 218-19. For the contrary opinion, see Christensen: 681-82.

[62] Cf. J.M.P. Smith: 225-230, Taylor: 1009, Edler: 54-56,67-69, 92, Krinetzki: 108-117 (he also provides a comparative analysis of the language of these verses), Pfeiffer: 601. According to Hyatt, the announcements against Moab and Ammon should be considered in the light of 2 Kgs 24:2, i.e., ca. 602 BCE. For Hyatt these announcements are among the main evidences for dating Zephaniah in the days of Jehoiakim (cf. Edens). It is noteworthy that Abrabanel (as well as Rashi, Radak) understood these oracles as grounded on the deeds of Moab and Ammon after the destruction of the Temple. He had no exegetical problem with such understanding because he considers Zephaniah's prophecy, or better the word of God, as directed to a future known to the deity.

[63] E.g., Ball, 1972/1988:129-49, Christensen, esp. 671-77, cf. Kapelrud,1975: 34-35.

that the reasons based on contents proposed by the other scholars are unconvincing;[64] and by arguing that announcements of judgment against Moab and Ammon are not impossible in Josiah's days,[65] or that they, along with the other oracles against the nations in this book correspond exactly to the political situation in the time of Josiah, ca. 628-621.[66]

Concerning v. 7, expressions like שׁב שׁבותם, שׁארית בית יהודה and the theme of restoration are considered clear signs of lateness (see point b, above).[67] On the other hand, other scholars deny that these expressions should be viewed as exilic or post-exilic or that the prophet Zephaniah was devoid of nationalistic feelings, and accordingly they consider the verse Zephanic.[68]

If all these verses are Zephanic, the message of the prophet included an announcement of territorial expansion beyond the Judean limits for the future Judean remnant (or, according to another position, for his contemporaneous Judeans) and an announcement that YHWH will cause the other gods to shrivel and that all the peoples will bow down to YHWH. If none of the verses is Zephanic, the message of the prophet included two main oracles against the nations, namely, against Assyria and Philistia. These countries are considered by many scholars the main enemies of Judah in the Josianic era. Accordingly, the relative weight of the political and earthly elements in Zephaniah's message tends to be stressed. On the other hand if vv. 8-9[a] are Zephanic, there may be grounds for an understanding of the message of Zephaniah in terms less dependent on concrete political-historical circumstances.

---

[64] E.g., Gerleman, 1942: 40; S.R. Driver: 342; Bic: 62-63.

[65] E.g., Rudolph,1975: 281-82, Bic: 63, Eiselen: 519, cf. G. A. Smith: 42, Eissfeldt: 424, who do not take a definite position. The supposedly Scythian threat over all the area is considered by some scholars a possible background for the prophecies of Zephaniah, and proposed lines of advance for the Scythian army are sometimes brought into the discussion (e.g., G.A. Smith: 42; J. M. P. Smith: 230; cf. Ball, 1972/1988:286), but see Edler: 49-51, and D. L. Williams,1963: 79-83.

[66] E.g., Christensen, esp. 677-682.

[67] Among those scholars who consider late either v. 7 or at least the phrases containing the language mentioned above, one may mention Rudolph, 1975: 275, 280; Elliger: 67; J. M. P. Smith: 219-20; Langhor, 1976:26; Edler: 84-86; Taylor: 1112.

[68] E.g., Kapelrud: 67-68; Gerleman,1942: 35-36; cf. Ball, 1972/1988: 105, 114-129.

Many scholars have considered the unit consisting of Zeph 3:8-20 to be non-Zephanic. The basic assumption underlying this position is that words of salvation or comfort and especially the motif of universal salvation, occur mainly (or only?) in exilic and post-exilic literature.[69] If Zeph 3:8-20 is late, the message of the prophet would have no (or almost no) words of salvation, or comfort. Renaud allows the possibility of Zephanic elements in vv. 11-13*, and for Edler these verses are Zephanic with the exception of שארית ישׂראל and מחריד ואין ורבצו ירעו כי המה.[70] The issue at stake is obviously not whether to add another two verses to Zephaniah or not. It concerns the entire message of the prophet. If these two verses fall, then Zeph 2:3 would have probably the same fate,[71] and therefore the social-ethical message of the prophet Zephaniah would fall as well. Other scholars consider vv. 9-13 Zephanic, mainly on the basis of their relation to vv. 1-8, or because they consider the idea that the peoples will serve YHWH to be preexilic, or both.[72] If these verses are Zephanic, the message of the prophet would have also included the image of a universal salvation and the "universalistic" image of all the peoples serving one God, YHWH. Finally, if vv. 14-20, or most of the material included in these verses, are "authentic," then they would receive a totally different meaning than what the address in second person may suggest. For these verses would not be a call of joy for the prophet's audience (like many Psalms), but a call of joy for the future Jerusalem envisaged by the prophet, a future Jerusalem that will come only for the "poor and humble" and only after the awesome judgment of the Day of YHWH.[73]

---

[69] Cf. J. M. P. Smith: 248-263; Taylor: 1113; Langhor,1976: 26; Sandmel, 1963: 106,110-111; Pfeiffer: 601. This proposal goes back to Wellhausen, Stade, Schwally and others. Seybold (1985, 58-62,112; 1985a, 43-44) acknowledges the existence of a Zephanic kernel, but his proposed reconstruction of the text leads to a meaning that sharply differs from the MT.

[70] See Renaud: 19-33; Edler: 219-228.

[71] Cf. Scharbert: 242-45.

[72] Cf. Eiselen: 520; Kapelrud,1975: 79-80; Rudolph,1975: 256, 295-97; Boadt, 1982: 223-26.

[73] So Kapelrud, 1975: 89-90.

Most modern scholars accept as historical the information given in Zeph 1:1, according to which Zephaniah prophesied in the days of Josiah. The main issue remains: When in the days of Josiah? Before the reform, at the time of the reform, or after it? The arguments brought on behalf of the idea that he prophesied before the reformation are basically: (a) The king is not mentioned in Zeph 1:4-9, and especially in v. 8 where the officers and "the sons of the king" are mentioned, therefore one may infer that the king had no real influence and power, i.e., Josiah was a minor (cf. 2 Kgs 22:1).[74] (b) The cultic notice in Zeph 1:5 reflects the situation before the reform but not after.[75] (c) The harsh words of Zephaniah make sense if they were addressed to such a syncretistic community. If this picture is correct, then the message of Zephaniah may have prepared the ground for the reform. Arguments (b) and (c) may also be interpreted as pointing to the time of the reform.[76] If that is the case, then Zephaniah's message reflects the ideas of the group that welcomed and advanced the deuteronomic reform in Josiah's days. Moreover, the contents and the language of Zeph 1:4-5 show clear similarities to deuteronomic language and ideas.[77] Christensen, as mentioned before, goes further. According to him, Zephaniah had something to do not only with the cultic reform but also with Josianic politics.[78]

However, it is noteworthy that the message of the prophet, if taken on its face value, was not: mend your ways, reform the cult and live. Instead, it announced that whatever the community does the day of judgment will come, and only those "humble" people who seek YHWH will perhaps live. If this "literal" understanding is accepted,[79] it seems difficult to reconcile with Deuteronomy, or with a real reformative

---

[74] E.g., J. M. P. Smith:196; Bic: 42; Keller: 181.

[75] E.g., Rudolph,1975: 255.

[76] In this case, Josiah and Zephaniah would be on the same side.

[77] E.g., Scharbert, Langhor.

[78] See, Christensen: 669-682.

[79] E.g., Hunter: 259-72.

policy.[80] Alternatively, if Zephaniah was active in the reform then his
sayings should not be understood in a "literal" sense.

The proposal that Zephaniah prophesied after the reform is based on
understanding שאר הבעל in Zeph 1:4 as "the remnant of Baal."[81]
Provided that this understanding is correct,[82] one may assume that
Zephaniah knew about the reform, and in spite of it, or because its success
was only partial, prophesied the coming judgment.

Obviously, after the reform may also be after Josiah. Accordingly,
Hyatt considers שאר הבעל, understood as "the remnant of Baal," one of
the items in Zephaniah that fits more the days of Jehoiakim than those of
Josiah.   The second item from the religious realm is Zeph 1:12.
According to Hyatt, the cynicism expressed there can be explained by the
failure of the Josianic reform and by the real outcome of his foreign
policy. He finds further support for his position in the section containing
the oracles against the nations, including those against Ammon and Moab
(cf. 2 Kgs 24:2).[83] The oracle against Assyria then would be after the
event and not before; the "historical motivation of Zephaniah would be the
Babylonian advance in the reign of Jehoiakim;"[84] and the failure of the
deuteronomic reform and the Josianic policies would be the background of
the Zephaniah's words.

Finally, Smith and Lacheman wrote a comparative and linguistical
analysis of the book. They found many expressions pointing to an exilic
or post-exilic date. If the book was always a unit, as Smith and Lacheman
think, then it is obvious that it cannot antedate the latest of its elements.
Thus, the Book of Zephaniah should be considered post-exilic. Smith and

---

[80] G. A. Smith copes with this difficulty by separating Zephaniah from the reformers.
According to him, Zephaniah had no interest in the reform. See G. A. Smith: 45-54.
Obviously, another form of coping with this tension is to propose a post-reform date for
Zephaniah. See D. L. Williams, 1963, esp. 79,83.

[81] E.g., Hitzig.

[82] This understanding seems to be erroneous, see notes on Zeph 1:4.

[83] See Hyatt. See also D. L. Williams.

[84] D. L. Williams,1963: 83.

Lacheman go beyond that and on the basis of the apocalyptic contents of chapter 3, conclude that the book was written ca. 200 BCE.[85]

The question of the audience of Zephaniah is closely related to the question of date. No one really doubts that Zephaniah (or the author of the book) was a Jerusalemite and that he spoke or wrote to his contemporaries. The issue is who were these contemporaries? In what religio-political and social circumstances did they live? The meaning given to the message of the prophet would be dependent on the response to this question.

The last question concerns the social location of the prophet. It seems quite obvious that no one can write a biography of Zephaniah. But D. L. Williams holds that he was one the most important priests of the Jerusalemite Temple (the one mentioned in 2 Kgs 25:18).[86] If this is the case then the Book of Zephaniah would be a document for the understanding of the priestly theology of the late monarchic period. From this perspective, the message of Zephaniah would have had a somewhat different sound.

The present survey of the modern history of research has shown the main historical-critical questions that have been asked and the main answers that have been proposed to them. It is clear that there is no consensus concerning the social location of the prophet, his historical circumstances, the scope of his sayings, the message conveyed by his sayings, and the identity of the addressees. It should be noted that the main questions, and obviously the proposed responses to them, concern the message of the prophet Zephaniah. Both the possible message and the socio-historical background of materials that were considered non-Zephanic have received much less attention.

---

[85] Smith and Lacheman: 137-42.

[86] D. L. Williams, 1963: 85-88. Most scholars do not support Williams' suggestion because of the lack of concrete evidence for the identification of Zephaniah with Zephaniahu, the priest. There have been other proposals, e.g., royal origin (e.g., J. M. P. Smith: 183), Temple slave origin (Bentzen, II: 153) and African roots (Rice). All are based on particular interpretations of Zeph 1:1. None of these interpretations is widely accepted today, but if they are considered compelling, they would be significant for the understanding of Zephaniah's message.

3. Textual, Linguistic and Comparative Notes

3.1 Preliminary Remarks

The purpose of the textual, linguistic, and comparative notes is twofold: to explain the meaning of words and expressions occurring in the Book of Zephaniah and to compare the use of these words and expressions in this book with their use in other biblical material.

The importance of a careful explanation of the meaning of words and expressions for a historical-critical analysis of the book, as the present one, is self-evident. The first step in any analysis of the text is the study of the "plain" level of meaning of its expressions, including an examination of their most probable usage. To a large extent, it is correct to say that before this step we have no real text but only a cluster of dots, bars and blank spaces to be deciphered. Since this stage provides the data for any subsequent analysis, it is crucial that it not be biased by presuppositions concerning the expected results of the subsequent steps. One cannot reach, for instance, an unbiased understanding of the meaning of the expressions occurring in a certain unit if one presupposes beforehand that the unit is a part of a cultic liturgy or a speech of a social reformer. In order to minimalize circular reasoning, one should examine first the meaning of the expression, and then, and only then, weigh the evidence for possible settings, dates, and socio-historical circumstances.

In addition, the pattern of occurrence of expressions in the Old Testament may point to a network of texts in which a certain set of expressions carrying a specific meaning tends to occur. The potential importance of such networks for a historical-critical analysis of the book has been discussed more fully in chapter 1 (Methodological Guidelines).

Thus, the goal of the following notes is to establish and examine the evidence concerning the meaning of words and expressions occurring in the Book of Zephaniah. Special attention will be given to the text of those units that have served as main points of support for scholarly positions concerning the Book of Zephaniah, or its different units. The results of the studies reported in these notes will be the basic set of data to be interpreted in the commentary section (chapter 4). Thus, while the notes section provides the data for the historical-critical analysis, the analysis is developed in the commentary section of this work.

From a historical-critical perspective, the book (at any of its presumed or reconstructed redactional stages), as well as any traditions that may be embedded in it, is a communicative object, that is, an object that was produced by a community or communities in dialogue with its or their own actual, or self-perceived, circumstances. Since this is so, one cannot fully understand the meaning conveyed by the text to the community that produced it without knowing about the community, its historical circumstances, its self image, the system of religio-cultural presuppositions held by the community, and the social role of the text (its reading or its listening) in the specific community. The purpose of this work is to shed light on these issues in order to understand the text/s as functional communicative object/s of the community/ies in which it has been shaped.

But, obviously, one cannot understand the meaning conveyed by the text to the community that produced it if one does not carefully analyze the most probable plain sense of the words and expressions that provide the "material" basis of the text. To illustrate this with one example: One may wonder about the real significance of a simple English expression like "I love you," in a certain text, or in a certain social occasion. But, undoubtedly, any possible conclusion in this respect will be entirely misleading if one assumes that, in its simplest level of meaning, "I love you" means "you love me," or if one assumes beforehand that "I love you" is used mainly, or even only, in relation to religious or cultic activities; or if one assumes that the substitution of "you" by "thee" will not change the meaning of the expression. This almost ridiculous example points to the necessity of a careful grammatical reading, of a careful textual and linguistic analysis of the expressions in the text, and of a careful consideration of the pattern of their occurrence, before beginning the analysis of the communicative significance of the text. In other words, the notes are an indispensable step before the commentary.

3.2 Notes on Zephaniah 1

3.2.1. Zeph 1:1

The superscription (Zeph 1:1) is one of the type "The 'word' of YHWH (דבר ה') that came to X," in which X stands for the name of the prophet.[1] This type is also attested in the prophetic superscriptions of the books of Hosea, Joel, Micah and Jeremiah (LXX),[2] and it may be considered a superscriptional variant of narrative openings like the "word event formula" (i.e., ויהי דבר ה' אל X, "the word of YHWH came to X")[3] and of similar expressions.[4]

---

[1] Other types of prophetic superscriptions are: (a) the "words of X, who . . . " (see Jer 1:1; Am 1:1); (b) those who use different kinds of *hazon* formulas (e.g., Isa 1:1, 2:1; Obad 1:1; Nah 1:1b); and (c) those who use different *masa* formulas (e.g., Isa 13:1 15:1, 17:1, 19:1, 21:1,11,13, 23:1, 30:6; Nah 1:1a, Hab 1:1; Zech 9:1, 12:1; Mal 1:1).

[2] See Hos 1:1; Joel 1:1; Mic 1:1; Jer (LXX) 1:1. Cf. Zech 4:6. On Jer 1:1, see Mc Kane: 2-3.

[3] This formula occurs many times in Jeremiah and Ezekiel (e.g., Jer 1:4,11,13; 2:1, passim; Ezek 3:16, 6:1, 7:1, passim), and elsewhere in Latter Prophets in Isa 38:4; Jonah 1:1, 3:1; Zech 4:8, 6:9, 7:4,8, 8:18. It is noteworthy that this pattern of occurrence cannot be the result of blind chance. This formula occurs elsewhere in the OT in 1 Sam 15:10; 2 Sam 7:4; 1 Kgs 6:11, 13:20, 16:1, 17:2,8, 21:17,28. For the formula in general, see, for instance, Rendtorff, 1986: 116.

[4] Such as X-ל היה דבר ה' (e.g., Isa 28:13) and X-אל היה דבר ה' (e.g., Jer 1:2; Hag 2:10,20; Zech 1:1,7, 7:1). In addition to their occurrences in Latter Prophets, these formulae (with slight variations) occur in Gen 15:1; 2 Sam 24:11; 1 Kgs 18:1. See also the expression מאת ה'

The superscriptional idiom "the word of YHWH that came to X" does not mean that the following text consists of words spoken directly by YHWH to X. This is clear from the fact that there are passages in Hosea, Joel, Micah, Zephaniah and Jeremiah (LXX) in which either YHWH or the prophet or both are mentioned in the third person (i.e., passages that do not claim to contain the word spoken by YHWH to the prophet X). Thus, on the basis of the content and on the basis of the attested meaning of דבר in many of its occurrences as nomen regens, one may conclude that דבר ה' in the superscription means: the matter from (of) YHWH.[5] Accordingly, the superscription formula in Zeph 1:1 is to be understood as: "The matter from YHWH that came to X."

Zephaniah is presented in Zeph 1:1 as the son of Cushi, son of Gedaliah, son of Amariah, son of Hezekiah. Zeph 1:1 is the only superscription in the Latter Prophets in which a list mentioning five generations occurs.[6] Moreover, Zephaniah is the only prophet who is introduced in such a way in these books.[7] Furthermore, identifying a person by a genealogical list going back four generations, or more, is a very uncommon feature in the entire OT except in Ezra, Nehemiah and 1-2 Chronicles.[8] In the OT a

---

הדבר אשר היה אל ירמיהו (Jer 7:1, 11:1, 18:1, 34:1,8, 35:1, 40:1). It is worth noting that there is a certain tendency in the Book of Haggai to use the preposition ביד instead of ל or אל , see Hag 1:1, 3; 2:1 (cf. Mal 1:1 and 1 Kgs 16:7).

5 Cf. the Siloam inscription, line 1 (. . . וזה דבר הנקבה . . .) and cf. זה דבר הרצח in Deut. 19:4, for further undoubtedly cases of דבר meaning "matter" see, for instance, 1 Sam 4: 6, 10:2; 1 Kgs 15:5; Job 19:28.

6 A superscription mentioning five generations occurs in Tob 1:1, and other mentioning six generations in Bar 1:1. It is noteworthy that in both cases all the fathers and forefathers of the "hero" have exactly the same theophoric element at the end of their names (e.g., Baruch son of Neriah, son of Mahseiah, son of Zedekiah, son of Hasadiah, son of Hilkiah), but strangely enough in both cases the name of the "hero" (i.e., Tobit and Baruch) stands outside this pattern. Cf. the last three names in the genealogical line of Zephaniah. Besides Zeph 1:1, the longest genealogical list in prophetic superscriptions is Zech 1:1 (cf. Zech 1:7). But the list there goes back only to the grandfather of Zechariah, and is probably the result of a secondary addition due to an erroneous identification of Zechariah, the prophet, with the one mentioned in Isa 8:2 (cf. Ezra 5:1). On these issues, see below.

7 Another prophet (Jahaziel son of Zechariah son of Benaiah son of Jeiel son of Mataniah the Levite, of the sons of Asaph) is presented by mentioning four generations, but in 2 Chr 20:14. The recurrence of the same theophoric element in three out of the four fathers is noteworthy.

8 The most common way to identify a person in the OT is by mentioning his name and his father's name (e.g., Isa 1:1, 2:1,13:1; Jer 1:1; Ezek 1:3; Hos 1:1; Joel 1:1; Jonah 1:1.). Sometimes a gentilic or a "professional" or a geographical note (or a combination of

person is introduced in this way four times: (a) in Zeph 1:1; (b) in Num 27:1 (// Josh 17:3); (c) in 1 Sam 1:1; and (d) in 1 Sam 9:1. The reason for the mention of the fourth forefather (i.e., Manasseh) in the story of the daughters of Zelophehad (Num 27:1) is clear, namely, the story is about their claim to their portion in the tribal inheritance of Manasseh. The person who is introduced in 1 Sam 9:1 is Kish the father of king Saul, but actually the latter is the one who is introduced, obliquely. Similarly, although Elkanah, the father of Samuel, is presented in 1 Sam 1:1, it is Samuel who is introduced, again in an oblique way. Thus, clearly, the long genealogical list in Zeph 1:1 is indeed an uncommon feature. Since it is generally accepted that genealogical lists do not simply pile up names but assert claims for certain social relationships,[9] then how can one explain the unusually long list in Zeph 1:1? [10]

---

them) is added to his name (e.g., 1 Sam 26:6,27:3; Hab 1:1; Mic 1:1), or to his name and the name of his father (e.g., Exod 31:6; 2 Kgs 13:1; Isa 39:1; Jer 20:1). There a very few cases in which only the name of the person is given (e.g., Obad 1:1, but cf. Mal 1:1). Also there are some genealogical lists that go back to second generation (e.g, 2 Kgs 22:3, Jer 36:11), or even to the third generation (e.g., Num 16:1; Jer 36:14). For epigraphic evidence for the mention of the third generation in some material from the late monarchic period, see bullae 21, 23, 79, and 113 in Avigad, 1986: 38, 39, 65.

There are seven lists in the OT that go back four generations (without counting parallels and including Zeph 1:1). Four out of these seven lists are in Ezra-Nehemiah-1-2 Chronicles. Moreover, all the twelve lists (without counting parallels) that go back more than four generations occur in Ezra-Nehemiah-1-2 Chronicles. For the lists and a for a discussion on ways of identification in ancient Israel, and their implications, see Auprecht.

[9] On the general issue of genealogy and social claims, see Wilson, 1977; see also Halpern, 1988: 245, and esp. 271-75

[10] Obviously, modern scholars are not the first to figure out that there is something "strange" in Zeph 1:1. The Babylonian Talmud explains this according to the rule that when the father of a righteous person is mentioned this is done in order to underline that he was also a righteous person (and vice versa if the person is a wrongdoer). ᶜUlla (עולא) said that if the name of the father of a prophet is mentioned, it is because he was a prophet (See B Meg 15a). Cf. Jerome, In Sophoniam i, 4-13 (p. 656). Ibn Ezra thought that the list goes back to Hezekiah, king of Judah, the most important of Zephaniah's ancestors (Ibn Ezra on Zeph 1:1). Since he explicitly gives an answer to the chronological objections that such proposal may provoke, one may conclude that such objections were already made. Radak claims that there is no evidence supporting the identification of Hezekiah as king Hezekiah (for this question see below). According to Radak, the persons whose names have been quoted in Zeph 1:1 were גדולים, i.e., important figures. Abrabanel considered them respectful persons or perhaps prophets but he strongly denied that Hezekiah is Hezekiah, king of Judah. Calvin knew about ᶜUlla's proposal and rejected it; however, he thought that it is possible that all the persons mentioned in Zeph 1:1 "excelled in piety" (Calvin: 184). According to Luther, they belonged to the order of the prophets (see Luther: 320, cf. Luther: 129).

Two names focused the attention of the scholars: Cushi and Hezekiah. The first may be understood as a gentilic.[11] If this is the case, Zephaniah's family came either from a "Bedouin" tribe[12] or from כוש = Nubia.[13] But Cushi may also be a personal name,[14] and actually functions in Zeph 1:1 as a personal name (equivalent to Gedaliah, Amariah and Hezekiah). Of course, if Cushi is (or was understood) only as a simple personal name it will not explain the existence of the long genealogical list in Zeph 1:1.

The name Cushi also occurs in a three-generation list in Jer 36:14 (the text is questionable).[15] There Cushi is the last name of the list. Accordingly, it is possible that Cushi in Jer 36:14 was (or was understood as) pointing to a foreign origin, and that the three-generations were related to the qualifications for being a member of קהל ה' (i.e., congregation of YHWH) in Deut 23, and especially to that laid down in Deut 23:8-9 ("children born to them—Egyptians—may be admitted into the

---

11 For instance, Num 12:1; Jer 38:7, 10,12; 2 Chr 14:8

12 See Hab 3:7; 2 Chr 14: 8-14 (esp. v. 14), 21:16 . Probably the historical kernel of the war that Othniel the son of Kenaz (see Josh 15: 5-19) fought against Cushan Reshataim (Judg 3:7-10) is related to these Cushites, who dwelt near the Southern borders of Judah. Perhaps such understanding is in the background of the tradition attested in the Lives of the Prophets, according to which Zephaniah was from the tribe of Simeon (i.e., Southern Judah), but this is obviously only a speculation. For alternative proposals concerning the historical kernel of the Othniel story, see Bartlett, 1989: 45 and especially 93-94 and the bibliography mentioned there.

13 According to Bentzen, כוש is a gentilic and Zephaniah came from a temple-slave family. See Bentzen: II, 153. According to Rice, Gedaliah, the grandson of king Hezekiah married an Ethiopian woman. Their son Cushi was named after the mother's country of origin, breaking a familiar tradition of Yahwistic names. Rice proposes the existence of several marriages between members of the Jerusalemite elite and Ethiopians . He relates them to the period of close relationship between the Judah and the 25th (Nubian) dynasty in Egypt, and especially to the days of the anti-Assyrian pact (ca. 705-701 BCE). See Rice.

14 For instance, Ps 7:1 (but not 2 Sam 18:21) and probably also Jer 36:14, see Carroll, 1986: 659. The name כשי is attested epigraphically, see Lawton: 340, J. M. P. Smith,184. An Aramean Ku-sa-a-a is mentioned in Haran, another in Nineveh (second part VII century). The name Ku-si-i is attested in Calah (the sh>s shift in Akkadian transcription of Western Semitic names is well known, e.g., הושע -A-u-si-i'). A Phoenician KS(h)Y wrote his name at Abu Simbel during the VIIth century, and the name Kus(h)i occurs also in Elephantine. See Lipínski, 1975: 689. For objections to Lipínski's understanding of Cushi, see Rice: 23-25.

15 This list may be the result of the obliteration, by chance or intentional, of an original ואת, which put together two names of the regular type, Z son of X. See Carroll,1986: 659 and the bibliography cited there.

congregation of YHWH in the third generation"), provided that (a) Cushi
means Nubian, and (b) that the law concerning the Egyptians was also
applied to the Nubians.[16] If this is the case, the aim of the relatively long
list in Jer 36:14 would be to prove that the "officer" (שׂר) Yehudi was
(qualified to be) a member of the "congregation of YHWH."

However, since the list in Zeph 1:1 opens with "Zephaniah son of
Cushi," this explanation is completely inadequate for Zeph 1:1. This does
not rule out the possibility that a later scribe, who thought that a foreign
ancestor was something inappropriate for a prophet of YHWH, added to
the original "Zephaniah son of Cushi" the names of three former
ancestors, each of them with a theophoric element יה, in order to prove
that Zephaniah was of Judean origin. If this is the case, Zeph 1:1 would
propose a solution to the problem concerning the relative foreignness of a
prominent Judean, as it is presented, for instance, by Deut 23:8-9. Of
course, this solution is different from the one in Jer 36:14. According to
Zeph 1:1, Cushi would not have been a Nubian but the son of a Judean
family who had clung for generations to the worship of YHWH.
Moreover, it can hardly be an accident that the third name that the late
scribe added to the list—according to this proposal—is the name of the
pious king Hezekiah. To sum up: According to this proposal, because of
the "emendation" of the original genealogical list, Zephaniah turned out to
be not only a "pure" Judean but also a member of the royal family, and no
less than kin of a king who supposedly reformed the cult in a way similar
to that "preached" by the prophet.[17]

It should be noticed that the main hypothesis in this proposal is that the
long list was written by a scribe who understood, or was afraid that others
could understand, Cushi as a gentilic. Accordingly the acceptance of this
theory implies two conclusions: (a) there is no historical ground for the
royal origin of Zephaniah, and (b) the original meaning of Cushi remains
an open question.

---

[16] Cf. Gen 10:6

[17] See Heller.

According to others, the long list was original and its purpose was to stress the fact that Zephaniah was a descendant of the king Hezekiah.[18] Obviously, the name Hezekiah need not necessarily be understood as referring to the king,[19] but in the vast majority of its occurrences in the OT it does refer to him. Moreover, if the genealogical list was "original" then the unusual reference back to four generations seems to make sense only if Hezekiah was the king. Alternatively, if the list was a literary list that tried to "clean" the name of Zephaniah, again, the most probable Hezekiah referred to is the king.

On the other hand, the existence of a reading חלקיה instead חזקיה in the Peshitta[20] (which may be considered as pointing to an alternative Hebrew reading), as well as in some MT MSS,[21] is hardly understood if an "original" or "scribal" tradition concerning the king Hezekiah was known. Significantly, although Hezekiah was considered the prominent king of Judah during the monarchic period, there is no evidence pointing to the existence of traditions connecting king Hezekiah with Zephaniah. Quite the contrary, there are places in which references to a royal origin are expected to be mentioned (e.g., Lives of the Prophets, b. Meg 15[a]), but they do not occur. Instead, one may find notes that are clearly incompatible with the idea of Zephaniah's royal origin (e.g., Lives of the

---

[18] For instance, J. M. P. Smith: 183; Taylor: 1009; Rice, especially pp. 21-22; cf. Pfeiffer: 600. Also see footnote 9.

[19] See 1 Chr 3:23; Neh 7:21, 10:18. Yet, חזקיהו refers only to the king and the late form יחזקיהו (forty-one occurrences) refers to someone other than the king only in 2 Chr 28:12.

[20] For the critical text of the Syriac Zephaniah, see *Vetus Testamentus Syriace* , published by "The Peshitta Institute", Leyden. This reading was probably the source behind Barhebraeus' claim that Jeremiah and Zephaniah were relatives, i.e., Hilkiah, the father of Jeremiah was the same (or a relative?, see below) of the Hilkiah mentioned in Zeph 1:1. See Gerleman, 1942:1. The obvious objection against the claim that the two Hilkiah were in fact one is chronological. One is described as Jeremiah's father (Jer 1:1), and the other as the grandfather of the grandfather of Zephaniah (Zeph 1:1). But Zephaniah and Jeremiah were contemporaneous.

[21] This is one of the forty-nine cases where the Peshitta to the "Twelve Prophets" is in accord with several masoretic MSS against the common MT. For the full list, and for the Syriac text of the "Twelve Prophets" as a testimony for a masoretic text of the "Twelve Prophets" that slightly deviates from the received MT, see Gelston: 120-21, 125.
The ancient masoretic text of the "Twelve Prophets" from Wadi Murabba'at (second century CE), is not extant at Zeph 1:1; see DJD II, Texts:200. For the list of the masoretic MSS reading חלקיה, see J. M. P. Smith: 185 . See also J. M. P. Smith: 185 for an Armenian Ms. that might point to a Greek tradition reading "Hilkiah".

Prophets).[22] How can one explain that just this Hezekian "tradition" concerning Zephaniah's ancestors "disappeared," in a period when traditions and legends about this king flourish?[23]

Thus, it seems that, in ancient times, the Hezekiah mentioned in Zeph 1:1 was not understood as king Hezekiah. Moreover, such understanding is not strange at all. To the contrary, it seems to be based on the general way in which people are introduced into OT units, and especially kings. Namely, when the name of the king is mentioned for the first time in a certain unit, there is an explicit reference to his father, or to the fact that he is a king, or in most of the cases to both (e.g., Isa 1:1, 7:1, 36:1, 39:1; Jer 1:3, 22:11, 18; 27:6; Ezek 1:2; 29:18, 33:2; Am 1:1, 7:10; cf. Prov 1:1, 25:1; Qoh 1:1; etc.).[24] Thus, the mention of the "bare" name Hezekiah could not reasonably prompted the "careful" reader to the assumption that this Hezekiah is king Hezekiah, but probably to the opposite assumption. Therefore, it seems unlikely that the "author" of the superscription (or of the addition of the name Hezekiah to an original list) had as its (main) goal to stress the royal origin of Zephaniah.[25] Thus, one may ask, what was his/her intention?

---

[22] A Simeonite origin is incompatible with a royal origin. See, Lives of the Prophets, Zephaniah 1.

[23] At least from the time of the author of the Book of Chronicles and thereafter Hezekiah was considered the most pious king of Judah (except David) . His image came to be very close to the image of the Messiah, at least in post-70 CE Judaism. Several messianic verses were interpreted as concerning him, (see for instance b. San. 94a). It is not surprising, therefore, that there are more legends concerning Hezekiah and his time than concerning all the other kings of the divided monarchy. None of these legends, however, mentions the genealogical relationship between Zephaniah and Hezekiah.

[24] The supposedly exceptions in Isa 44:28, 45:1 are not such. The text makes clear who is this Cyrus, and the expression "my shepherd" conveys the royal meaning. Any reference to "Cyrus, the king" in these texts is both unnecessary and diminishing. Actual exceptions to this rule are relatively few and most of them are relatively late, such as the superscription to Canticles or the superscriptions to individual Psalms. Zech 1:1 is worthy of a study as part of a more comprehensive study on the compositional and redactional history of the book, and its probable relationship with the compositional and redactional history of Haggai. Non-royal figures are also presented by their name and any combination of the name of their father, a title, a place name, or a gentilic. See Auprecht.

[25] It is noteworthy that King Hezekiah is never called חזקיה or חזקיהו in the prophetic superscriptions (as in Zeph 1:1) but יחזקיה or יחזקיהו, see Isa 1:1; Hos 1:1; Mic 1:1.

If the Hilkiah reading is sustained, all three names following Cushi would be names of priests in the restoration period.[26] Two of them (Amariah and Hilkiah) are also attested as the names of two supposedly High Priests from the monarchic period.[27] Amariah and Hilkiah are mentioned among the ancestors of Ezra (Ezra 7:1), and the two names are widely attested as names of priests. The third name, Gedaliah, is mentioned as the name of a priest from the line of Jeshua the son of Jozadak (the High Priest in the days of Zerubabel). This Gedaliah is one of the four priests (two of them with the theophoric element יה in their names) from this family who sent away their "foreign" women, according to Ezra 10:18. This action reflects an ideological position similar to the one that may have made necessary the long genealogical list in Zeph 1:1. Even if the coincidental explanation cannot be dismissed, these data clearly point to the possibility that the scribe who added three further names after כושי had in mind a priestly image of Zephaniah and not a royal one. If this is the case, the ancestors' list of Zephaniah could be a source for the study of the writer's time but not a source concerning the historical Zephaniah, the son of Cushi.

Nevertheless, this proposal is not without serious objections. The most important of them is that while the change from ז to ל is easily explained as a scribal error due to the similarity between the two letters in Syriac,[28] such graphical error is much less likely in Hebrew. However, it is noteworthy that there are several MT Mss reading Hilkiah, and the Peshitta agrees with "deviant" readings within the masoretic textual tradition in no less than 49 cases.[29] Thus, one cannot rule out the possibility that there were parallel (and alternative) Hebrew traditions. Obviously, the existence of two parallel Hebrew traditions does not imply that the "Hilkiah" reading should be the original, but only that it may have been the original. The

---

[26] See Ezra 7:3, 10:18; Neh 12: 7,12, 21.

[27] See, for instance, 2 Kgs 22:4; 2 Chr 19:11.

[28] See, for instance, Gerleman, 1942 : 1.

[29] See footnote 20.

existence of ancient parallel traditions certainly does not support the proposal that Hezekiah in Zeph 1:1 was understood as the famous king.[30]

Whether the name of the ancestor is Hezekiah or Hilkiah, one thing is clear: three clear Yahwistic names are mentioned before the name Cush. If Cush could have been understood as pointing to a non-Israelite origin, the list claims that he was a member of an "old" Yahwistic family, i.e., an Israelite (or Judean) family. Certainly, the existence of three generations of names ending with יה is possible in the late monarchic period.[31] However, lists of three consecutive names ending with יה occur rarely in the OT. They do occur as a part of longer list in Ezra 7:1, and Neh 11:4, 12:35. In this respect, it is noteworthy that list in Ezra 7:1-5 includes the names of Amariah and Hilkiah, and the list in Neh 11:4 also mentions the name Amariah (cf. Zeph 1:1). However, in the other three occurrences of such lists in the OT (Jer 35:3, 37:13, 51:59) the people who are introduced in this way[32] are supposed to be roughly contemporaneous with Zephaniah.

Finally, one cannot but notice that in general terms, the unusual relatively long genealogical lists become less unusual in the latter layers of the OT; that a prophet is introduced by genealogical list going back four generations in 2 Chr 20:14 (apparently without any special reason); and

---

[30] In this respect it should be noticed that if the name Hezekiah does not point to king Hezekiah (see above) then there is no reason to consider the Hezekiah reading the "easier" of the two.

[31] See the prosopographic list in Tigay: 47-63 that shows a relatively significant number of persons who carry a name ending with יהו and whose fathers also carried these kind of names. About half of the persons from the late monarchic period whose bullae have been published by Avigad and whose name ends with יהו have also a father whose name ends with יהו, see Avigad, 1986: 137-39. The probability that a person who has a name ending with יהו will have a father and grandfather with a name ending in the same way is approximately the square of the percentage of people whose name ends with יהו have a father whose name ends with יהו. Applying this calculation to the case of Avigad's bullae, the probability that a person mentioned there and whose name ended in יהו had a father and a grandfather whose names also ended with the theophoric element יהו is about 0.25. Of course, this calculation holds true only if the pattern of giving names remained unchanged through the generations.

[32] They are among the five persons mentioned in Jeremiah who have a name ending in יה and whose father's name and grandfather's name is mentioned. The other two are Micaiah son of Gemariahu son of Shaphan (Jer 36: 11) and Gedaliah son of Ahikam son of Shaphan (e.g., Jer 40:5).

that in sharp contrast with the prophetic superscriptions, the superscriptions of Tobit and Baruch mention five and six generations (Tob 1:1, Bar 1:1). Moreover, in Baruch the list is the result of a lengthening of an original shorter genealogical notice: "Baruch son of Neriah son of Mahseiah (Jer 32:12)." This list was expanded with other names ending in יה. Also the list in Tobit is built on names whose endings are identical, except for the hero of the book. These cases may suggest that there was a tendency to lengthen genealogical lists with names built according to a same pattern. Thus, if Zeph 1:1 had a shorter genealogical list that was lengthened later, then the way in which this lengthening would have been done is similar to the one found in Baruch, and similar to the way in which the artificial genealogy of Tobit has been written.[33]

To conclude, it is clear that the long genealogical list removes a possible suspicion concerning the origin of Zephaniah that may have been derived from the occurrence of the name Cushi. Since Zeph 1:1 is the only prophetic superscription that contains such a long list, one may assume that the list occurs because it "cleans" the name of Zephaniah from suspect. It seems possible, but unprovable, that there was a shorter original genealogical list including only Zephaniah and Cushi, or Zephaniah, Cushi and Gedaliah, and that later this list was lengthened. If there was such a lengthening, its date cannot be asserted, though the data mentioned above may suggest a date later than the early post-exilic period. In any case, one can conclude that the mentioned Zephaniah was considered the son of Cushi, and that Cushi, here, is nothing but a name (like Gedaliah, or Amariah, or Hezekiah), and that this name is well attested epigraphically in West Semitic languages. Any answer to the remaining question: why this Cushi was named Cushi, and not יה-X, can only be a matter of sheer speculation.[34] It is also clear that there are no real grounds for the assumption that Zephaniah was a descendant of

---

[33] Tobit, the earliest of the two, was probably written ca. third century. See Doran: 296-99, esp. 299 and the bibliography cited there.

[34] Cf. Rice.

Hezekiah, king of Judah. These considerations lead to an obvious conclusion: The social location and personal background of Zephaniah cannot be derived from the superscription.

3.2.2. Zeph 1:2-3

(a) The quest for the original form of the אָסֹף אָסֵף in v. 2 and of the אָסֵף in v. 3 is a permanent issue in Zephaniah's studies.[35] In the MT, the first is a rare combination of the abs. inf. of the root אסף in its qal form and a hiphil, cohortative or jussive, form of the root סוף, i.e., אָסֵף, which occurs also in v. 3.[36] There is no doubt that these expressions are meaningful and have a "striking assonance." Nevertheless, according to the normal rules of Hebrew grammar, the verbal form composed by an abs. inf. and a finite form of the verb requires that the two come from the same root.[37]

Two main critical positions have been developed: The first one accepts the reliability of the MT, and the second emends it so that the two verbal forms would be from the root אסף. The Peshitta, the Vulgate, and probably the Targum (for v. 2, but not for v. 3) seem to support these emendations.[38] Those who tend to accept the MT reading point to the fact

---

[35] Cf. Gerleman, 1942: 2-3; Sabottka: 5-7; Ball, 1972/1988: 14-17; Kapelrud, 1975: 21-22; Rudolph,1975: 261; Lipínski: 688; Irsigler,1977: 6-11; Krinetzki: 253-54. For a general review of the question and the different proposals see Irsigler, above

[36] Another possibility is to consider אָסֵף a *hiphil* , imperfect form, see Radak, cf. Sperber, 436; Andersen and Forbes: 174-75. For Lipínski's alternative proposal see below.

[37] See GKC 113 w, note 3. In fact, this rule "fails"three times (in Isa 28:28; Jer 8:13; and Zeph 1:2). But these are commonly considered textual errors (see GKC 72 aa, 113 w, note 3). It is noteworthy that Rashi (and later Abrabanel depending on Rashi) claimed that the second verb in Zephaniah should be written אאסף. This is, according to them, only one of the occasions in which an *aleph* is missing. They provide the example of Isa 13:20. There, according to Rashi, ולא יהל should have been written ולא יאהל (cf. D. W. Thomas' proposal in BHS). Both Rashi and Abrabanel consider that both verbal forms in Zephaniah are from the root אסף.

[38] The usual proposal is to read אֹסֵף instead of אָסֵף in vv. 2-3 (e.g., GKC 72 aa [cf. GKC 68 h], Elliger [BHS]). Thus, the consonantal text remains unchanged, but also the reading אֲאַסֵף (e.g., Wellhausen, cf. Rashi, Abrabanel; see Mic 2:12) has been proposed. If this is the case then a simple haplography could have brought to the present consonantal MT. For

the masoretes thought that the present combination of two verbs of different roots is acceptable Hebrew, provided that the two verbs have a similar sound and meaning.[39] In addition, Ball considers that rhetorical arguments support the MT.[40]

Alternatively, Lipínski has argued that אָסֵף is really the first person singular imperfect of the root אסף. According to him, the first vowel is like יָאֱצֹל (Num 11:25), but since in first person two א come together, one א drops out (GKC 68 g). The second vowel is like תֹּסֵף (Ps 104:29). Therefore, there is no need for emendation.[41] The root סוף or אסף (Lipínski) in its *hiphil* form is attested only four times in the OT;[42] three אָסֵף forms in Zeph 1:2-3, and in the expression אָסֹף אֲסִיפֵם (Jer 8:13). This expression is almost identical to the one in Zeph 1:2.[43] Thus, his proposals cannot be checked against the inner testimony of the Biblical sources. In any case, both the proposals for emendations of the OT and the proposed understandings of the MT, as it stands, do not change (or almost do not change) the overall meaning of אָסֹף אָסֵף in v. 2.[44]

---

these proposals and for the discussion of the testimony of the different ancient versions see Ball, 1972/1988, 1972: 15-16.

Sabottka and Kapelrud proposed an emendation of the vocalization that retains the problem of the two different roots. According to them, these two roots had been אסף and יסף. Thus, the ET of the original verse reads "I shall again sweep . . . ". They claim that "again" refers to the flood (Gen. 6:5 ff.). See Sabottka: 6-7; Kapelrud,1975:103, but cf. Kapelrud, 1975, 21-22. This proposal is not based on a grammatical difficulty (for its presupposition is that the occurrence of two verbs from different roots in the grammatical construction of v. 2 is grammatically acceptable), or on a hardly understandable reading, but on the "feasibility" of a change in the vocalization that brings about new meaning that fits a beforehand accepted position concerning the relationship between Zeph 1:2-3 and the account of the flood.

39 Cf. Gerleman, 1942: 2-3.

40 Ball, 1972/1988: 16-17.

41 Lipínski,1975.

42 Besides the *hiphil* forms, the main occurrence of the root סוף in Biblical Hebrew tends to be late. It occurs in Ps 73:19 (probably post-exilic), Isa 66:17, Esth 9:28, Qoh 3:11, 7:2, 12:13, Joel 2: 20, 2 Chr 20:16 and seven times in the Aramaic parts of Daniel. However, it also occurs in Am 3:15.

43 Similarly, אָסֹף אֲסִיפֵם is emended by Gesenius, and many scholars after him, to אָסֹף אֹספֵם (GKC 72 aa). For other proposed emendations, see Carroll,1986: 231 . For the position that the MT should be retained, see Mc Kane: 189.

44 Except for Sabottka's proposal, see above. Also, according to Gaster the language in v. 2 points to the "Ingathering Festival" (חג האסיף) mentioned in Exod 23:16, which he considers the occasion and the background of Zephaniah's preaching (Gaster, 1969). Gaster translates אָסֹף אָסֵף as follows: "I will make an ingathering" (Gaster, 1969: 679).

Qal forms of the root אסף, meaning 'remove,' 'sweep away,' 'destroy' are well attested in the OT (e.g., Gen 30:23; 1 Sam 14:19, 15:16; 2 Kgs 5:3,6,7,11; Isa 4:1; Jer 16:5; Ezek 34:29; Job 34:24; Ps 104:29). However, thematically and linguistically two occurrences seem to be important for our discussion. The first is Jer 8:13[45] (see above). The second in Hos 4:3 (there, the verb is in a *niphal* form that conveys a passive variant of the *qal* meaning):

בחית השדה ובעוף השמים וגם דגי הים יאספו . . .

This language resembles Zeph 1:3. The verb is the same (?); the objects to be destroyed are very similar; and the destroyer is the same.[46]

The verbal form אָסֹף occurs three times in the entire OT: (a) אָסֹף אָסֵף (Zeph 1:2), (b) אָסֹף אֲסִיפֵם (Jer 8:13; there followed by נאם ה', cf. Zeph 1:2); and (c) אָסֹף אֶאֱסֹף יעקב כלך (Mic 2:12; G seems to have read כלו instead of כלך).[47] But, in spite of the fact that the forms are very close, with or without emendations, the meaning conveyed by the expression in Mic 2:12 is totally opposed to the meaning conveyed in Zeph 1:2 and in Jer 8:13.[48] Unlike Jer 8:13, Mic 2:12 is generally considered post-exilic.[49]

(b) The word כל in v. 2, meaning 'everything' and fulfilling the role of the noun by itself, has a widespread occurrence in the OT that cuts across different layers and genres (e.g., Gen 9:3 [P], 33:11; Num 11:6; Deut 8:9, 28:47; Prov 16:4, 26:10, 28:5, 30:30; Qoh 3:19, 20; Ps 145:15; Isa 44:24; Jer 44:18). As with any 'everything,' the real content of this 'everything' is not clear. Verse 3 fulfills the role of an explanatory note.

Kapelrud thinks that "Gaster may be right in his guess about the occasion . . . The facts are mostly inaccessible to us, and in such cases only guesswork is left and a possibility to evaluate the guesses" (Kapelrud, 1975: 43 and cf. Kapelrud, 1975: 51). However, Kapelrud does not follow Gaster in his translation of the text (Kapelrud,1975: 103), but see, for instance, de Roche, 1980 a.

[45] For its meaning and its relation to the context, see Mc Kane,1986: 188-89.

[46] Buss has pointed out that Hos 4:1-3 contains " a number of elements not found elsewhere in Hosea's oracles." He suggests a cultic background for the unit. See Buss, 1969: 89.

[47] Mm. 2496.

[48] For Jer 8:13, see Mc Kane, 1986: 188-89, Carroll, 1986: 230-32.

[49] See Sellin,1922: 275; Mays,1976: 174 f. For a different and inconclusive position, see Hillers,1984: 39-40.

(c) With the exception of Gen 8:8, the occurrences of the language מעל פני האדמה in the OT are related to destruction. The verbs occurring in expressions containing this language are from roots that clearly convey this meaning. For instance, מחה (Gen 6:7, 7:4), שמד (Deut 6:15; 1 Kgs 13:34; Am 9:8), כרת (1 Sam 20:15; 2 Kgs 9:7; Zeph 1:3), and also כלה (Ex 32:12), שלח in its *piel* form (Jer 28:16), and כחד in its *hiphil* form (1 Kgs 13:34).[50] Obviously, both the expression in Zeph 1:2 (either emended or unemended) and the one with the verb from the root כרת in v. 3 fit well in this semantic field.

It is worth noting that מעל פני האדמה does not point by itself to a universal scenario of destruction, but to the entire destruction of a specific object or objects. In fact, the object is clearly universal, as their contexts show, only in two of the cases mentioned above (Gen 6:7, 7:4). It is undoubtedly non-universal in Exod 32:12; Deut 6:15; 1 Sam 20:15; 1 Kgs 9:7, 13:34; Jer 28:16; and Am 9:8. Therefore, one should conclude that from the use of מעל פני האדמה one cannot infer that the destruction announced in Zeph 1:2-3 is universal.[51] Any conclusion in this respect has to be made on the basis of the context of the expression in the unit.[52]

(d) Both the short utterance אָסֹף אֲסִיפֵם in Jer 8:13 and פני האדמה אָסֹף אָסֵף כל מעל in Zeph 1:2 are followed by נאם ה'. Although a discussion of the expression נאם ה' is beyond the scope of this work,[53] it is noteworthy that in its two (probably) earliest occurrences of this expression (both outside the prophetic books, namely, Ps 110:1; 2 Kgs 9:26), it actually means YHWH's utterance. In both cases, the divine

---

[50] Cf. גרש (Gen 4:14) that even if does not convey the meaning of utterly destruction has a very clear negative sense and implies that the previous situation is no more. Gen 4:14, 6:7, 7:4, 8:8 are considered a part of the "J layer" in the Pentateuch.

[51] It is noteworthy that there are two occasions in which the word אדמה has a double function, that is, (a) an element in the language מעל פני האדמה, and (b) a meaningful word by itself. In both occasions the non-universal meaning of אדמה is the one which is conveyed by אדמה ("soil" in Gen 4:14 and "a specific territory" in 1 Kgs 9:7). Jewish medieval commentators tended to understand אדמה in Zeph 1:2-3 in a restricted territorial sense, namely, the land of Israel (e.g., Ibn Ezra, Radak, Abrabanel). The same holds true for Christian commentators such as Luther and Calvin.

[52] Cf. Abrabanel.

[53] See Rendtorff, 1954; Wolff,1975: 143 and the bibliography there.

utterance is a short one, such as in Zeph 1:2. In Ps 110:1 the utterance consists of the words "said" by YHWH in a ceremony belonging to the "royal cult," in the Temple, in Jerusalem;[54] and in 2 Kgs 9:26 of a short divine oath/oracle.[55] The occurrence of נאם ה' after a short divine utterance is also attested in the post-exilic period (e.g., Hag 1:13), but this is not the main use of נאם ה' in the prophetic literature (i.e., the Latter Prophets).[56]

Summing up points a-d, the meaning of v. 2 seems to be clear: "YHWH said: I will entirely destroy everything."

(e) Since Gen 6:7 reads מאדם עד בהמה עד רמש ועד עוף השמים, it has been suggested (and generally accepted) that v. 3a is related thematically and linguistically to the flood tradition.[57] De Roche has proposed that Zeph 1:2-3 points to the "sweeping" of the creation and is related thematically and linguistically to Genesis 1.[58]

---

[54] See Anderson,1972: 767 -72. Whether this is a "royal Psalm" or a post-exilic messianic Psalm that uses traditional motifs of the monarchic period is irrelevant to the present discussion because in any case v. 1 would represent an "ancient" tradition. It is noteworthy that this is the only place in Psalms where the expression נאם ה' occurs.

[55] For date, origin and intention of the story in 2 Kgs 9:21-26, see Rofé, 1988: 95-97.

[56] In most of its occurrences in the prophetic literature, נאם ה' follows a divine utterance much longer than those mentioned above (e.g., Hos 2:15; Am 3:15, 4:11; Isa 37:34). The function of the expression there is to underline the divine origin of the preceding words by means of a concluding note. In addition, and fulfilling the same legitimating function, נאם ה' tends to occur in the second half of the opening verse in ביום ההוא pericopes (e.g., Hos 2:18, 23; Am 8:9; Mic 4:6, 5:9; Obad 1:8; Zeph 1:10; cf. Am 2:16; 8:11). The pattern of occurrence of נאם ה' in the different prophetic books is far from being uniform. For instance, it occurs 21 times in the Book of Amos (including four occurrences of נאם אדני ה' [Am 3:13, 4:5, 8:3,9,11]), and 175 times in the Book of Jeremiah. The expression נאם אדני ה' occurs 81 times in the Book of Ezekiel, while the shorter and usual נאם ה' occurs only four times in this book (for אדני ה' in Ezekiel see, Zimmerli, 1983: 558-561, Mc Gregor: 57-74 and the bibliography cited in these works). נאם ה' occurs only four times in Hosea (Hos 2: 15,18,23, 11:11), only twice in Micah (Mic 4:6, 5:9), and eleven times (including related forms) in Isaiah 1-39 (Isa 1:24, 3:15, 14:22,23, 17: 3, 6, 19:4, 22:25, 30:1, 31:9, 37:34). See Rendtorff, 1954. A study of these occurrences and their history is beyond the scope of this work.

[57] If it were the case and the material could be dated to the late-monarchic period, then it would be an important point for the study of the religious traditions and the theological thought of the period, with the J and P accounts for comparison.

[58] See de Roche, 1980; de Roche, 1980 a. Cf. with the midrash on Qoh 1:2 attributed to R. Judah son of R. Simon: "The seven 'vanities' mentioned by Kohelet correspond to the seven days of creation . . . On the fifth day, *Let the waters swarm with the swarms of living creatures* (Gen I, 20); but it is written, *And I will consume the fowls of heaven, and the fishes of the sea* (Zeph. 1:3). On the sixth day, *And God said: Let us make man in our*

Actually, in Zeph 1:3, two expressions occur: אדם ובהמה and הים
עוף השמים ודגי. The first one is a typical merism[59] conveying the
meaning of "everyone" or "everything" that stands between "(hu)man" and
beast. This merism is relatively common in the OT.[60] It occurs with the
root כרת in the *hiphil* form, as perhaps implied in Zeph 1:3, in Ezek
14:13,17,19,21, 25:13, 29:8 (significantly, none of these refers to a
universal scenario of destruction). Furthermore, in Ezek 14:13 and 25:13,
the complete speech includes the language נטה יד, with YHWH as the
subject, which is the opening phrase of Zeph 1:4. אדם ובהמה also
occurs in Jer 36:29, again in a non-universal doom context. Significantly,
it appears in a positive context in Zech 2:8 and Ps 36:7, both post-exilic.[61]

The addition of "the birds of the sky and the fish of the sea" to the usual
"(hu)man and beast" (in v. 3) accommodates the sense of "completeness"
given by "(hu)man and beast" to a tripartite vision of the world: ארץ
(earth), ים (sea), and שמים (sky, air); cf. Ps 69:36, 96:11; Job 12:7-8;
Deut 30:11-13.[62] Obviously, as this list of biblical references shows, this
vision is not restricted to the creation story and does not refer necessarily
to the flood story. Thus, one cannot simply assume that the language of
Zeph 1:3 refers to a specific set of traditions. Since the tripartite vision is
not always expressed by the same—or similar—language, a comparison
between the specific language in Zeph 1:3 and that of other texts

---

image (Gen I,26); but it is written, *And I will cut off man from off the face of the earth*
(Zeph. loc. cit)" (Qoh. Rab. [Soncino ET] p. 6).

[59] Following Krasovec, the most important characteristics of merism are: "Firstly, merism
is the art of expressing a totality by mentioning the parts, usually the two extremes,
concerning a given idea, quality or quantity; consequently polar expression is the most
usual form of merism. Secondly, merism is substitution for abstract words such as "all,"
"every," "always." Thirdly, the mentioned parts have figurative or metaphorical sense;
literal interpretation proves to be in many cases totally incongruous. Fourthly, merism
should not be confounded with antithesis, for in contrast to merism in antithesis opposed
extremes do not express the same aspects of the same idea in its totality, but opposite
aspects of the same idea in their mutual exclusion" (Krasovec, 1983: 232).

[60] See Krasovec, 1977, esp. 37, 74. Krasovec's list (p.74) mentions Gen 6:7, 7:23; Exod
8:13,14, 9:9,10,19,22,25, 12:12, 13:2, 15; Lev 7:21, 27:28; Num 3:13, 8:17, 18:
15,15, 31: 11, 26, 47; Jer 7:20, 21:26, 27:5, 31:27, 32:43, 33:10,10,12, 36:29, 50:3,
51:62; Ezek 14: 13,17, 19:21, 25:13, 29:8, 36:11; Jon 3:7, 8; Zeph 1:3; Hag 1:11; Zech
2:8; Ps 36:7; 135:8; Qoh 3:19. See also Ben Shoshan (entry בהמה).

[61] Concerning the date of Ps 36 see Gerstenberger,1988:154-57 and Fohrer,1970: 287.

[62] Cf. Krasovec, 1977: 35.

containing this kind of vision may help to evaluate the supposedly clear references to (or the case for dependence on) particular traditions in Zeph 1:3.

The expression עוף השמים occurs many times in the OT; however, the phrase עוף השמים ודגי הים occurs only twice. Besides Zeph 1:3, this phrase occurs only as the second part of the list in Hos 4:3 (where יֵאָסְפוּ also occurs). The first part of this list (like the one in the J creation story [see Gen 2:19-20], but unlike the first story of creation [see Gen 1:24-26]) does not mention the reptiles (רמש) as a different class.[63] Instead, it contains the general term חית השׂדה, which occurs also in Gen 2:19-20. It is noteworthy that חית השׂדה does not occur in P,[64] and that the alternative term used in the first story of the creation is הארץ חית (Gen 1:24-26). Significantly, both accounts of the flood do mention the reptiles (see Gen 6:7,20, 7:8,23, 8:17, 9:2,10). Since the reptiles are also mentioned in 1 Kgs 5:13, but not in Ps 8:8-9, probably a post-monarchic psalm,[65] their presence or absence does not point to different layers but to different traditions.[66]

The expression דגי הים occurs eight times in the OT (Gen 9:2; Num 11:22; Ezek 38:20; Hos 4:3; Hab 1:14; Zeph 1:3; Ps 8:9; Job 12:8). It is noteworthy that it does not occur in the creation stories in the first two chapters of Genesis and only once in relation to the account of the flood. It is also worth noting that the fish are neither slaughtered nor hunted but "gathered" (see כל דגי הים יאסף in Num 11:22); therefore, the two אסף forms with fish as the object of the action (Hos 4:3 ; Zeph 1:3)

---

63 According to the MT. The LXX added the reptiles, probably influenced by Hos 2:20, see Elliger (BHS).

64 חית השׂדה does not occur in P. In the Tetrateuch, it occurs in Gen 2:19,20, 3:1,14; Exod 23:11,29; Lev 26:22 (the curses at the end of the so-called Holiness Code.)

65 See Gerstenberger,1988: 67-72, esp 70-72. See also Fohrer,1970: 286 and the bibliography cited there.

66 It was suggested that the reptiles are not mentioned in Zeph 1:3 because of metric reasons. However, the existence elsewhere of a classification of the animals that does not include the reptiles undermines such proposal. Moreover, the hypothetical reference to the reptiles is needed only in order to make the compatible with a previous presupposition, i.e., that the flood story stands behind Zeph 1:3.

probably involve a play on double meaning (namely, the root אסף meaning "gathering" (the fish) but also "destroying").

A very similar phrase to עוף השמים ודגי הים occurs in Ps 8:9 (also in connection with tripartite vision of the world), but there צפור שמים stands instead of עוף השמים. The phrase צפור שמים occurs nowhere else in the Hebrew parts of the OT, but it does appear in Aramaic in Dan 4:9, 18.

(f) The phrase והמכשלות את הרשעים is commonly considered a gloss.[67] There are several reasons for this widespread view. The phrase contains two terms concerning those who are going to be wiped out. Both terms convey a negative judgment (רשעים, מכשלות). This is in sharp contrast with the use of entirely neutral terms for the objects of destruction elsewhere in verses 2 and 3 (עוף השמים, דגי הים, אדם, בהמה). Moreover, והמכשלות את הרשעים lacks the characteristic repetitive sound structure of vv. 2-3.[68] It also seems to disrupt the metrical balance of the verse, and cannot be considered a supplement to the meaning of entirety conveyed by the reference to the three basic elements of the world : earth, water/sea, and air/sky. In addition, the phrase appears in the G textual tradition at a late stage.[69]

However, if והמכשלות את הרשעים is an addition, then its purpose is explanatory. But accepting what appears to be the MT reading (i.e., מכשלות as the plural of מכשלה = ruins; see KBL[3], cf. Isa 3:6), does

---

[67] So, for instance, J. M. P. Smith: 186; Lipínski, 1975; Kapelrud,1975: 22; Irsigler, 1977: 11-14; Edler: 14, 100-01; Krinetzki: 182; Renaud, 1986:4.

[68] E.g., אדמה - אדם and אדמה - אדם - אדם - אדם and אסף - אסף אסף - אסף, as well as the two occurrences of נאם ה' מעל פני האדמה in these two verses.

[69] See Irsigler, 1977: 11 and the bibliography mentioned there, esp. see Jerome, Zeph I-2.3 (p. 658). For a comparison of the readings of different versions as well as different LXX readings, see Ball, 1972/1988: 17. The phrase is also lacking in La^S (i.e., the OL according to fragmenta Sangallensia) but, other important OL readings seem to imply a Hebrew text closer to the MT; see Oesterley: 76, 384. On the basis of the absence of the phrase from the supposed LXX* text, Krinetzki (198) proposes a date for this gloss: ca. 150 BCE, i.e., the time in which LXX* was probably concluded. However, it should be noticed that even if one accepts the existence of a Hebrew Vorlage of the LXX* that did not include this phrase, one cannot conclude on these grounds that no contemporaneous Hebrew text include the phrase. The data from Qumran clearly proves that divergent Hebrew texts existed at one time (and place).

not serve this purpose, at least for us. Moreover, since the ancient versions contain clearly divergent readings,[70] each of them seems to be an attempt to translate the MT והמכשלות את הרשעים. One may assume therefore, that the ancient translators also had difficulties in understanding this verse.[71]

Since the word רשעים conveys the meaning of "wicked", it seems likely that the addition of והמכשלות את הרשעים is related to, or express ethical sensibilities.[72] Obviously, the question is, in which way? Several proposals for textual emendations of the puzzling word המכשלות have been suggested, among them הכשלתי, כשלתי, and מכשלים.[73] The proposal והכשלתי את הרשעים has on its behalf the obvious parallelism, and the rich assonance with the following expression: והכרתי את אדם. However, this proposal is not supported by the ancient versions. Moreover, it seems difficult to explain how a reading that is so clear, well balanced, and so rich in assonance can lead by a scribal error to the perplexing והמכשלות את הרשעים. What are the alternatives?

Lipínski and others consider מכשלות[74] the normal feminine plural of the *hiphil* participle of כשל, which in this case is followed by a regular accusative ("the wicked").[75] The remaining question is, why a feminine

---

[70] Obviously, except for those MSS in the LXX tradition that do not contain any reference to this phrase.

[71] The question whether the LXX translator had a Hebrew Vorlage without והמכשלות את הרשעים or omitted the phrase because of its difficult meaning (cf. Zeph 3:10) remains somehow open --even if the first alternative seems more likely-- because of tendency in the LXX text of Minor Prophets to show a very free translation of these problematic phrases instead of just omitting them (see Ziegler, 1944: 107-08; Gerleman, 1942: 3; Irsigler, 1977: 11-12).

[72] Similar sensitivities brought to the addition of the כל רשיעיא notes in the Targum to Zephaniah. See Targum Zeph 1:7, 18, 3:8. See also Ribera Florit: 131.

[73] See, the summaries of modern research in J. M. P. Smith: 191; Ball, 1972/1988: 17-18; Irsigler, 1977: 12 and the bibliography mentioned these works. For a suggestion of an original reading much more removed from the MT, see Kauffmann, 1938-56, III: 349 n.2. Kauffmann also considers possible that מכשלות means "kingdoms whose regime is lawless (פרוע)," see there.

[74] Or מכשלות, see Edler: 14; but see, Andersen and Forbes, 174-75.

[75] For a similar use of the *hiphil* participle of כשל see b ᶜAbod. Zar. 11 b; cf. Gen. Rab. 28.6, midrash on . . . מאדם ועד בהמה (Gen 6:7). See Lipínski, 1975: 688; see also del Olmo Lete: 298. Del Olmo Lete wrote on this issue in reaction to Sabottka's proposal of

participle?   Rudolph[76] thinks that it points to בהמה, which unlike
עוף השמים and דגי הים is feminine, but it is more likely that all the
mentioned animals are referred to by means of a feminine plural that point
to a collective noun (e.g., הבקר היו חֹרשׁות, Job 1:14).[77]   It should be
noted that in Zeph 1:3 (or Zeph 1:2-3) nothing is said about the specific
way in which the animals caused "the wicked" to stumble.   The animals
are not mentioned again in the text as a cause of "stumbling", so any
suggestions in this respect remain entirely speculative.[78]

3.2.3. Zeph 1:4

(a) The expression נטה יד על-X occurs in the "plagues tradition", in
both the J and P narratives.[79]   In these narratives, X refers to natural
elements (e.g., skies, rivers, soil) and they are not to be destroyed.   The
action is a symbolic one.   It is performed by Moses or Aaron or both, but
not directly by God.   The only exception appears in Exod 7:5 (P), in an
explanatory note concerning the reasons for the plagues that is not a part of
the narrative as such.

Among prophetic announcements of judgment, the expression occurs in
Isa 23:11, which is probably non-Isaianic, and may be dated to the 7th

---

"congeneric assimilation" of the roots ממכ/מוכ and כשׁל. See Sabottka: 8-10. For other
scholars who consider מכשׁלות the fem. pl. pt. of כשׁל see Rudolph, 1975: 262; Irsigler,
1977: 12-13; Edler:14.

[76] Rudolph, 1975: 262.

[77] See GKC 145c. Cf. Irsigler, 1977: 13 n.14.

[78] This does not mean that people have refrained from proposing causes and ways in which
the animals cause the "stumbling." From ancient times there have been two main lines of
proposals. According to Gen. Rab. 28.6, abundance is the source of the "stumbling." b.
cAbod. Zar. 55a implies an understanding that points to idolatry. Among modern
scholars, the second alternative is more popular, see Irsigler, 1977: 13-14; Edler: 100-
01; Wolfe: 110; cf. Gerleman, 1942: 4-5. In relation to the second alternative, the
suggested comparison with Deut. 4:16-19 (e.g., Edler: 100-01) only shows that Deut
4:16-19 and Zeph 1:2-3 share a common tripartite vision of the world, and that Deut 4:
16-19 stands against any image whatsoever.

[79] In J narratives, Exod 8:1,2; 9:22; 10:12,21,22; cf. Exod 8:12-13. In P narratives Exod
7:19; 14:16,21,27 .

century,[80] there X is the sea, and obviously the judgment is not against it. X refers to the persons, peoples or countries against whom the divine judgment comes forth in Jer 51:25 (a relatively late exilic unit),[81] in Zeph 1:4, and eight times in Ezekiel.[82] Moreover, in Ezekiel half of the units whose punishment section opens with נטה יד על-X contain also a *hiphil* form of כרת (see Ezek 14:13, 25:7,13,16) as in Zeph 1:4. Furthermore, in two of these unit the object of the "cutting off" is אדם ובהמה (Ezek 14:13, 25:13), and cf. Zeph 1:3.[83]

(b) The expression על יהודה ועל כל יושבי ירושלם occurs in Jer 35:17 (with אל instead of על). A similar expression, namely, ירושלם על כל עם יהודה ואל כל ישבי occurs in Jer 25:2 and the expression כל ישבי ירושלם is attested in Jer 13:13, 17:20. The pair ירושלם איש יהודה - ישבי occurs in Jer 4:4, 11:2,9, 17:25, 18:11, 32:32, 35:13. Pairs consisting of ישבי ירושלם - X יהודה occur several times in the Book of Jeremiah (see above), in 2 Kgs 23:2, Zeph 1:4; Dan 9:7 and several times in 2 Chronicles. To conclude, these apparently common expressions occur nowhere in the prophetic literature but in the Book of Jeremiah and in Zeph 1:4.[84] Besides clearly late literature (Daniel, 2 Chronicles) there is only one occurrence of a similar expression in Kgs 23:2 (i.e., כל איש יהודה וכל ישבי ירושלם).[85]

---

[80] See Clements,1982: 191-96 and the bibliography cited there. For the view that it is Isaianic, see Hayes-Irvine:292.

[81] See Carroll,1986: 841-44 and the bibliography cited there.

[82] Ezek 6:14, 14:9,13, 16:27, 25:7,13,16, 35:3

[83] A similar form occurs in Ezek 14:9, where the root שמד appears instead of the root כרת, without changing the meaning.

[84] Even a so expected language as ישבי ירושלם, which occurs 16 times in Jeremiah, occurs elsewhere in the prophetic literature only in Ezek 12:19, 11:15, 15:6; Zeph 1:4; Zech 12:5; 13:1. In addition it occurs only in 2 Kgs 23:2; Dan 9:7; Neh 7:3, and 2 Chr 20:11,13,15,18,20, 31:4, 32: 22,26,33, 33:9, 34:30,32, 35:18.

[85] Cf. יושב ירושלם ולבית יהודה (Isa 5:3); ליושב ירושלם ואיש יהודה (Isa 22:21). Note the order of the two elements and the "singular" form in יושב ירושלם. Significantly, ישבי ירושלם does not occur in Isaiah, see note above. On these topics, and especially on the question of the order in which Judah and Jerusalem are mentioned cf. Jones, 1955: 239-40. It is noteworthy that the order in which the two elements of the pair and the singular form of יושב ירושלם may be interrelated features, for there is a tendency to include the element in plural form in the second spot. See Berlin, 1985: 45.

(c) The most probable location referred to by מן המקום הזה, "from this place," is Jerusalem (cf. Jer 19:12), though another possibility, which is supported by several scholars, is that the place is the Temple (cf. Deut 12:3, 26:9; Jer 7:3; Hag 2:9).[86] This may be the case but it is not necessarily so because in prophetic literature מן המקום הזה is not always a terminus technicus for the Temple.[87] Thus, the meaning of "this place" in any specific unit is dependent on the context. The difficulty with Zeph 1:4 is that the immediate context provides no clear answer. Verse 4 claims that it contains the words of YHWH (YHWH is mentioned in the first person) but it claims nothing concerning the audience and the circumstances in which the divine speech has been transmitted. It seems likely that the reference to those who dwell in Jerusalem, which immediately precedes the phrase מן המקום הזה, may have led readers to the assumption that Jerusalem is "this place."[88]

The phrase מן המקום הזה is commonly considered a gloss.[89] This is so because the phrase seems to disrupt the metrical balance of the verse and because of its contents. The ancient versions do support the MT reading but, clearly this is no reason for ruling out the possibility that הזה מן המקום is a gloss.[90] On the other hand, metrical reasons alone are not

---

[86] See, for instance, Edler, 1984: 14, 101-02; Renaud, 1986:4. On the basis of similar expressions in Deut 12:3, 26:9 (cf. Jer 7:3) they consider this use of "this place" a deuteronomistic feature. So, Edler, 1984: 14, 101-02; Renaud, 1986:4, cf. Kapelrud, 1982:23.

[87] For instance, Jer 16:2,3, 19:6,7, 51:62 cannot refer to the Temple.

[88] However, v. 4a does not mention the inhabitants of Jerusalem alone, or for their sake only, but as an integral part of the pair, Judah (i.e., people of Judah) - dwellers of Jerusalem; a pair that conveys the meaning of the entire population of Judah. Thus, a more careful reading of the text may lead to the idea that "this place" is the entire land of Judah. However, such understanding of the phrase stands at odds with the meaning of מקום. This term occurs hundreds of times in the OT referring to a spot, to a building, to a city, to an area. That is, the range of meanings of מקום quite overlaps the range of meanings of the English word "place." It is noteworthy that מקום as a (probable) synonym for ארץ, as required for the understanding of "this place" as a reference to the land of Judah, occurs in the OT (Num 20:5, 32:1), but is rarely used in this way. For an advocate of the understanding of מקום as a reference to the entire land of Judah, including Jerusalem, see Ball, 1972/1988: 59.

[89] E.g., Elliger (BHS); Gerleman, 1942: 6, 67; Krinetzki: 182; Rudolph, 1975: 262; Edler, 1984: 14, 101-02; Renaud, 1986:4.

[90] There is no reason to suppose that all the glossators lived—at the very earliest—after the crystallization of the Hebrew Vorlage of any specific text in the LXX or that their work

a compelling reason for the the determination of glosses. Moreover, the expression . . . מ הכרתי followed by a direct object and seemingly introducing no additional knowledge occurs elsewhere in the OT (e.g., Ezek 14:13,17, 21:8; Am 2:3; Nah 2:14). Also a מן (/...מ) clause occurs in many sentences whose verbal clause contains כרת in its hiphil form (e.g., Josh 7:9; Ezek 14:8,13,17; Am 1:5,8, 2:3; Mic 5:9,11,12,13; Nah 2:14; Zech 9:10; Ps 34:17; 101:8). Ironically, one may conclude that either the writer of the unit wrote in accordance with a common Hebrew form, or the glossator introduced his/her note in way that turns one common Hebrew form[91] into another common Hebrew form. But, this is not exactly the case because the specific מ clause in Zeph 1:4 is quite uncommon in prophetic literature. It is noteworthy that expressions containing the phrase מן המקום הזה occur more than twenty times in Jeremiah (e.g., Jer 7:3,6,7,20, 14:13, 16:2,3,9, 19:3,4,6,7, 22:3,11, 24:5, 27:22, 28:4,6, 29:10, 32:37, 33:10,12, 40:2, 42:18, 44:29, 51:62) but elsewhere in the Latter Prophets only in Zeph 1:4 and Hag 2:9.[92] This may suggest that the writer responsible for "from this place" was influenced by or shared certain stylistic features of the Book of Jeremiah. Therefore, the extent of such influence, or sharing, in the relevant unit in Zephaniah (Zeph 1:4-6*), and in the entire Book of Zephaniah, may become a helpful hint for discerning the original meaning and date of "from this place" in Zeph 1:4.

From the standpoint of the content, it is noteworthy that the phrase "from this place" introduces a spatial emphasis that does not exist elsewhere in Zeph 1:4-6. This is especially true if "this place" refers to Jerusalem or to the Temple, and not to the entire land of Judah.[93]

---

should be absent in the Hebrew Vorlage behind non-Hebrew ancient versions. For a different approach, see Kapelrud,1975: 23.

[91] For sentences containing an *hiphil* form of כרת but without a מן/מ clause see, for instance, Lev 26:22; Josh 23:4; Judg 4:24; 1 Sam 24:21; 1 Kgs 18:4; Isa 10:7, 48:9; Jer 44:11; Ezek 17:17; Obad 1:14; Zeph 3:6, Ps 109:13.

[92] Elsewhere in the OT, expressions containing the language המקום הזה occur several times in 1-2 Kings, 1-2 Chronicles, and in Gen 20:11, 28:16; 1 Sam 12:8.

[93] See note 88.

(d) . . . והכרתי . . . את שאר הבעל את שם הכמרים

The term שְׁאָר הבעל commonly translated as "the remnant of Baal".
Accordingly, some scholars have proposed that the term reflects the
writer's awareness of the existence of the Josianic reform. Consequently,
the putative time of the verse, and for many scholars, the putative time of
the prophet Zephaniah, is after the Josianic reform.[94]

However, שאר הבעל does not stand alone as the direct object of the
verb. Zeph 1:4 shows a parallel structure שאר הבעל // שם הכמרים,
i.e., שאר // שם.[95] The pair שאר - שם occurs also in Isa 14:22.[96]
Moreover, since שאר means "remnant" = שארית, then it is noteworthy
that the closely related pair שם and שארית is attested in 2 Sam 14:7.[97]
The word שם occurs with verbs like הכרית, מחה, השמיד (Josh 7:9;
Zech 13:2; Isa 24:22; Deut:9:14, 29:19; Ps 9:6). In all these cases the
meaning is identical: absolute destruction, absolute "cut off." It is
significant that this meaning is conveyed by the pair שאר - שם and not by
שאר alone. Thus, even if שְׁאָר is repointed שְׁאֵר (i.e., "flesh",

---

[94] Radak considers possible that this refer to the circumstances in the last days of the
monarchy, after Josiah's death (או אמר על חרבן הארץ כי מלכי יהודה אחר יאשיהו עשו הרע בעיני השם).
Similarly, several modern scholars (Hyatt, Edens and Williams) have proposed that
Zephaniah proclaimed his message in Jehoiakim's days or later in the monarchic period.
Hyatt refers to the expression "the remnant of Baal" as a supporting piece of evidence for
the proposal. See Hyatt, esp. pp. 25-26, cf. Edens: 31-33, 56-57, 77-78. Alternatively,
it may be proposed that Zephaniah proclaimed his message during the reform or after the
reform but in Josiah's days. Among the supporters of this alternative, one may mention
Calvin (191-92), Kapelrud (1975: 23) and see the bibliographic note in J. M. P. Smith:
187. Yet, there is a third possibility, i.e., that Zephaniah proclaimed these words in the
minority period at the first years of Josiah's reign—before the reform—but at a time when
the worship of Baal was already in decadence and therefore only a "remnant" of Baal
existed in Judah, see Kauffmann, 1938-56: III, 349-50. Clearly, all these proposals
depend upon the understanding of שאר as remnant.

[95] That is, in Zeph 1:4, the words שם and שאר are semantical and grammatical equivalent. The
LXX reads "name", i.e., שם twice. Although the LXX is secondary (see Gerleman, 1942: 6-
7; Rudolph: 262) it points to an interpretative attitude that reflects the existent
parallelism.

[96] According to Ginsberg, Zephaniah was influenced by Isaiah, in style as well as in
contents. The similarity between Zeph 1:4 and Isa 14:22 is part of the supporting
evidence that he provides in order to prove the case. See Ginsberg, 1953: 258-59. The
fact that there are similarities between the two books (i.e., between the Book of
Zephaniah and the entire Book of Isaiah, cf. Zeph 2:15, Isa 47:8) is undeniable but,
clearly, Ginsberg's interpretation of the data is not the only possible one. See
commentary, below.

[97] Cf. זכר // שם in Prov 10:7; Job 18:17.

"offspring"),[98] the meaning would remain unchanged, because the reconstructed pair שֵׁם - שְׁאָר would be only a special form of a common basic pair: "heir" - "name"(= שֵׁם; cf. Isa 14:22, 66:22; Job 18:17-19). This pair also conveys the meaning of "entirety", of "completeness."[99] Thus, our verse may be understood as " I [YHWH] will totally wipe out" X. What does this X (the direct object of the divine action) represent in Zeph 1:4?

The usual direct objects of כרת in its hiphil form[100] are individual persons, a group of persons mentioned by a collective name or by a geographical term,[101] or in several cases, animals.[102] Significantly, neither deities nor cultic objects are its direct objects in Deuteronomy, or in the dtr. history, or in Jeremiah. However, illegitimate cultic objects worshiped by Judeans/Israelites are the direct object of the verb in Mic 5:11-12; Zech 13:2; Lev 26:30.[103] Which kind of direct object do we have in Zeph 1:4?

---

[98] Sabottka has proposed to change the masoretic שְׁאָר to שָׁאֵר i.e., literally "offspring of Baal. " He understands this phrase as "worshipers of Baal." See Sabottka,1972: 15-18. Cf. Dahood, 1976: 270; Watson (1976: 270) accepts Sabottka's repointing of the text. One of the main objections against this hypothesis is that while שָׁאֵר is attested with the sense of blood-relationship it does not occur elsewhere in a collective sense (e.g., Lev 18: 6,12,13, 21:2, 25:49; Num 27:11); see Gerleman, 1973: 253, but cf. Irsigler, 1977: 17 n.53. In any case if שָׁאֵר is a synonym to "offspring," this does not mean that the meaning conveyed by the sentence containing the parallel structure שֵׁם // שָׁאֵר is to be understood according to the "literal" meaning of שָׁאֵר alone. If שָׁאֵר means "offspring" the pair שָׁאֵר // שֵׁם would be only a special form of a common basic pair: "heir" // "name"= שֵׁם, which is attested in the OT in Isa 14:22, 66:22; Job 18: 17-19

[99] This basic pair occurs in the OT and in ancient Near East material, on this issue see Watson, 1988: 192-93, Irsigler 1977, 17-18.

[100] For the use of the *hiphil* form of כרת see point a, above.

[101] About seventy times in the OT. Also Nah 2:14; Ps 34:17, 109:15 refer to the "cutting off" of persons or certain group of persons. Even the occurrence in 1 Sam 28:9 refers to the "cut off" of persons, not of "ghosts", (see the second part of the verse).

[102] E.g., Exod 8:5; Mic 5:9.

[103] It is noteworthy that these three instances are considered exilic or post-exilic. The occurrence of the term חמנים in Lev 26:30 points to the exilic period or later; see Fritz, 1980, and the bibliography cited there. Zechariah 13 is commonly considered post-exilic (for a summary of modern critical approaches to Deutero and Trito-Zechariah, see Soggin,1980: 347-51 and the bibliography mentioned there). Mic 5:11-12 is either late monarchic or most probably post-monarchic. See Mays,1976: 124-25. The attempt to date it to Hezekiah's time relies mainly on the existence of the Hezekian reform, but no pre-dtr source mentions this reform. It is entirely doubtful that there was a Hezekian reform, except for the removal of the bronze serpent (2 Kgs 18:4), and I have written on this issue elsewhere (Ben Zvi, 1987: 131-41). Moreover, even those who accept the

Baal as the name of a deity occurs many times in the OT. The polemic against the cult of Baal in Judah (with, and perhaps, the exception of the Athaliah's pericope in 2 Kgs 11) is in fact a polemic against Yhwistic cult carried out in "illegitimate ways," from the point of view of the deuteronomic/deuteronomistic movement. Thus, in these polemic texts, Baal actually stands for YHWH, but YHWH who is worshiped "illegitimately".[104] Consequently, Baal in Zeph 1:4 cannot be considered a separate transcendental deity who is to be "cut off" by YHWH. But, regardless of this, or any other identification, Baal can hardly mean a deity in Zeph 1:4. As seen above, if this were the case it would be a very rare use of the *hiphil* form of כרת. Moreover, since one can "cut off" only what exists, it would imply that the Judean have been worshiping a transcendental deity, Baal. This deity, although inferior to YHWH, would continue to exist until the day in which YHWH will cut it off. Although the theme of "bringing down" the other gods is attested elsewhere in the OT (e.g., Zeph 2:11; Ps 82), it never occurs in announcements of judgment against Israelites or Judeans, even if in numerous cases these announcements are based on a cultic indictment.[105]

Alternatively, Baal may mean the cult of Baal. In the dtr. note that summarizes and evaluates Jehu's cultic actions (2 Kgs 10:28-31) the term Baal refers to the cult of Baal, as the account of his actions (2 Kgs 10:18-

---

historical reliability of the account in the Book of Kings, could hardly fit vv. 9-10 with their putative time, and if v. 13a is also an addition, what remains of the text?
The "cutting off" of their carved and graven images of Assyria, in Assyria, in Nah 1:14 is another touch of the painter's brush in the picture of the utter destruction of Assyria. This is not a polemic note against illegitimate cult.

[104] See Ben Zvi, 1987: 356-63.

[105] "Ashera", either in singular or in plural forms, is often mentioned as an object to be "cut off." A general discussion on the issue of "Ashera" is beyond the scope of this work. It seem sufficient for our purpose here to point to the fact that the "Ashera" that is supposed (or ought) to be cut off cannot be a transcendental deity and see Exod 34:13:
כי את מזבחתם תתצון ואת מצבתם תשברון ואת אשריו תכרתון
Not only that "ashera" is mentioned together, and in equivalency, to altars and pillars but also it is impossible that the text commands the Israelites to "cut off" a transcendental deity.

27) clearly shows.[106] It is noteworthy that this meaning of Baal occurs only in the dtr. summary but not in the narrative proper.

There is also a third option, closely related to the last one: Baal may mean a cultic object representing the deity. The polemic use of the name of the worshiped deity when the reference is actually to a non-legitimate cultic object is very common in dtr. literature,[107] but significantly, it is not attested in pre-dtr material.[108]

To conclude: Our verse may be understood as " I [YHWH] will totally wipe out the object that represents Baal (or the cult of Baal, see below) and the priestlings from this place[109]" or in an English translation that keeps the flavor of the Hebrew text but is inconclusive about the meaning of Baal : " . . . I will wipe out from this place every vestige of Baal and the name of the priestlings . . . " (NJPSV).

The word "priestlings" translates the Hebrew word כמרים. Related nouns from the root kmr with the meaning of "priest" are well attested in Old Akkadian, in Mari texts, and in Akkadian texts from Canaan and Syria (13th-15th century BCE), as well as in Aramaic, Punic, Nabatean, Palmyrian, and Syriac texts.[110] However, it occurs only three times in the entire OT and only in a pejorative sense. In Hos 10:5 this term refers to the priests who served YHWH at Beth-el and Samaria, but who served as priests of an idolatrous cult whose idol was the calf, according to the

---

[106] The alternative attested reading for the verse וישמד את בית הבעל מישראל (see Jepsen, BHS) probably reflects an attempt to sustain the common meaning for Baal and at the same time not to read that Jehu destroyed a "deity". Clearly, the MT version is the most attested for this verse and also represents the difficult reading. For further discussion on 2 Kgs 10: 28-31, see Montgomery and Gehman, 1951: 411-12, 416; Gray,1970: 508; Jones,1982: 472 and the bibliography cited there.

[107] The phenomenon is attested tens of times in the dtr. literature. An extreme case is Jer 2: 28, where even אלהים is used not as a transcendental "being," but as a an object made by human hands.

[108] Not even in the Book of Deuteronomy, except its first four chapters, and Deut 28: 36,64 where עץ ואבן are probably dependent on Deut 4: 28.

[109] "With the priests" is probably a late gloss, see J. M. P. Smith: 187-88. Rudolph, 1975: 262; Edler: 102; Elliger (BHS), and see below.

[110] See CAD, values "kumru" and "kumirtu"; Sivan,1984: 238; Jean-Hoftijzer: 122, entry כמר‏II. In the days of Assurbanipal,the term is attested only for the priestess of the Arabian goddess Delebat. It was proposed also that the origin of the name Qumran is related to this root (oral shift from k to q). See Bowman.

polemic claim of the text.[111] According to 2 Kgs 23:5—from a pre-dtr H source,[112] the כמרים were the priests placed by the kings of Judah, in the cities of Judah, to "bring offerings" (לקטר) at the bamot. The cult at the "bamot" was YHWH's cult, but it was considered illegitimate and idolatrous by the deuteronomic movement. The third occurrence of כמרים is in Zeph 1:4. It is noteworthy that this term does not occur elsewhere in the OT. Even priests that are clearly considered illegitimate, such as the northern priests (e.g., 1 Kgs 12:31,32, 2 Kgs 23:19-20), the priests of the bamot (e.g., 2 Kgs 23:8, 9), and even a Jerusalemite Baal priest (2 Kgs 11:18) are called כהנים. The term כהנים is also employed for Egyptian, Midianite, Philistine, Moabite and Ammonite priests in the OT (Gen 47:22; Exod 2:16; 1 Sam 5:5, 6:2; Jer 48:7, 49:3). Obviously, none of them were YHWH's priests. Thus, although the term כהנים has been used for Yhwistic, either legitimate or illegitimate, priests and for non-Yhwistic priests, the term כמרים in two of its occurrences (Hos 10:5, 2 Kgs 23:5) clearly refers to illegitimate priests of YHWH.[113] Therefore there is no ground for the idea that the term כמרים itself conveys the meaning of priests of an alien transcendental deity distinct from YHWH, be it Baal or any other "alien" god. The term כמרים only conveys the meaning of wrong worship. The connection made sometimes between the כמרים and the cult of a separate transcendental deity called Baal depends mainly on a certain set of assumptions concerning the nature of the cult of Baal in Judah.[114]

---

[111] For the text see Wolff,1974: 171; cf. Elliger (BHS).

[112] See, for instance, Spieckerman, 1982: 83, 425

[113] Pace, for instance, Ball, 1972/1988: 24; Sabottka, 1972: 18.

[114] Obviously, those who think that Baal in Zeph 1:4 refers to the cult of a separate transcendental deity, at least from the point of view of its worshipers, may deduce from this "fact" that כמרים are the priests of this cult. However, it is worth noting that this is only an inferred meaning based on a certain presupposition. Consequently, as any inferred conclusion, its validity is dependent on the validity of the presupposition. Certainly, it cannot be used to support the validity of the presupposition.
In my opinion, only when the claims made in the midst of the polemic begun to be considered the "historical" truth about what happened in the last days of monarchic Judah, when a generation that did not produce even one clear name with Baal as its theophoric element (see Tigay, Avigad, 1986) but abundance of Yhwistic names turned out to be considered a generation of Baal (the deity) lovers who have abandoned YHWH,

(e) "With the priests" (i.e., עם הכהנים) commonly considered a gloss.[115] This is mainly because, (a) the phrase is lacking in the LXX, (b) it is supposed to be an explanation of the difficult term כמרים, (c) it disturbs the metrics of the unit, and (d) the phrase seems to be superimposed over a well structured unit.

The first argument is not conclusive by itself, because of the reasons mentioned above in the discussion on והמכשלות את הרשעים.[116] Since it seems that the translators of the LXX Hos 10:5 and the LXX 2 Kgs 23:5 were uncertain concerning the translation of the term כמרים,[117] and since the term occurs only three times in the entire OT, it has been suggested that the phrase "with the priests" explains the meaning of כמרים. This is possible, but taking into account that the gloss was introduced into the Hebrew text, the main question would be whether the Hebrew readers would have difficulties in understanding כמרים. In this respect it is noteworthy that the Aramaic term כמרים (meaning priests in Aramaic,[118] but especially priests of "foreign" gods in Jewish Aramaic/s) is not so rare as it is in Biblical Hebrew. For instance, in the Aramaic of the Jews of Elephantine the term כמר (in different related forms) is attested in Cowley 13 line 13, Cowley 27. 3,8,14 (the latter, reconstructed), and Cowley 30. 5. There, the term כמר is used always for non-Yhwistic priest, and mainly for the priests of Khnub. In sharp contrast, at Elephantine, the term כהן is used only for the priests of

---

then the Judean Baal was unequivocally considered an "alien" deity, and therefore the μyrmk, its priests. This process led to the identification of μyrmk with "idolatrous" priests in Jewish Aramaic (or Aramaics) since the the days of the Elephantine and all the way along, and to the same identification in "Midrashic" Hebrew; see below.

[115] E.g., J. M. P. Smith: 187-88; Taylor: 1112; Gerleman, 1942:6; Elliger (BHS); Rudolph, 1975: 262; Krinetzki: 182; Sabottka, 1972: 18; Kapelrud, 1972: 23; Irsigler, 1977: 18-22; Edler: 15, 102; Renaud, 1986: 4-5; Langhor, 1976:6. RSV and NRSV delete (!) the phrase in the translated text. The phrase is also lacking in NJB, REB and NEB; the latter in its 1971 edition of the OT and Apocrypha went further and deleted also the footnote with the reference to the Hebrew reading, which is supported by most of the ancient versions.

[116] For the discussion on the LXX evidence concerning this phrase, see Gerleman, 1942: 6, Ball, 1972/1988: 25; Irsigler, 1977: 18-20

[117] See Gerleman, 1942: 6, Ball, 1972/1988: 25.

[118] Jean-Hoftijzer: 122, entry כמר II

YHWH.[119] The same meaning of כמר is attested in Gen. Rab. 26,[120] and in a Hebrew pericope in Gen. Rab. 65.[121] The term, with the same meaning of priest of "foreign" gods, is attested in both Talmuds,[122] and in Targum Jonathan to the Prophets.[123] It is noteworthy that the Targum to Zeph 1:4 translates the Hebrew עם הכהנים by עם כומריהון. The aim of this translation is to make explicit what was according to the translator the implicit meaning of MT כהנים, i.e., priests of "foreign" gods.[124]

Summing up: If the Hebrew readers knew Aramaic, then they may have been able to understand כמר without the help of an explanatory note.[125] Concerning the third argument, metrical reasons by themselves are not a conclusive reason for considering a phrase a gloss. The fourth argument deals with the structure and meaning of the unit.

Following "I (YHWH) will cut off from this place" (v. 4), a series of direct objects occurs. Each of these direct objects is preceded by the preposition את, and each refers to some group that is to be "cut off" in a way that explicitly refers to the reason for the "cutting off."[126] Since the list of direct objects is the main element in the unit, and since these direct objects are not characterized by their socio-political identification but by their cultic deeds, it is clear that the emphasis in the unit relies on the

---

[119] See Cowley 30 line 1,18 and Cowley 81: 8.39.

[120] ויראו בני האלהים, midrash on (Gen 6:2), כומריה נגבך אלהיא . . .

[121] רבקה שהיתה בת כומרים לא היתה מקפדת על סנופת עבודה זרה, see Gen. Rab. 65, midrash on תהיין מרת רוח ליצחק ולרבקה (Gen 26:35). Gen. Rab. was written ca. 400-450 in the land of Israel.

[122] See, for instance, the bibliographical references of Jastrow's dictionary.

[123] See, for instance, Ribera Florit 150-51; Jastrow.

[124] Cf. Targum Jonathan to Judg 17:5,13, 28:30, in which also the MT כהן is translated כמר. Clearly, if the Hebrew כהן here is equivalent to the Aramaic כמר then the question is how to understand the difference between the two terms that exists in the Hebrew text. That is, what the Hebrew כמר may mean if it cannot be understood as the Aramaic כמר? The translator of the Targum solves the problem by a free translation of the Hebrew כמריו as פלחידון.

[125] The fact that in extant Palestinian Aramaic texts and inscriptions from the late second Temple period the term כמר is not attested does not prove that it was not known. In this respect it is worth noting that none of the occurrences of the term כהן in this corpus is exchangeable with כמר (see 2QJN frag. 4 line 14,15; 11QJN frag. 14 line 6; Givaat Hamivtar Abba Inscription line 1; 1QapGen xxii 15; 1QTLevi i, 2). For the texts, see Fitzmayer and Harrington: 52, 80, 124, 168.

[126] For v. 5b, see below.

identification of the non-legitimate cultic actions that brought upon these groups the divine announcement of punishment (see vv. 4-6). Baal (the cult of Baal) and the כמרים are related to each other by the pair שם - שאר. The grammar of the text stands against the reading: "I will cut off the כמרים." What is about to be cut off is שם הכמרים. This being the case, שם makes it impossible to read כמרים without the reference to Baal. Thus, the pair שם - שאר combines Baal and כמרים into one functional unit of meaning explicitly pointing to a kind of illegitimate cultic activity.

The note עם הכהנים does not introduce the priests as a regular member of the series of direct objects; they are not preceded by את. Although they are included in the first group of the indicted, they stand outside the structure built upon the pair שם - שאר, and therefore they are not necessarily related to Baal. Since they are not explicitly related to Baal there is no direct reference to any illegitimate cultic activity that may explain the reason for their future punishment. One may only assume that if they are mentioned here, they probably have done something wrong.[127] In all these aspects, the note עם הכהנים does not resemble the rest. These differences may suggest that עם הכהנים has been superimposed over a well structured unit. The idea of a secondary origin for this note is supported by the semantic equivalence[128] between הכהנים and כמרים. This semantic equivalence is supported by the structure of the verse which connects the two words by עם, which means in this case "along with" (e.g., Gen 18:23 "will you destroy the innocent along with [עם] the guilty").[129] The stress on the equivalence of the two also explains why כהנים is not introduced by את as a regular direct object of the "cutting

---

[127] Since this is only an assumption, Abrabanel who, for historico-theological reasons and because of his "historical" exegesis, held that also the "just" were eventually "cut off" from Jerusalem (i.e., they were slain, or went to the exile) pointed to this verse as an example supporting their position. See Abrabanel.

[128] Since כהנים is preceded by עם, it stands in the text in equivalence to כמרים. If כהנים would have been introduced by את it would have been in equivalence with שם כמרים and בעל שאר.

[129] Sabottka has proposed, following van Hoonacker, that עם here means "aus" (Sabottka, 1972: 18), but see, for instance, Rudolph, 1975: 262 and Irsigler, 1977: 20-21.

off," because had it been the case, the structure of the verse would have point to an equivalence between שם (or שם הכמרים) and כהנים. But equivalence does not mean synonymity; to the contrary the phrase "the priestlings along with the priests" makes sense only if the priests are not the priestlings. As seen above, the differentiation between כהנים as YHWH's priests, either righteous or wicked, and כמרים as priests of "alien" gods is not attested elsewhere in the OT, but it is attested in the Elephantine papyrus and in the "rabbinic" literature (mainly in Aramaic but also in Hebrew). It seems that at a certain time, and because of the interpretation given to כמרים, a clear differentiation between this term and כהנים was developed. This differentiation had almost no influence in the text of the OT, and therefore is probably late.

3.2.4. Zeph 1:5

(a) The worship of the heavenly bodies is neither mentioned in Judean prophetic literature from the period before the beginning of the deuteronomic movement nor condemned in any pre-D source. On the other hand such worship is mentioned and condemned in Zephaniah, Jeremiah and Ezekiel.[130] The biblical evidence concerning asherah and baal shows the same pattern.[131] Obviously, a triple coincidental theory is hard to sustain.[132]

It is worth noting that all the key "idolatrous" terms found in Zeph 1:4-5 (Baal, host of heaven and priestlings), appear in the account of Josiah's reform in 2 Kings 23.

(b) ואת המשתחוים הנשבעים לה' והנשבעים במלכָּם

---

[130] For a discussion on the cult of the Host of Heaven in monarchic Judah, see Ben Zvi, 1987: 377-90.

[131] See Ben Zvi, 1987: 356-63, 364-76.

[132] For the implications of this pattern of occurrence for the reconstruction of the religio-cultic history of Judah, see Ben Zvi,1987: 356 ff.

According to the MT and most of the ancient versions, YHWH is mentioned in the third person in v. 5ᵇ. Accordingly, the form of the direct divine speech, which is attested from v. 2 to 5ᵃ, comes to an end.

Elliger (BHS), following Nestle, Marti, and others, proposes to read "moon" instead of YHWH.[133] This proposal may solve the (modern?) problem caused by a possible interpretation to the reference to worshipers of YHWH and to worshipers of Malcam in the two sides of the parallel structure,[134] but there is no textual evidence favoring this emendation, nor any compelling reason supporting it.

Many scholars consider that the MT shows a disturbed metrical balance in this verse. These considerations led to several proposals concerning the original Hebrew text. Although the word משתחוים in this phrase (this is the second time it occurs in v. 5) is lacking in several important texts in the LXX textual tradition (some texts in the LXX tradition lack the entire phrase "those who bow down and swear to YHWH"),[135] the tendency in modern research has been to consider הנשבעים (and not המשתחוים) secondary and dependent on the second נשבעים in this verse.[136]

The opposite proposal has also been advocated, i.e., that משתחוים is secondary and that it was introduced by a scribal error induced by the משתחוים in v. 4.[137] Yet another option has been suggested, namely, that נשבעים and משתחוים represent variants in the tradition, and

---

[133] See also Elliger, 1951: 55, 59. For a general overview of different textual proposals on v. 5, see Jeppesen: 372.

[134] Obviously, Abrabanel consider this parallelism another evidence supporting his idea that both the righteous and the wicked will be cut off from Jerusalem; see above. The Targum, and some Medieval Jewish commentators, propose that the verse refers to those who although bow to and swear by YHWH, do not swear only by YHWH (see Rashi, Ibn Ezra, Radak). According to Calvin the verse refers to those who did not only reject "the law of God" but also were boasting that they are worshiping God (Calvin: 196-97).

[135] See, Ziegler, 1967; J. M. P. Smith: 192; Gerleman, 1942: 7; Ball, 1972/1988: 25; Irsigler, 1977: 23.

[136] E.g., J. M. P. Smith: 188; Elliger (BHS); Rudolph, 1975: 262; Krinetzki, 1977: 254; Edler: 15; Renaud, 1986:5.

[137] E.g., Ehrlich: 456. Therefore, he translates: "die zu JHVH sich bekennen, aber bei Moloch (oder Milcom) schwören." Cf. Calvin's exegesis of this verse. Also Jeppesen (following Hitzig) considers מתשחוים secondary, according to Jeppesen נשבעים לה' refers to the use of "heathen oath formulas in connection with Yahweh's name" and he compares this text to Hos 4:15. See Jeppesen: 373.

therefore the present verse is another case of double readings (e.g., 2 Kgs 11:13; note the asyndetic form in which the two readings are connected).[138]

Finally, they are also those who consider the MT text as it stands the original text.[139] They point to the fact that an asyndetical structure of two participles is not impossible in Biblical Hebrew.[140] Moreover, this asyndeton may introduce a mood of "passion" (e.g., Exod 15:9; Am 5:21) that may be relevant to the message of the text.[141] Accordingly, and since there is no את before הנשבעים במלכם, verse 5 may describe those who are about to be "cut off" as: those who bow, take oaths of loyalty to YHWH (again and again), yet they swear by Malkam (again and again).[142]

Thus, the entire v. 5 mentions only two groups of people whose cultic activities are condemned. These two groups are sharply contrasted by the literary emphasis on the similar opening, and by the use of the same verbal form משתחוים ל with a total different object (YHWH instead of the Host of Heavens). This conveyed meaning seems to be reinforced by the asyndeton that brings the theme of the oath of loyalty to YHWH, only in order to blow it up by the differential use of the two closely related verbal forms להשבע ל and להשבע ב and their indirect objects.[143]

Obviously, the contrast between the two verbal forms mentioned above does point to a central contrast, the one between YHWH and מַלְכָּם. While the MT מַלְכָּם means "their king"; G[L], Vg and S read "Milcom,"

---

[138] Cf. Gerleman, 1942: 7; Talmon.

[139] See, for instance, Ball, 1972/1988:26-30; House, 1988: 118, 127.

[140] See GKC § 120 g,h; and especially § 154 a note 1.

[141] For further examples, see GKC § 154 a note 1.

[142] For ו with the meaning of "but", "yet," see, for instance, Gen 6:8; Lev 2:12; etc. See GKC § 154 a; Williams: 71.

[143] להשבע ל is similar to "take an oath of loyalty to" (e.g., Exod 32:13; Isa 45:23; 2 Chr 15:14) yet the expression להשבע ב is more close to "sworn by X." Sometimes biblical authors underscored the substantial difference between two concepts by the use of the same verbal form followed by different prepositions(cf. לבסח על מצרים in 2 Kgs 18: 21,24 and לבסח אל ה' in 2 Kgs 18:22, 30). For the general case of grammatical contrast in biblical parallelism, see Berlin, 1985: 31-63.

(i.e., the national Ammonite god) instead of מִלְכָּם.[144] Who is this
מִלְכָּם?

In the OT, the X in the expression X- נשבעים ב means YHWH in
almost all the cases in which the one who "swears" is a person. Slightly
different is Lev 19:12, in which X means the name of YHWH, i.e., a
concept that represents him.[145] However, in Jer 12:16 X refers to Baal
and in Am 8:14 it means "אשמת שמרון."[146] Thus, X in this language
means either a deity or something which represents it. Accordingly,
מלכם should be understood in one of these two ways. Since the context
of the verse precludes the possibility that YHWH and מלכם are identical,
three divine identities have been proposed for "malkam":

(1) "Malkam" refers to Milcom, the Ammonite deity. This suggestion is
supported by some ancient version as mentioned above. Nevertheless,
according to this proposal the national Ammonite deity would be one of
the principal deities of the ruling Jerusalemite elite. Since the members of
the socio-political center of power of Jerusalem had their own national
deity, and since its traditions served as their source of legitimacy and
strength and as a necessary and existential unifying factor in society, then
it seems utterly strange that this elite, by their own will, had chosen to
worship the deity of the Ammonite center of power, instead of their
own.[147] Furthermore, there is no corroborative evidence suggesting that
Milcom's worship was one of the sins of the Judean elite in the late
monarchic period.[148]

---

[144] So RSV, NRSV, REB; NJPSV translates: "Malcam," and in the footnote explains:
"apparently identical with "Milcom, the abomination of the Ammonites." Cf. 1 Kings
11:5.

[145] The idiom in Gen 31:53 deserves a complete discussion, which stands beyond the scope
of this work.

[146] YHWH as worshipped in the Northern Kingdom?, the image (the calf)?

[147] It could not be the result of Ammonite coercion. Not only that no historical source
points to this coercion, but also the relative strength of Ammon precludes it. The
Assyrians, who had the necessary power, if they ever compelled vassals kingdoms to
any cult, they would have probably compelled them to an Assyrian-Mesopotamian cult,
and in any case not to an Ammonite one.

[148] 2 Kgs 23:13 cannot be used as such an evidence, cf. 1 Kgs 11:7 (see BHS).

Yet, there is a possibility that the reference to Milcom is a sheer hyperbole. If this is the case, the phrase והנשבעים במלכם would only point to a common knowledge that Milcom was a foreign deity, and to the fact that the author of the text was highly critical of the cultic behavior of certain Judeans.[149] Significantly, not only monarchic Judeans knew that Milcom was the Ammonite deity, but also readers of 1-2 Kings (see 1 Kgs 11:5,33; 2 Kgs 23:13). This leads to the question which reading, Milcom or Malcam, would have been more likely to lead to the other. The literary (quasi) equivalence between YHWH and Milcom/Malkam clearly suggests that the latter is a deity. Milcom is a known deity but Malkam is not.[150] Consequently, it seems more likely that a puzzling Malkam give rise to the relatively well-known Milkom in the ancient versions mentioned above than that an original Milkom turned because of a scribal error to Malkam.[151]

(2) Malkam refers to Baal. This suggestion is based on the commonly accepted picture of the state of the cult or religion in Jerusalem at that time. The widespread worship of "baal" as described in dtr. texts is nothing but forms of YHWH's worship that were regarded as illegitimate in D, dtr. and post-D literature.[152] However, even if the classical picture is accepted, there is no support in the text, or in any textual tradition, for the reading "baal", unless Malkam is understood as Molek, and Molek is understood as Baal.

(3) Malkam refers to Molek, the deity that was worshipped in the Valley of Ben Hinom and that, according to this line of thought, has nothing to do with YHWH.[153] However, all the occurrences of Molek in the OT are related to one particular kind of ritual and probably to one place.[154] Zeph

---

[149] Cf. Ezek 8: 14.

[150] Malkam as a personal name occurs only in 1 Chr 8:9. There Malkam is the name of a Benjaminite. For the Chronicler, Malkam was not the name of a foreign god.

[151] A likely original Milcom is rendered Molek in 1 Kgs 11:7. But Molek was understood as a deity, and therefore the textual case of 1 Kgs 11:7 does not parallel the one in Zeph 1:5.

[152] See Ben Zvi,1987: 356-63.

[153] For the opposite proposal, see Ben Zvi,1987: 391-412.

[154] Except for 1 Kgs 11:7, in which Molek is probably not the original reading; see above.

1:5 suggests a widespread religious attitude (not a specific cultic activity), not attested elsewhere in the OT, unless it is supposed that Molek is a reference to Baal. However, this would imply that the Baal's proposal is accepted.

There is an alternative approach: to understand "malkam", as it stands in the MT, i.e., "their king." The meaning of this "their king" may be derived from Jer 2:28:

ואיה אלהיך אשר עשית לך

יקומו אם יושיעוך בעת רעתך

כי מספר עריך היו אלהיך יהודה

It seems clear that the purpose of the verse is not to state that each city had its own transcendental deity. Nowhere in the Old Testament is such a statement made. In the phrase אלהיך אשר עשית לך , here, as well as in the related phrase אלהי אשר עשיתי (Judg 18:24), אלהים must be understood as an object, like an image, a statue, etc., which represents a transcendental god. As pointed out before, in dtr. literature, especially when the worship mentioned is illegitimate, the same terms may be used for both the god and the objects representing it. For example, here, something made by human beings is called "your god" (אלהיך), and in 1 Kgs 12:28, in the famous expression הנה אלהיך ישראל, the word אלהיך refers to each of the two calves of gold. In the three mentioned instances, a term normally used for YHWH appears with a possessive suffix (i.e., not as a proper noun), and refers to something representing the deity (in the second case, obviously the God of Israel). A common feature in all these cases is that the referred representation of the deity is considered illegitimate from a deuteronomistic point of view.

Malkam in Zeph 1:5 is probably nothing but the exact parallel of אלהיך. Since YHWH was considered and referred to as מלך,[155]

---

[155] There is epigraphic evidence for names such as מלכיהו, מלכיהו. The names מקנמלך (cf. מקניהו 1 Chr 15:21) and מלכיהו are attested in late monarchic Jerusalem, in the same group of bullae (the name מקנמלך is attested also in Ammon, there it probably refers to the— local—national god of Ammon). See Avigad,1986: bullae 98,99,120, 174, 175 and Lawton,1984: 339. For a discussion on מלך as referring to YHWH, and not to an hypothetical god Molek, see Ben Zvi,1987: 391-412, esp. 405-10.

malkam here may be understood as something representing YHWH. From the negative context in which the term occurs, it has to be concluded that this form of representation was considered illegitimate after the deuteronomic reform.

From a stylistic point of view, it is worth noting that the observed literary pattern of contrasts by means of apparent similarities reaches its climax in the opposition of YHWH (i.e., rightly worshiped, or rightly conceived and therefore rightly worshiped)[156] and Malkam (i.e., YHWH wrongly worshiped, or wrongly conceived and therefore wrongly worshiped).

3.2.5. Zeph 1:6

(a) The verbs used in the deuteronomic literature[157] with X מאחרי (X stands for YHWH, or for a clear reference to YHWH) are from the roots סור and שוב (e.g., Deut 7:4; Jos 22:16,18,23,29; 1 Sam 12:20,15:11; 1 Kgs 9:6). These sentences always have a negative sense. They appear also in Num 14:43 (non-P), 2 Chr 25:27, 34:33 (which has no parallel in Kings) and in Job 34:27.[158] Hos 1:2 has זנה in the explanatory comment attached to the strange divine command: אשת זנונים וילדי זנונים לך קח לך, probably because of stylistic literary reasons. Significantly, this language does not occur in the Book of Ezekiel. There the verbs used with X מאחרי are from the roots תעה and נזר (Ezek 14:7, 11). Finally, the only form really close to Zeph 1:6 occurs in Isa 59:13.[159]

---

[156] One may assume that in ancient Israel, worship was not unrelated to the image of god of the worshiper.

[157] For the exception see 2 Kgs 17:21. The verb there is probably נדח; see Montgomery,1951: 479.

[158] Also in Jer 3:19, but given its metaphoric context it should be better considered as a special case. For Jer 3:19 see Carroll,1986: 151-53; Mc Kane (1986): 77-83.

[159] For מאחר instead of מאחרי see also 2 Sam 7:8; Ps 78:71 (probably late monarchic, see Anderson,1972: 561-77).

(b) The pair דרש - בקש, with YHWH as the direct object, occurs in Ps 105:4 = 1 Chr 16:11 (post-exilic[160]), and in Ps 24:6 (post-exilic[161]), but in an inverse order. Not referring to YHWH, and also in the inverse order, i.e., בקש - דרש, it occurs in Judg 6:29 and Ezek 34:6.[162]

3.2.6. Zeph 1:7

(a) The word הס (Silence !) is an interjectional form of the imperative of הסס in its *qal* form.[163] Rudolph considers הס a cultic call,[164] but it seems clear that the meaning of any הס (silence!, be quiet!) can only be inferred from the context in which it occurs.[165] The complete expression occurring in Zeph 1:7 is: X-מפני הס, in which X='אדני ה. With X=YHWH, this expression occurs in Hab 2:20 (late monarchic period?) and in Zech 2:17 (post-exilic). Despite the similarities, it is worth noting that unlike Hab 2:20 and Zech 2:17, Zeph 1:7 contains no reference to the "holy abode" (קדשו היכל) or to the "holy dwelling"(מעון קדשו).

The audience of this "silence!" are clearly those who are asked to be in silent. This audience may be real (i.e., those who heard the speech), or an implied literary feature (i.e., the implied audience of the speech in the

---

[160] See for instance Fohrer,1970:291, Anderson (1972): 726. This Psalm presupposes the Exodus story in its Pentateuchal form.

[161] These terms function as technical terms for the community of the faithful in this Psalm. See Gerstenberger,1988: 118-19.

[162] This pair, as the basis of a parallel structure, occurs neither in 2 Chr 20:3-4 nor in Deut 4:29. The idiom in Deut 4:29 is composed by בקש and מצא; cf. Am 8:12.

[163] See GKC § 307 a; Meyer, II: 145,182. The LXX and the Peshitta translate הס or הסו in the sense of "be afraid," "fear" (cf. OL; Oesterley: 384). For a brief discussion on these translations, see Gerleman, 1942: 7-8. Instead of the MT "be silent before Adonai YHWH," Tg. Neb. reads "all the wicked have come to an end before YY," (י קדם מן רשיעיא כל ספו). This reading concerns the history of interpretation of Zephaniah. It does not point to an original divergent Hebrew text. It is noteworthy that the Targumic renderings of Zeph 1:6,7 contain several clear deviations from the MT.

[164] Rudolph, 1975: 266.

[165] For instance, הס in Am 6:10 is clearly not a cultic cry/call. The verse means: "Hush! so that one may utter the name of the LORD"(NJPSV). הס in Am 8:3 may be the result of a textual corruption (cf. Elliger [BHS]), but in any case it cannot be considered a cultic call. Also הסו in Neh 8:11 is not a cultic call.

book), or even an implied literary feature from the standpoint of the implied audience. That is, the audience that is implied in the book is not the one who is called to be in silence, but instead they are told that someone else is called to be in silence. Moreover, this "someone else" may include the audience (real or implied) without overlapping it.[166]

To whom is הס "said" in Zeph 1:7? Clearly, Zeph 1:7 provides no answer. Furthermore, neither the entire first chapter of Zephaniah nor any of its different units claim to be directly addressed to the various kind of people who are either indicted and going to be punished, or to any hypothetical pious group. Indeed, no one is ever referred in the second person in Zephaniah 1. Thus, since there is no clear reference to real or literary addressees (i.e., to someone mentioned in the second person, or mentioned as addressee in a reported speech),[167] there are no grounds for identifying these addresses. It is noteworthy that also in this respect Zeph 1:7 is unlike Hab 2:20 ("be silent before YHWH all the earth") and Zech 2:17 ("be silent all flesh before YHWH").

The cry הס expresses the normative attitude of human beings before the appearance of YHWH. It stresses the imminence of God's appearance. This sense of imminence is explicitly conveyed by the subsequent phrase, "for the day of YHWH is near."

(b) "For the Day of YHWH is near" (כי קרוב יום ה'). This phrase is a common expression in the " day of YHWH" (hereafter, DOY)[168]

---

[166] Cf. Hab 2:20; Zech 2:17

[167] This feature is quite common in DOY literature (see below), but also in many other prophetical pieces (e.g., Isa 13:6-16; 3:1-12, respectively).

[168] If יום ה' was indeed a terminus technicus, then the precision in the language cannot be disregarded. The term יום ה' occurs only in Isa 13:6,9; Ezek 13:5; Joel 1:15, 2:1,11, 3:4, 4:14; Am 5:18; Obad 1:15; Zeph 1:7,14; Mal 3:23. Alternatively, if יום ה' is not a "terminus technicus", but refers to past or future events, which are conceived as specific actions of YHWH that stand far beyond the "regular" flowing of events, then other terms are to be considered as pointing to DOY. For instance, expressions like יום לה' אלהים, יום חרון אפו, יום אף ה', יום לה', יום לה' צבאות, and almost any prophetic announcement of judgment in which the word יום is included—YHWH is a constant factor, either explicitly or implicitly—will point to this category. Since several literary features of the description of DOY are common to many of the units containing the expression/term יום ה', it seems appropriate for the purposes of this work to refer to them as "DOY literature". Since there are some literary units that lack this precise expression, but show a large degree of similarity with DOY literature (e.g., Ezek 30:2[b]-3/5), the above

literature (e.g., Isa 13:6; Joel 1:15, 4:14; Obad 1:15; cf. Ezek 30:3; Joel 2:1; Zeph 1:14). The meaning of the phrase is clear. It points to the imminence of DOY and in doing so accomplishes a clear rhetorical function. Although Zeph 1:7 presupposes an audience who knows what DOY is about, it also presupposes an audience who is not aware that DOY is at hand, and therefore, it is certainly relevant for the assumed audience.[169] To sum up, Zeph 1:7b contributes, as do Zeph 1:7a (see above) and Zeph 1:7c,d (see below), to the emphatic formulation of this meaning.[170]

(c) The sacrificial term זבח is used as a "technical" term in relation to YHWH's punishment in Isa 34:6 (post-monarchic [171]); Jer 46:10 (non-

---

mentioned way of defining DOY literature may be too minimalist. Thus, this definition will be used only as an affirmative group of reference (i.e., in order to prove the existence of certain features in the DOY literature). The negative group of reference (i.e., the group of reference used in order to prove the absence of certain features in DOY literature) will include all variations in the prophetic literature of "day" and "YHWH", which are commonly considered as pointing to DOY.

If Zeph 1: 7-13* originally belongs to the DOY literature (for the opposite idea, see Edler: 184 ff.), then the non-eschatological character of this day, here, and especially its limited geographical realm are noteworthy (cf. Am 5:18-20; Ezek: 13:5). The opposite holds for many other pieces in DOY literature (cf. Isa 13:6,9; Obad 1:15; Zeph 1:14-18 and the descriptions in the Book of Joel). For a discussion on the "Day of YHWH" in Zephaniah, see the relevant section in this work.

[169] To argue that the main point in the "saying" : "the Day of YHWH is at hand" is to convince someone who thinks that DOY is not about to come soon that DOY is indeed coming and soon, is quite obvious, and almost tautological. This point has been explicitly stated many times all along the history of interpretation of Zephaniah (e.g., Radak, Calvin: 204).

[170] It has been proposed that the phrase "the Day of YHWH is at hand" has additional meanings. These proposed meanings are directly related to certain scholarly hypotheses concerning the concept of DOY. For instance, von Rad considers this phrase a "coined formula of tradition," and proposes that "the Day of YHWH is at hand" may have been the "stereotyped call with which the troops were summoned to take the field in the holy wars." See von Rad,1959: 108. Since this use of the phrase is attested nowhere in the Old Testament, this proposal relies entirely on von Rad's hypothesis concerning the origin of the concept of DOY (see von Rad, 1959; for a criticism of von Rad's position see Weiss, 1966, van Leeuwen, 1974 and the bibliography mentioned in the latter, see also Everson, 1974, and Hoffman, 1981). Everson claims that "the day of YHWH is at hand" points emphatically to the imminence of the day, i.e.,the position expressed in the body of this work (see Everson, 1974: 331). Hoffman, who maintains that "one of the most important aspects of the concept of the Day of the Lord is the emphasis that it is a day of judgment for the wicked," thinks that the root קרב has legal connotations (Hoffman, 1982). Since no one denies that the word קרוב may mean "at hand"/ "near in the axis of time," for it is well attested conveying this meaning, Hoffman's proposal depends, to a large extent, on his understanding of DOY.

[171] See Clements,1982: 271-74, and the bibliography cited there.

dtr, late monarchic?[172]); Ezek 39:17,19, and Zeph 1:7. זבח refers metaphorically to the sacrificial slaughter in Isa 34:6 and Jer 46:10, but to the "offered," or probably to the meal, after the slaughter in Ezek 39:17,19.

What does זבח mean in Zeph 1:7? The use of the hiphil form of כון is compatible with the two possible meanings.[173] Therefore, the only way to decide between these two possible understandings is by means of קְרֻאָיו הקדיש.

However, הקדיש קְרֻאָיו may convey the two purports, depending on which of two possible imports of הקדיש is preferred. According to the first, הקדיש refers to an object that is sanctified in order to be "offered" to YHWH (see Lev 27:26).[174] Obviously, if it is the case in Zeph 1:7, then those who are consecrated in order to be sacrificed are the invitees (קְרֻאָיו). That is, they are the direct object of the verb, and therefore, according to the context of Zeph 1:7, this hiphil form of קדש is to be understood in a metaphorical way. Such a metaphorical meaning of קדש is attested elsewhere (Jer 12:3). It is obvious that, according to this interpretation, the verse makes ironical use of the widespread custom of inviting (קרא) persons to the sacrifice and to the sacrifice meal (see 1 Sam 16:5, cf. Ezek 39:17-21). According to this reading, so does YHWH in Zeph 1:7. Also YHWH has invitees, but the invitees are not going to enjoy the "offering." Instead, they are to be sacrificed. Moreover, they have already been set apart for the offering. Furthermore, if the Leviticus conception of sanctification (=set apart for YHWH) is implied, these invitees are irredeemable because any sanctified object that can be offered in the altar cannot be redeemed.[175] Thus, the fate of the invitees has already been sealed. Even more, their sacrificial slaughter is imminent for

---

[172] For a discussion on Jer 46: 3-12, see Carroll,1986: 761-65. It is quite impossible to date Jer 46:3-12 precisely. Probably, it refers to the battle of Carchemish, and may belong to the late monarchic period.

[173] הכין זבח does not occur elsewhere in the Old Testament. The fact that כון in its hiphil form may refer to the "offered" is clear from Num 23:1,29.

[174] See Milgrom, 1976: 783 § 4b.

[175] See, Milgrom, 1976:783.

"the sacrificer" is about to come (Zeph 1:7a). But who are these invitees?
Zeph 1:7 provides no answer; it only provokes the question.

There is, however, a second and alternative interpretation of קְרֻאָיו
הִקְדִּישׁ.

YHWH may have sanctified his/her guests for the meal (i.e., the
alternative understanding of זבח) with him/her.[176] This image, without
mentioning the sanctification, occurs in Ezek 39:17. YHWH's guests are
clearly identified there: birds of every sort and all beasts of the field. But
Zeph 1:7 does not identify the guests.[177] Zeph 1:7 does not identify even
the one who is about to be sacrificed in order that others will have the
"meal."

Some modern scholars have supported the first alternative and some the
second.[178] There is yet a third possibility that becomes clear when one
analyses v. 7 as a unit. This unit is composed by four versets.[179] The
first verset makes clear that YHWH is about to come but leaves

---

[176] See, Milgrom, 1976: 784 §6.

[177] Certainly, ancient and modern commentators tried to fill the information gap. Basically,
there have been two models of interpretation. According to the first, the guests are
those who are about to execute the divine punishment. For instance, Jerome, Abrabanel
and Calvin proposed the Chaldeans (cf. "Nebuchadnezzer, my (YHWH's) servant" [Jer
25:9]; already mentioned by Jerome in his commentary on Zephaniah). Among modern
scholars, who consider this verse part of (or a reflection of) an actual address given by
Zephaniah in the days of Josiah, the Chaldean theory could not be accepted because of
historical reasons. Instead, there was a tendency to think first in terms of Scythians
(e.g., Eiselen:525), and later on, because of the widespread rejection of the Scythian
hypothesis, in terms of "enemies of Judah" without any further differentiation (e.g.,
Boadt, 1982: 210). According to Ginsberg the phrase is another example of Isaiah's
influence on Zephaniah (see Isa 13:3). He suggested that Zephaniah was inspired by "the
purified guests" who will execute YHWH's wrath against Assyria (according to
Ginsberg's interpretation of Isa 13, "Babylon must here (Isa 13) be regarded by the
prophet as the capital of Assyria"). See Ginsberg, 1953: 258. The same text in Isa 13
have suggested other scholars that Zeph 1:7 refers to the gathering of an army in order
to wage a holy war (cf. Edler: 194). Moreover, it has been suggested that the "holy
army" should not have been restricted to human soldiers, and therefore, the guests may
have been "heavenly beings" (cf. Sabottka: 34-35, Elliger, 1951: 60).
The main alternative to these proposals is based on Ezek 39:17 and claims that that the
guests are the birds and the beasts. It was already proposed by Radak, and since then
stands as the main alternative to the "hosts" interpretation (cf. Ball, 1972/1988: 65).

[178] There is a relatively large number of articles and references to this issue. See Irsigler,
1977: 285-88 and the vast bibliography cited there.

[179] Following Hrushovski and Alter, the line-halfs, as well as the line-thirds in triadic
parallelism, are designated versets in this work. See Hrushovski: 1201-02; Alter,
1985:9.

unanswered questions of place, audience, and the specific characteristics
of this coming. The second verset points to the imminent coming of
YHWH and attaches it to the impending DOY (i.e., this is not a usual
theophany, but the kind of theophany related to the DOY). The second
verset presupposes an audience who is not unaware of the concept of
DOY, but of the fact that DOY is at hand. The second and the third verset
begin with כי . This is a common device for stressing the connection
between two subsequent versets.[180] In other words, the double opening
with כי suggests the two versets should be read together. This reading
brings a sense of heightening, not only that DOY is at hand but even more,
that YHWH has already "prepared" an offering.[181] Not only is DOY
"near," but also YHWH has been active in bringing the day upon
someone, who is not specified.[182] Granted that there is an ongoing
heightening in the message, that each verset shows an emphatic character
in relation to the preceding one,[183] one expects the climax in the fourth
verset הקדיש קראיו. Clearly, this is the climax of the unit if the
identity of the "offering" is made known, i.e., the invitees are the offering
and they have been already "set apart" (cf. Jer 12:3) in order to be
"sacrificed." But since there is no זבח with the participation of the
"sacrificer" and the "sacrificed" alone, the understanding of the verset as
saying not only that YHWH has already prepared the offering but also has
already sanctified the guests, and therefore they are ready, along with

---

[180] See, for instance, Isa 40:2, Jer 4:30, 50:11; cf. Isa 15:5-6, in which a כי functions as the
common opening. Clearly, although the versets may show grammatical equivalency
(e.g., Isa 40:2, Jer 4:30, 50:11), they may also stand in grammatical contrast (e.g., Ps
41:12; Isa 15:9, 63:16; Zeph 1:7). On this issue, see Berlin,1985: 31-63.

[181] One can persuade a person that A is B by saying that also C is B only if the other person
accepts beforehand that C is B and that A and C are related. Persuading someone that
DOY is at hand by saying that YHWH has already prepared the "offering" makes no
sense if the person is unaware of the relationship between the "offering" and DOY, or if
he/she considers much more impossible to believe that YHWH has prepared his/her
"offering" than to believe that DOY is at hand.

[182] What exactly has been prepared by YHWH (i.e., "the animal", or the slaughter, or the
meal) is irrelevant in this context because all the possible alternatives convey the same
meaning. Consequently, any explanatory note will be digressive here whereas the
present ambiguity is not.

[183] Cf. Alter, 1985: 18 ff.; esp. 18-22.

YHWH, to bring about the DOY can be interpreted as a further emphasis in the line of imminence. Moreover, those who consider קְרֻאָיו a reference to some kind of hosts[184] that are about to bring a historical, as well as metahistorical change, DOY may consider the last verset as the emphatic line saying that the "hosts" have been already released. This would bring an overarching structure in the unit: it begins with a worldly action that is brought about by an anticipated divine action ("Silence!"), and concludes with an expected worldly action that is brought about by a divine action. This interpretation may be supported by a comparison between the grammatical occurrence of YHWH at the beginning of the text ("*before* YHWH) and in its conclusion (*his* guests), with YHWH as a subject in the middle of the unit. Since, each verset contains a reference to YHWH, and since this feature is unique in the verse, it is clear that YHWH is a key term in the unit. Consequently, one cannot rule out this proposal, for it closely follows this key term.

Thus, both interpretations seem to be correct. What does it mean? Clearly, the author of Zeph 1:7 was not incapable of expressing his/her points in a straightforward and emphatic manner; to the contrary he/she did it in neat and well structured form. Since both the well structured form and the linguistic meanings of הִקְדִּישׁ קְרֻאָיו point to ambiguity, it is likely that verse 7 expresses, and even emphatically expresses, an intentional ambiguity. Why? For rhetorical reasons. The reader/hearer of the verse is told that DOY is at hand. Since he/she is aware of the connection between the זֶבַח image and DOY, the author uses a vivid and credible image in order to convince the reader/hearer of something difficult to believe, namely, that DOY is indeed at hand.[185] Nevertheless, the vivid image turns out to be uncertain because of the ambiguity of the last verset. The ambiguity brings uncertainty concerning the identity of the guests and the sacrificed, and therefore, calls attention to question. Ambiguity leads

---

[184] See, footnote, above.

[185] The perfect "tense" of verbs related to offering in this verse is noteworthy. They convey the sense that: this has been done, so DOY is really at hand (קָרוֹב) i.e., adjectival form.

to reflection on what was read, or heard. Thus, the total vagueness about the audience who is told to be silent, or concerning place, begins to seem more relevant than before. Finally, the reader/hearer cannot but leave the verse with a clear sense that something terrible is about to happen, but he/she does not know for sure what. Puzzled by questions of identity, the reader/hearer is ready for the subsequent unit in the Book of Zephaniah.[186]

(d) It is noteworthy that the double divine name/title אֲדֹנָי ה' occurs only in once in the Book of Zephaniah, in the expression מִפְּנֵי אֲדֹנָי ה' הס (elsewhere in chapter 1 YHWH is referred as ה'). The expression ה' אֲדֹנָי occurs 280 times in the Old Testament, among them 213 times in the Book of Ezekiel,[187] and only seventy-seven times elsewhere in the Old

---

[186] The functional role of the image of זבח in Zeph 1:7 (i.e., that it occurs only in order to draw the attention of the reader/hearer to certain questions) is supported by the lack of any further use of this motif in the entire book, in any of its redactional levels; except for Zeph 1:8[a] that makes explicit what is implicit in the functional role of verse 7, namely, that it is an introduction to the following verses.

[187] The "authenticity" of the double divine name/title (אדני ה') in general and especially in the Book of Ezekiel has been questioned. Mainly because of the occurrence of a single "kyrios" in the hypothetical original text of LXX of Ezekiel. It has been assumed that the early LXX text reflects an early Hebrew Vorlage containing only YHWH. Accordingly, the MT double divine name was explained as the result of relatively late pious additions of the perpetual *qere* of YHWH to the text. Divergent inner LXX renderings (which are the majority) were explained by assuming either different translators or partial editing/s of the LXX text/s in order to bring it closer to the MT. See, for instance, Cooke: 33-34, Eichrodt:12, Elliger [BHS]. The main evidence for the "original" LXX reading came from LXX967. For a comparative table of MT, OL and the attested LXX renderings of the divine name in Ezekiel, see Mc Gregor: 223-257. For the history of research on the LXX renderings, see McGregor: 57-74, Zimmerli, 1983: 558-61 and the bibliography cited in these works.

More recent studies on the LXX readings of the divine name in Ezekiel have tend to reject the idea that LXX points to a Hebrew Vorlage containing only a single divine name. For the Septuagint question, see Zimmerli, 1983: 558-62 and the bibliography cited there, and McGregor: 79-93.

In addition, a close examination of the occurrence of the double name in MT Ezekiel (and in MT in general) shows that the above mentioned proposal is unacceptable. For instance, the double divine name/title occurs in the phrase כה אמר אדני ה' no less than 122 times in Ezekiel, but there is no occurrence there of the close expression כה אמר ה' צבאות, which is, for instance, so widely attested in Jeremiah. Moreover, there are also eighty-one occurrences of נאם אדני ה' in Ezekiel, but the double divine name occurs only five times in an address to God, and there are only four instances of כה אמר ה' and another four of נאם ה' in the entire Book of Ezekiel (they occur in the—likely to be—later layers of the book, see Zimmerli, 1983: 556). Furthermore, it is clear that these figures are not due to a general reticence in Ezekiel to use the name ה' without אדני. The name ה' alone occurs 218 times in Ezekiel, there are eighty-seven instances of אני ה' and ninety-four instances of the name ה' at the end of construct chain (e.g., יד ה', "hand of YHWH"; see

Testament. This double divine name occurs only four times in the
Pentateuch, twice in Genesis (Gen 15:2,8), and twice in Deuteronomy
(Deut 3:24, 9:26); only once in Joshua (Josh 7:7), twice in Judges (Judg
6:22, 16:28), six times in 2 Samuel chapter 7 (vv. 18,19[2],20,22,28,29),
and twice in 1-2 Kings (1 Kgs 2:26, 8:53). With the exception of 1 Kgs
2:26, in all these texts אדֹנָי ה' occurs in the context of direct human
speech to YHWH.[188] In prophetic literature (except Ezekiel) the term
occurs forty-nine times. They include eight occurrences in Jeremiah (Jer
1:6, 2:22, 4:10, 7:20, 14:13, 32:17,25, 44:26), four in Isaiah 1-39 (Isa
7:7, 25:8, 28:16, 30:15), thirteen in Isaiah 40-66 (Isa 40:10, 48:16,
49:22, 50:4,5,7,9, 52:4, 56:8, 61:1,11, 65:13,15), twenty in Amos (Am
1:8, 3:7,8,11,13, 4:2,5, 5:3, 6:8, 7:1,2,4[2],5,6, 8:1,3,9,11, 9:8) but only
one each in Micah, Obadiah, Zephaniah and Zechariah (Mic 1:2; Obad 1:1;
Zeph 1:7; Zech 9:14). It is worth noting that the context in which the
expression occurs in the Latter Prophets is clearly not confined to direct
human speech to YHWH. Finally, in the Writings, אדֹנָי ה' occurs only
three times in Pss (Ps 71:5,16; 73:28).[189]

The described pattern of occurrence of אדֹנָי ה' is clearly not a random
one. Also, there is at least one specific expression אהה אדֹנָי ה' in
which the divine name is always אדֹנָי ה' (see Josh 7:7; Judg 6:22; Jer
1:6, 4:10, 14:13, 32:17; Ezek 4:14, 9:8, 11:13, 21:15). However, there is
no such uniformity concerning Y- הס מפני. Y may stand for אדֹנָי ה',
as in Zeph 1:7, but also for YHWH as in Hab 2:20 and Zech 2:17. Thus,

---

Mc Gregor: 60-1, Zimmerli,1983: 556-58). Thus, there can be no doubt that there is a
clear pattern of occurrence, and that this pattern is not the result of a random choice of
terms. Obviously, the selective occurrence of אדני ה' cannot be explained in terms of
pious addition of the perpetual *qere* to the ineffable name. It is worth noting that when
there was indeed a real attempt to avoid the name YHWH in Biblical literature, i.e., in
the so-called Elohistic Psalter (Pss 42-83), אלהים occurs instead of ה', not אדני.

[188] For the use of אדני in direct speech to a superior, see Lande: 28-35, 81.

[189] Cf. Even-Shoshan, 17-18. For a different counting, see Boadt,1978: 494. The double
divine name אדני ה' is to be differentiated from the name/title אדני ה' צבאות that occurs in
Isa 3:15, 10:23,24, 22:5,12,14,15, 28:22; Jer 2:19, 46:10[2],49:5, 50:25,31; Am: 9:5;
Ps 69:7 but not even once in Ezekiel. The form אדני ה' occurs in Hab 3:19, Pss 68:21,
109:21, 140:8, 141:8.

there are no clear parallels to the occurrence of אֲדֹנָי ה' in Zeph 1:7 elsewhere in the Old Testament.[190]

3.2.7. Zeph 1:8

(a) As mentioned above, verse 8a and its preceding verse are the only place in Zephaniah in which there is a reference to the זבח issue. The phrase in v. 8[a], namely, "on the day of YHWH's zebach," does not claim to be YHWH's speech. To the contrary, since it mentions YHWH in the third person like v. 7—and unlike vv. 8[b]-9—it claims to be a connective note, as well as an interpretative key, for the divine speech in vv. 8[b]-9, but not a part of it.[191]

The phrase in v. 8[a], along with similar introductory sentences, occurs in verses 10 and 12. It seems to be a part of a compositional or editorial framework that turns the three blocks of material in vv. 8-13* into one tripartite divine speech. These three phrases are commonly considered secondary,[192] i.e., they are not considered among the original sayings of

---

[190] Only one may note that in "third Servant Song" (Isa 50:4-9), in v. 5 YHWH is called ה' אֲדֹנָי (as anywhere in this song, see vv. 4,5,7) and that the same v.5 contains phrase נְסוּגֹתִי לֹא אָחוֹר. Both are comparable with Zeph 1:6-7. Also in verse 8 in the same song one reads קָרוֹב מַצְדִּיקִי (i.e., "my vindicator is at hand) and cf. Zeph 1:7. This cluster of comparable terms and idioms exists in spite of the clear generic difference between the two units.

For the proposal that אֲדֹנָי ה' may have been used because of the occurrence of בֵּית אֲדֹנֵיהֶם in Zeph 1:9, see Ball, 1972/1988:65. Ball consider his proposal a support for his understanding of בֵּית אֲדֹנֵיהֶם as a reference to the Temple (i.e., the House of YHWH); see Ball, 1972/1988: 70.

[191] It is worth noting that the connection between v. 7 and vv. 8[b]-9, which is made explicit by v. 8[a], exists independently of the phrase in v. 8[a]. Since the contents of v. 7 point to questions and issues that remained entirely unsolved in the framework of the verse, one had to assume that the verse cannot stand alone but as a part of a larger unit of meaning. The proximity between v. 7 and vv. 8[b]-9, and the way in which the latter answer the open questions of v. 7 (see above, and below) indicates that the two could have been blended into one unit of meaning without the supportive claim made by v. 8[a] Clearly, the proposal that v. 7 or vv. 8[b]-9 are included in one unit of meaning in the given text, does not rule out the possibility that either v. 7 or vv. 8[b]-9, or both, could have had a previous textual "life."

[192] See, for instance, Gerleman, 1942: 67-68; Edler: 7-8, 103-04; Elliger (BHS); Rudolph, 1975:267.

the prophet Zephaniah. Obviously, such a position implies that one may point to a certain corpus of sayings that contains the actual words of the prophet, or at least that closely reflect them. This position presupposes the acceptance of the claim of the superscription and interprets it as real authorship. Such a presupposition characterizes the prophet-oriented approach mentioned in the introduction of this work. But, according to the text-oriented approach in which one begins the analysis from the received text back to their original units, the main question is not whether Zephaniah said these words or not, but whether they are secondary additions to an existent text of Zephaniah (or proto-Zephaniah), or compositional devices used in order to compose the text out of pre-existent units, or redactional devices used to attach a certain unit to an existent text (proto-Zephaniah).[193] Obviously, one cannot choose one of these alternatives only on the basis of the temporal and connective phrase "on the day YHWH's zebach," and therefore, the issue will be discussed in the commentary section.

It is worth noting that the phrase in v. 8[a] connects the preceding and the subsequent verse by means of an explicit reference to the preceding verse which also functions as an interpretative note. The urgent sense of the imminence of the divine action in v. 7 is sharply diminished or vanishes entirely: "On the day of YHWH's zebach, YHWH will punish the officials . . . (v. 8)." It is worth noting that post-monarchic generations probably considered that the destruction of the Temple and Jerusalem was the fulfillment of the announcement of judgment in Zeph 1:8-13*.[194] It is hardly possible that these generations thought that the mentioned historical events occurred in the reign of Josiah. Thus, if Zeph 1:8-13* was related in the post-monarchic period to Zephaniah (i.e., a prophet who lived and prophesied in Josiah's days), then either the prophet prophesied

---

[193] For proposals concerning the redactional history of these units, see, for instance, Kapelrud, 1975: 18-19; Scharbert; Irsigler, 1977: 95-96, 440-42; Renaud, 1986: 9-10 and the bibliography cited in these works.

[194] Cf. the descriptions in Lamentations. It is worth noting that pre-critical commentators consider the destruction of Jerusalem and the Temple as fulfillment of this prophecy. So, for instance, Jerome, Radak, Abrabanel, Calvin.

concerning a future not too distant from his days but by no means imminent, or his prophecy did not come true.[195]

(b) The exact expression ופקדתי על (see also vv. 9, 12) is attested several times as one of the verbal forms occurring in a series of perfect forms that indicates a set of related actions of the deity and whose general purpose is judgment, i.e., punishment. This form is attested in monarchic as well as in post-monarchic material, in Exod 32:34 ; Hos 1:4, 2:15, 4:9; Am 3:14; Isa 13:11 (post monarchic),[196] and about ten times in Jeremiah, including dtr-Jeremiah (e.g., Jer 15:3).[197] Significantly, it never occurs in the Book of Ezekiel.[198] This verbal form occurs several times, after a temporal . . . והיה form—as in Zeph 1:8—or any other temporal form,[199] and in most of instances is the first perfect of the series, or the only one if the series contains one perfect.[200] Moreover, the form ופקדתי never occurs after והכרתי את or והכרתי על or ונטיתי ידי, in a series of perfect verbal forms. This pattern of occurrence does not support the

---

[195] Obviously, the meaning of this "delay" depends on the historical circumstances in which these notes have been written. For instance, Kapelrud thinks that they were added to the words of the prophet at an early stage, probably by one of his disciples, because it was too risky to proclaim an imminent judgment against the powerful leaders of the state (Kapelrud, 1972: 17-19, 28). Leaving aside the question if Kapelrud does justice to the text, and to the severe indictment of the leaders, which remains unchanged by any addition (pace Kapelrud, who thinks that "neither the שרים not the בני המלך needed to feel themselves offended" because of this text [Kapelrud, 1975:19]; cf. Edler's criticism of Kapelrud's position [Edler: 105-06]), his proposal illustrates how the proposed date for the notes leads to a certain set of possible meanings and preempts an alternative set of meanings.

[196] See for instance Clements, 1982: 135. For a different opinion, see Hayes and Irvine, 1987: 220-21.

[197] See for instance Mc Kane,1986: 335-36. The position that Jerusalem and the Temple were destroyed because of the sins of Manasseh is one of the main topics of the dtr. history (more precisely, dtr. H).

[198] Other qal forms of פקד על conveying the meaning of punishment occur in the OT, many of them in Jeremiah (e.g., Jer 11:22, 13:21, 25: 12, 29:32; 44:13, cf. Jer 5:9, 29— where על may have a double function) but also in other books (e.g., Hos 4:14, 12:3; Am 3:2; Zech 10:3). פקד על does not occur all in Ezekiel, and does not occur, with this meaning, in LBH (i.e., late Biblical Hebrew; see Polzin, 1976) literature.

[199] E.g., Exod 32:34; Jer 9, 24, 51:47, 52; Am 3:14; Hos 1:4.

[200] E.g., Exod 32:34; Isa 13:11; Jer 15:3, 21:14, 23:34, 36:31; 51:44, 47, 52; Hos 1:4, Am 3:14. But see Hos 2:15.

idea that vv. 8ᵇ-9 originally followed vv. 2-5 (or 4-5).[201] It is worth noting that the speaker in the expression פקדתי is always YHWH.

(c) ... בני המלך ... שרים [202] probably means "the officials ... the royal family ... "

Gaster proposes that Zephaniah spoke against the background of a Canaanite, pagan festival of "ingathering" and made constant reference to characteristic features of the festival. Accordingly, for him בני המלך refers to the "royal entourage" who are "likened satirically" by Zephaniah to the youngsters (sons and grandsons of the invited guests), who were also brought to the divine banquet ceremony.[203] Sabottka proposes that מלך refers to Baal. Accordingly, "the Baal's sons" are a metaphorical designation for Baal's worshipers and שרים refers to a cultic officer.[204] According to Heider, שרים can [sic] denote cultic officials, he proposes that מלך refers to Molek, instead of Baal, and accordingly "sons of Molek" (Heider's reading of the phrase) refers to "the victims (or perhaps the cult-members) of the cult of Molek." He admits the conjectural character of his proposal but considers a "secular" understanding of "sons of the king" even more problematic, not only because Zephaniah's favorable view of Josiah but also because "his [Josiah's] sons can hardly have been old enough (Jehoiakim, the eldest son was twelve years old when the reform began) to draw the prophet's ire in this oracle."[205]

However, the well attested meaning of שרים in the OT is royal officials and not cultic officials or priests. Even Am 1:5; Jer 48:7, 49:3 (that allegedly support the latter proposal) do not point to this possibility unless the text is emended on—and only on—the grounds of presuppositions

---

[201] For such proposal, see Scharbert.

[202] LXX reads "the king's house" for בני המלך." However בית and בני point to the same meaning. In Gen 45:11; Exod 16:31; and Josh 17:17, 18:5, the MT reads בית but the LXX בני; in Ezek 2:3; 1 Chr 2:10 the MT reads בני and the LXX בית ; in Jer 16:14 MT and LXX read בני ; in Hos 1:7 both read בית. Also cf. Neh 7:28 (MT and LXX) with Ezra 2:24 (MT and LXX).

[203] See Gaster, 1969: 678-85, esp. 681-82.

[204] See, Sabottka, 1972: 36-38.

[205] See Heider: 334-35.

concerning the existence and social extension of "foreign cults."[206] Similarly, there is no textual ground for reading "Molek" instead "king." Heider's reading is an integral part of his hypothesis concerning the worship of Molek in Judah, but is neither a requirement of the text nor its straightforward meaning. In any case, the term שׂרים meaning royal officials is well attested in the OT and causes no interpretative problem in this verse, unless it is emended.

The second term, the title בן המלך, is well attested in epigraphic material from the monarchic period.[207] It is also attested in neighbor countries and in biblical literature. From the time of Clermont Ganneau (ca.1888) there are scholars who claimed that this title refers to an officer of middle or even low rank; i.e., "king's son" means "king's servant". According to some scholars, this "servant" had a role in "internal security affairs" (see 1 Kgs 22:26-27; Jer 36:26, 38:6). Moreover, in 1 Kgs 22:26 and Zeph 1:8 the supposedly crown prince is named after other officers, and it may reflect his relative rank.[208] However, both the testimony of extra-biblical sources from the ancient Near East and the improbable degree of ambiguity for an administrative 'terminus technicus' (many times in the OT the son of the king is clearly the prince and not a police officer, e.g., 2 Kgs 15:6) point against this proposal. Furthermore, the existence of "king's sons" whose task is not what it is expected for the "crowned prince" can be explained by the fact that the title refers to the enlarged royal family and not only to the biological sons of the king (see 2 Kgs 10:1).[209] This family included many persons, and one should not expect to find each of them at the highest rank of the administration.[210]

---

[206] On the general issue of "foreign cults" in monarchic Judah and specially on Molek's cult, I wrote elsewhere. See Ben Zvi, 1987: 356-412, esp 391-412.

[207] See, for instance, Avigad, 1969, 1981, 1986; Histrin and Mendels, 1978; Bourdreil and Lemaire,1979.

[208] For these proposals see, for instance, Grin,1967, and De Vaux,1965: 119-20.

[209] Although the number seventy is not to be taken literally but as a way of conveying a sense of entirety, it obviously implies a relative large number.

[210] For this point of view, see Rainey,1975; and Lemaire,1979.

The pair שרים - בני המלך conveys the meaning of the entire Judean elite (except for the king) in Jer 52:10.[211] The reference to the "officers" is lacking in the parallel account in 2 Kgs 25:7.[212]

Many scholars think that the literary and ideological context of the unit makes a reference to the Judean king unavoidable, if only there were a ruling Judean king. Thus, since the "sons of king" and the "officers" are mentioned but not the Judean king, these scholars have inferred that the text was written during the days when Josiah was a minor and had no real power (see Zeph 1:1; 2 Kgs 22:1).[213] Clearly, this inference is valid only if the premise is true and if it leads unequivocally to the proposed inference. In other words, if it is true that (a) if there were a ruling king, he must have been mentioned and condemned in this text, and (b) if the preceding sentence is true then the only possible explanation is Josiah's childhood. The absence of any reference to the king in similar accounts in the prophetic literature (e.g., Isa 1:21-23 [-26]; Mic 7:3) or even a positive reference to him (see Lam 4:13, 20) in a context of condemnation are clear indications that the answer to the two conditions mentioned above cannot be affirmative. This does not necessarily rule out the possibility that the text refers to or reflects the days of Josiah's childhood, but rules out the idea that the text necessarily points to these days.[214]

---

[211] Although it is hardly questionable that there is a historical kernel to this narrative, it is worth of noting that the text implies that the only remaining members of the Davidic family, along with the officers who served the legitimate dynasty, are those who are around Jehoiakin in Babylon (except for the blind and heavily condemned Zedakiah; for the contrast between the two kings, see Carroll, 1986: 861). Such a claim is particularly important in relation to the tension between the exiles in Babylonia and those who remained in Judah (cf. Ezek 11: 14-21, 33:23-29).

[212] The "officers" are mentioned in Jer 39:6 (a third parallel account) but instead of שרים the text reads חרים. Jer 39: 4-13 are lacking in LXX Jeremiah (ch. 46).

[213] Cf. Eiselen: 507-13; J. M. P. Smith: 196; Kauffman: 349 (Heb.); Rudolph, 1975: 267; Edler: 124-25; Lohfink, 1984: 101. It is noteworthy that traditional commentators gave almost no attention to the lack of mention of the king. For instance, Calvin felt no need to explain why the king was not mentioned but he did feel the need to explain why the simple people are not mentioned in these verses (Calvin: 207-08, and cf. the editor's note).

[214] For more comprehensive discussion on this issue, see the commentary section.

(d) The term מַלְבּוּשׁ occurs in 1 Kgs 10:5 (= 2 Chr 9:4); in 2 Kgs
10:22 (but see BHS); Isa 63:3; Ezek 16:13; Job 27:16. These
occurrences, and especially 1 Kgs 10:5; Ezek 16:13; Job 27:16, seem to
imply that מלבוש in the OT refers to an expensive cloth (cf. the popular
שׂמלה; e.g., Gen 44:13; Exod 19:14 ; Deut 10:18; 2 Sam 12:20; Isa 4:1;
Ruth 3:3). The occurrences of מלבוש in Job 27:16 and 1 Kgs 10:5 do
not support the idea that מלבוש is necessarily a cultic garment.[215]

The language מלבוש נכרי occurs only in Zeph 1:8. The meaning of
the term נכרי in the OT quite overlaps the meaning of the English term
"alien." The main interpretative question is therefore, in which sense are
these clothes alien.   נכרי clearly means "foreign" in most of its
occurrences in the OT (e.g., Exod 2:22, 18:3; 21:8; Deut 29:21; Judg
19:12; 2 Sam 15:19; 1 Kgs 8:41,43, 11:1, 8; Ruth 2:10; Lam 5:2; Ezra
10:2, 10,11,14,17,18,44; Neh 13:26, 27). Nevertheless, in several of its
occurrences נכרי does not have the connotation of "foreign" but of "not
yours, stranger to you" (e.g., Prov 5:20—cf. v. 18—6:24, 23:27),[216] or
"not you, but someone else who is a strange to you" (e.g., Prov 20:16,
27:2,13; Qoh 6:2). In addition, it is obvious that נכריה in Isa 28:21 and
Jer 2:21 does not mean "from another country" but "strange to YHWH."
Since, נכרי means "foreign" in the vast majority of its occurrences in the
OT—except Proverbs—and the context in Zeph 1:8 is compatible with this
meaning, there is no reason to prefer the alternative readings. Moreover, it
is worth noting that נכרי meaning "foreign" may also convey a sense of
"inappropriate for you" (e.g., 1 Kgs 11:1, 8; Ezra 10:2, 10,11,14,17,18,
44), and this is clearly the case in Zeph 1:8. Undoubtedly, the author of
Zeph 1:8 thought that these foreign clothes should not be worn by the
Judeans.   Thus, the author's use of the term נכרי points to the
association of "foreignness" with "unfitness" for Judeans.   This

---

215This idea was suggested many times and it relies on 2 Kgs 10:22. Cf. Rashi;
  Gaster,1969: 682; Sabottka, 1972: 38; Watts, 1975: 159; Bic: 56; also cf. Targum
  Zeph 1:8. Critical approaches to this idea are also old. See, for instance, Radak, Ibn
  Ezra, and Calvin.

216 Radak, in the name of his father, brought an explanation based on this meaning of נכרי.

association occurs elsewhere in relation to foreign women (e.g., 1 Kgs 11:1, 8; Ezra 10:2,10,11, 14,17,18,44; Neh 13:26, 27), but there is no reference to "foreign women" in Zeph 1:8. On the other hand, Zeph 1:8 is the only case in the OT of indictment for wearing foreign clothes.

3.2.8. Zeph 1:9

(a) The expression כל הדולג על המפתן as a way of characterizing a group, and at all, occurs only in Zeph 1:9. The divergence among the readings of the ancient versions points to the difficulties that the translators had with this expression.[217] For centuries there have been two main exegetical lines concerning כל הדולג על המפתן. According to the first, the expression refers to non-Israelite cultic behavior (see Targum Zeph 1:9, y. ᶜAbod. Zar. 3.2, Rashi); according to the second, to crimes in the social sphere (see Peshitta, Ibn Ezra, Radak, Abrabanel, Altschuler, Calvin). In modern scholarship there is an almost overwhelming preference for the first option.[218] However, there is no consensus on the literal meaning of the expression. This is due to the differences concerning the meaning of the words דלג and מפתן. In general terms, one may say that there are two main approaches to this question. The first translates the expression as "those who leap over the threshold," and most scholars relate this custom to Philistine, Assyrian, or the general ancient Near Eastern "magical" world. The second approach translates as follows:

---

[217] For comparative summaries of the diverse readings in the ancient versions, see J. M. P. Smith: 208-09; Gerleman, 1942: 8-11; Ball, 1972/1988: 36.

[218] For modern studies on this question, see, for instance J. M. P. Smith: 208-09 ; Ehrlich: 456-57; Bennet,1918-9; Frazer,1923: 313-322; Gerleman, 1942: 9 -13; Donner,1970; Ball, 1972/1988: 36-37; Irsigler, 1977: 39-49 (including a comprehensive bibliographical data and a brief discussion of this data); Krinetzki,1977: 56-57; Edler: 129-131.
Since so much has been written on this topic and in order to prevent an unnecessary lengthening of the notes, references to previous works will be kept to the illustrative minimum in this section.

"to mount the platform", upon which a statue of the god, or the king's throne stood.[219]

The word מפתן should be understood as the threshold of the gate in Ezek 46:2, and as the threshold of Dagon's temple in 1 Sam 5:4-5,[220] but as the platform upon which the Temple stood in Ezek 9:3, 10:4,18, 47:1. Therefore, it seems that מפתן served as a general word for an elevated surface.

Words from the root דלג occur only five times in the OT (2 Sam 22:30 [=Ps 18:30]; Isa 35:6; Zeph 1:9; Cant 2:8).[221] The two basic meanings proposed for דלג (i.e., "to climb up" and "to leap") are possible for דלג in 2 Sam 22:30 (=Ps 18:30),[222] but the second fits better the context in Isa 35:6. Furthermore, דלג parallels קפץ in Cant 2:8, pointing clearly to the second proposal.[223] To sum up, since only the meaning "to leap" is compatible with all the biblical occurrences of דלג, and since according to the old Newtonian rule one should refer the same effect to the same cause (i.e., one should propose only the necessary [minimum] number of explanations to a given phenomenon), then one has to prefer the understanding of דלג as "to leap" in Zeph 1:9. Accordingly, since people can leap over a threshold, but not over the platform of the building, Zeph 1:9 should be understood as " I will punish all who leap over the threshold" (NRSV).

---

[219] A clear illustration of the weaving between the two position is given by the two widely used Hebrew lexicons, BDB and KBL. BDB (1907) renders דלג as "leap," KBL (1953) renders it as "hinaufsteigen", i.e., "ascend" but KBL[3] (1967) renders it as "springen", i.e., going back to the BDB rendering.

[220] For the text, see BHS. "Dagon" at the end of vs 4 refers to Dagon's trunk. Winkler and Gerleman, proposed "pedestal" for מפתן, and interpreted it as the pedestal upon which Dagon's statue stood. This meaning is impossible for Ezek 46:2.

[221] In four out of these five occurrences, the attested form is a piel form. The exception is the qal participle in Zeph 1:9. The difference of meaning between the two *binyanim* , if any, may be related to the sense of intensification given by *binyan piel* .

[222] For instance, compare the RSV (and NRSV) rendering of the expression in both cases ("leap over a wall") with the NJPSV rendering ("scale a wall").

[223] It is worth noting that דלג in Sir. 36:31 (מי יאמין בנדוד צבא המדלג מעיר אל עיר) means to bound, to leap, and in "mishnaic" Hebrew it also means to leap or to skip (see m. Ohol. 8.5 [*qal* form]; m. Meg. 4.4 [*piel* form, metaphorical sense]; t. Dem. 3.17; cf. Sop. 11:6.

Modern readers must ask themselves what custom is this. Clearly, since those responsible for the ancient versions were puzzled by the expression, one can assume that they were unfamiliar with this custom, and asked themselves this question. The Targum related the custom to the Philistines, i.e., a midrashic interpretation based on 1 Sam 5:4-5. Certainly, 1 Sam 5:4-5 is a Judean pejorative story concerning the origins of the "leaping" custom at the temple of Dagon. But this story just implies that this custom was not a common behavior.[224] A more common custom of burying holy objects under the threshold of the houses is attested in the area at different times, including the Assyrian period. The idea was that the gods and spirits under the threshold prevent the entrance of evil spirits, demons, etc. Accordingly, to stand upon them was considered not only an impious act but also a dangerous one.[225] Against this background, it has been proposed that the prophetic message is a reversal of this position. Not to rely on YHWH,i.e., to rely on these "spirits", is not only a sin but also leads to doom. Since this custom was unknown to the (original) writers of 1 Sam 5:4-5, but supposedly common when Zeph 1:9 was written (or proclaimed orally) then scholars, who assume an early date for 1 Sam 5:4-5 and a Josianic date for Zeph 1:9, tend to consider this custom to be an example of Assyrian influence on Judah.[226]

Nevertheless, it is strange that this supposedly common custom was neither mentioned nor condemned in the large amount of biblical material concerning cultic and religious sins.[227] Is Zeph 1:9 the only extant evidence of a furtive custom? Or was the custom condoned, later? Or was it only by chance that no other reference to this custom survived in the biblical literature? One cannot ruled out such possibilities. But what kind of support can be brought on their behalf? Moreover, what kind of evidence supports the basic presupposition from which all these proposals

---

[224] Cf. Irsigler, 1977: 48 and the bibliography cited there.

[225] Cf. Donner, 1970.

[226] Cf. Edler: 130-31.

[227] Isa 57:8 is undoubtedly a difficult verse, but by no means can be interpreted as pointing to the custom referred in Zeph 1:9.

spring, namely, that leaping over the threshold has a cultic/religious meaning?

The notice in 1 Sam 5:4-5 implies only that leaping over the threshold was a remarkable custom of the Ashdodite priests and uncommon in Judah. The broad divergence in the ancient versions of the OT implies that the custom was not known in their days (at least from the second century BCE). Even the Targum, in its religious/cultic interpretation of the phrase, refers only to a textual tradition (1 Sam 5:4-5) relating the custom to the Philistines, i.e., an ancient people who no longer exists by the time of the Targum to the Prophets. Moreover, even the Targum felt the need to explain explicitly what "leaping over the threshold" means. Both the existence of this need and the given explanation support the idea that the mentioned custom was unknown in his (or her) days.[228] Clearly, the evidence mentioned above points to two periods, one presumably before the last years of monarchic Judah and the other several centuries after, but it is worth noting that there is no evidence, whatsoever, for the existence of a cultic/religious leaping over the threshold in monarchic Judah. There is only a proposed interpretation of Zeph 1:9. What evidence does remain in order to support the cultic/ religious interpretation of Zeph 1:9? The existence of popular beliefs concerning the magic features of the entrance of the house in general, and especially of the threshold. But these beliefs are so widespread that they cannot be unequivocally related to a specific time and place.[229] Moreover, against this general background, the evidence mentioned above (regarding "leaping over the threshold" as an uncommon or unknown custom) seems to be even more impressive. Furthermore, if despite the points made above, one keeps holding to the

---

[228] The custom of "leaping over the threshold" was unknown also in the Talmudic period in Palestine, as it is clear from the following saying: "R. Jeremiah in the name of R. Hiyya bar Ba said 'The nations of the world made a single threshold, but Israel made a great many thresholds' (y. ᶜAbod. Zar 3.2, ET J. Neusner, *The Talmud of the Land of Israel. Vol 33. Aboda Zara* [Chicago: University of Chicago Press, 1982] 119). The scriptural proof for this statement is as follows: "On that day I will punish every one who leaps over the threshold (Zeph 1:9)."

[229] Cf. the "modern" custom of the groom lifting the bride in his hands and passing her over the threshold of their home after the wedding.

idea that "leaping over the threshold" was a magic-related behavior in late monarchic Judah, why should a magic-related behavior be non-Yhwistic? Clearly, one should not expect Judeans to have developed an entirely distinct magic-behavior. But, for instance, the existence of Judean amulets does not necessarily point to a non-Yhwistic tendency, as the famous amulet from the late monarchic period containing the priestly blessing (Num 6:24-26) clearly illustrates.

What remains to support the commonly accepted idea that "leaping over the threshold" has a cultic import? Perhaps, genre recognition. But, (a) to hold fast to a proposed genre before a critical analysis of the language of the unit, and accordingly, restricting the possible meaning of the phrases and idioms in the literary unit to those that are compatible with the presupposed genre is a clear methodological flaw, which leads to uncritical circular thinking; (b) the basic genre of the unit including Zeph 1:9 is "prophetic indictment." In general terms, in prophetic literature, Israelites, Judeans, and Israel, have been condemned because of both cultic sins and socio-moral sins (both were "religious" sins).   Therefore, genre recognition cannot be referred to as a clear support for the idea that "leaping over the threshold" has a cultic import. Consequently, it seems that the only "evidence" supporting the cultic interpretation is the presupposition that Zeph 1:8^b-9 should be read in the light of Zeph 1:4-5. But even if these verses were parts of an original text or speech (which is very questionable, see commentary),[230] this does not mean that the writer, or the prophet, should have condemned the people either on cultic grounds or on social grounds but not on both (cf. the Decalogue).

To sum up: The evidence supporting the cultic or magic interpretation of "leaping over the threshold" is far from convincing. Is there any alternative to such understanding?

---

[230] For the opposite position, see, for instance, Scharbert.

Without the secondary ביום הוא ("on that day") in v. 9, which even in the present form of the text should be read as a phrase closed by parentheses,[231] the verse reads:

ופקדתי על כל הדולג על המפתן

הממלאים בית אדניהם חמס ומרמה

The clause opening with הממלאים is a regular relative clause beginning with "he (ה) + participle" (e.g., 2 Kgs 22:18).[232] Thus, this "leaping people" not only leap over a certain threshold but also "fill their master's palace with lawlessness and fraud" (NJPSV). The plural form הממלאים points to a collective understanding of the noun-phrase כל הדולג על המפתן (see 1 Kgs 20:20, cf. Gen 4:15; Exod 12:15; 1 Sam 3:11; 2 Sam 5:8). Therefore, they represent a group. This condemned group is not characterized by each of the mentioned features separately but by both of them, simultaneously.[233] Accordingly, the "leaping" group is also the characterized by the clause opening with הממלאים, and therefore, since they have a master (אדון) they are servants (עבד), all of them. But, whose servants?

The expression בית אדניהם probably does not mean the Temple.[234] It would be a very strange and unattested way of referring to the

---

[231] The expression . . . הממלאים בית אדניהם, following the "on that day" clause, has no independent meaning; it is clear related to the expression preceding the "on that day" clause. Thus, this temporal clause not only that does not link the immediately preceding text to the following one (unlike the similar clauses in vv. 8,10,12), but also separates a clause from its referent. This "on that day" has been added in order to make explicit the implicit claim of the text, namely, that the "day of YHWH's offering" is the "that day." A claim already made in v. 10 (and v. 12 in a different language). It is noteworthy that the tendency to make explicit the implicit is one of the characteristic features of the material existent in MT Jeremiah but not in the LXX Jeremiah (See, Tov, 1985: 225-27).
Obviously, considering "on that day" in v. 9 secondary does not mean that the phrase has to be disregarded. It points to a stage in the interpretative process. A central topic is why the phrase was introduced in its present place, instead of being at the beginning of v. 9, as one expects in the light of Zeph 1: 8,10,12 as well as Zeph 3:16, 20.

[232] See, R. J. Williams: 90 § 539; cf. GKC § 126 b.

[233] Cf. "to the king of Judah, who sent you . . . (2 Kgs 22:18). The addressee is not characterized as the king of Judah and as the one who sent the commission but as being both at the same time.

[234] This line of interpretation goes back to the LXX and the Vg. Several modern scholars uphold this understanding of the verse. See, for instance, Gerleman, 1942: 11; Ball, 1972/1988: 37-38

Temple.[235] To go even further and to propose that "their masters/lords" = "foreign gods"[236] is obviously to go beyond the explicit meaning of the text.

Closely related expressions to בית אדניהם occur several times in the OT (Gen 39:2, 40:7, 44:8; 2 Sam 12:8; 2 Kgs 10:3; Isa 22:18, Zeph 1:9). In all of them, the master is a human being, and not Gor or a god.[237] Moreover, words composed of the noun אדון with different pronominal suffixes occur hundreds of times in the OT. Significantly, these words refer to YHWH, as the master/lord, only six times in the OT (Pss 8:2,10, 135:5, 147:5, Neh 8:10, 10:30), and always in a context that preempts ambiguity. It is noteworthy that while all of these occurrences are probably post-exilic,[238] those who proposed that אדניהם refers to YHWH based themselves on their reconstruction of the cultic situation in Manasseh's days, in the monarchic period.

Thus, אדניהם, "their master,"refers to the owner of the house, or palace, and he is human. His identity may be derived from the comparison of the two פקדתי sentences:

ופקדתי על השרים ועל בני המלך

ועל כל הלבשים מלבוש נכרי

ופקדתי על כל הדולג על המפתן

הממלאים בית אדניהם חמס ומרמה

The first sentence first mentions the high officers, the royal family in its comprehensive meaning, and later it refers to everyone who dresses so

---

[235] This proposal depends overwhelmingly on: (a) the historicity of the deuteronomistic picture of the religious situation in the days of Manasseh; (b) the presumption that the wrongdoers in this unit are apostates; and (c) a cultic related understanding of the term מפתן as well as on the custom of leaping, which was considered out of question for YHWH's faithful people. Neither these assumptions seem to be proved nor the attested meaning of בית אדניהם is "the Temple" (see below). This is another illustration of the method of "illuminating" phrases, idioms, and simple words in the text in the restricting light of a beforehand accepted hypothesis.

[236] Cf. Sabottka's proposal, self-described "wenig wagemutig," see Sabottka, 1972: 42-43. Among the critical responses to Sabottka's proposal, one may mention del Olmo Lete: 298 and Rudolph, 1975: 262.

[237] Contrast with בית אלהיהם in Judg 9:27.

[238] See Gerstenberger, 1988: 67-72; cf. Anderson: 839, 944.

and so, even if they were neither high officer nor nobles. The second sentence seems to have its point of departure, linguistically as well as thematically, at the end of the first, it further popularizes, mentioning now every servant/officer—whatever his rank and social circle—who enters the royal palace and brings iniquity into it.

(b) Although the terms חמס and מרמה are well attested in the OT, the pair חמס ומרמה occurs only twice, in Zeph 1:9 and in Isa 53:9.

The word חמס is commonly paired with שׁד (Jer 6:7, 20:8; Ezek 45:9; Am 6:3; Hab 1:3; Isa 60:18). Phrases containing piel forms of the root מלא and the noun חמס occur many times in the OT (e.g., Gen 6:11,13; Ezek 7:23, 28:16; Mic 6:12, Ps 74:20). This is not the case with מרמה, but the phrase בתיהם מלאים מרמה, which resembles the expression in Zeph 1:9, occurs in Jer 5:27.[239] There, מרמה means "wealth gained by fraud."[240] The term חמס clearly means "wealth gained by violence," and not violence itself in Am 3:10. Thus, it is possible, but by no means certain that the verse in Zeph 1:9 says: "who fill . . . with wealth gained by violence and fraud" (cf. Am 3:10) instead of "who fill . . . with violence (or, "lawlessness [NJPSV]) and falsehood." (cf. Mic 6:12,[241] Isa 53:9). Obviously, there is a third position, i.e., that the text is intentionally ambiguous. It is likely that the author responsible for the entire book, or most of it, understood the verse in its ambiguous sense, for this interpretation would have pointed simultaneously to the social emphasis (cf. Zeph 2:3, 3:12) and to the emphasis on "language", "words," (cf. Zeph 3:9,13) that characterizes important sections of the book.

---

[239] A post-monarchic piece. See, Carroll, 1986: 189.

[240] See, Mc Kane, 1986: 133.

[241] The date of Mic 6:12 is an open question in modern research, see Mays, 1976: 143-49 and the bibliography cited there. See also Hillers: 80.

3.2.9. Zeph 1:10-11

(a) Verse 10ᵃ connects the preceding with the following verses by means
of the temporal clause "on that day" (cf. Zeph 1:8,12, 3:11,16,20). The
general aspects of these clauses in Zeph 1:8.10,12 has been discussed in
the notes to Zeph 1:8.

The addition of נאם ה' to these temporal clauses has no parallel in the
Book of Zephaniah, but נאם ה' occurs many times after ביום ההוא in
the Latter Prophets (see Isa 22:25;[242] Jer 4:9, 30:8, 49:26 [but not in LXX
Jer], 50:30; Hos 2:18 [cf. Hos 2:23]; Am 2:16, 8:3, 9;[243] Obad 1:8; Mic
4:6, 5:9; Hag 2:23;[244] Zech 3:10,12:4, 13:2;[245] cf. Am 9:13; Joel 2:12).
It is noteworthy that this combination of phrases is attested neither in
Ezekiel nor in Isaiah (except for Isa 22:25).

The claim of נאם ה' is that the following verses (i.e., the rest of v. 10
and v. 11) are divine speech, but obviously the divine speech does not
include the phrase נאם ה'. Both the phrase נאם ה' and the temporal
clause are an introduction to the following unit, but not an integral part of
it. It has been proposed that the addition of נאם ה' turned a former unit
in which the speaker was the prophet into a unit in which the speaker is
YHWH.[246] This proposal is based in two arguments: (a) there was a
former unit that contained the rest of v. 10 and v. 11 but not vv. 4, 5, 8ᵇ,
9, 12,13;[247] and (b) the "prophet" is the first person singular behind the
former text. The first argument points to general issues of sources,
compositional level, and redactional levels, that cannot be resolved on the
narrow basis of notes to a specific verse. The second argument points to
the specific contents of vv. 10-11, from קול צעקה to the end of v. 11.

---

[242] נאם ה' צבאות instead of נאם ה'.

[243] נאם אדני ה' instead of נאם ה' in Am 8:3,9.

[244] נאם ה' צבאות instead of נאם ה'.

[245] נאם ה' צבאות instead of נאם ה' in Zech 3:10, 13:2.

[246] See, Irsigler, 1977: 96; Renaud, 1986:9; cf. Asurmendi: 9.

[247] Obviously, if the temporal clause + נאם ה' is a part of the original unit, or if the original
unit contains any of the mentioned verses, then YHWH will be the speaker of the entire
unit. See, for instance, Scharbert, 1982.

These lines are entirely impersonal. Moreover, while YHWH is mentioned in the third person in some similar laments in prophetic literature (e.g., Jer 25:36-37), many others are clearly impersonal insofar as it concerns their contents and divine speech according to their superscription (e.g., Jer 48:1b-10 [see esp. vv. 3-5]; Isa 15:1b-9). Some of these units contain not only a superscription that claims that the subsequent lament is divine speech but also either a concluding note or one to several notes within the lament (or added to the original lament), or both, making the same claim (e.g., Jer 49:1-6, 7-11). To sum up: A unit containing only verse 10 from קול צעקה to the end of v. 11, and occurring in the prophetic literature is not necessarily a prophet's speech. Moreover, there is a certain tendency, in prophetic literature, to attribute many of similar sayings to YHWH, and not to the prophet.[248]

(b) The "Fish Gate" is mentioned in Neh:3:3, 12:39; 2 Chr 33:14 (without parallel in Kings). Mishneh is a quarter[249] mentioned in 2 Kgs 22:14 (// 2 Chr 34:22) but not in late Biblical sources[250]. "Machtesh" is probably another quarter of Jerusalem, not mentioned elsewhere in the OT.[251] The literary way in which the "blow" upon Jerusalem is described

---

[248] Clearly, this conclusion does not rule out the possibility that these units may reflect literary units outside the prophetic literature. But in this case, one cannot refer the original unit to the "prophet."

[249] The LXX, the Peshitta and the Vg interpreted it as "a second gate". The Targum identifies it with the Ophel.

[250] משנה in Neh 11:9 does not refer to a quarter of the city but to the officer, as a title, see Rudolph, 1949:182-83; Myers,1965: 184, Michaeli, 1967: 348

[251] It is noteworthy that the "authors" of the ancient versions were completely unfamiliar with these topographic marks. For instance, the LXX reads "the gate of men slaying" instead of "the Fish gate" (probably reading שער הרגים instead of שער הדגים, i.e., a simple and attested scribal error in Hebrew, but a possible error only if one is unfamiliar with the name of the gate). The LXX and the Vg consider משנה as a gate in Jerusalem; yet the Targum translates משנה as עופלא, i.e., "Ophel." Due to a scribal error עופלא turned into עופא (cf. Rashi) in several MSS of the Targum, and was perpetuated in the text of the Targum printed in Miqraot Gedolot. Other MSS of the Targum (e.g., Ms Eb. 80; see Ribera Florit:138, 15) and the one used by Radak read עופלא; see the critical apparatus in Sperberg's edition of the Targum. The identification of משנה with עופלא is certainly mistaken. The Targum also translates מכתש as "the valley of Kidron," probably a reference to a well known place instead of מכתש, which is not mentioned elsewhere in the OT and whose location in Jerusalem was unknown to the "author" of Tg. Neb. For a summary of the evidence, and a short discussion, see Gerleman, 1942: 13-15; Ball, 1972/1988:38-39; Seybold, 1985: 29, esp. n.32.

(that is, the general situation of the city is described by references to the severe distress in particular geographic points that belong to the mentioned geographico-political unit) is found also in Mic 1:8-16;[252] Isa 10:28-29,[253] 15:1-2, Isa 16:7-8. It is noteworthy that the latter two make quite obvious that in this literary pattern, the entire geographical area is described as struck (or going to be struck) and not only the particular places explicitly mentioned. The comparison of the first two examples with the latter two shows that when the writer is close to the place (and time) he (or she) tends to include several places well known to him (or her) and to his (or her) contemporaries, but that may leave no further remarks in our sources. They were important for them, but probably not so much for subsequent generations. Obviously, in this respect Zeph 1:10-11 stands in the same category as Mic 1:8-16 and Isa 10:28-29.

(c) The language עם כנען . . . כל נטילי כסף occurs only in Zeph 1:11. נטילי is the plural construct form of נָטִיל, a קָטִיל form that theoretically may be passive or active.[254] Since עם כנען means "merchants" in this verse (cf. Isa 23:8; Job 40:30; Prov 31:24)[255] and the structure is based on parallelism, the active meaning of the *qatil* formation has to be preferred. The word כי here does not necessarily mean "because." Its literary role is emphasis, and it may also be translated as "surely", "indeed", or "yea" (cf. Ezek 11:16; Zeph 2:4, cf. also Gen 4:23-24; Isa 3:1; Am 6:11,14).

The apparently common expression שבר גדול occurs in Zeph 1:10 and six times in the Book of Jeremiah (Jer 4:6, 6:1, 14:17, 48:3, 50:22,

---

[252] Elsewhere I wrote that the list of places—or its kernel—is related to the 701 BCE events in Judah, see Ben Zvi,1987: 233-41.

[253] It also may refer to an itinerary. Concerning Isa 10:28-29; see Clements, 1982: 117-20 and the bibliography cited there.

[254] See GKC 84 § 1.

[255] So Ibn Ezra, Radak, Calvin, Altschuler, Duhm, J. M. P Smith, Gerleman, Elliger, Ball, Kapelrud; Sabottka; Rudolph; Krinetzki; Asurmendi; Scharbert; Zurro and Alonso Schöckel; Edler; House, etc. For a different point of view, see Rashi, "others" whose ideas were rejected by Calvin, Even-Shoshan, and hesitantly Boadt (Boadt, 1982: 211). The reference to the "canaanite" therefore, does not imply a condemnation on cultic grounds, and see below.

51:54), but nowhere else in the OT.[256] The expression . . . מ צעקה קול occurs only in Zeph 1:10 and in Jer 48:3 (there, close to גדול שבר). The other two occurrences of קול צעקה in the OT are in Jer 25:36 (// to יללה), and in a different context in 1 Sam 4:14. It is noteworthy that the mentioned verses in Jeremiah occur in units commonly considered either late monarchical or exilic, but not in dtr-Jeremiah.[257]

Remarkably, there is no reference in these verses to any cultic sin. The text itself does not point to a "ceremonial howling for the vanished god of fertility,"[258] nor restricts the merchants to those "who have profited by catering for worshippers in the sale of figurines and cult objects."[259] The cultic behavior of the Judeans is not compared with the common image of the cult of the "Canaanites"[260] not only because "canaanites" means merchants in v. 11,[261] but also because the parallelism with נטילי כסף. The absence of any explicit cultic reference in these verse makes a double or ambiguous meaning improbable.[262] This double meaning is even more improbable. Different forms of the term "canaan" meaning "merchant" occur in Isa 23:8; Ezek 16:29, 17:4; Hos 12:8; Zech 14:21; Job 40:30; Prov 31:24. Significantly, in none of these cases the term implies or refers to the cultic behavior of the Canaanites.[263] Furthermore, in Ezek

---

[256] The closest expression elsewhere is in Lam 2:3.

[257] Zeph 1:10-11 also resemble Jer 49:3, and in general terms, but only in general terms, Isa 15: 1-9. On the poetic aspects of Zeph 1:10, and especially on the poetic relationship between יללה, שבר גדול, and צעקה; see Irsigler, 1977 a.

[258] So Gaster, 1969: 683.

[259] So Watts,1975: 160.

[260] This comparison is explicitly made in the Targum. But clearly, here, as well as in many other places, the Targum bears testimony to its own interpretative line, and not to a different textual tradition. The LXX also compares the people to be punished (i.e., the Jerusalemites) with the Canaanites, on the basis of its reading נדמה as it were from the root I דמה (i.e., "to resemble") instead of II דמה (i.e., "to cease, to cause to cease," "to destroy"; cf. Isa 15:1; Jer 47:5). See Gerleman, 1942: 15-16; Rudolph, 1975: 263. Among modern scholars, very few understand עם כנען as "those who behave as Canaanites" (i.e., not in the sense of merchants); see, for instance, Ehrlich: 457.

[261] See note above.

[262] For the proposal of a double meaning, see Bula.

[263] This includes Zech 14:21; see, for instance, the note on Zech 14:21 in NJPSV. Zech 11:7,11 may provide two further examples of this use of "canaan" in the sense of merchant (in this case sheep-merchant, see LXX), again without any reference to the cultic behavior of the Canaanites.

16:29, 17:24 even the term ארץ כנען loses its common geographical meaning, and there the "land of traders" referred to is none but Babylonia (Chaldea).

3.2.10. Zeph 1:12

(a) The phrase והיה בעת ההיא anchors the subsequent verses to the ongoing text claiming that the future events described in vv. 12-13 will be contemporaneous with those described in vv. 7-11. Following this introductory and temporal remark, the description of the events begins with a simple imperfect (without *waw*) verbal form (אחפש). Thus, the verbs in v. 12 belong to a new chain of verbal forms, unrelated, at least grammatically, to the chain of vv. 8-9. Clearly, both the new temporal introduction and the imperfect form אחפש point to a break between vv. 8-11, or 10-11, and vv. 12-13. Significantly, it is a conspicuous feature of prophetic literature that temporal linking clauses[264] that introduce a description of a future event are followed by a verb in the imperfect.[265] This general feature strongly suggests that the phrase beginning with אחפש and the temporal introduction are interrelated.[266]

(b) The phrase אחפש את ירושלם בנרות occurs only in Zeph 1:12. The speaker (the first person singular) is obviously YHWH (cf. על ופקדתי, the next form in the verbal chain). The object of the search is obviously not the city of Jerusalem but the people of Jerusalem.[267] Since they have to be "searched," one should infer that they have been "hiding."

---

[264] E.g., והיה ביום ההוא, והיה בעת ההיא, והיה ביום ההוא, והיה בעת ההיא.

[265] For instance, Isa 2:20, 3:7,18, 4:2, 7:18,20, 21,22,23, 10:20, 11:10, 12:1, 17:4,7, 18:7,19:16,18,19,23,24, 22:25, 24:21, 26:1, 27:1,12,13, 28:5, 31:7; Jer 3:17, 4:9,11, 8:1, 30:8, 31:1, 50:4; Ezek 24:26,27, 29:21, 30:9, 38:10, 18, 39:11; Hos 2:18, 23; Joel 4:18; Am.8:13, 9:11; Mic 2:4, 4:6; Zeph 3:11,16,20; Hag 2:23; Zech 3:10, 13:1,2,4, 14:6,8,9,13,20. In contrast, waw-perfect forms, occur only rarely (e.g., Isa 22:20, Hos 1:5; Am 8:9, Mic 5:9).

[266] Pace, for instance, Kapelrud, 1975: 17-18.

[267] This metonymic use of the name of cities or countries is well attested in the OT. See, for instance, 2 Sam 8:6; Jer 51:24; Am 1:3,6,9,11 (note the plural forms following the name of the city or country).

They were hiding because YHWH is to "reach"[268] the Jerusalemites and for judgment.[269] Since YHWH will search for the people of Jerusalem with lamps, one should conclude that the people of Jerusalem were imagined as hiding in dark places. Obviously the most probable hiding places in Jerusalem are neither swamps nor distant islands (as in Assyrian descriptions of kings trying to avoid the anger of the Assyrian king, as well as of the Assyrian gods), but places that are out of sight in a city. Most of them are dark places (caves, dark rooms, etc.). Clearly, in v. 12 there is all the potential for the widespread contrast between "light"= G/god=G/godly and "darkness"= sinners=sin. Also the image of the sinners clinging to their darkness and hiding themselves from the "light" is potentially implied in this sentence. Significantly, not only that these images are not developed in the MT, but the plural form "lamps" clearly points to a worldly image. YHWH is not searching with "the light" but with (oil) lamps. Moreover, many lamps (as expected of worldly lamps) are necessary for the task.[270] The plural form "lamps" occurs in the MT,

---

[268] Note that the general meaning of פקד is "reaching" someone in order to change his or her present situation, for good (mainly in the form פקד את, e.g., Gen 50:24; Exod 13:19;1 Sam 2:21; Isa 23:37; Zech 10:3; Ps 65:10), or for the worse (mainly in the form פקד על, e.g., Exod 32:34; Isa 13:11; Jer 21:14, 44:13, 50:18; Hos 2:15,12:3).

[269] Certainly, the image of people futilely trying to avoid the Deity, or deities, from reaching them is a common place through the ages. For example, one may mention that in a modern Palestinian version of the ancient idea of the Day of Judgment, the wrongdoers are described as trying to find shelter from the "yellow wind" in caves, and obviously failing (cf. Rev 6:15-17). See, D. Grossman, HaZeman haZahov (Tel Aviv: HaKibbutz Hameuchad, 1987; in Hebrew): 64. In OT literature one may mention, for instance, the futile attempt of Jonah (Jonah 1:2-3) and the forceful piece in Am 9:1-4, Obad 1:4.

[270] Although the Day of YHWH is described as a day of darkness in Zeph 1:15 (cf. Am 5: 18-20; Isa 13:9-11; Ezek 32:7-8; Joel 2:10; the Balaam texts of Deir CAlla, I 1.6 [See Kyle McCarter, 1980]), the text in v. 12 does not imply that YHWH should search the Jerusalemites in the darkness because YHWH brought darkness to them (as in the units describing the the Day of YHWH). In Zeph 1:12, as in Am 9:1-4 (the two occasions in which the searcher is YHWH), YHWH is searching someone who has been trying to avoid YHWH. The fact that "the light" is not an image of either God, or godly, or salvation, or ideal world in the Book of Zephaniah works against the idea the image of "the light" contrasted "the darkness" is intended in this book.
Although during the "Akitu" festival, there were ritual processions with torches, this ceremony can hardly have something in common with the image of YHWH searching the hiding Jerusalemites in order to punish them. Only by attaching Zeph 1:12 to a supposed ritual of the "Day of YHWH" and by proposing a close relationship between this supposed (and unattested) ritual to the Akitu ritual, one may consider the procession of torches relevant to Zeph 1:12 (cf. Gaster, 1969: 683). Sabottka proposes that this

is already attested in the "MT" text from Murabba'at, and is attested in the Vg. Reflection on this verse probably caused the multiple lamps[271] to transform into o n e lamp (a less worldly image) in the LXX.[272] Probably influenced by the LXX, also the Peshitta shows a singular form.[273] Reflection on this verse also brought the Tg. Neb. to avoid the anthropomorphic image of YHWH searching with lamps by "translating": "I (YHWH) will appoint searchers who will search those who live in Jerusalem like the people who search with lamps." These versions are important for the history of interpretation of the text but not as textual witness to an ancient (and original) Hebrew text.[274]

It is noteworthy that not only החיא בעת והיה is related to the אחפש phrase but also that the latter is meaningless without the following

---

verse, as well as Prov 20:27, reflects a demythologized form of the Ugaritic image of the sun as the "lamp of the gods" (Sabottka, 1972: 47-48; for a critical response to this proposal, see, for instance, del Olmo Lete: 299). Also superimposed to the text is the meaning suggested by the common comparisons between Zeph 1:12 and the sentence ב9 חדרי כל חפש אדם נשמח ה' נר in Prov 20:27. In Zeph 1:12, YHWH is not looking for "inner motives," "occult sins," (cf. R. L. Smith: 131; Watts, 1975: 161; Boadt 1982: 211-12—it will be a day in which nothing shall escape Yahweh's eyes) but YHWH is looking for the Jerusalemites.

271 This is the attested meaning of נרות in Hebrew. נרות as the plural of נר occurs about twenty-five times in the OT (e.g., Exod 25:37; Lev 24:4; Num 8:2; 1 Kgs 7:49; Zech 4:2). Although, the plural form of a noun may point to the intensification of the idea of the stem (e.g., תבונות Isa 40:14; see GKC 124 § a,e), this "possible" meaning of נר is attested nowhere in the OT. The same holds true for Sabottka's proposal that נרות is a an abs. fem. singular form (Sabottka, 1972: 47). The clearly attested meaning of נרות in the OT is: lamps. According to the basic critical principle that one should propose only the necessary (minimum) number of explanations to a given phenomena (in our case to the meaning of נרות), one should not add new proposals concerning the meaning of נרות unless it is absolutely necessary, i.e., unless the accepted meaning of the word makes no sense at all in its context.

Why does "the searcher" need lamps and one lamp is not enough for him? Different answers may be proposed, for instance, that one lamp may burnt out too early (cf. Rudolph, 1975: 263), that there was a need for more light than the light that one lamp may provide, that several places were illuminated at the same time, etc. In any case, the reference to multiple lamps points to the worldly character of these lamps. These are not "the lamp/light" of YHWH but lamps.

272 The MT reading is clearly a "lectio difficilior" (cf. Edler: 16). The amount of scholarship on this MT reading underlines this fact (see, for instance, the bibliographical references in Irsigler, 1977: 245).

273 For cases in which the LXX text of Zephaniah have influenced the Peshitta text of Zephaniah, see Gelston,1987: 162-63.

274 The well-known image of Zephaniah searching with a lamp, which is based on the image in the cathedral of Reims, is due to a misreading of the text, but significantly, a misreading that avoids the anthropomorphic image of YHWH.

sentence (. . . ‏ופקדתי על‎). Moreover, according to v. 12b, YHWH is going to act and punish. That is, the putative conception of those undisturbed people (‏שמריהם הקפאים על‎), who said YHWH will do nothing, good or bad (v. 12c), is refuted.[275]

(c) Zeph 1:4 opens with a general announcement of judgment (there, against Judah and the inhabitants of Jerusalem) that in the subsequent phrases becomes much more focused (i.e., against people doing so and so, see above); the same holds true for Zeph 1:12. YHWH will search for the Jerusalemites, according to the opening phrase, but will punish a specific group of them, according to the subsequent phrase:

‏ופקדתי על האנשים הקפאים על שמריהם‎

‏האמרים בלבבם לא ייטיב ה' ולא ירע‎

Both the participles preceded by ‏ה‎ and the use of the phrase ‏פקדתי על‎ recall Zeph 1:8-9. What kind of relationship exists between the two units? Obviously, an answer to this question must take into account the results of textual, linguistic and comparative analyses of the phrase in Zeph 1:12.

(c.1) Concerning ‏פקדתי על‎, see above.

(c.2) It has been proposed that the expression ‏ופקדתי על האנשים‎ should be completed to ‏ופקדתי על האנשים השאננים‎, or emended to ‏ופקדתי על השאננים‎.[276]

The word ‏שאנן‎ occurs in Jer 48:11 and is related there to the image of the undisturbed wine. However, according to MT, "the people" (‏אנשים‎) are modified by the adjectival phrase ‏הקפאים‎ . . . . The form X- ‏ה‎ ‏האנשים‎, where X is a participle, is attested elsewhere in the OT (e.g., 2 Sam 23:17; Isa 66:24) and presupposed by the "completion" theory. It seems that there is neither need for the emendation (or completion) nor evidence supporting it.[277] Whether the text is emended or not, the basic meaning remains unchanged.

---

[275] See below.

[276] See, for instance, J. M. P. Smith : 201, 209; Rudolph, 1975:263; Elliger (BHS).

[277] Cf. Edler:16; House: 128.

(c.3) The phrase הקפאים על שמריהם occurs only in Zeph 1:12. It
seems to be misunderstood by the LXX, the Peshitta,[278] and the OL.[279]
Yet, it has been translated literally by the Vg.; Tg. Neb. drops out the
image entirely, but attempts to convey its meaning.[280] Thus, it seems that
this metaphorical expression caused difficulties by the time of the ancient
versions. The image, and partially the language of the phrase, occurs in
Jer 48:11. But, on the surface, the concept seems to be a positive one in
Jer 48:11-12, for it is contrasted with going into exile. Moreover, in Jer
48:11 Moab, which is compared with wine, is described as follows, " He
[Moab] has settled on his lees; he has not been poured from vessel to
vessel" and therefore (see the causal על כן) "his [Moab's] taste remains
in him and his scent is not changed." However, the Moabites so described
in Jer 48:11 are about to be punished by YHWH. Moreover, the
description there is considered the reason for the punishment of Moab (vv.
12-13; note the לכן, at the beginning of v. 12).[281] Thus, according to Jer
48:11-13 as a unit, undisturbed lack of activity is indeed appropriate for
producing wine but is also the kind of behavior that leads to YHWH's
punishment. In a similar way, the main image conveyed by the phrase
הקפאים על שמריהם in Zeph 1:12 is immobility (cf. Exod 15:8, Job
10:10), lack of activity.[282]

---

[278] See Gerleman, 1942: 16-17.

[279] Oesterley: 384.

[280] דשלן שליוא על נכסדהון. See Ribera Florit, 1982: 138,152. Cf. the modern Good News Bible,
"I will punish the people who are satisfied and self-confident."

[281] Also cf. Jer 48:10.

[282] Whether the wine will be spoiled because of its resting on the lees or not is irrelevant.
Jer 48:11-13 clearly shows that even if the wine turned out to be superb this does not
mean that the attitude of the people described by the metaphor is the right attitude.
Similarly, if a person is compared with a hibernating bear, the most likely meaning is
that the person is indolent, even if the bear does not hibernate because it is slothful.
For the question of the wine and its fermentation, see G. A. Smith: 50-51; J. M. P.
Smith: 202; Ball, 1972/1988: 41; Edler: 143.
Sabottka suggests a more concrete and direct meaning than the proposed in this work,
namely, "die starr/betäubt sind von ihren feinen/schweren Weinen" (Sabottka, 1972:
48-49; cf. NEB, "who sit in stupor over the dregs of their wine"). Sabottka proposes
that שמרים in Zeph 1:12 means, metonymically, "wine" (as in Isa 25:6), and that the root
קפא may also mean "stupor." Sabottka's proposal was accepted by Gerleman, see
Gerleman, 1973: 253. See also Asurmendi: 160; Alonso Schöckel- Valverde (*Nueva
Biblia Española*); cf. R. L. Smith: 131; Watts, 1975: 161. It is remarkable that words

(c.4) The persons who are to be punished are described as,

האמרים בלבבם לא ייטיב ה' ולא ירע, i.e., "those who say in their hearts (i.e., to themselves) YHWH will not do good nor bad. Clearly, to do good and to do bad are two extremes that convey the sense of entirety (e.g., Isa 41:23), and therefore this is a typical case of merism.[283] Accordingly, the phrase means: "those who say to themselves YHWH will do nothing."[284]

The sharp contrast between the people's saying YHWH will do nothing on the one hand and YHWH's saying: "I will search . . . I will punish . . . [those] saying YHWH will do nothing" on the other, is self evident. Moreover, the people are those who "rest immobile on their lees," those who are unable to produce any change in their situation. Contrary to their thinking, YHWH is active and will produce a change.

The conception that YHWH will do nothing occurs also in Ps 10:11,13 (probably exilic or post-exilic).[285] Since YHWH/God (אלהים) appears, mainly, as a "functional deity" in the OT,[286] it is hardly surprising that this line of thought leads to the expression אין אלהים, "there is no God," in Ps 10:4, 14:1= 53:2 (also exilic or post-exilic).[287] The main difference

---

from the root קפא occur in a clear context only twice in the OT, in Exod 15:8, Job 10:10. Neither קפאו (Exod 15:8) not תקפיאני (Job 10:10) can mean stupor. Words from the root קפא occur in less clear contexts in Zeph 1:12 and in Zech 14:6.

283 See Krasovec,1977: 106; cf. 102-03.

284 Similar expressions, describing the powerlessness of divine beings, occur in Isa 41:23 and Jer 10:5 (both from the post-monarchic period; concerning the date of Jer 10:5, see Carroll, 1986: 252 ff. esp. 257-58; Mc Kane,1986: 216 ff., esp. 220; for a different approach, see Holladay,1986:325-26). There, however, the powerless are "gods" and not YHWH.

285 See Fohrer,1970: 286 and the bibliography cited there, see also Kraus, 1978:79 and Gerstenberger,1988: 72 ff., esp. 75.

286 The issue stands beyond the scope of this work, but it is clear that the image of YHWH/God in the OT is much closer to a functional, acting power in the universe and among the peoples—including, or perhaps especially including Israel—than an object of metaphysical reflection.

287 See Fohrer,1970: 286, 288 and the bibliography cited there and Gerstenberger,1988: 218-21. According to Gerstenberger, the setting of Ps 9-10, 14, 53 are Jewish communities in the Persian period.
These expressions and the thought expressed by them should be clearly distinguished from expressions of disbelief concerning prophetic sayings (e.g., Jer 17:15). The latter do not question the capability or willingness of YHWH to act; they question the authenticity, and legitimacy, of the message of the prophet. For a different approach, specially concerning Zeph 1:12, see Rose, 1981.

between Zeph 1:12 and the Psalms mentioned above is that the latter refer to אלהים and not to YHWH. This is quite expected in general considerations about the deity.[288] In Zeph 1:12, however, YHWH is mentioned. This is probably due to the "personal" confrontation between YHWH and the people who are about to be punished.

Significantly, Ps 10 and Ps 14 // Ps 53 contrast the godless wealthy people who had not suffered distress with the community (of believers) whose concept of God is implicitly defined by the description of the godless (i.e., inversion of attributes, see below) and whose fate was not so good. The expectancy of divine judgment is clear. Zeph 1:12-13 also assigns a godless conception to the undisturbed wealthy people (see v. 13), implying what the position and belief of the writer are. These considerations lead to the crucial question: What is the function of the quotations of sayings of wrongdoers and wrongthinkers in prophetic literature,[289] as well as in Psalms? Are they straightforward quotations that one has to accept at face value?

The fact that many times the quotation is attributed to Israel (or Judah or Jerusalem) in general (e.g., Jer 2:27; Ezek 12:27; Am 6:13-14) or in some cases to a certain group in Judean society (e.g., Ezek 8:12; Am 9:10; Mic 3:9) but not to a specific person, and even more the fact that many of these quotations are attributed to a foreign nation, or city, in its "entirety" (e.g., Isa 37:24-27, 47:8; Ezek 25:3,8, 28:2, 29:9; Obad 1:3; Zeph 2:15) clearly shows that these are not actual quotations.[290] Thus, the authors of the quotations are not to be found among the wrongdoers and wrongthinkers but among the authors of the prophetic units and Psalms. Why, then, did they write these quotations, and even more precisely: What is the communicative significance of these quotations? In order to answer this question one may think in terms of the author, the audience and the

---

[288] See Redford, 1970:110-130.

[289] E.g., Isa 5:19, 42:17, 47:8, 65:5; Jer 21:13, 27:14, 32:43; Ezek 25:3,8, 28:2, 29:9; Am 6:13, 9:10; Mic 4:11; Zeph 2:15; Pss 10: 11,13, 14:1, 40:16, 53:2.

[290] For a study on the quotations in the Book of Ezekiel, see Clark; on quotations concerning foreign indicted peoples in Ezekiel, see Clark: 276-80, and the bibliography there.

specific claim made by the text. Since, in several cases, the wrongdoers and wrongthinkers are foreign peoples, and in others clearly outsiders, one concludes that the audience does not necessarily include the people to whom the saying is ascribed. Accordingly, the main point of the piece is not to reform the wrongdoer or wrongthinker whose putative saying is quoted but to stress that what the saying says should not be thought or believed. By whom? By the audience of the prophetic piece or Psalm. Thus, the quotations, by their stress on a set of ideas and beliefs that should be rejected, point to a set of ideas and beliefs that should be accepted. Accordingly, the communicative significance of Zeph 1:12 is that YHWH can and will do something, and not only something, but judgment upon those rich people (see v. 13) who believe that YHWH will do nothing. If this is the communicative message of Zeph 1:12 to the author's community, then one may assume that there were people in this community who were, at the very least, insecure concerning YHWH's capability or willingness to exert judgment, or quite despaired because the expected judgment has not yet come and the world remained upside down and therefore they became less confident, or both. The only alternative to this approach is to propose that the author wrote a direct and strenuous attack on a position that no one held. Although for rhetorical reasons the language of the author may be—and clearly is in certain cases— hyperbolic, the very rhetorical use of a hyperbole indicates, that underlying the exaggeration there are real issues at stake in his or her community.[291]

---

[291] An obvious illustration of this relationship between author, community and putative characteristics of outsiders is the anti-Judaism tendency in Pauline literature. The issue at stake was not what the Jews really thought at that time but "Jewish" attitudes in the Christian communities addressed by the Pauline literature. Certainly, as the Pauline literature, at least on its face values, cannot be used as a reliable base for the understanding of the contemporaneous Jewish thought, so the putative quotations of indicted sinners in the prophetic books cannot be taken in its face value as historically reliable sources for any reconstruction of the thought of the indicted group.

3.2.11. Zeph 1:13

The verse opens with והיה חילם. Most modern translations tend to
read: "Their wealth . . . "[292] However, the והיה form conveys a clear
meaning of an expected result.[293] That is, what will happen to the
wealthy, the owners of goods and houses, according to v. 13 is the
explicit result of their attitudes, as described in v. 12.

Words from the root שסה, with the general meaning of "plunder," occur
several times in the OT (e.g., Judg 2:14,16; 1 Sam 14:48; 2 Kgs 17:20;
Isa 17:14, 42:22; Jer 30:16, 50:11). The word מְשִׁסָּה occurs in 2 Kgs
21:14 (dtr); Isa 42:22, 26; Jer 30:16 (probably post monarchic); Hab 2:7
and Zeph 1:13.[294] Except for its occurrences in Zeph 1:13 and Hab 2:7,
the word appears paired with בז.

It is remarkable that according to this verse, at the day of judgment or
later, Jerusalem will be plundered. Nothing is said, however, about the
identity of the plunderers. Nothing is said about actual warfare.

Several scholars consider the last part of the verse, (i.e., "they shall
build houses . . . ") an addition,[295] which was probably triggered by the
preceding word בתים. The expression seems to stand at odds with the
image in vv. 13a and 14a, provided that the latter is taken literally.
According to vv. 13a and 14a, the wealthy people are already dwelling in
good houses, which will be a waste in the imminent day of judgment. So,
it seems that there is no time for building and planting.

---

[292] See, for instance, Kapelrud, 1975:104; House: 120; O'Connor: 245; Edler:8; RSV;
NRSV; NJPSV; REB; Nueva Biblia Española. On the other hand, KJV translates:
"Therefore their goods . . . ", and Rudolph: "Da verfällt ihr Besitz der Plünderung . . . "
(Rudolph, 1975: 261).

[293] See, Meek, 1955: 40-43.

[294] The word was probably written משוסה in 4QpZeph. See Horgan, 1979: 191-92 and the
bibliography mentioned there. Cf. *ketiv* Isa 42:24 according to the L. codex (but not
according the Aleppo codex ; on this question see Andersen-Forbes: 95 and the
bibliography cited there).

[295] See, for instance, J. M. P. Smith: 203, Elliger,1951:56; Elliger (BHS); Edler: 81-82.
For the contrary position, see, for instance, Sabottka: 50; Rudolph, 1975: 269; Watts,
1975: 161; Asurmendi:160.

A similar expression occurs in Am 5:11, and the same meaning is conveyed by equivalent expressions in Deut 28:30-34,38-42; Lev 26:16; Mic 6:15. The image in Am 5:11 and Zeph 1:13 appears also in Ezek 28:26; Isa 65:21, but in the latter as an ideal future (there, the verbs are not negated). Thus, one may conclude that the image occurring in Zeph 1:13 is a relatively widespread metaphor for societies in which people cannot (or can, if the verb is not negated) enjoy the fruit of their own work. The central point of the horrible curses in Deut 28:30-34,38-42; Lev 26:16; Am 5:11; Mic 6:15; Zeph 1:13 is that any work, all, will be in vain. It is self-evident that this curse does not point to a day of judgment but to a time of judgment.[296] Accordingly, some scholars among those who think that underlying the text of the Book of Zephaniah lies the speech of the prophet concerning the imminent Day of YHWH (hereafter, DOY) tend to consider the expression "they shall build houses . . . " a later addition.[297] However, neither v. 12 nor v. 13 refers to DOY or contains any of its typical expressions (see below). Moreover, the supposed contradiction between the rest of vv. 12-13 and the expression"they shall build . . . " in the same v. 13 rests on the reading of vv. 12-13 in the light of v. 14, but does not exist at all if vv. 12-13 are read in their own light. To the contrary, in that case instead of thematic contradiction one finds thematic completion. The wealth of the indicted is to be destroyed and their efforts to restore it will be in vain.[298]

3.2.12. Zeph 1:14

Verse 14 contains four versets. Only the first of them has provoked no scholarly controversy. The imminence of the DOY is conveyed in v. 14a as in Zeph 1:7[b] by the expression קרוב יום ה'. The same, or very

---

[296] Significantly, none of the biblical references mentioned is related to material concerning the Day of YHWH.

[297] E.g., J. M. P. Smith: 203

[298] Similar patterns of completion occur elsewhere in the OT (e.g., Lev 26; Deut 28).

similar expressions, occur elsewhere in DOY material (Isa 13:6; Joel 1:15, 2:1, 4:14; Obad 1:15). The expression יום ה' הגדול occurs in the context of DOY in Joel 3:4, and slightly different in Joel 2:11, but in Joel גדול occurs along with נורא, so the expression reads הגדול והנורא יום ה' (cf. Deut 1:19,7:21; 8:15, 10:17, 21; 2 Sam 7:23; Ps 97:3; Mal 3:23 [DOY]; Dan 9:4; Neh 1:5, 4:8, 9:32; 1 Chr 17:21).

The main problem in the second verset concerns the word מַהֵר. Several scholars have proposed that מהר here means "soldier."[299] This meaning is clearly attested in other Semitic languages,[300] but not in biblical Hebrew. On the other hand, מהר meaning "quickly" is well attested (e.g., Exod 32:8; Deut 4:26, 7:4, 22, 9:3,12,16, 28:20; Josh 2:5; Judg 2:17, 23; Ps 69:18; 79:8;[301]102:3; 143:7; Prov 25:8). Moreover, it is obvious that if one understands מהר as "soldier" or "hero," מְאֹד cannot be understood as usual, i.e., "very." Accordingly, Sabottka has suggested reading מאד as מָאֵד meaning "der Große" (i.e., "the grand"). Although Dahood has proposed the existence of an original reading מָאֵד in several Psalms, it is noteworthy that in sharp contrast with the hundreds of times the word מְאֹד occurs in the MT, the word מָאֵד occurs nowhere in the MT.[302]

Other scholars consider מַהֵר an infinitive absolute of the root מהר in the piel pattern.[303] If this is the case, and since the infinitive absolute may have an adverbial meaning,[304] one may translate מהר מאד as "very quickly," "most swiftly" (NJPVS). קרוב in the second verset, at least, can be understood as an infinitive absolute of קרב in the qal pattern (see

---

[299] See Sabottka, 1972: 50-52; R. L. Smith: 129, 131; cf. Watts, 1975: 162.

[300] See Sabottka, 1972: 51 and the bibliography mentioned there.

[301] Pace Dahood II: 252, Sabottka: 51.

[302] See Sabottka, 1972: 51 and the bibliography mentioned there.

[303] See, for instance, Meyer III: 62. Other scholars consider מהר either the *piel* participle of מהר (i.e., a *piel* participial form without the prefix מ see GKC § 52 s; Gerleman, 1942: 18-19) or an abbreviation—probably due to haplography—of the participial form ממהר (e.g., Edler:16).

[304] The most common examples are הֵיטִיב, and הרבה. For a clear adverbial use of מהר see Josh 2:5. For the infinitive absolute with adverbial meaning, see Meyer III: 62; R. J. Williams: 37 § 204.

Qoh 4:17). An infinitive absolute may also function as a verbal noun (e.g., Isa 22:13). Thus, קרוב in the second verset may be translated as "coming." Summing up: The first two versets can be translated: "The great day of YHWH is near; coming and most swiftly." This translation is in accordance with Hebrew grammar, is based on meanings clearly attested elsewhere in the OT, and provides a sense of ongoing intensification from first verset to the second one, which is a well-known feature of many biblical Hebrew verses,[305] and thus is to be preferred.

The scholarly discussion concerning the third verset has focused on the meaning of the words קול and מר (if the latter is not emended).[306] In addition, due to the difficulties that the fourth verset has raised, several proposals for emendation of the third and fourth verset together have been suggested.[307]

קול usually means either "voice" (e.g., Gen 27:22), or in a more general sense, "sound" (e.g., Ezek 37:7; Nah 3:2; Hab 3:10; 1 Kgs 14:6; Lam 2:7).[308] However, when קול occurs at the beginning of a clause and is followed by a genitive it may function as an exclamatory "Hark!."[309] Several scholars support this exclamatory meaning in Zeph 1:14.[310] It is noteworthy that in almost all the cases in which an

---

[305] See, for instance, Alter,1985: 18 ff., esp.18-22; and Kugel, 1981: 1-58.

[306] According to the masoretic division of the text, מר belongs to the fourth verset. Rashi and Radak interpreted the text on the basis of such division. Also according to Ibn Ezra and Abrabanel, the sound of the day was *mar*. It is noteworthy that although the Vg. translates this verset word for word, it relates מר to the third verset. Significantly, also Tg. Neb. implies such a reading.

[307] For instance, Elliger (BHS) suggests the reading קל יום ה' מֵרָץ וְחָשׁ מִגִּבּוֹר, i.e., "the day of YHWH is swifter than a runner and faster than a hero." This proposal is supported, for instance, by Krinetzki (84), Alonso Schöckel- Valverde (Nueva Biblia Española) and Edler (8,16); also cf. Job 9: 25a. Gaster considers the possibility that the cultic background of this saying is a "ritual race—a not uncommon feature of seasonal festival;"see Gaster, 1966:684. Brockington accepts the BHS suggestion but proposes גדוד instead of גבור , and accordingly, the second comparison turns out to be, "faster than a band of raiders" (cf. NEB). Undoubtedly, the proposed meanings suit the context, but they are dependent on a relatively large amount of textual emendation which is the last resort in biblical exegesis. In addition, they have no support in ancient versions.

[308] According to Sabottka and Watts, קול means "noise" Zeph 1:14 (see Sabottka, 1972: 52; Watts, 1975: 162.

[309] See GKC § 146 b, 147 c; BDB, entry קול § 1 f.

[310] E.g., Rudolph, 1975: 273 (He also proposes this meaning for the קול in v. 10).

interjectial meaning is possible, the context clearly indicates that the addressees are asked to listen a sound, a voice (e.g., Gen 4:10; Isa 13:4; 40:3; 52:8; Jer 4:15; 50:28); in none of them is an "implied" meaning "sound", "voice" incongruent with the context. Thus, it seems that the question of קול in Zeph 1:14 is not one of "either . . . or", but perhaps, of "both."[311] Accordingly, the verset may be translated: "(Hear!) the sound of DOY is *mar* ."

There has been some scholarly discussion concerning the meaning and textual originality of מר.[312] On the basis of the evidence of the OT, it is clear that the word מר, from the root מרר, may mean "bitter," in its restricted sense (e.g., Prov 27:7) as well as in its metaphorical sense (e.g., Isa 33:7). The issue at stake is, whether this is the only possible meaning. For instance, Kutler has pointed (again) to the possibility of a second meaning for מרר, "be strong."[313] Probably the most clear example in support of this position is Gen 49:23. Such a meaning of מרר and even more a double meaning of "bitterness" and "strength" (i.e., something like "fierce") suits also the context in Judg 18:25; 1 Sam 22:2; 2 Sam 17:8, Hab 1:6, and cf. Qoh 7:26. The similarities between Hab 1:6 and Zeph 1:14, as well as the use of the image of the גבור ("hero") and the term צרה in the fourth verset (see below) point to a "military" image. So one may translate the entire verset "(Hear!) the sound of DOY is fierce."

The fourth verset has already caused difficulties for the authors of the ancient versions, which diverge in their renderings.[314] The same holds true for modern scholars.[315] Concerning this verset, the main question is

---

[311] Cf. Barthelemey, 1980: 374.

[312] KBL3 proposes a slight emendation from מר to המר (textual error due to simple haplography). For Elliger's (BHS) proposed reading and for Brockington proposal, see above. Sabottka does not propose to emend the text but understands מר as "stark", "gewaltig" (Sabottka, 1972:52); Watts translates מר as "overpowering" (Watts, 1975: 162).

[313] See Kutler and the bibliography mentioned there.

[314] For a summary of several different renderings, see Ball, 1972/1988: 41; on this issue, see also Gerleman, 1942: 19-21; Irsigler, 1977: 52-53; Ribera Florit: 138, 145, 153; and the bibliography mentioned in these works.

[315] See, for instance, the bibliography mentioned in Irsigler: 1977: 52-56.

not the meaning of the individual words but the meaning of the verset, as a unit, as a part of the poetic line. There is consensus that גבור here means "warrior." The word שם occurs hundreds of times as an adverb of place but it may convey, in poetry, the sense of time (e.g., Pss 14:5// 53:6, 36:13, Ps 132:17).[316] Since the word שם in Zeph 1:14 does not occur in narrative but in poetry, and since the verse stresses the dimension of time but does not mention at all the dimension of place, it seems likely that also in Zeph 1:14 שם means, "then."[317] Words from the root צרח (I)[318] occur only twice in the OT, in Zeph 1:14 and Isa 42:13 (*hiphil* form). There is a wide consensus that the general meaning of the root is "to cry out," "to utter a roar." This consensus is supported by the evidence of the cognate languages and fits the biblical context in its two occurrences.

To conclude: The verset may be translated : "at that time a warrior utters a roar (or cries out)." This way of reading the text is already presented in Rashi, and underlies the midrashic version of Tg. Neb. that explicitly refer to DOY as the day in which the "warriors" or "heroes" will be killed; that is, providing the answer to the question why the "heroes" will cry out.

Alternatively, one may consider that the "warrior" who will cry out is the one who is the active force in bringing the DOY, none but YHWH.[319] One finds support for this proposal in the language and image of Isa 42:13. There YHWH is referred to as כגבור and YHWH אף יצריח יריע. If this is the case, צרח in Zeph 1:14 can be paralleled with יצריח in Isa 42:13, and תרועה in Zeph 1:16 (another line in the DOY poem) with יריע. It is noteworthy that YHWH is described as גבור also in Zeph 3:17. There, in the context of a reversal of the situation in Zeph 1, YHWH is (again) called גבור, but this time one reads גבור יושיע.

---

[316] Significantly, these Pss are probably post-monarchic. Note the (messianic ?) expression אצמיח קרן לדוד in Ps 132:17 (cf. Ezek 29:21). For a different approach concerning the date of Ps 132, see Anderson: 879-80. For a list of the various opinions in modern research see Lorentz,1979: 286. Concerning Pss 14 (// 53) and 36, see Gerstenberger, 1988: 153-57, 218-21; Anderson: 130-31; 286.

[317] So, for instance, Ehrlich: 458. For an alternative interpretation of שם ("see"), see Sabottka, 1972: 53-54; Sabottka is supported by Watts (162).

[318] For צרח II, see Judg 9:46 and 1 Sam 13:6.

[319] See, for instance, Gerleman, 1942: 19-20; Ball, 1972/1988: 42.

Moreover, the poetic line has a clear heightening sense if it is read with YHWH as the "hero." In that case, the sense of imminence in the first two versets leads to description of the day itself. The description begins with an indirect element, with a result of the action that is taking place, with "the sound of the day of YHWH" (note the genitive position of the noun YHWH). Then after the assertion that this sound is fierce; the last verset heightens the image by contrasting the grammatical case of YHWH (genitive) in the third verset with the case of YHWH in the fourth verse (nominal, subject of the sentence) and by contrasting YHWH (third verset) with its equivalent "warrior" (in the fourth).[320] By the end of the poetic line it is clear that YHWH is the warrior whose shouting is the source of the fierce sound of the DOY, and that YHWH is the one who bring distress in such a day.[321] It is noteworthy that as in Zephaniah 3 (see below) where YHWH is described as bringing salvation without any human intermediary; YHWH in Zeph 1:14 is bringing punishment without any intermediary.

3.2.13. Zeph 1:15

Verse 15 contains five versets. Each opens with the word יום in the construct state (*nomen regens*) and, except for the first, each contains a pair of nouns connected with each other by their similar meaning, by the conjunction *waw* , and by the fact that each function as *nomen rectum* of the same *nomen regens* (i.e., יום, "day"). The use of pairs (or even triads) of nouns in such way is attested elsewhere in the OT (e.g., 2 Kgs 19:3 // Isa 37:3; Isa 22:5) and conveys the meaning of a superlative.[322] Thus, a dynamic translation of יום חשך ואפלה renders "a day of

---

[320] On contrasts as poetic devices in Biblical Hebrew poetry, see Berlin, 1985.

[321] For YHWH as a divine warrior, see P. D. Miller, 1973 and Kang, 1989 (especially pp. 197-204).

[322] Cf. GKC § 133 l

extreme darkness" instead of the common "a day of darkness and gloom" (RSV).

The structure based on the word יום and the repetition of this key word (six times) in the verse are stylistic devices that call immediate attention to the main issue in the verse: The day (DOY).[323] The first verset is a nominal phrase that introduces the description of the day. Its structure, as well as its general meaning, recalls Isa 37:3 // 2 Kgs 19:3.[324] The day described in Isa 37:3, however, is היום הזה, i.e., "this day" as required by the narrative there. The day of YHWH, as a future day, is referred to as היום ההוא in Jer 46:10.[325] There, the "day" is a day of judgment upon Egypt.

The "day of YHWH" is described in the first verset as a "day of wrath,"[326] יום עברה. Although the word עברה ("wrath") is attested several times in similar contexts,[327] the expression יום עברה, however, occurs elsewhere only in Prov 11:4. The closely related expression יום עברות appears only in Job 21:30, and the expression יום עברת ה' only in Zeph 1:18 and Ezek 7:19, but the latter is commonly considered a gloss based on Zephaniah.[328]

Although יום צרה occurs many times in the OT (e.g., Jer 16:19; Obad 1:14; Hab 1:7 [cf. Jer 16:19], Hab 3:16; Pss 20:2, 50:15; Prov 24:10, 25:19), the expression יום צרה ומצוקה appears only in Zeph 1:15.

---

[323] On repetition in poetry as a stylistic device and specially on the repetition of a key-word as an structural element, see Alonso Schöckel, 1988: 75-83, 192-93.

[324] The verse occurs in the so-called account B1 (Isa 36:1-37: 9a + 37:37-38) of the campaign of Sennacherib. See, for instance, Clements, 1982: 280 ff. This account is commonly considered non-Isaianic.

[325] והיום ההוא לאדני ה' צבאות The word צבאות lacks in the LXX. Compare the expression כי זבח לה' צבאות in Jer 46:10 with the one in Zeph 1:7.

[326] This is the source of the Christian "Dies irae, dies illa" (according to the Vg. translation of יום עברה היום ההוא) in the opening of the Sequence in Mass for the dead. This day of "wrath" was related to the Gehinnom and to Gehinnom's retribution in the Rabbinical tradition. By such a move the dreadful day turns out to be a characterization of the punishment of a special group: The sinners. See b. Sabb. 118a; b. ᶜAbod. Zar. 18b; b. B. Bat. 10a. Clearly, such concept of Gehinnom does not occur in the Hebrew Bible and stands beyond the scope of this work.

[327] For instance, in DOY literature in Isa 13:9,13; as בעברת ה' צבאות in Isa 9:18; see also Ezek 22:21,31, 38:19 and Lam 2:2.

[328] See Zimmerli,1979: 211; Greenberg,1983: 152.

The pair צרה ומצוקה occurs elsewhere in Pss 25:17, 107:6,13, 19, 28—probably post-monarchic Psalms—[329] and in Job 15:24.

The expression שאה ומשואה is unique, and both יום שאה and יום משואה do not occur elsewhere in the OT. But the pair משואה - שאה occurs also in Job 30:3, 38:27.[330] The word משואה occurs elsewhere, in its plural form, in Ps 73:18; 74:3, both psalms are probably post-monarchic. It is noteworthy that Ps 73 shows some affinities with the Book of Job.[331] One may conclude that the language of this verset shows far more similarities with probable post-monarchic Psalms and wisdom literature than with other pieces of prophetic literature, including DOY descriptions.[332]

The last two versets in Zeph 1:15, חשך ואפלה יום ענן וערפל יום, occur word for word in Joel 2:2.[333] The motif of darkness is very common in DOY literature (e.g., Am 5:18-20; Isa 13:10; Joel 2:2, 3:4, 4:15, cf. Ezek 30:3). It also occurs in a non-biblical equivalents to DOY. To illustrate, in the Balaam text from Deir Alla, it is characterized by darkness (Combination I, lines 6-7).[334] Egyptian images of the chaotic days out of which the "savior" will rise and establish the correct order of society, as well as of the universe, are also characterized by darkness.[335]

---

[329] See Fohrer,1970: 287,291 and bibliography cited there; Gerstenberger, 1988: 119-21; Anderson: 206-7, 749.

[330] The defective writing משאה instead of the משואה is not uncommon in the Book of Job; cf. שאה in Job 30:14, 38:27, but שואה in Job 30:3.

[331] See Anderson: 529-47, esp. 529, 537-38; Fohrer, 1970: 289 and the bibliography cited there.

[332] Pace Kapelrud who wrote: "they [most of the words referred above] show that the prophet's vocabulary contained words that were not ordinarily in use (i.e., in the Old Testament, but they do not seem to be words used in daily language either)." See Kapelrud, 1975: 62. Whether these words were used in daily language or not is open to discussion but the language used here does occur in the OT, in certain Psalms and in Wisdom literature.

[333] The sentence is commonly considered secondary in Joel 2:2 and original in Zephaniah (see for instance Wolff, 1975: 44). However, it is worth noting that the main reason for this assumption is that "Zephaniah precedes Joel."

[334] See, for instance, Kyle McCarter, 1980; Lemaire, 1985.

[335] See, for instance, Koenen and the bibliography mentioned there. The motif of darkness also occurs in the Sumerian "Lament over the Destruction of Ur." See ANET 611 ff. See also Buss, 1969: 93 and the bibliography there.

The pair אפלה - חשך occurs in Exod 10:22 (non-P),[336] and compare with Isa 8:22, 29:18.[337]

The expression יום ענן וערפל occurs also in Ezek 34:12, and וערפל ענן also occurs in relation to the theophany at Sinai in Deut 4:11, 5:22. Neither in Deuteronomy nor in Ezek 34 is the expression related to the dreadful acts of YHWH in DOY but to the contrary, to YHWH's merciful deeds toward Israel. In Ps 97:2, probably a post- monarchic Psalm,[338] the expression ענן וערפל appears in relation to the "image" of what surrounds YHWH.[339] Finally, the expression יום ענן appears in a DOY-like piece, in Ezek 30:3, but this DOY is the day of judgment of Egypt (and Nubia), not of Israel, or Judah.

3.2.14. Zeph 1:16

The expression יום שופר ותרועה occurs only in Zeph 1:15, as does the expression יום שופר. The term יום תרועה occurs in Num 29:1, there it refers to the feast of the first day of the seventh month. This can hardly be the meaning of the expression in Zeph 1:15. The pair תרועה - שופר occur many times in the OT. The pair may occur in the description of a theophanic and non-war like set of circumstances (e.g., Ps 47:6, cf. Pss 98:6, 150:2-5), of a special cultic occasion (e.g., 2 Sam 6:15 // 1 Chr 15:28), and of the proclamation of the jubilee (Lev 25:9). But in many cases, the pair points to war activities (e.g., Josh 6:5; Am 2:2; Jer 4:19, 49:2; Job 39:25). In addition, the expression may carry a metaphorical military character. That is, the expression may be used for describing a clearly non-military situation by means of war imagery (e.g., Joel 2:1). Moreover, this variety of meanings is attested also for each of the words

---

[336] Perhaps a conflate reading. On conflate readings, see Talmon, 1976 and the bibliography mentioned there.

[337] Also cf. Job 3:4-6

[338] Cf. Anderson: 686-87; see Fohrer, 1970: 290.

[339] Among the theophanic elements that occur in Ps 97, one finds "fire goes before him [YHWH] and burns up his adversaries round about" (Ps 97:3, RSV) and cf. Zeph 1:18.

of the pair separately.[340] As a result only the context may clarify the meaning of the pair in Zeph 1:15.

The contents of the next two versets, הבצרות ועל הפנות הגבהות על הערים, (i.e., "against the fortified cities and against the high battlements") points either to a real or metaphorical war imagery. The pattern על ... ועל clearly recalls Isa 2:12-16, and since the expression הפנות הגבהות is an equivalent to כל מגדל גבה (cf. 2 Chr 26:15) and הערים הבצרות to כל חומה בצורה, the expression in Zeph 1:16 recalls especially the one in Isa 2:15, מגדל גבה ועל כל חומה בצורה ועל כל. The expression there is in the context of a description of the events of the day of YHWH (יום לה' צבאות). The imagery is clearly war-like, but no earthly army is mentioned; moreover, the present context shows that YHWH is indeed the real "warrior." The (present) context of Zeph 1:16 points to a similar conclusion (see, vv. 14, 15,17). This is congruent with the results of the comparison between the text and language of Zeph 1:14,16 and those of Isa 42:13 (על איביו יתגבר ה' כגבור יצא ... יריע אף יצריח).[341] Neither the verse itself nor the context in which it occurs points necessarily to a worldly event. To the contrary, the context of v. 16 suggests a non-worldly event in which the only active agent is YHWH. Thus, one may conclude that if the verse was ever historically dependent, in its present form it is not, and intentionally not. In this respect, one may note that nowhere in Zeph 1 are earthly armies mentioned. However, even if this is indeed the claim of the text, the question concerning the significance of the text to its original community remains open. This is so because the significance depends on the date of the composition of the text and on the ideas and point of view of the community. For instance, a crucial question is whether the text was considered a prophecy concerning the future that was said by a prophet in

---

340 Concerning שפר (or the sound of "shofar") alone see, for instance, Jer 42:14 (war and disaster); Ps 150:3 (cultic hymn); Isa 27:13 ("salvation"); 1 Kgs 1:34, 39 ("coronation" ceremony); Exod 19:16 (Sinai theophany). Concerning תרועה , see, for instance, Am 1:14 (war); Lev 23:4 (cultic); Ps 33:3 (cultic-hymnic); Num 10:5 (military imagery).

341 Cf. Gerleman, 1942:19.

the past and already fulfilled[342] or a prophecy yet to be fulfilled.[343] If the first possibility is accepted then one may ask about the possible historical events that the community may have considered to be fulfillment of the prophecy.[344] Obviously, the list of possible candidates depends on the proposed dating of the community (i.e., monarchic or post-monarchic). This issue can be resolved, if at all, only in the light of the entire evidence concerning the book of Zephaniah in general and its DOY section in particular, and therefore, it will be discussed in the commentary section.

The war-like imagery is also the key to the understanding of the surface meaning of these versets. The "warrior" will reach, and overcome, the strongholds of the "enemy," so its defeat will be complete. There will be no escape from the hands of the "warrior."[345] Thus, one may compare the message conveyed by these versets with Am 9:1-4 and Obad 1:4, even if the latter use different metaphors and different language.

The expression ערים בצרות occurs many times in the OT (e.g., Num 13:28; Deut 1:28, 3:5, 9:1; 2 Kgs 19:25 // Isa 37:26; Hos 8:14; Neh 9:25; 2 Chr 32:1, 33:14). In sharp contrast פנות גבהות occurs only in Zeph 1:16. The term פנה is used in relation to fortifications only in Zeph 1:16, 3:6; 2 Chr 26:15 and Neh 3:24, 31,32.[346]

---

[342] Traditional commentators (e.g., Jerome, Calvin, Abrabanel, Altschuler) have considered this section of the Book of Zephaniah as a prophecy that was fulfilled, at least partially, in the days of the destruction of the monarchic Jerusalem and the First Temple.

[343] There is a third possibility: a prophecy that was proclaimed and never fulfilled because of a change in the attitudes of the addressees (e.g., Jonah 3) or even a prophecy that failed to be fulfilled and yet no explanation is given to the failure (e.g., Hag 2:23). However, it should be noted that even these prophecies are related to a historical or supposedly historical events.

[344] Sometimes, the biblical text explicitly points to the historical events to which the generalized imagery of DOY refers to (e.g., the destruction of Babylon by the Medes in Isa 13:1-22 ; concerning this text see Clements: 132-38 and the bibliography cited there). In Zephaniah, the context limits the geographical choices to either Judah or Jerusalem or both.

[345] Obviously, these versets cannot be understood as restrictive, namely, as if their meaning were that the "warrior" will fight only, or even mainly, against walled cities and battlements. The war imagery and the context clearly indicate that Jerusalemites would not be safe only if they manage to walk outside Jerusalem nor Judeans (non-Jerusalemites) had no reason to worry because they lived in the countryside.

[346] The use of פנה in שער הפנה (e.g., 2 Kgs 14:13; Jer 31:38; Zech 14:10; 2 Chr 26:9) or closely related languages does not necessarily point to the use of פנה in the sense of "battlements." שער הפנה there may be translated as the "Corner Gate" (so RSV; NRSV;

3.2.15. Zeph 1:17

(a) YHWH is the subject and the speaker in the expression לאדם
הצרתי. There is a similar occurrence of צרר ל in its *hiphil* verbal form
in Jer 10:18.[347] Significantly, the outcome of YHWH's action in Jer
10:17-18 is deportation, not destruction as in Zeph 1:17. The other
occurrences of *hiphil* forms of צרר ל in the OT are Deut 28:52; 1 Kgs
8:37 // 2 Chr 6:28 (Solomon's prayer); Neh 9:27; 2 Chr 28:20,22, 33:12
(non-parallel accounts).

There has been a tendency in modern research to understand vv. 17-18
in universalistic terms.[348] Insofar as it concerns v. 17, the key term is
אדם. Traditional commentators (e.g., Rashi, Abrabanel, Calvin) did not
understand the word אדם as pointing to humanity in general and the same
holds for several modern scholars, such as J. M. P. Smith and House.[349]

The word האדם is a collective noun and as other collective nouns it may
refer to an individual member (or individual members) of a group, or to
the generic meaning of the group.[350] For instance, אשה means "woman"
in Judg 19:26 and in many other occurrences but "women" (in general) in
1 Sam 21:5-6 and Qoh 7:26. Obviously, in Zeph 1:17 האדם does not
refer to "the 'man' " but to "humans." In this sense האדם stands in polar
opposition to non-האדם, i.e., non-humans. The comprehensive pair,

---

NJPSV). Thus, one concludes that the term פנה in such cases may convey its well attested
meaning, i.e., "corner" (see Exod 27:2, 38:2;1 Kgs 7:34; Ezek 43:20, 45:19 ; Job 1:19;
Prov 7:12; 2 Chr 28:24). The term פנה by itself clearly conveys the meaning of
"fortification" or "battlement" only in the occurrences mentioned above.

[347] On Jer 10: 17-18 see Carroll,1986: 259-60; Mc Kane, 1986: 228. See Bright,1965: 67-
74 for the proposal that Jer 10:17-18 originally followed Jer 9:21. Also Rudolph
supports this idea. The proposed dating is the late days of the Judean monarchy.

[348] E.g., Taylor: 1112; Elliger, 1951: 62-63; Gese: 1901; Renaud, 1986:7-8. These
scholars trace back these verses to a redactor. According to Renaud these verses belong
to the framework of Zeph 1 (Zeph 1:2-3, 17-18) that brackets the Zephanic material.
Others, such as R. L. Smith and Kapelrud do not deny that the destruction envisaged in
these verses is universal but they trace the verses to Zephaniah, the prophet (See
Kapelrud, 1975: 30-31; R. L. Smith: 30-31.

[349] See J. M. P. Smith: 205-06; House: 70. Edler proposes a diachronic understanding of the
word האדם, according to him, a later redactor understood the word as pointing to
"mankind" (see Edler: 200).

[350] See GKC § 123 a, 123 b

באדם ובבהמה, occurs in Exod 8:13,14, 9:10, 13:2; Num 8:17, 18:15, 31:11,26. Certainly, in all these cases האדם does not mean "all the human beings on earth" but "the people" to which the context refer, in other words it is entirely clear that neither all mankind suffers the plagues of Egypt nor the laws of first-born in the Book of Numbers apply to humankind as a whole (cf. Num 8:17). In addition, it is noteworthy that only once in the OT, in the relatively late Jer 32:20,[351] does the language האדם convey the sense of the general (humankind), while carrying on a preceding statement concerning the particular (Israel), as proposed by the universalistic approach to Zeph 1:17. To conclude, the proposed universal meaning of the phrase cannot be supported by, or derived from, the term האדם. On the other hand, the term האדם does not contradict a universal understanding of the verse, even if such use of האדם is only occasionally attested.

(b) The theme of עור ("blind") and specially the comparisons with עורים are very common in late "First-Isaiah," and in Deutero and Trito-Isaiah, e.g., Isa 29:18, 35:5, 42:7,16,18,19, 43:8, 56:10, 59:10. In the Isaianic tradition it stands in dialogue with the blindness and deafness of Isaiah's call (Isa 6:10).[352] In addition, a similar metaphor occurs in Deut 28:29.

(c) The function of the expression כי לה' חטאו in Zeph 1:17 is clear, namely, to stress that the described punishment is a response to wrong behavior. In this respect one may compare this note with את הרשעים והמכשלות in Zeph 1:3,[353] but also with similar notes occurring only in Tg Neb Zeph 1:7,18. The value of the latter as textual evidence for the original Hebrew text of Zephaniah is nil but this is not the case insofar as the focus is history of interpretation. However, it is noteworthy that nothing but interpretation is the driving force in the redactional history of a biblical text, until it reaches the status of "received text" to which nothing

---

[351] See Carroll, 1986: 624-25 and the bibliography mentioned there.
[352] See Clements, 1985: 101 ff.
[353] So, for instance, Gerleman, 1942: 21.

can be added or deleted (and therefore the oral or written interpretation takes the form of an independent work). Thus, the Targum to Zephaniah points to the existence of common interpretative lines influencing first the Hebrew text of Zephaniah and later the Targum to Zephaniah. Interpretative lines come out of a certain community living under certain circumstances and produce a communicative message to the community. Therefore, one may ask about the circumstances that may have made necessary—again and again—a clear stress on the culpability of those who are punished by YHWH. It seems that this stress is pointless if there were no (explicit or implicit) doubts about divine justice in the community. Unfortunately, questioning divine justice cannot be related to a particular historical event but is as ubiquitous as perceived and real unjust suffering is, and as ubiquitous as human beings' thinking of God as just, merciful and powerful.

The expression חטאה לה' כי occurs in Jer 50:14, and fulfills there the same role that חטאו לה' כי fulfills in Zeph 1:17. Significantly, the expression does not occur in the LXX Jer and most scholars consider it a pious gloss.[354] In a similar way, most scholars considered לה' חטאו כי in Zeph 1:17 to be a gloss. This is so mainly because the expression interrupts the divine utterance, by changing the speaker,[355] and seems to destroy the metrical balance and to hinder the flow of the discourse in v. 17.[356] Closely related expressions occur as a confession of the sinners, as an expression of their awareness that they deserve the divine punishment, in Jer 3:25 and 8:14. There the expressions are an integral part of the speech and not a narrator's comment, as it is in Zeph 1:17.

(d) The word לָחֶם occurs also in Job 20:23, but this text is highly controversial.[357] The ancient versions read in Zeph 1:17 either "their

---

[354] See for instance, Carroll, 1982: 822.

[355] J. M. P. Smith proposes to emend the expression to כי לי חטאו. Accordingly, he does not consider the emended expression a gloss.

[356] See, for instance, Gerleman, 1942:21; Rudolph, 1975: 263-64; Elder: 17,106, and the bibliographical list in J. M. P. Smith: 206.

[357] See, for instance, Gerleman, 1942: 21; Dahood,1957: 314-15; Pope, 1965: 140.

flesh," "their corpse," or an unambiguous "their carcass" (Tg. Neb.). The probable relation between this word and the Arabic *lahm* , "flesh," is already mentioned in a saying attributed to R. Levi in Exod. Rab. 42:4, and mentioned many times since then.[358] Obviously, this implies a metaphorical sense for שָׁפַך, "pour out." The use of שָׁפַך beyond its narrowly defined literal meaning is well attested in the OT (e.g.,1 Sam 1:15; 2 Sam 20:10; 1 Kgs 13:5; Ezek 20:33,34; Ps 22:15; Lam 2:11), and it fits well the text in Zeph 1:17.[359] Moreover, if this is the case the pair לחם and דם will be equivalent to the well known pair בשׂר and דם, "flesh" and "blood," which does not occur in the OT but occurs in Sir 14:18 and many times in "rabbinical" Hebrew.

Alternatively, the text has to be emended in order to render a liquid equivalent to "blood." For instance, one may propose to drop the second מ as a dittography (or retain it as an enclitic מ) and to read לֵחָם (cf. Deut 34:7), i.e., "their sap of life".[360] It is worth noting that a similar problem exists in Jer 11:19 where בְּלַחְמוֹ cannot be taken as a reference to flesh or to a corpse. The proposed textual emendations for Jer 11:19[361] are almost the same as those for Zeph 1:17.

Both alternative renderings may be correct,[362] but it seems preferable not to emend a comprehensible biblical text, which is supported by the ancient versions, in order to propose a certainly possible biblical text but one without any evidence supporting it.

---

[358] Either accepting it (e.g., Rashi, Gerleman) or mentioning it in order to reject it (e.g., Abrabanel, Rudolph).

[359] Especially because of its double function, as the verbal form for "their blood" and for "their flesh= carcass." On this point, see, for instance, Ball, 1972/1988: 43.

[360] See for instance Sabottka (1972): 56-8; Gerleman (1973): 253; Rudolph, 1975: 264; Watts, 1975: 163; R. L. Smith: 149.

[361] See Mc Kane, 1986: 257, Carroll, 1986: 275.

[362] Although the two mentioned alternatives are the main ones, several other proposals have been made. For instance, BDB, as well as in NEB propose that לחמם means "bowels" (cf. 2 Sam 20:10); and for a list of different proposals, see BDB and J. M. P. Smith: 210.

3.2.16. Zeph 1:18

(a) The expression גם כספם גם זהבם . . . ביום עברת ה' occurs, with slight changes, in MT Ezek 7:19, but not in the LXX. It is commonly considered a gloss in Ezekiel, probably taken from Zeph 1:18.[363]

The form גם . . . גם occurs more than fifty times in the OT, in almost every biblical genre and across boundaries of time. The motif of gold and silver as useless objects in the day of judgment does not occur in the DOY literature.[364] But it occurs in Prov 11:4. Significantly, as mentioned above, the expression יום עברה occurs only in Prov 11:4 and Zeph 1:15, and יום עברת ה' only in Zeph 1:18 and Ezek 7:19, which is the only other occurrence (even if slightly different) of the expression ה' גם כספם גם זהבם . . . ביום עברת in the OT.

The message of the phrase is clear: "silver and gold," i.e., material riches will not save their owners on the "day of wrath."[365] Certainly not every person can even think about the possibility of being saved by his or her wealth, only those who have "silver and gold" can, or can be described as hoping to do so. The writer of this sentence betrayed here his or her own understanding of the character of the condemned people. Unless the writer considered all human beings, or all Judeans, wealthy, one should conclude that he/she qualified האדם in v. 17: Instead of every human being, or every Judean; the wealthy.

Obviously, the explicit negation of the possibility that wealth can buy personal salvation in the "day of wrath" can arise only against the background of a society in which wealth can buy personal "salvation" in the normal course of the events. The point made by the writer is that

---

[363] See Zimmerli; 1979: 211; Greenberg,1983:152

[364] Including Isa 13:6-8, 9-16. In Isa 13: 17-22 a similar thought is expressed, but it does not belong to DOY literature, see Clements, 1982:132, 136-38.

[365] According to Sabottka and Watts, silver and gold may point to the "idols." See Sabottka: 58; Watts, 1975: 163; cf. Ball, 1972/1988: 91. The question of idolatry is not mentioned in this unit. Moreover, "idols" is neither the usual meaning of "gold" and "silver" nor the necessary one in v. 18.

although the wealthy cannot be punished in the normal course of events because their wealth is their shield,[366] there will be one day, namely, the "day of wrath," when things will be different, then their riches will be no longer a shield for them and they will not avoid YHWH's judgment.

The sentence also serves as a "midrashic comment" to v. 6, i.e., those men instead of seeking God for salvation thought of their money as their savior (cf. דרשו לא in v. 6), and may be considered a further development of the motif of חיל (wealth) in v. 13 (cf. ‏..‏ זהב ‏...‏ כסף. חיל in Ezek 28:4 and Zech 14:14). In addition, the expression 'ה גם כספם גם זהבם ‏...‏ ביום עברת also suits the war-like imagery of the preceding verses (cf. Isa 13:17). Although Isa 13:17 is a post-monarchic piece,[367] people trying to "bribe" murderers in order to save their lives is a timeless fact, as well as, a timeless literary image.[368]

(b) The expression באש קנאתו ‏...‏ כל הארץ occurs also in Zeph 3:8, with YHWH in the first person as expected from the context of divine speech. There the expression is the emphatic closing statement made by YHWH in the judgment section. Moreover, the importance of the expression is explicitly stressed in Zeph 3:8 by the use of the כי (e.g., Zeph 3:8b, 9, 10, 12, 20). This is not the case in Zeph 1:18. The expression there opens the narrator's apodosis that concludes the chapter[369] and the כי phrase is, as expected, the concluding one, i.e., כי כלה אך נבהלה יעשה את כל ישבי הארץ.

---

[366] Cf. Job 21: 28-33.

[367] See, for instance, Clements, 1982:132, 136-8 and the bibliography cited there. For a different dating, see Hayes-Irvine, 1987: 220-23.

[368] The text provides no support to the suggestion that the reference to the "silver and gold" in this verse reflects the payment given by Psammetichus I, King of Egypt, to Scythians in Palestine, in order to persuade them not to come further, according to Herodotus I, 105 (cf. Taylor: 1010, Lods: 131; for the general historical question, see Spalinger, 1978). Such a proposal is based on a set of presuppositions: (a) Zephaniah, a prophet who lived in last quarter of the seventh century BCE, said or wrote the relevant part of v. 18; (b) Zephaniah's speech necessarily reflected contemporary political events; (c) Herodotus' report is a historical reliable source; and (d) there are no other candidates but the Scythians for the role of an invading army in the days of Josiah. Cf. Eiselen: 509-10; Cazelles; Taylor: 1010; Pfeiffer: 600.

[369] The sentence opening with באש קנאתו האכל כל הארץ is formally connected to its direct antecedent, i.e., 'ה עברת ביום ‏...‏ כספם גם by a *waw*. Obviously, the connectedness between the two is not dependent on the existence of the *waw* ; as a reading without the

It is noteworthy that while אש and קנאה occur in relation to YHWH or
to YHWH's theophany many times in the OT, the language קנאת ה'
באש (i.e., "in the fire of YHWH's jealous wrath" [RSV modified])
occurs only in Ezek 36:5[370] and in Zeph 1:18, 3:8. In a different form,
the same metaphor occurs in Ps 79:5, probably a post-monarchic
psalm.[371]

(c) Concerning the phrase . . . כי כלה אך נבהלה יעשה את. The
expression . . . עשה כלה את occurs several times in the OT in either late
monarchic or post-monarchic pieces, e.g., Jer 5:18, 30:11, 46:28; Ezek
11:13, 20:17; Neh 9:31.

The word נבהלה is a probably a *niphal* participle. A similar expression
but with נחרצה instead of נבהלה occurs in Isa 10:23, 28:22;[372] Dan
9:27. In the latter it seems to be a coined expression, and in the former
two it does not occur in phrases containing the expression . . . כלה את
עשה (cf. עשה כלה ב in Isa 20:23).

The word נבהלה is understood as "in haste" in the LXX and in the Vg.
Several scholars consider this translation the correct one.[373] This is so
because such an understanding of בהל fits well with both the grammatical
requirements and the context, and above all because words from the root
בהל conveying the general meaning of "to hasten" do occur in Biblical
Hebrew, mainly in post-monarchic Hebrew in Prov 20:21 (qere), 28:22;

---

waw clearly shows (cf. RSV, NJPSV; on the general issue of semantic connectedness,
see Berlin, 1985, esp. 91-94 and the bibliography mentioned there). Since the
connectedness depends on the syntagmatic relationship between the . . . תאכל כל הארץ
באש קנאתו and its precedent, the meaning conveyed by this relationship cannot be
clarified but by contextual meaning. The sentence opening with . . . קנאתו תאכל כל הארץ
באש does not represent a new element in the description of the punishment but a kind of
conclusion, namely, "so, in the fire of YHWH's jealous wrath . . . " (pace Alonso
Schöckel-Valverde who translate "cuando el fuego de su celo . . . ; see Nueva Biblia
Española).

[370] Cf. Ezek 38:19.

[371] See Anderson,1972: 577; Fohrer,1970:289 and the bibliography cited there.

[372] Isa 28:22 is commonly considered post-monarchic and Isa 10:23 either post-monarchic
or late monarchic, see Clements, 1982: 114, 232 and the bibliography mentioned there.
For a different dating, see Hayes-Irvine: 203,329-30.

[373] See, R. L. Smith: 129; House:121; Bula; cf. RSV, NEB.

Qoh 5:1, 7:9; Esth 2:9, 6:14, 8:14; 2 Chr 26:20, 35:21.[374] However, words from the root בהל usually convey the general meaning of "to terrify," "to cause dismay" (e.g., Gen 45:3; Exod 15:15; Lev 26:16; Judg 20:41; Isa 13:8; Jer 51:32; Ezek 7:27; Job 23:15,16) and accordingly several scholars support the proposal that the participle נבהלה functions as an adjective meaning "terrible."[375]

There is also an alternative approach. If נבהלה in Zeph 1:18 (cf. נחרצה in Isa 10:23, 28:22) is equivalent[376] to כָּלָה, "complete destruction", one may conclude that נבהלה is a noun. If this is the case, נבהלה will probably mean "terror," or even "sudden terror."[377] However, the lack of clear examples of proposed nominal patterns[378] weakens this position.

(d) Undoubtedly, the expressions תאכל כל הארץ and ישׁבי הארץ כל, both in v. 18, sharply raise the interpretation dilemma of "universal destruction" against "local destruction." Does הארץ in כל ישׁבי הארץ refer to "all the land of Judah/ Israel" or to the entire world? The common modern answer is that Zeph 1:18 refers to all the world.[379] A

---

[374] It is noteworthy that the meaning "to hasten" for בהל is well attested in Aramaic, and therefore it has been proposed that the use of words from the root בהל with this meaning is an Aramaism. For this position, see, for instance, Wagner: 33. For the opposite proposal, i.e., internal development in Hebrew, see Fredericks: 214, 218. See also the bibliography mentioned in Fredericks on behalf of each position. For Aramaic influence in Biblical Hebrew in general, see, for instance, Kutscher, 1982: 71-77.

[375] E.g., Ball, 1972/1988: 44; Kapelrud: 105; J. M. P. Smith: 207; cf. NJPSV; NRSV. Among other proposals one may mention that Sellin emends נבהלה to בהלה.

[376] אך has an asseverative meaning in Zeph 1:18. See GKC § 153; Williams § 389.

[377] See Gerleman, 1942: 22 and the bibliography mentioned there; cf. Sabottka: 59; Rudolph, 1975: 264.

[378] Abstract, verbal, nouns derived from the *niphal* pattern. On these nouns in general, see Meyer, III 17. On nouns with a prefixed *nun* due to the *niphal* pattern, see GKC § 85 n. However, the nouns mentioned there (e.g., נפתולים, "wrestlings," Gen 30:8) do not show the proposed form of נבהלה.

[379] This answer appears neither in Calvin's commentary nor in the medieval Jewish commentaries. Moreover, in such commentaries there is no polemic against the "universal" approach to these verses. They simply presuppose a Judean setting for the verse.
Also among modern scholars, there are several who remain undecided, see G. A. Smith: 58; J. M. P. Smith: 201; and a few hold that הארץ means Judah, e.g., Eiselen: 529. For the widespread "universalistic" approach, see, for instance, Duhm, 1910: 67; S. R. Driver: 341; Gerleman, 1942:22; Taylor: 1112; Ball, 1972/1988:290; Irsigler, 1977: 112-13; 138; Boadt, 1982: 212-13; Kapelrud, 1972: 30-31; Martin: 19, 22; O'Connor:

reassessment of this general assumption may lead to a less conclusive
position.

The word ארץ is well attested in the two meanings, i.e., as "land" and
as "earth."[380] The same holds true for the entire phrase, ישבי הארץ
כל. In Joel 1:14 כל ישבי הארץ are the Judeans, or even their
representatives, but the same phrase probably refers to all the inhabitants
of the earth in Zech 11:6. Even narratives where the "doom" of "the land"
is accompanied by cosmic features, most of them resembling the DOY's
features, show no unequivocal meaning for ארץ. For instance, Jer 4:19-
22 enlarges the perspective of Jer 4:11-18, which is clearly focused on
Jerusalem and the Judeans. Nevertheless the term כל הארץ in v. 20
clearly refers to Judah and not to the entire earth. The vision goes further
in the following verses (Jer 4:23-26): The "land" returned to primeval
chaos, the mountains shaking, the light gone, no human beings (אדם
אין), all the arable land and cities destroyed, and so on. Although this
appears to be a vision of universal destruction, the text also says נדדו
וכל עוף השמים, i.e., all the birds have fled (to somewhere). Certainly,
they have not been annihilated. So even this vision implies that the
"speaker," and the writer as well, actually thought in terms of a large but
geographically limited destruction. Deut 32:22 provides another example.
There one reads: "For a fire has flared in My wrath and burned to the
bottom of Sheol, has consumed the earth (ארץ) and its increase, eaten
down to the base of the hills" (NJPSV), but from the context it is clear that
while Israel is being punished, humankind continues to exist (see vv. 26-
27). Therefore, these verses do not seem to imply the destruction of the
entire world. Summing up, the two meanings are well attested and
theoretically possible in Zeph 1:18. Clearly, neither the language nor the

---

248; Edler:82; Renaud, 1986: 7-8. A good illustration of the general change concerning
the interpretation of the term ארץ is the move from the English rendering "land" for ארץ
in KJV to "earth" in RSV (the "earth" meaning is kept in NRSV).

[380] For instance in a clear non-universal meaning Gen 35:12; Exod 12:19; Josh 9:9; 2 Kgs
17:16; Isa 7:24; Jer 40:4; Ezek 39:18; Hos 1:2; Joel 1:14; Am 3:11 but in a universal
meaning Isa 6:3 (?); Jer 10:10,12; 50:23; 51:7; Nah 1:5. This second meaning is
probably related to meaning of ארץ as the opposite of שמים (e.g., Gen 1:1), and since the
heavens are universal, also the land is.

context in Zeph 1:18 point decisively to either of the two alternatives. Even if the verse is interpreted in the light of the DOY's images (vv. 14 ff.), this will not provide solid support for any critical decision. To be sure, one may prefer one reading over the other on the basis of a previously accepted hypothesis concerning the message of either the prophet or a redactor, but such reading does not explain the most conspicuous feature in the text: The text is ambiguous. Moreover, the text is not ambiguous because biblical writers could not determine how to overcome the ambiguity of their language, as the unambiguous use of the word ארץ clearly proves.[381]

The ambiguous meaning of ארץ in v. 18 can be interpreted as a sophisticated literary double entendre. It can also be interpreted as an expression of the feelings and thoughts of Judeans for whom their annihilation (as described in the verse and in the preceding verses) is subjectively tantamount to a total destruction, and therefore only by means of a double meaning term they are able to express both the objective and the subjective reality.[382] Obviously, these two interpretations are not incompatible. As mentioned before, ambiguity as a rhetorical device, grasps the attention of the reader or hearer. Thus v. 18 not only emphatically concludes the description of the judgment but also calls attention to those who are to be punished, to כל ישבי הארץ. The following verses, Zeph 2:1-3, are directed to them and focused on them.[383]

---

[381] See the preceding footnote. It is worth noting that biblical writers overcame the double meaning of ארץ not only by means of the context but also by the use of תבל instead of ארץ (e.g., Job 37:12; Isa 14:21; Jer 10:12= 51:5).

[382] It is noteworthy, that even in our days, " the land" has also an ambivalent meaning in several modern languages. The use of "the land" in figurative ways is probably attested through all history. This can hardly be the result of blind chance. One may ask for instance, what is implied in the classical saying of Richter (XIX century): "Providence has given to the French the empire of the land; to the English that of the sea; to the Germans that of the air." Obviously, Richter claims for the existence of a certain, assumedly "objective," politico-cultural reality in his days. But he obviously betrayed his own subjective reality, one in which England, France and Germany, and their overseas territories, constitute "the world."

[383] Obviously, a clear rhetorical function does not necessarily mean that the verses occurred together already at the compositional level. Such a proposal would imply that only the one responsible for the compositional level had literary capabilities.

3.3 Notes on Zephaniah 2

3.3.1. Zeph 2:1

(a) The language הִתְקוֹשְׁשׁוּ וָקוֹשׁוּ[384] was understood by the LXX, the Peshitta, the Vg and Tg. Neb. as "gather together."[385] As pointed in the MT it is a combination of two imperatives forms of the root קשׁשׁ, one according to the *hitpoel* (*hitpolel*) pattern and the second to the *poel* (*polel*) pattern.[386] Such combinations of two imperatives connected by a copulative *waw* [387] occur in the Hebrew Bible and in these cases the second verb refers to the fulfillment of the action mentioned by the first one.[388] The use of two verbal forms of the same root but in two different patterns (e.g., *qal* and *niphal* , *piel* and *pual*, *qal* and *hitpael,* etc.) as pair words, either in parallel versets or in juxtaposition, is a common stylistic

---

[384] According to the Murabba'at text, הִתקשׁשׁו וקשׁו. The Murabba'at text slightly differs from the MT in this verbal form, and in Zeph 2:3, 3:9,11. See respective notes. The extant fragment of 1QpZeph points to the common masoretic writing (see Horgan, 1979: 63-65 and the bibliography mentioned there). The masoretic writing also occurs in b. San. 19a. The Aleppo Codex reads הִתקשׁשׁו while the Leningrad Codex (B 19a) and the printed Second Rabbinic Bible reads הִתקשׁשׁו. Whether in this case, as in other cases (e.g., Mic 6:7 ברבבות [L, SRB]; ברבבות [A]) one should read with simple *shewa* or composite *shewa* was open to vivid discussion in Medieval times (see *Minhat Shai*, to Gen 12:3).

[385] Resh Lakish, one of the most important Amoraim of the second half of the third century, interpreted it as "take away the straw from yourselves and then take the straw from the others," and therefore similar to "adorn yourselves (by living in accordance to God's will) and then adorn the others." This interpretation served as the "biblical" support for the general principle that one cannot require the other to emend his or her ways before requiring the same from oneself. This principle was used, for instance, to support the idea that one can judge others only if one can be judged (e.g., a king cannot judge if he cannot be judged). See b. Bab. Bat 60b; b. San 18a; b. San 19a; Lam Rab. 3. 40 (there, the words: "Koshu (Zeph II, 1), i.e., men should correct (koshet) themselves and the correct the others" [Soncino ET] are assigned to R. Joshaiah, an Amora who lived one generation before Resh Lakish). An evaluation of the principles mentioned above is beyond the scope of this work. In any case such interpretation of התקשׁשׁו וקשׁו is unlikely the "original" one in Zeph 2:1, and points much more to the interpreter and his /her community than to the writer of the book of Zephaniah and his/her community.

[386] See GKC 67§ l. Note the *dagesh* in the שׁ of קשׁ.

[387] For the vocalization of this *waw*, see GKC 104 § d-g. The vocalization with *qametz* in Zeph 2:1 is the expected one. See GKC 104 § g.

[388] See GKC 110 § f-a.

feature in the OT (e.g., Josh 6:1; Jer 20:14, 23:19).[389] One can find examples of juxtapositions of a *hitpael* verbal form and of a *qal* one of the same root, as in Zeph 2:1, in Isa 29:9 and Hab 1:5, and the inverse order occurs in Isa 24:19.

The root קשש occurs in its *qal* form in Exod 5:7,12; Num 15:32,33; 1 Kgs 17:10,12. The meaning of "gathering" (either "straw" or "wooden sticks") is a common feature in these occurrences. This meaning not only supports the renderings of the ancient versions, but also fits its context. Similar calls for gathering occur in the context of "on the eve of the judgment" several times in the OT (e.g., Lev 26:25; Jer 4:5, 8:14; Joel 1:14; 2:16).[390] The probable background for these gatherings is a ritual of penitence. Such rituals are reflected, for instance, in Am 5:14-15; Jonah 3:7; Joel 1:13-14, 2:12-17; Jer 3:22b-25 (?); 2 Kgs 22:11,19; 2 Chr 20:3-19. The contents and the structure of the rest of v. 1 and vv. 2-3 support this understanding.[391]

---

[389] On this topic, see Berlin, 1975: 36-40 and the bibliography cited there.

[390] Perhaps also Jer 4:5, 8:15.

[391] Cf. See Raitt, 1971. However, the expression in Zeph 2:1 is an hapax and words from the root קשש in the *hitpoel* pattern do not occur elsewhere in the OT. This fact, along with a sense that the proposed meaning does not fit the context, led several scholars to propose alternative readings and in modern times, also to textual emendations.
Already Calvin in his commentary on Zephaniah discusses several proposals that were known to him. Among them, (a) that the word comes from the root קשש ; (b) that the word comes from the root קוש ; (c) that the word comes from the word קש. He also mentions the following proposed readings : "gather yourselves, gather"; "search yourselves . . ."; "gather the chaff, gather the chaff" ("as though the Prophet (sic) ridiculed the empty confidence of the people"). See Calvin: 229-30. Calvin's position, however, is clear: "I consider the real meaning of the Prophet to be - 'Gather yourselves, gather;' for this is what grammatical construction requires" (Calvin: 229).
Among modern proposals for the emendation of the consonantal text, one may mention the proposed original forms התבוששו and בושו (e.g., BDB, Ehrlich: 458) and התקדשו וקדשו (Procksch). For a list of different proposals, and the relevant bibliography, see J. M. P. Smith: 211-12.
Deleting the *dagesh* in the *shin* of קושו, which marks the assimilation of one of the *shin* of the root, Sabotkka proposes to derive it and התקוששו from the root קוש, "to set a trap", which occurs only in Isa 29:21 (but see BHS). See Sabottka: 61-62. For a critical response to Sabottka's proposal, see del Olmo Lete: 299; Hunter: 262.
Rudolph also proposes that the word comes from the root קוש, but meaning "bent, bent back." See Rudolph, 1975: 271. Although this meaning is attested in Arabic, it is not attested in Hebrew.
Others due to their stress on the denominative character of התקוששו and therefore the focus on קש, "straw, " propose translations such as, "Gather yourselves as stubble, and remain as stubble" (Hunter: 261; see del Olmo Lete: 299; Hunter: 261-62; Gerleman, 1942: 24,

Obviously, a ritual of penitence is not the setting of a literary piece that tells about such a gathering. Even if the written words are an exact transcript of what the prophet said in his/her call to the people, from the very moment that the words of the prophet were written in order to be read later, one stands before a literary piece that calls a certain public—not necessarily, and probably not at all, the public of the proclaimed word—to reflect upon the meaning of the described event. Writing a "story" about a prophet calling the people for repentance, in order to produce the material basis for personal or communal reflection, is an entirely different activity than actually calling the people to repentance.

(b) The expression נכסף לא has been translated and interpreted in many different ways. All these interpretations, however, concur in one point: The expression conveys a negative evaluation in Zeph 2:1. This is so because of the context, or in more precise words because of genre recognition based on the meaning of the other parts of the unit (Zeph 2:1-3.) This unit seems to be a prophetic summons to repentance. If a prophetic summons to repentance includes a vocative, then it will be either neutral, such as "Children of Israel" (2 Chr 30:6; cf. Ezek 18:30) or condemnatory (e.g., Jer 3:12, 14, 22).[392] Since הגוי לא נכסף cannot be considered a neutral term, such as "House of Israel," one must conclude that the phrase has a condemnatory meaning.

The word נכסף is a *niphal* participle of כסף. The verbal form ל נכסף is attested in the OT (Gen 31:30, Ps 84:3) with the meaning of "long for." Since instead of נכסף ל-X Zeph 2:1 has only נכסף, there is

---

69). This stress may be misleading insofar as one is concerned with meaning and not with etymology. Forms from the root קשש in *polel* occur elsewhere without any conveyed meaning of "gathering straw" but simply "gathering" (e.g.,Num 15:32,33; 1 Kgs 17:10,12). In addition, it is noteworthy that other roots that convey a general meaning of "to gather" in stems other than the *hitpael* (such as כנס, קבץ, and אסף) also have *hitpael* forms whith meanings such as "gather themselves", "gather together," i.e., similar to the proposed meaning of the *hitpael* התקושש. Obviously, the occurrence of מן in v. 2 does not necessarily point to a "dictionary" meaning of the התקושש related to קשש; the occurrence of the two words in closely textual vicinity may well be a pun on words. For the proposal that קשש "might be used here in the sense "be hard, stiffen,"as it were קשה, see Gray, 1953. Such a meaning of קשש is not attested elsewhere in the OT.

392 Cf. Raitt, 1971.

a line of interpretation maintaining that X-ל is implied in Zeph 2:1 (cf. Ps
10:13; Deut 13:15), i.e., that this is an elliptical clause. If this is the case,
then the task of the interpreter is to make explicit what is implicit in the
text. For instance, Tg. Neb. translates הגוי לא נכסף as "people who
do not desire to return to The Torah." Of course, here the religious
thought of the author of Tg. Neb. comes to the forefront. The MT book
of Zephaniah does not refer to The Torah, and one can hardly expect that
this was the implicit meaning of phrase. Much more in accordance with
the thought and language found in the Book of Zephaniah is Hunter's
proposal,[393] namely, "which has no longing for YHWH" (Hunter: 261-
62; and cf. Zeph 2:3). In addition it has been proposed that "X" has a
general and comprehensive meaning,[394] and therefore the phrase means,
"which has no aspirations" and points to either indifference or
resignation.[395]

Alternatively, one may consider the verbal forms נכסף ל and נכסף to
be separate forms, in terms of meaning. If this is the case then the latter
may be understood as either a passive *niphal* or reflexive *niphal* [396] of
כסף, which occurs in the OT in *qal* forms and means "to desire," "to
long" (Job 14:15; Ps 17:2). Accordingly, the phrase may be translated
either "people which is not desired" (Kapelrud:105; cf. the Vg.) or "the
people who do not long for itself", and therefore has sinned and brought
upon itself the day of judgment (cf. Ps 37:28). Obviously, the first
alternative does not solve the quest for the implicit meaning, for it leads to
the question, not desired by whom? As in the case of the Tg. Neb., the
quest for the implicit meaning may bring to the forefront the interpreter's
own world. For instance, according to Calvin and Altschuler, God is the
answer to the "whom." But, both Calvin and Altschuler qualified the

---

[393] See also Ball, 1972/1988: 98.

[394] According to Sabottka, this meaning is conveyed by לא in v.1, which functions as a
substantive, "Nichts". See Sabottka: 62-63.

[395] See Irsigler, 1977: 62 and the bibliography mentioned there.

[396] GKC 51§c, e.g., ועמשא לא נשמר (2 Sam 20:10). Compare the use of the reflexive נשמר
without ל in Deut 2:4 with the one of נשמר ל in Deut. 4:15, Josh 23:11.

literal meaning of the text, each according to his own theological perspective. Thus, Calvin explained that the people were not worthy of God's love, but God loves them, and that this love is a "remarkable proof of the unfailing grace of God" (Calvin: 230); Altschuler, underscored the temporary character of the situation.

In addition to these understandings of נכסף, other suggestions have been made. For instance, since in Aramaic and Arabic the root כסף may be understood as meaning "be ashamed", it has been proposed that נכסף הגוי לא means "O shameless nation" (RSV, NRSV; already Radak, in the name of his father, pointed to this interpretation). It is noteworthy that this "Aramaic" meaning is not only unattested elsewhere in Biblical Hebrew, but also the Targum provides a different rendering. Furthermore, there is no clear support for this meaning in the ancient versions. Several scholars related the root כסף to כֶּסֶף , i.e., "silver." Accordingly, the metaphorical meaning "not broken" (cf. Zeph 1:10) has been proposed (cf. Rudolph, 1975: 271), as well as "without money," (cf. Seybold, 1985: 37). Gray suggested that נכסף should be emended to נכפס and that further textual emendations should be carried out in this verse (see above). He translates Zeph 2:1 as follows: "Stiffen yourselves and stand firm, O people without cohesion (Gray: 1953).[397]

One of the main methodological principles in critical studies is that one should not multiply unnecessarily the number of explanations given to closely related phenomena.[398] Accordingly, one should not multiply unnecessarily the number of proposed meanings for a given verbal form in Biblical Hebrew, for instance, כסף. The existence of different shades of meanings or even different meanings in a cognate language may be suggestive of but certainly does not necessarily point to the existence of

---

[397] For a summary of the different proposals concerning the meaning of הגוי לא נכסף, and the relevant bibliography, see Irsigler, 1977: 62; Hunter: 263; Rudolph, 1975: 271-72; J. M. P. Smith: 222. For כסף meaning "be broken, depressed" see also Barr, 1968: 320 n. 177 and the bibliography mentioned there.

[398] Cf. the second rule in Newton's "Rules of Reasoning in Philosophy": "Therefore, to the same natural effects we must, as far as possible, assign the same causes." See Isaac Newton, *Mathematical Principles of Natural Philosophy* (ET A. Motte, F. Cajory, Berkely, 1934): 398-400.

these meanings—or shades of meanings—in biblical Hebrew.[399] Consequently, on the basis of the principle mentioned above, one should conclude that those proposals anchored in clearly attested biblical meanings of verbal forms of כסף should be preferred, namely, the proposals mentioned in the first two paragraphs. But, which of them?

The question of the most probable meaning of the phrase cannot be resolved on strictly textual grounds. But it seems that the context and especially the comparisons with other prophetic summons to repentance may be of some help. The context, and the genre in general, points to two main actors, human beings and YHWH and to their interacting. Thus, if one has to supply an implicit element in the vocative phrase in Zeph 2:1, the most likely candidate is YHWH. This, leaves two options: (a) the people are not desired by YHWH; (b) the people do not long for YHWH. Both are possible, but a comparative analysis of other derogatory vocatives, including explicit and implicit calls for repentance, indicates that they tend to refer to the people's attitude and not to the (real or deserved) attitude of others towards the people (e.g., Jer 3:12, 14, 22; cf. Isa 5:8,11,18, 20,21,22). The same holds true if one analyzes the negative attributes of גוי in the OT (e.g., גוי לא חסיד, Ps 43:1; גוי חטא, Isa 1:4; גוי חנף, Isa 10:6; גוי נבל, Deut 32:21; גוי אבד עצות, Deut 32:28). Thus, it is more likely that the phrase tends to say "the people who do not long for YHWH" rather than "the people who are not desired by YHWH" or "not worthy of being desired by YHWH." But, it is noteworthy that the phrase does not say it straightforwardly. The phrase contains an ellipsis and a great deal of ambiguity. This ambiguity underlines two themes at the same time: (a) peoples longing for YHWH,

---

[399] Moreover, even if two words are etymologically related they may have different meanings in different languages. On the methodological questions concerning the use of cognate language, see J. Barr, 1961, 1968.
The dismissal of the two principles mentioned above can lead and has led to a plethora of proposals, none of which has an attested anchor in biblical Hebrew. The task of the historical-critical interpreter is not to use his/her knowledge of cognate language, and in some cases his/her imaginative power as well, in order to support a reading that seems subjectively sound, i.e., that fits beforehand conceptions concerning the text. He/she should be constrained by the evidence of biblical Hebrew except for cases in which the result is an utterly meaningless expression.

which in prophetic literature (and probably in the entire OT) is not an ethereal attitude but is related to (or even used as a synonym of) behavior according to God's desire (e.g., Am 5:14; Isa 1:10-17; and esp. Zeph 2:3); and (b) God's attitude toward the people. The two themes are at the heart of the message of Zephaniah 2:3.

3.3.2. Zeph 2:2

The first two versets in Zeph 2:2 have raised a large scholarly debate concerning their meaning and their original Hebrew text.[400] However, the "literal" rendering for MT בטרם לדת חק, i.e., "before the decree is born (i.e., comes out),"[401] is understandable in the context of the verse. The sense of "the time is quickly running out" that governs the entire verse[402] is also clearly perceived if one renders כמץ עבר יום literally as "like chaff a day has passed away" (RSV footnote).[403]

Although בטרם is attested more than thirty times in the OT,[404] the expression בטרם לא is a hapax. Moreover, it cannot be explained by the fact that the event which is coming is undesirable (cf. Jer 38:10; Prov 18:13). Furthermore, the form is בטרם without לא in other utterances that refer to the eve of the judgment (e.g., Jer 13:16; Zeph 2:2a; and cf.

---

[400] For different approaches and proposals concerning this verse, see, for instance, Gerleman, 1942: 25-26; Ball,1972:98-100; Sabottka,1972: 64; Rudolph,1975:272; Irsigler, 1977: 62-64; Hunter 263-64; Barthelemey, 1980: 374-75. In general terms, one may say that the BHS proposal, to emend the text to בטרם לא תדחקו, "before are you driven away" (RSV; NRSV) is widely accepted.

[401] For another instance of a "highly" figurative use of ילד, see Prov 27:1; cf. Job 15:35; Isa 33:11; 55:10; 59:4. For חק referring to divine decree, decision, see Ps 2:7.

[402] That this is the case is clear from the use of the expression כְּמֹץ (cf. Hos 13:3; Isa 17:13, 41:15; Ps 35:5, and esp. Isa 29:5). Because of the parallels in 2:2b and 2:2c, the meaning of the entire verse is unequivocal: Something has to be done and very soon, before the Day of Wrath comes.

[403] Cf. Barthélemy, 1980: 374-75.

[404] E.g., Gen 27:33; Lev 14:36; Deut 31:21; 2 Kgs 2:9; Jer 13:16; Isa 8:4, 66:7; Ezek: 16:57; Ps 39:24; Prov 18:13; Job 10:21. It does not occur in Ezra-Nehemiah-Chronicles but probably in Ruth 3:14. Cf. מטרם in Hag.2:15.

Ezek 16:57). Significantly, the similar language עד אשר occurs elsewhere without לא, but as עד אשר לא in Qoh 12:1,2,6.[405]

3.3.3. Zeph 2:3

The interpretative problems that one faces in v. 3 are different from those faced in vv. 1-2. Unlike the scholarly situation concerning vv. 1-2, there is scholarly agreement concerning the meaning of the words and expressions in v. 3. The question is how to understand v. 3. Moreover, because of reasons that will be self-evident in the following discussion, the understanding of verse 2:3 seems to be crucial for the understanding of Zeph 2:1-3 as a unit.

On the surface the MT makes little sense. It seems difficult to suppose that the addressees are כל ענוי הארץ, and even more difficult to suppose that the message to them is: בקשו ענוה.[406] In addition, how can one reconcile the first vocative, הגוי לא נכסף, with the second one, כל ענוי הארץ?

A traditional response to the last question has been that the vocatives do not refer to the same public: הגוי לא נכסף refers to the sinners and כל ענוי הארץ to the righteous.[407] Accordingly, the real issue is why the righteous are asked to seek righteousness, and the meek humility. This question almost asks for theologically oriented responses. Thus, one reads:

> for we hence learn that even the best are roused by God's scourges to seek true religion with greater ardour than they had before done. Though then it be our object to serve God and to follow his word, yet when calamities arise and God appears as a judge, we ought to be stimulated to greater care and diligence; for it never is the case that any one of us fully performs his duty (Calvin: 235).

---

[405] The presence of two negatives in the same sentence emphasizes the negation. See GKC §152 y.

[406] Although metric considerations are never conclusive, one may note that 2:3a stands at odds with the metrical form of 2:3b and 2:3c.

[407] See for instance, Radak, Abrabanel, Calvin, Altschuler. Among modern scholars who support this approach one may mention Hunter (see below).

Radak and Abrabanel, one their part consider the first בקשו את ה' as pointing to prayer. The righteous should pray for the "coming back" of the sinners to God's ways. But the righteous have not only to pray for the "coming back" of the sinners but also to seek righteousness and humility with the sinners, so they will return to the right way (Radak).

Whatever the merits of the theological principles implied in these interpretations, it is clear that these interpretations do not suit the Book of Zephaniah if the latter is analyzed according to historical-critical criteria. To seek YHWH is neither synonymous with a request to pray for the correction of the ways of the sinners nor the last part of the verse with human efforts in such direction. In addition, it is hardly acceptable that summons to repentance, real or literary, will open with a vocative condemning the people in order to leave the same people aside, without asking them to do anything, but turn to a selected and praised group in order to ask this group to keep their ways, so perhaps they will be saved; for the others are already damned (e.g., Jer 3:12, 14, 22). Even when the vocative is neutral, or even only implied, the addressees are always asked to repent (e.g., Joel 2:12-13; Am 5:4-6, 14-15; Jonah 3:7-9; Zech 1:2-3; Mal 3:7; Isa 1:16-17, 55:6-7; Jer 3:12-13, 4:1, 18:11; Ezek 18:30-32; 2 Kgs 17:13; 2 Chr 30:6-9). [408]

Since the addressees are those who are being called to repentance, a second approach to the question of how to reconcile the first vocative, הגוי לא נכסף, with the second one, כל ענוי הארץ, is needed. Theoretically, at least, the simplest approach is to propose that there is only one group of addressees, that this is the group who is called for repentance, and that it is called by two different vocatives. The obvious

---

[408] Pace Hunter who writes: "The apparent contrast in address between "the nation" and "all humble of the land" can be explained by postulating different audiences for the two parts of the utterance, the first in vv. 1-2 being directed to the bulk of the people... and the second to a smaller and less influential group who have remained faithful to Yahweh. We must picture Zephaniah speaking on an occasion when representatives of both groups were present" (Hunter:267). "For the first time, according to my analysis, we have a prophetic exhortation that is not directed toward the very people whose sins have prompted the announcement of judgment, but to a group which would be inclined to heed the prophet's words" (Hunter: 269-70). See Hunter: 264-71.

objection to this approach is that the differences between the two vocatives and the description of the groups is too large. Leaving aside a *sui generis* explanation that the righteous are intentionally called sinners in order to shake them, or their confidence, it seems that the proposal concerning one audience necessarily leads either to textual emendation or to the idea that Zeph 1:2-3 is a composite unit.[409]

The simplest and the more likely proposal of textual emendation is that haplography has occurred, namely, a כ before כל ענוי הארץ has been dropped.[410] This textual emendation radically changes the meaning of the unit. It presupposes that the addressees who are going to be punished are only a part of the people. Outside them, there is a group of righteous people referred to as כל ענוי הארץ and whose behavior is presented to the addressed evildoers as a model to be followed. The speaker probably is a member of this group or at least sympathizes with it. Accordingly, both the historical-sociological picture and the theological message of the unit are totally different after the addition of the second כ. However, is it a well grounded textual change? The ancient versions do not support it. Even more important, there is no real reference to such a group in Zephaniah 1, except, perhaps, and only very indirectly in v. 18. Significantly, the term כל ענוי הארץ occurs in Ps 76:10 (see below), and there it refers to the people who will be saved by YHWH.[411]

Alternatively, if the MT is retained, then it is to be assumed that at least some part of verse 3 is an interpretative note on vv. 1-2. In order to

---

[409] For instance, according to Elliger the last בטרם לא phrase in v. 2 and the the first sentence in v. 3 (until פעלו) are secondary (see Elliger, 1951: 64-65). Irsigler considers secondary only the mentioned sentence in v. 3 (Irsigler, 1977: 116-17, 172). According to J. M. P. Smith, the text from בטרם לא יבוא (v. 2) to the end of v. 3 is secondary. The "dropping" of v. 3 in its entirety allows him to relate v. 1 and the first line of v. 2 to the Philistines' section. (See J. M. P. Smith: 213-15).

[410] See Rudolph,1975: 274; Krinetzki: 257, Edler:18.

[411] There are other proposals of textual emendations, for instance Ehrlich emends ענוי הארץ to עמי הארץ on the basis of Zeph 3:20. According to Ehrlich, "the peoples," not the Judeans, are those who are asked to seek YHWH, to seek righteousness, and humility. Accordingly, he interprets אשר משפט פעלו as a reference to God's use of "the peoples" in order to punish Judah. See Ehrlich 458-59.

evaluate this possibility, the language, as well as the message of the entire verse, has to be examined.

The idea that doing "good" is the right thing to do in order to avert YHWH's wrath is a commonplace in the OT.[412] The possibility that ethical behavior may be (אולי) useful in order to avoid the divine punishment, even in the "eve of the day of judgment", occurs also in Am 5:15 and cf. Dan 4:24.[413] The stress on the possible, but not necessary, character of any specific divine response to human behavior (see v. 3) occurs elsewhere in the OT (e.g., Am 5:15; 2 Kgs 19:4 //Isa 37:4; Exod 32:30).

The expression עני ארץ, according to the Murabba'at text,[414] occurs in Ps 76:10 and Isa 11:4. Both Isa 11:4 and Ps 76:10 are likely to be post-monarchic.[415] It is noteworthy that while the second part of Ps 76:10 is almost identical to a phrase in Zeph 2:3, the first part of the verse clearly recalls Zeph 3:8.

Unlike the well attested and general בקשו את ה' in v. 3a,[416] neither בקשו צדק nor בקשו ענוה (v. 3b) occurs elsewhere in prophetic literature, or in the entire OT. The pair צדק - ענוה occurs another time in the OT, in Ps 45:5, but whether it is a part of the original composition or the result of a messianic interpretation of kingship in the early days of

---

[412] The concept that "good deeds" and "walking in YHWH's ways" lead people to life and keep them away from YHWH's wrath is found all across the entire OT: Pentateuch, prophets, proverbs, psalms, most historiographical works, etc. The widespread acceptance of this concept and specially its problematic relation with human experience are central to Job, to certain Proverbs (e.g., Prov 24: 16, 19-20) and to a certain degree to the dtr. redactions of the books of Kings.

[413] It is possible that this "teaching" was related to rituals of repentance, where such instruction may have been given to the people (e.g., Am 5:14-15., cf. Dan 4:24). Compare with Akkadian S(h)urpu texts. They contain a long list of sins, many of them of moral character. The person, who is looking for forgiveness from the gods, has to confess them as a part of the ritual of penitence, in order to avoid the divine wrath. Even if they do not include instructions in positive languages, they are implied in the negative form of the confession. See Reiner, 1958: 1, 13-18 (Cf. the אשמנו, בגדנו... list in the Jewish liturgy of Yom Kippur; also cf. Jer 3:19-25, Pss 32, 103).

[414] The MT reads עני הארץ.

[415] See, for instance, Clements: 121-22 and Fohrer, 1970: 289.

[416] Cf. Exod 33:7; Deut 4:29; Hos 3:5 (probably non Hoseanic; cf. Buss, 1969: 70, 109), 5:6; Jer 50:4; Zech 8:21, 22; Ps 105:2 = 1 Chr 16:11; 2 Chr 11:16, 20:4 (without parallel in Kings).

the Second Temple period is open to discussion.[417] In any case, in Ps 45:5 these terms are not mentioned in relation to common people. Even the word ענוה occurs in Zeph 2:3, but nowhere else in prophetic literature. Significantly, it is attested in Prov 15:33; 18:12; 22:4; Ps 45:5 (see above).[418] It is worth noting that its occurrence in Prov 22:4 may explain why ענוה was singled out in Zeph 2:3. One reads in Prov 22:4: "the effect of humility (ענוה) is fear of the LORD, wealth, honor and life" (NJPSV). That is, ענוה is a (or the) human attitude that leads to the establishment of the correct relationship between YHWH and human beings. Its importance, therefore, is self-evident.

The term צדק occurs many times in different pairs with משפט (e.g., Deut 16:18; Hos 2:21; Ps 72:2, 89:15; 119:121; Prov 1:3; Qoh 5:7). Thus, the occurrence of משפט in second part of verse 3a is hardly surprising. The expression אשר משפטו פעלו, may recall Mic 6:8 (עשות משפט). But in Zeph 2:3 the root פעל occurs instead of עשה. The idiom עשה משפט occur more than twenty times in the OT[419] but פעל משפט only once, in Zeph 2:3. An analysis of the pattern of occurrence of verbal forms from the root פעל instead of the usual עשה forms shows that the former occur mainly, but not only, in wisdom literature, post monarchic psalms and post-monarchic material (e.g., Prov 30:20; Job 7:20, 36:23; Isa 43:13, 44:12,15; Ps 141:4).[420] The stress on צדק and the use of פעל instead of עשה in Zeph 2:3 calls attention to the form פֹּעֵל צֶדֶק which occurs only in Ps 15:2, a psalm whose setting is in a post-monarchic, non sacrificial early Jewish community.[421] In this respect it is worth noting that the term עניו, or closely related terms, occurs in many psalms whose probable setting is in the cult of such

---

[417] See Gerstenberger,1988: 186-90; Anderson: 346-49; Bardtke (BHS).

[418] For Ps 18:36 (// 2 Sam 22:36), see Anderson: 163 and the bibliography mentioned there. Cf. NJPSV, RSV. The meaning "humility" is contextually impossible there.

[419] E.g., Gen 18: 19,25; Deut 10:18; 2 Sam 8:15; 1 Kgs 3:28, 8: 45, 49,59, 10:9; Jer 5:1, 7:5, 9:23; Ezek: 45:9; Mic 6:8; Ps 9:5, 17, 119: 121, 146:7, 149:19; Prov 21:3, 7, 15.

[420] The expression פעל און counts for almost half of the occurrences of verbal forms from פעל.

[421] See Gerstenberger,1988: 86-89.

communities (e.g., Pss 10, 22, 25, 34, 37, 69, 76, 147).[422] Moreover, in these psalms both the motifs of צדק and משפט and the idea that God "saves," in this world, the righteous, who are those ענוים, are a commonplace.[423] Since Zeph 3:11-13 informs the reader that "a poor humble people" (עם עני ודל) will remain after the judgment, then it seems probable that in these communities, these "poor and humble people" were identified with "all the humble of the land" (כל ענוי הארץ), and accordingly with those who accepted the advice of v. 3b.

If one turns to the issue of the interpretation of received traditions by these post-monarchic communities, it seems clear that the main interpretative question for them was: How to understand, in their days, previous catastrophic announcements of judgment concerning the day of the wrath of YHWH .

These communities could not understand them as literally fulfilled in the past. Even without the information of Zeph 3:11-13, and other similar notes, their very existence was the most convincing proof that it was not the case. It seems that three alternatives remained to them:

(1) To denounce these announcements as false prophecy, and to consider the prophet to whom the announcements are attributed as a false prophet. If this were the case, these false prophecies would not be transmitted from generation to generation.

(2) To understand the prophecy as looking to a distant future. This alternative led to eschatological interpretations.

(3) To understand that the prophecy was partially fulfilled, or metaphorically fulfilled. Why so? Zeph 2:3 and the mentioned above Psalms, relate "salvation" to righteous ways.[424] If they assumed that in the past there were not only evildoers but also pious people, YHWH may not have destroyed them but saved them. But who are the pious? Taking

---

[422] See Ps 10:12,17, 22:27, 25:9, 34:3, 37:11, 69:33, 76:10, 147:6. On the setting of these psalms, see Gerstenberger,1988: 75,112-13, 121, 159-60.

[423] These ענוים are generally contrasted with ungodly, wicked, oppressors and wealthy people (see, for instance, Ps 10; 22:27-29; 34; 37; see Gerstenberger, 1988: 75).

[424] Although there is no claim that righteous ways lead necessarily and unequivocally to salvation (note the אולי in Zeph 2:3), there is a clear claim of relationship.

into consideration their communal point of view on ethics, divine reward, the meaning of history and the very fact that they had remained, one may conclude that "all the humble of the land" are suitable candidates.

3.3.4. Zeph 2:4

(a) The particle כי at the beginning of the verse is translated "for," mainly by those scholars who relate v. 4 to vv. 1-3 (or parts of it),[425] but כי may also be understood as "indeed", "certainly."[426] Moreover, the rhetorical use of כי at the beginning of a clause, in order to emphasize it, is widely attested in the OT.[427] Thus, one may conclude that the particle כי does not necessarily point to the close connectedness of the vv. 1-3 and v. 4, but to the contrary it may point to the beginning of a new literary unit.[428]

(b) According to a South-North, and then West-East axis (i.e., towards the Judean border) four Philistine cities are mentioned in v. 4: Gaza, Ashkelon, Ashdod, Ekron. Notes concerning the disaster that will befall an entire country are often written as a series of short notes describing the future situation in its mains cities and places (e.g., Isa 15; Jer 48:1-5, 49:3; Am 1:7-8). These short notes do not intend to be an exact and literal account of what will happen in each city but convey all together the sense of general disaster that will befell the country (see below). Accordingly, the specific contents of a note concerning the fate of a city may be dependent, or even mainly dependent, on literary concerns. For instance, it is self-evident that the expressions עזה עזובה תהיה and תעקר עקרון (Zeph 2:4) are based on paronomasia.[429] Thus, the question why

---

[425] E.g., J. M. P. Smith: 215. See also RSV, NRSV.

[426] See NJPSV. Sabottka proposes "Seht!" (Sabottka: 70).

[427] See Muilenburg, 1961.

[428] E.g., Ps 47:3; Isa 15:1.

[429] Cf. Hos 10:30; Mic 1: 10,13,15; Am 5:5; Zech 9:3. On paronomasia, see Alonso Schöckel, 1988: 30-31.

Ekron "shall be uprooted"[430] but Gaza[431] "shall be deserted" is not to be answered in historical terms, but only in literary terms. The case of Gaza and Ekron has clear implications concerning reading competence[432]: These notes are not supposed to be "historically reliable sources," neither for discerning specific Judean attitudes concerning individual foreign cities nor as trustworthy accounts of historical events that actually befell each of these non-Israelite cities.

The Philistine cities mentioned in Zeph 2:4 are those noted in Am 1:7-8; Jer 25:20; Zech 9:5-6.[433] The cities in Zeph 2:4 are grouped in two pairs that are identical to those in Jer 25:20, though their internal order is inverted. Gaza is the first city in three of these lists (Am 1:7; Zeph 2:4 and Zech 9:5) and the second in Jer 25:20 because of the inversion of the pair.

The clear paronomasia in the first and last verset has led several scholars to suggestions concerning the original paronomastic text of the other versets, especially the one referring to Ashdod. Certainly, a reading אשדוד בצהרים ישדדוה is as paronomastic as עקרון תעקר or עזה עזובה תהיה. But this argument leads to the conclusion that the present text is the most difficult reading. One may understand why a person may have tended to complete the paronomastic pattern but one can hardly understand how a scribe will destroy such a self-evident pattern

---

[430] The expression עקרון תעקר is unique in the OT. Words from the root עקר do not occur in any other announcement of judgment in the OT. The harshness of the announcement against Ekron led to the midrashic, "typological" equation of Ekron with Caesarea on the sea in a saying attributed to R. Abbahu; see b. Meg 6a.

[431] The English term "Gaza" goes back to the LXX transliteration of the name עזה. Since the LXX transliterated ע sometimes as "gamma" (e.g., Gaza) but sometimes omitted it at all (leading for instance, to the English name Jacob for the Hebrew יעקב), and since these transliterations follow, in general terms, the Arabic differentiation between ʿayin and ghayin, the data suggests that the letter ע stood for two phonemes. The same holds true concerning the letter ח. See Kutscher,1982: 17-18. These studies have obvious implication on the research concerning the sound value of these pieces.

[432] On reading competence and its conceptual importance in OT studies, see Barton, 1984: 11-19.

[433] These cities are the same cities mentioned as kingdoms in neo-Assyrian and neo-Babylonian sources (e.g., the account of the third campaign of Sennacherib, see *OIP* II l. 54, 60-75, III l. 31-34).

without noticing it.[434]   Moreover, neither Mic 1:10-16, nor Am 5:5;
neither Zech 9:3 nor Isa 10:28-30 shows only or even mainly
paronomastic puns on words, although they were possible, at least in
several cases.[435]

The language אשדוד בצהרים is probably a good example of *double
entendre* (see שֹׁדֵד בצהרים, "a destroyer at noonday," in Jer 15:8; cf. Ps
91:6).[436] Similar cases of *double entendre* occur in Zeph 2:5 (כרתים
גוי; cf. Ezek 25:16), and Zeph 3:1 (העיר היונה).

3.3.5. Zeph 2:5

(a) The expression חבל הים occurs only in Zeph 2:5,6. Perhaps there
is an intentional play on words based on different meanings of חבל,
namely, "sailor" (Ezek 27:8,20; cf. Jonah 1:6 and "mast" in Prov 23:34);
"destruction" (Mic 2:10) and "region" (e.g., Deut 3:4, 13,14; Josh 19:29).

The כרתים, "Cherethites," are associated with the Philistines here and
in Ezek 25:16.[437] In both cases, the Cherethites are associated with the
inhabitants of the shore, but in Ezekiel the term is חוף הים instead of

---

[434] Cf. Gerleman, 1942: 29. For a list of proposed emendations, see Zalcman 366; Gordis,
1987: 487; Gerleman, 1942: 29. The ancient versions do not support these proposals.

[435] For the explanation that the described fate of the cities (metaphorically, women) is to be
understood as an ascending scale of women's suffering, see Zalcman and Gordis, 1987.
According to Ball and Deissler the MT provides "a more balances assonance as the two
middle lines utilize the שׂ sound while the first and fourth lines employ paronomasia."
See Ball, 1972/1988: 101 and the bibliography mentioned there.

[436] One may also consider a probable play of meanings between אשדוד (cf. Prov 19:26 where
משדד may mean "drives away") and ירשׁה. See Thomas: 63, Rudolph, 1975: 277. But it is
worth noting that שדד occurs in a *piel* form in Prov 19:26.

[437] The LXX translates כרתים as Cretans, here and in Ezek 25: 16. The tradition according to
which the Philistines came from Crete is attested in Am 9:7 (cf. Jer 47:4; archaeological
data clearly indicate the existence of close relationship between the Mycenian world
[not only Crete] and the Philistines). However, Crete is named Caphtor (כפתר) in these
biblical texts and closely related names for Crete exist in Ugaritic, Akkadian and
Egyptian (see, for instance, KBL3). On the other hand, the existence of double names,
especially if they originated in different families of languages, cannot be ruled out (cf.
Hatti and Kharu). If כפתר indeed referred to Crete, then this verse would reflect a tradition
relating the Philistines to Crete. For a very positive assertion in this direction, see
Delcor. Kapelrud goes further to consider the "Cherethites" as the people of Crete
(instead of Philistines) and therefore an "unknown danger" for the Judeans in the days of
Zephaniah's preaching. See Kapelrud: 52-53, and esp. 76-77.

חבל הים (see above). The Cherethites are mentioned another eight times in the OT (1 Sam 30:1, 2 Sam 8:18, 15:18, 20:7, 23, 1 Kgs 38:44, 1 Chr 18:17). Most of these occurrences are in relation to the mercenary army of David. From the references one can learn that the Cherethites were not Israelites, but nothing more specific. Only the reference to נגב כרתי ("Cherethite Negev") in 1 Sam 30:14 points to a certain geographical area, namely, in the nearby of the Judean Negev and probably West of it. On the basis of other sources, it is clear that Philistines settled down not only in the sea shore but also in agricultural settlements and cities in the coastal hinterland and East of it (e.g., Gath, Ekron, and Ziklag, see also Gen 20, Gen 26). Thus, the pair "dwellers of the seashore - Cherethites" is either a simple case of double vocative (cf. Isa 1:4) or a kind of merism conveying the meaning: "the entirety of the Philistines"[438] or both (i.e., double function).

The expression גוי כרתים is an intentional play on words;[439] i.e., כרתים as a gentilic but also as a negative attribute.[440] Unlike the LXX, both the Vg. and Tg. Neb.[441] follow the adjectival meaning of the play on words and do not translate כרתים as a gentilic.[442]

(b) The phrase דבר ה' עליכם is considered a gloss by many scholars.[443] YHWH appears here in the third person, but in the first person in the last sentence in v. 5. The exact expression occurring in Zeph 2:5 (i.e., X - דבר ה' על) occurs in Zech 12:1, as a second "title" that follows the first one, משא. The redactional character of its occurrence in Zech 12:1 is suggested by the fact that the text that follows the title "the word of YHWH concerning Israel" (Zech 12:1), does not mention the

---

[438] For merism based on the polar opposition ים ("sea") and שדה (field), see Ezek 26:5-6; Ps 96:12; 1 Chr 16:32 (the explicit polar opposition "sea shore"-"West" is attested in Ugaritic); see Krasovec, 1977: 108-09.

[439] Cf. והכרתי את הכרתים in Ezek 25:16. Cf. Zeph 2:5.

[440] For "גוי + negative attributes" see note on Zeph 2:1, above.

[441] Also Aquila, Theodontion and Symmachus translate in a similar way. See also Gen. Rab. 28.5. See also Jerome on Zephaniah 2: 5-7.

[442] The same holds true for their respective translations of והכרתי את הכרתים in Ezek 25:16.

[443] See, for instance, J. M. P. Smith: 217; Elliger (BHS); Langhor, 1976:27; Edler: 107-07.

term Israel at all.[444]   Moreover, a very similar double superscription, משא דבר ה' אל ישראל, occurs in Mal 1:1. Since the use of the term משא in prophetic superscriptions is generally associated with "prophecies of judgment" (cf. Isa 13:1;14:28, 15:1, 17:1, 19:1, 21:1,11,13, 22:1, 23:1, 30:6; Nah 1:1; Hab 1:1; Zech 9:1), then its occurrence along with X - דבר ה' על in a late superscription suggests that the latter was probably interpreted more as "prophecy against X" than "prophecy concerning X." The phrase X - דבר ה' על in Zeph 2:5 has a contextual meaning of "decreed doom."

Alternatively, one may consider the entire verse as a literary הוי unit.[445] Zeph 2:5 opens with a הוי cry followed by a participle like, for instance, Isa 5:8, 10:1, 33:1, 45:10; Jer 22:13,14; Mic 2:1; Hab 2:9. The second vocative in Zeph 2:5, גוי כרתים clearly recalls the opening of the woe-unit in Isa 1:4. In most of the woe units the addressees appear in the second person, after the vocative phrase;[446] and see והאבדתיך in Zeph 2:5. The speaker in a הוי unit may be the "prophet" (e.g., Isa 5:8,10:4; Mic 2:1) or YHWH (Jer 22:13-14; 23:1). But because of the reference to YHWH in the third person in the phrase דבר ה' עליכם, if Zeph 2:5 is interpreted as a unit then the putative speaker can only be the prophet. What does the prophet say in this unit? First he says: דבר ה' עליכם, that is, a title (see above; cf. Zech 12:1), and also an interpretative key[447] for the subsequent speech. Following the title, the "prophet" quotes the divine speech: "Land of merchants, land of the Philistines." This quotation functions both as a vocative and as an indictment (see below). The announcement of judgment immediately follows as expected: " I will destroy you, no inhabitants will be left."[448] Certainly, prefixing titles as

---

[444] Israel is not mentioned in Zech 12-14.

[445] On הוי units see for instance, Roberts, 1982: 296-300; Hillers, 1983; Buss, 1978: 169 and the bibliography there; cf. Gerstenberger, 1964, esp. 251-52.

[446] See Roberts, 1982: 299-300.

[447] Cf. House: 129.

[448] According to this interpretation of the text, והאבדתיך is a perfect preceded by *waw* , that is not a part of *waw* consecutive construction. Such verbal form may occur in the apodosis to causal clauses or their equivalents (e.g., Obad 1:8); see GKC § 112 nn. Sabottka considers this *waw* emphatic. See Sabottka: 75-78.

interpretative keys for subsequent texts is more likely to be a written literary enterprise, as the widespread use of titles in the redactional levels of the prophetic books clearly shows. But in Zeph 2:5 the employment of titles goes beyond their common use and is described as an integral part of the prophetic speech. This use of the title suggests a writer and a community that was so used to titles that they could imagine prophets, flesh and blood, introducing their speeches to actual audiences by titles.

(c) The phrase כנען ארץ פלשתים is commonly emended to אכנעך ארץ פלשתים,[449] but some scholars have preferred to delete כנען as a late gloss.[450] Alternatively, Ehrlich attaches כנען to the preceding phrase, and accordingly he considers the entire phrase a reference to the putative (for Ehrlich real) fate of the Canaanites during, and after, Israel's (putative) conquest of the land.[451] The main reason for these proposals is that Philistia is nowhere else called Canaan in the OT.[452] But even Chaldea may be considered ארץ כנען when כנען means "merchant" (see Ezek 16:29).[453] If one considers this meaning of כנען then כנען ארץ פלשתים is either a sequence of two vocatives referring to the same addressee (cf. Isa 1:4; see above) or a regular nominal sentence, " The land of the Philistines is a land of merchants."[454] Such a description of Philistia is not neutral in Zeph 2:5. The doom announcement that follows clearly suggest a negative evaluation. The negative connotation of "merchant" already occurs in Zeph 1:10 and both

---

[449] See, for instance, Rudolph, 1975: 277; Edler: 18

[450] See, for instance, J. M. P. Smith: 217; cf. Elliger (BHS). Also the reading כי נענה has been proposed, see J. M. P. Smith: 223. None of the proposed emendations is supported by the ancient versions.

[451] Ehrlich: 459.

[452] Perhaps the reading of the Peshitta: "Canaan and the Land of the Philistines" is already an attempt to cope with this difficulty. Obviously, this attempt leads to another question, what is Canaan ? Some modern scholars say: Phoenicia (cf. Irsigler, 1977: 118 and the bibliography mentioned there). Although Phoenicia may be called Canaan (cf. Gen 10:15), and even though there are announcements of judgment against the Philistines and the Phoenicians in which they are mentioned together (see Jer 47:4; Joel 4:4-8), the Phoenicians are not mentioned elsewhere in the unit, unlike the Philistines. Moreover, Canaan does not necessarily mean Phoenicia; see below.

[453] Cf. Hos 12:8; Prov 31:24; Job 40:30; Isa 23:8; Zeph 1:10.

[454] See Gerleman, 1942: 30.

uses may point to the socio-economical thought of the writer/s of these two notes and (to a certain extent) of their audience. Indirectly, they may point to their social location.

(d) The language והאבדתי with YHWH in the first person, occurs elsewhere in the Latter Prophets in Jer 25:10; 49:38; Ezek 25:7,16, 30:13, 32:13; Obad 1:8; Mic 5:9. The expression מאין יושב occurs twice in Isaiah (Isa 5:9, 6:11), twice in Zephaniah (Zeph 2:5, 3:6) and nine times in the Book of Jeremiah (4:7, 26:9, 33:10, 34:22, 44:22, 46:19, 48:9, 51:29,37; cf. Jer 2:15, 9:10). This expression tends to appear along with the theme of the destruction of a city or cities (e.g., Isa 6:11; Jer 4:7, 26:9, 34:22, 46:19, 48:9, 51:37) and with the adjectives שמה or שממה (Isa 5:9, 6:11, Jer 4:7, 34:22, 44:22, 46:19, 48:9, 51:29,37). This pattern of occurrence suggests that Zeph 2:5 is not independent from Zeph 2:4. Significantly, the divine והאבדתי occurs also in Ezek 25:16, in the announcement of judgment against the Philistines. As mentioned above, Ezek 25:16 is the only other place in the OT in which the Philistines are mentioned together with the Cherethites. Moreover, both contain a reference to the dwellers on the sea-shore (although the language is slightly different, see above).[455]

3.3.6. Zeph 2:6

(a) Concerning the pattern of occurrence of חבל הים, see above. The LXX reads Crete instead of חבל הים.[456]   On the surface, the LXX

---

[455] Also cf. שארית in Ezek 25:16 and שארית in Zeph 2:7; see below.

[456] This LXX reading and the feminine verbal form היתה that may point to the feminine ארץ instead of the probable masculine חבל (cf. v. 7) have led to the proposal that חבל הים is a late addition (e.g., J. M. P. Smith: 218; G.A. Smith:62; Eiselen: 532; Elliger, 1951: 66; Elliger (BHS); Rudolph, 1975: 277). Gerleman has pointed out that the LXX reading does not point to a different Hebrew text (see below), and in any case a LXX reading can only be supportive evidence. The presence of the feminine form היתה, which is the other main support for the proposal that the expression is a gloss, has been explained by the fact that חבל הים is the name of a land, and therefore feminine, or by pointing to the influence of the subsequent feminine forms or both (see Sabottka: 78; Ball, 1972/1988:

reading can be explained on the basis of a Hebrew *Vorlage* characterized by the presence of the expression נות כרת and the absence of הים חבל. But כרת there cannot be understood as Crete. Gerleman[457] proposed that the LXX simply equates Cretans with "dwellers of the sea region " (ישבי חבל הים) on the basis of its understanding of Zeph 2:5; accordingly the LXX rendering Crete in v. 6 is only a matter of choice of words—based on a certain understanding of the text—and therefore does not point to the existence of a different Hebrew Vorlage.[458]

(b) The exact meaning, and even the "original" text of נְוֹת כְּרֹת רֹעִים is controversial.[459] The idiom נאות הרעים[460] occurs in Am 1:2 and its meaning is clear, namely, " the pastures of the shepherds"(cf. Jer 9:9, 23, 25:37; Joel 2:19,20, 2:22, Ps 23:2, 65:13; Lam 2:2). The word כַּר means also "pastures" (e.g., Isa 30:23).[461] The gender of the noun כר seems to be masculine in Isa 30:23 and in Ps 65:14. Accordingly, one may expect that its construct form would be כרי. However, such a form would spoil the excellent repetition of consonantal sounds set up by the pair כרתים and כרֹת. Moreover, one may note that some masculine nouns show the ות- ending in their plural construct form, even if they have well-attested construct plural forms with the regular masculine ending (e.g., the form יְמֵי is attested hundreds of times in the OT but ימות occurs in Deut 32:7 and Ps 90:15);[462] moreover some masculine nouns have plural and construct forms ending with ות- instead or in addition to the regular masculine endings (e.g., דור, דורים, דרת [see Ps 145:4; Isa 51:8; Gen

---

303; cf. Radak). To the degree that these explanations hold so does the non-gloss understanding of חבל הים.

[457] Gerleman, 1942: 31-32.

[458] The Peshitta mentions both "the sea-region" and Crete, perhaps on the basis of its own understanding of the LXX that led it to the assumption that כרת in v. 6 means Crete. See Gerleman, 1942:30-31.

[459] See, for instance, Ehrlich: 459; J. M. P. Smith: 218, 223-24; G. A. Smith: 62; Ball, 1972/1988:103-04; Rudolph, 1975: 277; Edler:68; Barthelémey, 1980: 375-76.

[460] נאות and נות are two spelling variants of the same word. On spellings omitting א see Andersen-Forbes: 85-90.

[461] For כרת as a form of כר, in v. 6, see Sabottka: 78-79; Kselman, 1970: 581; Irsigler, 1977: 179.

[462] See GKC § 74n.

9:12], or אריות, אריה, אריים [see Jer 4:7; Zeph 3:3;1 Kgs 10:20]).[463] Furthermore, some words do not always occur with the same grammatical gender (e.g., כַּר that is masculine in Judg 7:16;1 Kgs 18:34 but feminine in 1 Kgs 17:14, 16; Qoh 12:6).[464]

If כרת רעים and נות רעים are synonymous, then it is likely that the present reading is a conflation of either two traditional variants (as in 2 Kgs 11:13) or, and more likely, of a reading כרת רעים (note the repetitions of sounds) and its explanatory gloss (i.e., נות).[465]

The pastures are mentioned together with the folds of the flock (גדרות צאן). Since the flock can be either in the pasture or in the enclosure, the combination of the two conveys the idea of entirety. In addition, it seems likely that "enclosure for flock" stands as an equivalent to the "enclosure for human beings", i.e., cities. The land of cities will be a land of flock enclosures (and of pastures for the shepherds).

Whatever the exact meaning of נְוֹת כְּרֹת רֹעִים, there is no doubt concerning the general meaning of v. 6: The sea-region, or the "land of the Philistines," which is now a country of cities, will become a pasture land, because of YHWH's judgment. The dichotomy city dwellers-shepherds, and probably also cities- enclosures for the flock, is worth noting. The implied conception here is that the destruction of the city, along with its social and political institutions, advances pastoralism. A similar conception occurs, for instance, in Ezek 25:5-6, where the Arabs are the shepherds that will settle down in the Ammonite territory. Who are the shepherds that will settle down in Philistia? Verse 7 brings the answer.

---

[463] See GKC § 74 m.

[464] See Meyer II: 42. For a similar rejection of the objections against כר-כרת based on the gender of כר in its other biblical occurrences, see Sabottka: 78-79.

[465] The alternative, i.e., an original construct chain of three nouns in which the first and the second are synonymous, is very unusual. On conflate readings see Talmon, 1976 and the bibliography mentioned there.

3.3.7. Zeph 2:7

(a) The word חבל in v. 7 has been commonly understood as "lot" (i.e., "portion;" cf. Deut 32:9; Ps 105:11).[466] Alternatively, it has been proposed that the original reading was חבל הים as in v. 5.[467] Those scholars who support the second alternative tend to consider חבל הים a gloss in v. 6, because חבל הים will occur as a grammatically feminine expression in v. 6 and as a masculine one in v. 7, if the MT חבל is emended to חבל הים. Significantly, neither proposal explains the third person plural pronominal suffix in עליהם, which supposedly refers to חבל, or to חבל הים.

Whether the MT reading is retained or הים is added, the general meaning of the phrase is clear, Philistine territory will be given to "remnant of the house of Judah" (שארית בית יהודה).

(b) The expression שארית בית יהודה occurs only in Zeph 2:7. Even its general form, i.e., שארית בית-X occurs only in Zeph 2:7 and in Isa 46:3. In the latter X means Israel, and the occurrence of בית ישראל instead of the expected ישראל is probably related to the occurrence of expression בית יעקב in the first verset of the same line.

The expression שארית יהודה occurs in the Book of Jeremiah (Jer 40:15, 42:15,19, 43:5, 44:12, 14, 28; cf. Jer 40:11), but nowhere else in the entire OT. Moreover, it appears only in those chapters of the Book of Jeremiah that describe Gedaliah's community, its collapse and the subsequent exile of Johanan son of Kareah. In these chapters, the term

---

[466] See, for instance, Gerleman, 1942: 33-34; Barthelémey, 1980: 376-77; NJPSV. This understanding of חבל already occurs in Tg. Neb.

[467] See, for instance, Duhm: 68; Rudolph, 1975: 277; Watts, 1975: 168; Elliger (BHS); RSV; NRSV. This proposal is supported by the LXX, as well as the Peshitta. The independence of the Peshitta rendering, however, is highly questionable.
One may conjecture that חבל הים in v. 6 is due to a former scribal note (gloss), mentioning the reading חבל הים in relation to חבל in v.7, and that later on the note entered into the text and before the phrase to which it originally referred (see Rudolph, 1975: 277). Obviously, this conjecture cannot be proved.
For a third alternative, see Sabottka:80 and the bibliography mentioned there. Sabottka's proposal, namely, that חבל means "flock" is based on Ugaritic but the only possible and very questionable biblical support for his rendering of חבל is Job 39:3.

שארית יהודה refers to those Judeans who either remained in Judah after the destruction of Jerusalem or returned to Judah in Gedaliah's days.[468] The more common, and general, expression שארית ישראל occurs in Jer 6:9, 31:7, Ezek 9:8, 11:13; Mic 2:12; Zeph 3:13; 1 Chr 12:39 [שרית], 2 Chr 34:9. Significantly, the terms ישראל שארית and שארית יהודה neither occur together nor seem to have been interchangeable.

(c) The expression עליהם ירעון . . . is probably the most difficult interpretative point in verse 7. The "remnant of the house of Judah" may be the subject of ירעון, as the context requires, because שארית is a collective noun and because although it is a feminine noun it represents also masculine persons (cf. Am 1:8).[469]

The verbal form רעה על occurs elsewhere in Isa 49:9; Cant 1:8 (cf. also Ezek 34:13). In Isa 49:9 the verb is intransitive and the preposition is locative, thus the verse says: "they shall pasture on (along) the roads;" in Cant 1:8 the verb is transitive and the preposition is locative. The subject of both the transitive and the intransitive רעה may be animals (e.g., Gen 30:31; Isa 11:7) or metaphorically, Israel (e.g., Ezek 34:13; Isa 49:9). In the present context, the verbal form ירעון על in Zeph 2:7 is intransitive (cf. ירבצון in the second part of the sentence, which is also intransitive).[470] Thus, taking into account that the subject of ירעון is "the remnant of the house of Judah" (see above), עליהם ירעון in v. 7 clearly means: "the remnant of the house of Judah shall pasture on them."[471] The problem is the identification of "them."

---

[468] Jer 43:5 claims that the entire שארית יהודה went to Egypt along with Johanan son of Kareah. This is an hyperbole and even Jer 44:12, 14, 28 implies that not all the Judeans leave to Egypt. From a historical point of view, there is no doubt that Judeans remained in Judah, even after Johanan son Kareah.

[469] See GKC § 145 b,e.

[470] The pair רעה - רבץ is intransitive if both verbs occur in the *qal* pattern and have the same subject (see Ezek 34:14). This pair, with an intransitive meaning occurs also in Zeph 3: 13. Compare ורבצו ואין מחריד in Zeph 3:13 with Job 11:19 and Isa 17:2. The image of Isa 17:2 recalls Zeph 2:6-7 but with one main difference, the "flock" in Zeph 2:6-7 is "the remnant of the house of Judah."

[471] Sabottka, Kselman and R. L. Smith propose to revocalize the MT עֹלֵיהֶם into עֻלֵיהֶם , i.e, "their young," or perhaps, "their babies" (see Isa 49:15; 65:20). See Sabottka: 80-81;

Theoretically, שארית בית יהודה may be the antecedent but in such case it can be neither the subject of ירעון nor the subject of ירבצון. One may perhaps think about the possibility of an indefinite subject for ירעון (implying God ?) and שארית בית יהודה as object, but such idea should be dismissed because of ירבצון. If שארית בית יהודה cannot be the "them," who can be? גדר, as well as כר is a masculine noun and the entire phrase: "the pastures of the shepherds and the folds for the flocks" is the best candidate for the wanted "them."[472]

(d) יפקדם ה' אלהיהם ושב שבותם (*ketiv*)

     יפקדם ה' אלהיהם ושב שביתם (*qere*).

Such pairs of *qere-ketiv* (*yod* vs. *waw*) are relatively common (several tens)[473] and according to Andersen-Forbes, they may be the legacy of the Herodian era.[474] The LXX, the Vg; the Peshitta and Tg. Neb. render captivity or exile for שבות/שבית in Zeph 2:7. Also traditional interpreters consider this phrase a clear reference to the "coming back from the Babylonian exile."[475] Obviously, they did not deduce from such an interpretation that the prophecy is post-exilic; for them, a prophecy to be fulfilled in the Babylonian exile was congruent with a dating in the days of Josiah and Zephaniah's authorship.

In general terms modern scholarship does not attempt to distinguish between the term שבית, which may be spelled שבות in the *ketiv*, and שבות. The very existence of *qere-ketiv* variants, such as cases of *ketiv* שבית but *qere* שבות (e.g., Jer 29:14, 49:39; Ezek 39:25; Job 42:10; Lam 2:14) and the explicit *qere* שבית for a word already spelled שבות

Kselman, 1970; R. L. Smith: 133,134. The fact that in almost all cases עליהם means the preposition על + the pronominal suffix, the existence of an attested verbal form רעה על, and the absence of any other reference to the "babies" in the text point against the proposed emendation. The problem with עליהם ירעון is neither grammatical nor semantical but contextual.

[472] Cf. Gerleman, 1942: 34. The emendation of text from עליהם to על הם (see, for instance, Elliger (BHS); Rudolph, 1975: 277; House: 129) although technically possible and contextually sensible, seems unnecessary.

[473] See, for instance, משוסה - משסה in Isa 42:24.

[474] See Andersen- Forbes: 149.

[475] E.g., Ibn Ezra, Radak, Abrabanel, Calvin.

but never שבות (e.g., Ps 85:2,126:4; Zeph 2:7) suggest that the words
were not simply interchangeable. If there was a difference, what kind of
difference was it ? The *ketiv* (without *qere* note) שבית in Num 42:10, as
well as the *qere* שבית in Jer 29:14, suggests that שבית is strongly
related to exile, captivity. Moreover, the *qere* שבות for the *ketiv* שבית
in Job 42:10, a place in which the word cannot imply exile, seems to
support this suggestion.[476] But, one should be cautioned that the *qere*
שבות for only three out of the five occurrences of שבית in Ezek 16:53
cannot be explained in these terms. Moreover, in Ezek 29:14, which also
seems to point to the meaning "exile, captivity," reads שבות with no *qere*
variant. Thus, it seems that no reliable systematic differentiation of שבות
and שבית can be drawn.[477] Obviously, this conclusion does not prove,
or even suggest, the opposite, i.e., that שְבוּת/שבית are systematically
interchangeable with שבות or that שְבוּת/שבית does not refer to "exile,
captivity."

In modern scholarship, two main approaches concerning the meaning of
the expression שוב שבית or שוב שבות have been developed.
According to one of these approaches (hereafter, the first approach), the
expression contains a reference to captivity, and in general terms conveys
the meaning of "return from the captivity." According to the other
(hereafter, the second approach), it conveys a general meaning of
"restoring a past fortune," "reversal of a previous judgment."[478]
Although the second approach implies a conception of a lost well being, it
does not necessarily imply either captivity in general or the Babylonian
exile in particular.

---

[476] Also the apparent relationship between שביה and שבית may support this suggestion.

[477] In addition, one may wonder to what extent the reading שבית reflected in the *qere* and in
the vocalization of the *ketiv* text, is not the result of an interpretative reading of a
consonantal שבות.

[478] Certainly, the expression refers either to the "image (concept) of the exile and the
related events" or to "the reversal of an image of previous judgment, misfortune." In
neither case does the expression refer to historical events "as they were." Any reference
to "previous judgment, misfortune" or "exile, captivity" in the following discussion is
to be understood according to this note.

While שבית in Job 42:10 (*ketiv* שבית; *qere* שבות)[479] does not point
to exile and שבית in Num 21:29 clearly points to captivity, the vast
majority of the occurrences of שבית/שבות can be interpreted either way.
Even more, insofar as it concerns post-monarchic literature, the two
approaches actually converge in any case in which the text deals with the
fate of Israel (or Judah) and not with the fate of a particular individual.
This is so because the theme of the return from the exile is not be
understood in a narrow literal sense.   For instance, if שביתם
שב שבותם/שב means "will bring them back from the exile," it is
obvious that such hopeful expression implies that they will be returned in
order to enjoy some kind of well being and, obviously, there will be a turn
in their fortunes. Beyond that, the hope expressed by the reversal of the
exilic conditions was a clear expression of either a general longing for
"restoration," which did not end even with the establishment of the Second
Temple, and even centuries thereafter continued to influence Second
Temple thought,[480] or a longing for the establishment of a new and ideal
reality (e.g., Jer 32:3 6-41),[481] or both.   In any case, the idea of the
reversal of the exile was not narrowed down to express only the physical
settlement of some previous deportees. Moreover, the interpretation of
שוב שבות as "reversal of judgment" implies that there has been a
misfortune, a judgment. One can safely assume that for an exilic or post-
exilic writer, and his/her community, the most significant misfortune that
befell Israel, as a whole, was the exile and the related events. Thus, the
second approach leads to the first just as the first leads to the second.

The convergence of the two proposed meanings, however, is limited to
the exilic and post-exilic literature. Since references to the return from
exile are commonly dated to the exilic and post-exilic period, the
interpretation that claims that the phrase שבות/שבית שוב does not
necessarily point to the exile, even if the text refers to Israel or Judah,

---

[479] See above.

[480] The Jerusalemite community in the days of Ezra is called נולה in Ezra 9:4, 10:4, 8. Cf.
Ezra also 9: 4-9; 1 Mac 14:41.

[481] On Jer 32: 36-41, see Carroll, 1986: 628-30.

allows a pre-exilic dating. If this pre-exilic dating is proposed, then a pre-exilic judgment (misfortune) stands in the background of the text.[482] This background is obviously different from the one proposed by the approach that from the very beginning related the expression to the exile.[483]

What is the background in Zeph 2:7? Obviously, the answer cannot be given on the basis of this phrase alone. One can only note in addition to the textual and comparative comments made above that the general image of Zeph 2:7, as well as the occurrence of the pair ב רבץ- על/אל רעה (see above) recalls Ezek 34:13-15, a piece which presumes the exile. It is worth noting that Ezek 34:13-15 is preceded by וערפל ענן ביום שם נפצו אשר המקומת מכל אתהם והצלתי ("I will rescue them from all places where they have been scattered on a day of clouds and thick darkness" (RSV); cf. Zeph 1:15). One may also compare שבותם שב in Zeph 2:7 with the similar expression, שבותיכם את בשובי in Zeph 3:20. See notes on Zeph 3:20.

3.3.8. Zeph 2:8

(a) The word גידוף occurs elsewhere only in Isa 43:28 and Isa 51:7. The pair גידוף - חרפה occurs in Zeph 2:8 and Isa 51:7. The word גדופה occurs along with חרפה in Ezek 5:15 and other forms of the general pair גדף- חרף (in the *piel* pattern) occur in 37:23 (//2 Kgs 19:22) and Ps 44:17. Further words from the root גדף in the *piel* pattern—the only one attested verbal pattern of גדף—occur in Num 15:30; Isa 37:6 (//2 Kgs 19:22); Ezek 20:27.

---

[482] Obviously, such a pre-exilic dating cannot be based on the thesis that שוב שבות/שבית does not necessarily point to an exilic or post-exilic dating. Even if the thesis is correct, it will only *allow* a pre-exilic dating.

[483] For a summary of the scholarly discussion on שבות/שבית in the last century, as well as a reappraisal of the question, see Bracke, 1985. See also, for instance, Dietrich, 1925; Borger, 1954; Holladay, 1958; Soggin, 1976, and specially concerning Zeph 2:7, Irsigler, 1977: 180-81 and the bibliography mentioned there.

(b) The verbal form X-על גדל in the *hiphil* pattern occurs in Jer 48:26, 42; Ezek 35:13; Ps 38:17, 41:10; 55:13; Job 19:5 and Zeph 2:8, 10. In most of the cases the meaning is clear: "to boast against someone" or "to vilify someone" (e.g., Jer 48:26, 42; Ezek 35:13; Ps 55:13;[484] Job 19:5). X means YHWH in most of the occurrences of this expression in the prophetic literature (Jer 48:26, 42, Ezek 35:13, and "the people of YHWH ZEVAOT" stands in the locus of YHWH in Zeph 2:10. In its three occurrences in Psalms (Ps 38:17, 41:10; 55:13) X means the first person of the Psalm, and Job is the one against whom the others speak in Job 19:5. Nowhere else but in Zeph 2:8 X does mean border or territory.[485] This pattern of occurrence and meaning, along with the attested meaning "to make great" for גדל in its *hiphil* pattern (e.g., Am 8:5; Ezek 24:9), have led to two approaches. According to the first, the Ammonites and Moabites enlarged their mouth, according to the second they enlarged their territory. Rashi, and Ibn Ezra pointed to the first alternative; Radak and Abrabanel supported the second. Calvin knows the "mouth" alternative but rejects it in favor of the "territory" alternative; today many modern scholars think the other way.[486]

Certainly, the close relationship between וינדילו על גבולם and עמי חרפו את favors the idea of boasting/vilifying (cf. Ps 55:13). Moreover, the closest antecedent to the pronominal suffix in גבולם is עמי (my [YHWH's] people; i.e., a collective noun that can be referred to in the third person plural).[487] Furthermore, הגדיל על pointing to territorial expansion is unattested. To sum up: the most likely translation reads, "(Moab and Ammon) made boasts against their territory" (RSV, NRSV). But, what does it mean to boast against a territory? The answer probably

---

[484] Equivalent to חרף as in Zeph 2:8.

[485] Sabottka proposes that על נבולם means "auf meinem Berg." נבל means "mountain" or "hill" (Heb. הר) in Ugaritic (cf. Arabic), and perhaps also in Ps 78:54. Sabottka considers the מ at the end of נבולם an enclictic *mem*. See Sabottka: 84-85.

[486] E.g., J. M. P. Smith: 226; Ball, 1972/1988: 292; Rudolph, 1975, 275,77; see also RSV, NJPSV. For the opposite position, see, for instance, Watts, 1975: 169; R. L. Smith: 133-34; Valverde- Schöckel (Nueva Biblia Española).

[487] See GKC § 135 p. The LXX reads "my."

lies in a similar text in Ezek 35:12, לאמר שממה לנו נתנו לאכלה
שמעתי את כל נאצותיך אשר אמרת על הרי ישראל ("I have heard
all the taunts you had uttered against the hills of Israel: 'They have been
laid waste; they have been given to us as to devour'."). Thus, הגדיל על
is probably another case of *double entendre*.

The description of the behavior of the Ammonites and Moabites here,
resembles the description of the Ammonites in Ezek 25:2-6 (after the
destruction of Jerusalem and the exile). The image of the Ammonites as
those who will be punished for taking Israel's territory occurs in Jer 49:1-
6 and Am 1:13, but is quite uncommon in reference to other peoples.
While announcements of judgment against Ammon tend to refer to
territorial encroachment (e.g., Am 1:13-15; Jer 49:1-6; cf. Judg 11:12-
28), announcements of judgment against Moab tend to mention its pride,
its boastful attitude (e.g., Isa 16:6, 25:11; Jer 48:26). Both themes are
combined in Zeph 2:8.[488]

While Ammon and Moab are frequently mentioned one after the other
(e.g., Am 1:13-2:3; Jer 48,49:1-6), it is unusual to find them together in a
full fledged announcement of judgment as in Zeph 2:8-9. The only other
example is Ezek 25:8-11, and there their occurrence together is probably
the result of redactional activity. The case in Zeph 2:8-9 is different as the
structure of parallel references in vv. 8,9 clearly shows.

It is noteworthy that in the series of announcements of judgment against
the nations in Zephaniah 2, only concerning Ammon and Moab, the
grounds for the judgment are related to their attitude towards "the people
of YHWH." In this respect, one may note that Ammon, because of its
geographical position, was not able to annex Judean territory. The most
Ammon could have done was to send (along with Moab)[489] bands against

---

[488] Whether these themes reflect somehow historical circumstances (and which historical
circumstances) or whether there are only literary stereotypes is a main interpretative
question. See the commentary section

[489] The only other case in which Ammon and Moab are mentioned together as attacking
monarchic Judah is 2 Chr 20. The account in 2 Chr 20 has no parallel in the Book of
Kings.

Judah as it is mentioned in 2 Kgs 24:2, in relation to Jehoiakim's rebellion.[490]

3.3.9. Zeph 2:9

(a) The expression ה' צבאות אלהי ישראל occurs elsewhere in 2 Sam 7:27, Isa 21:10, 37:16 (but not in the parallel account in 2 Kgs 19:15); 1 Chr 17:24 and more than thirty times in the Book of Jeremiah. However, the expression נאם ה' צבאות shows a different pattern of occurrence (Isa 14:22, 23, 17:3, 22:25; Jer 8:3 [not in LXX Jer], 25:29 [not in LXX Jer], 30:8, 49:26 [only נאם ה' in LXX Jer]; Nah 2:14, 3:5; Zeph 2:9; Hag 1:9, 2:4,8,9, 23; Zech 1:3,16,3:9, 10, 5:4, 8:6,11, 13:2, 7).[491] The function of the entire note (נאם ה' צבאות אלהי ישראל) is to identify the speaker in the unit, and by means of this identification to legitimate and to stress the validity of announcement. Thus, the presence of the common expression נאם ה' is essential to the role of the note, or in other words, נאם ה' belongs to the compositional level of the note.[492] It is worth noting that this is one of the few cases in which the conclusions based only on the function of a note are supported by different kinds of data. In the OT, the expression חי אני is followed by נאם ה' in all of its occurrences (see Num 14:28 [P]; Isa 49:18; Jer 22:24; 46:18; Ezek 5:11, 14:16,18,20, 16:48, 17:16, 18:3, 20:3, 31, 33, 33:11, 34:8, 35:6,11; Zeph 2:9),[493] but three (see Num 14:21, Ezek 17:19, 33:27).

---

[490] Ammon and Moab were also among the lands were Judeans took refuge immediately after the Babylonian conquest (Jer 40:11) and later Ishmael son of Nethaniah and his group crossed over to the Ammonites. According to Josephus (*Ant.* 10.9.7 § 181), Nebuchadnezzar fought against the Ammonites and Moabites in his 23th. year(cf. Jer 52:30), i.e., 582/1 BCE. The reason of Nebuchadnezzar's campaign was most likely rebellion.

[491] Moreover, it seems that the word צבאות entered in the LXX textual tradition only at a late stage (cf. Jer 49:26). Cf. Irsigler, 1977: 181 and the bibliography mentioned there; Elliger (BHS).

[492] The location of the note in the divine utterance, namely, shortly after the first divine words, is quite common (e.g., Jer 1:15, 16:16; Am 9:7, 8; Nah 2:14, 3:5).

[493] Jer 46:18 and Ezek 20:3 in a slightly modified form.

This pattern indicates that it is much more likely that אני חי entered the text with נאם ה' than without it, for in such case one would need to explain why the writer wrote in an unusual way. Moreover, since the expression נאם ה' צבאות אלהי ישראל (i.e., as if צבאות were an addition to Zeph 2:9) occurs nowhere in the Latter Prophets except in Isa 17:6,[494] one may assume that this expression is less likely to occur than a simple נאם ה' or צבאות ה' נאם. Significantly, the term צבאות ה' occurs in the Book of Zephaniah only in Zeph 2:9 and 2:10, and צבאות נאם ה' tends to occur more in late prophetic literature than in commonly considered monarchic prophetic literature (see above). The difference in the pattern of occurrence of נאם ה' צבאות and צבאות אלהי ישראל ה' suggests—and only suggests—an interesting convergence of Jeremianic style with some relatively typical expressions of late prophecy. The addition of אלהי ישראל to one of the common terms נאם ה' or נאם ה' צבאות is probably related to compositional reasons that are discussed in the commentary section.[495]

The biblical phrase for total destruction is אלהים את סדם ואת עמרה מהפכת. Such level of destruction leaves the country unsuitable for human living forever (see Deut 29:22; Isa 13:19-22; Jer 49:18, 50:40; cf. Isa 1:9).[496]

Although the exact meaning of the hapax ממשק חרול is open to discussion,[497] both the reference to "salt"[498] (made by the expression

---

[494] It occurs only one other time in the OT, in 1 Sam 2:30. Significantly, this verse is one of the most important interpretative keys of the deuteronomistic history as a whole. According to 1 Sam 2:30, YHWH says that although he has emphatically declared (אמור אמרתי) that the House of Eli will serve him forever (יתהלכו לפני עד עולם), now YHWH says: "Far from me; for those who honour me I will honour and for those who despise me..." (RSV). The implications of such position concerning the divine promise to David and his house are obvious.

[495] See commentary on Zeph 2:8-10.

[496] Deut 29:22; Isa 1:9,13: 19-22; Jer 49:18, 50:40 do not antecede deuteronomic/ deuteronomistic literature. A different image of the events of Sodom and Gomorrah appears in Am 4:11.

[497] The LXX turns ממשק into Damascus. Damascus is mentioned nowhere in Zephaniah and this reading is probably due to an inner Greek textual corruption. See Gerleman, 1942: 38, cf. Rudolph, 1975: 277. The word חרול occurs in Prov 24:31 and Job 30:7 and there the context points to some kind of undesirable weeds or thorns. מכרה is commonly

מכרה מלח which is another hapax) and the explicit expression
"desolation forever" (ושממה עד עולם) confirm the idea that in Zeph 2:9
the theme of "Sodom and Gomorrah" carries its usual meaning. Thus,
one may conclude the language seems unusual but not the meaning of the
line.

(b) The expression ינחלום (qere גויי) עמי יבזום ויתר גוי
שארית[499] introduces a new element. The "remnant of my (YHWH"s)
people" will plunder them and shall possess them." To whom does this
"them" refer? There are three possible answers: (a) the Ammonites and the
Moabites (see v. 8),[500] (b) the land of Ammon and the land of Moab (see
v. 9), (c) intentional double entendre. The verb בזז may take persons as
well as places as its direct object.[501] The verb נחל does not necessarily
imply territorial possessions but this is the case in most of its occurrences,
except for those in the Book of Proverbs.[502] The territorial connotations
of נחל turns the two versets into an ongoing emphatic line: not only that
"my people" will plunder the land, but also they will take it as their

---

either related to כרה, "to dig", and therefore מכרה is considered to mean "pit" or to the
Akkadian *karu*, "heap", and accordingly מכרה is translated as "heap."
An indication of the severity of the problems involved in the clarification of the
specific meaning of the expression ממשק חרול ומכרה מלח is Ehrlich's note saying that of
all these terms he only knows (for sure) what מלח is and the (certain) explanation of
these words has to wait until the coming of the prophet Elijah (see Ehrlich: 460). For
less agnostic remarks and proposals concerning the meaning of these phrases, see, for
instance, Gerleman, 1942: 37-39; Ball, 1972/1988: 106-07; Rudolph, 1975: 277;
Barthélemy, 1980: 377; see also Irsigler, 1977: 181 and the bibliography mentioned
there.

[498] Cf. Jer 17:6; Ezek 47:11; Ps 107: 33-34; Job 39:6. Also cf. Judg 9:45 and see Gevirtz,
1963.

[499] *Ketiv* גוי, Leningrad Codex *qere* גויי.The masoretic *ketiv* is one of the few cases of
defective spelling of î at the end of the word, see GKC § 8k; Andersen-Forbes: 111. See
also Radak and *Minhat Shai* on Zeph 2:9. GKC also mentions that, perhaps, the
spelling in Zeph 2:9 is the result of an error due to the preceding י. At any case, the
meaning is clear, "my people." The expression יתר גוי is parallel and synonymous with
שארית עמי. The word יתר is equivalent to שארית and גוי to עמי (see, for instance,Radak,
Altschuler, and most if not all modern scholars).

[500] Cf. J. M. P. Smith: 227-28; Irsigler, 1977: 122

[501] For human beings as its direct object see, for instance, Isa 10:2, 11:14, 17:14; Jer
30:16; for places, see, for instance, Gen 34:27; 2 Kgs 7:16; Isa 24:3. The root בז is
generally related with defeat in war, but significantly no military language is mentioned
in Zeph 2:8-9.

[502] E.g., Prov 3:35, 11:29, 14:18, 28:10.

inheritance. The stress on the reversal in the fate of Israel on one hand and on Ammon, along with Moab, in the other (see below), suggests a second dimension, the Ammonites and Moabites have acted against "my people"; "the remnant of my people" will not only plunder them but also disinherit them. That is, the Ammonites and Moabites had a temporary achievement at the expense of "my people;" but "the remnant of my people" will have a constant one (נחלה) at their expense. Thus, images of territory and its people merged together and convey a meaning that none of them alone can bring to the text.[503]

The question, however, is what will the " remnant of my people" inherit?[504] A barren land? This interpretation is very unlikely.[505] But if this land is worthy of living, what about the statement in the first part of v. 9?[506] Certainly, one may think about a two-stage fulfillment of the announcement (cf. Isa 58:12, 61:4)[507] but one may also think of a two-stage composition, especially because the horizon of vv. 8-9 (without . . . שארית עמי) does not include "Israel's" taking the possessions of Moabites and Ammonites.[508] Moreover, although a similar idea occurs in Zeph 2:7, the clear difference between שארית בית יהודה and עמי שארית (see below), both in meaning and in their pattern of occurrence cannot be overlooked.[509]

(c) The expression שארית עם referring to "Israel" occurs in Zeph 2:9; Hag 1:12, 14, 2:2; Zech 8:6,11,12; referring to the rest of Gedaliah's

---

[503] It is noteworthy that this *double entendre* is kept in most modern translations and it is so intelligible that even "popular" commentaries find no reason to explain it.

[504] Or at the very least, "will disinherit the Moabites and the Ammonites," see R. L. Smith: 134. But even this translation points to an implied remnant's ownership.

[505] Certainly to possess (נחל) a land was not understood as having a title of property and living elsewhere. See, for instance, Ps 69:37.

[506] Perhaps this is one of the reasons that caused Radak, who as most of the traditional commentators commonly considered these kind of announcements as references to the return from the Babylonian exile, to wonder if this is case concerning this special prophecy and to conclude without ruling out the possibility that the prophecy refers to the messianic days.

[507] To a large extent an "actualization" of Radak's line of thought.

[508] Cf. Rudolph, 1975: 281-82; Renaud, 1986:15.

[509] For a different approach, see Renaud, 1986:15.

community in Jer 41:16; and referring to those who are not included in the category of "heads of father's houses" in Neh 7:71.

It seems likely that the writer employed the term עמי in Zeph 2:9 in order to stress the theme of the reversal (cf. חרפו את עמי, v. 8, see above).[510]

(d) The expression יתר גוי occurs nowhere else with a similar meaning.[511] The use of the expressions שארית עמי and יתר גוי make the claim of the text unequivocal: Those who will possess former Moabites and Ammonites possessions are not "my people" but the "remnant of my people." A situation of strong distress before the "good days" is clearly envisaged. Those scholars who consider the entire text of Zephaniah, or most of it, as an address given by the prophet Zephaniah in the days of Josiah have to conclude, that the prophet spoke about an unavoidable doom for Judah. Only a few, a remnant will be able to survive, and to enjoy glorious days in the future. Thus, these scholars have to sustain the view that the prophet even when he mentions the expected fall of foreign nations is not providing any hope for most of the people. Accordingly, Kapelrud, for instance, claims that Zephaniah is a prophet of doom who, unlike "most of the other prophets," did not call his audience to change their ways: "the only task of the prophet was to preach that Yahweh now wanted to make a clean sweep and then start anew with a humble and lowly people."[512]

Obviously, the text conveys a totally different message to those who consider themselves a remnant (see the use of שארית העם in Hag 1:12, 14, 2:2; Zech 8:6,11,12).

---

[510] The theme of the reversal occurs in other places in the OT (e.g., Isa 14:2; Jer 49:2).

[511] Cf. Josh 23:12 and Hab 2:8.

[512] See Kapelrud, 1975: 77-78 (the quotation from p. 78).

3.3.10. Zeph 2:10

(a) According to Sabottka, זאת here means "shame."[513] But it seems more likely that זאת occurs here according to its very common use as a recapitulative particle,[514] and therefore can be translated as "this." If this is the case the entire verse introduces no new elements but only stresses the reason for the punishment. The language of the verse is basically that of v. 8. It is noteworthy, however, that the verse takes the language חרפו from v. 8 (חרפו את עמי) but changes the ויגדילו על גבולם (v. 8) into ויגדלו על עם ה' צבאות, that is, a second equivalent to חרפו את עמי.[515] This change does not support the idea that the entire verse is a statement supporting the last part of v. 9.[516] Another significant change is from עמי (in vv. 8-9) to עם ה' צבאות (in v. 10), i.e., verse 10 does not claim to be said by YHWH.

(b) The word גאונם is a clear reference to the theme of "pride," which is commonly related to Moab; see above.

3.3.11. Zeph 2:11

(a) The LXX and the Peshitta point to a Hebrew reading (or misreading) נִרְאֶה instead of נורא, i.e., as if it were from the root ראה instead of ירא.[517] Both readings are contextually possible but the MT is more forceful and therefore probably more appropriate. The comparison

---

513 See Sabottka: 88-89, Watts, 1975: 170-71. For a critical response, see del Olmo Lete: 300.

514 More than one hundred and fifty occurrences in the OT. See Even-Shoshan, entry זאת.

515 This is one of the reasons that this verse is commonly considered an addition to either Zephanic material or to a secondary material already added to the Zephanic layer; see, for instance, J. M. P. Smith: 228 and the bibliography mentioned there; Elliger, 1951: 69; Gerleman, 1942: 70; Renaud: 1986:15; Irsigler, 1977: 123; Edler:92.

516 Cf. Rudolph, 1975: 281-82.

517 The Vg. and Tg. Neb. follow the MT reading.

between Ps 96:4 (//1 Chr 16:25) and Zeph 2:11 provides further support to this position.[518]

(b) The specific meaning of רזה is doubtful. Words from the root רזה occur several times in the OT (Num 13:20; Isa 10:16,17:4, 24:16; Ezek 24:20; Mic 6:10; Ps 106:15). These words convey a general meaning of "loss of strength," "leanness." Accordingly, it has been proposed that רזה means "weakened."[519]   Other scholars, although accepting this general meaning, consider it necessary to emend the text to יְרַזֶּה (i.e., to a *piel* form), in order to make the verb transitive and causative (cf. Jer 10:4). If this is the case, the absence of the י from the text would be a simple haplography.[520] The *piel* form of this verb is, however, unattested elsewhere. Moreover, one may note that the *qal* form ויחלש in עמלק ויחלש יהושע את (Exod 17:13) is either causative ("to make Amalek weak") or conveys the second meaning of חלש (i.e., "to rule, command, overwhelm"). Significantly this latter meaning is attested in the form על חלש (see Isa 14:12).[521]   Certainly, the example of חלש is highly suggestive concerning רזה. Moreover, in Prov 14:28, רזון (from the root רזה) stands in parallel with "king."[522] Furthermore, in Aramaic the root רזה is attested with the sense of "to be strong, hard." Thus, Sabottka may be right in his proposal that רזה here means "beherrscht,"[523] but רזה may also be a causative, "to weaken," as in Exod 17:13. The conveyed meaning of the sentence will remain the same whatever choice is made.[524]

---

[518] See, for instance, Sabottka: 90. For a different position see Elliger (BHS); Krinetzki, 1977: 259; Edler: 19.

[519] See, for instance, Rashi (החיש כחם), R. L. Smith: 134., Kapelrud, 1975:106.

[520] See, for instance, Elliger (BHS), Krinetzki, 1977: 259; Edler: 19. For a critical approach to this proposal, see, for instance, Gerleman, 1942: 39.

[521] Cf. Sabottka: 91, n. 109 and the bibliography mentioned there. Also cf. Burns.

[522] Cf. Judg. 5:3; Hab 1:10; Isa 40:23; Prov 8:15, 31:4.

[523] See Sabottka: 90-91. Cf. Ps 97:9.

[524] This holds true even if רזה is emended to רדה (e.g., Ehrlich: 460, Rudolph, 1975: 278) is accepted. This is so because the scholarly discussion on רזה was carried out on the basis of a general agreement concerning the conveyed meaning of the sentence.

(c) Although the phrase כל אלהי הארץ referring to all the gods occurs nowhere else in the OT, similar phrases conveying a similar meaning occur in Ps 95:3, 96:4 (4-5), 97:9,[525] all of them are among the psalms "celebrating the kingship of YHWH."[526] Also the theme of all the peoples accepting YHWH and bowing to YHWH (see Zeph 2:11)[527] is present in these psalms (e.g., Ps 96:7-10, 97:6-7).

The conception, or image, of YHWH as superior to other gods, or even "killing" them, occurs also in Exod 15:11 (מי כמכה באלם ה') ; in Ps 29:1; 82:2, 6; and probably in a pre-masoretic text of Deut 32:8,43.[528] However, unlike Zeph 2:11 and the psalms celebrating the kingship of YHWH, none of them refers to the gods as כל אלהי הארץ but as אלם or בני עליון or אלהים.

It is significant that all these notes, except Zeph 2:11, are in poetry. Especially in poetry (and worship) one cannot rule out the possibility that ancient formulas are used, and therefore the text literally understood expresses neither the beliefs of the writer of the piece nor those held by the community.[529] But one cannot claim that this is one of such cases until one proves that there is an ancient formula that precedes the composition of the text and that the text supports a metaphorical understanding. For instance, one can hardly consider Deut 32 and Ps 82 as referring to non-existent, metaphorical figures. But it has been proposed that the

---

[525] Cf. Ps 99:2, see BHS.

[526] See Anderson: 33-35, 680-1. These psalms are also called "Enthronement Psalms." They include Pss 47, 93, 96-99.

[527] Cf. Zeph 3:9 but note that the relationship between the "peoples" and YHWH is never described in these Psalms in the terms found in Zeph 3:9, nor the worshiping community is described in terms of "humble and lowly people."

[528] The proposed text for Deut 32:8 reads יצב נבלת עמים למספר בני אלים ... בהנחל עליון. See Rofé, 1982: 70-72 and Mayes, 1981: 384-85 and the bibliography cited in these works; see also BHS. The proposal is based on 4QDeut and the LXX. The Qumran text for Deut 32:43 reads: השחחו לו כל אלהים, the LXX suggests כל בני אלהים השחחו לו; see Rofé, 1982: 73-79; Mayes, 1981: 393 and the bibliography mentioned in these works. On the religious thought expressed by Ps 82 and Deut 32, see Rofé, 1982: 67-84.

[529] The use of biblical texts in modern liturgies is a good example of that. For instance, Jewish prayerbooks written in this century contained all Exod 15: 11 and the verse is actually sung every week in modern Jewish communities. This does not mean that people in these communities believe in the existence of a plethora of gods—as existential beings—and compare them to YHWH.

references to the gods in the psalms celebrating the kingship of YHWH do not express the beliefs of the Psalmist or his/her community.[530] This may be the case but this position cannot be derived from expressions referring to the superiority of YHWH over other gods (e.g., Ps 95:3) or from the use of pejorative names (e.g., Ps 96:5). Different is the case in Ps 97:7 (which recalls the so-called Deutero-Isaiah), but even there, one cannot rule out a play on words between פסל, "image of god," and אלהים, "god" but also "image or object representing god" (e.g., Judg 18:24).

Moreover, is a clear theological concept, as well as belief, concerning the non-existence of gods to be expected in such communities, or is that a modern way of thinking? Certainly, these communities believed in one God, but does it necessarily mean that they ruled out the existence of heavenly beings that, though clearly inferior to YHWH are not human? Evidence concerning the belief in angels (and demons) in the second Temple period (and thereafter) leaves the question open.[531]

(d) The expression כל איי הגוים has been understood by the ancient versions as referring to "the islands of the nations." Such understanding is, however, contextually difficult because the previous locative remark was הארץ, meaning "the world." Moreover, this is not a unique feature: In Ps 97:1 (see above) איים רבים also occurs in a parallel structure to הארץ meaning "the world." In addition, a more general meaning like "habitable lands" (which metaphorically may refer to "all the inhabitants of all habitable lands") seems to be contextually more suitable than a restricted "islands" (or "coastlands", or their inhabitants) in Isa 40:15, 41:1,5, 42:4,10, 49:1; 51:1.[532]

---

[530] See, for instance, Anderson: 683.

[531] See, for instance, Dan 10:13, 20-21, 12:1. For the relationship between other gods and "Israelite" angels; see Rofé, 1979.

[532] Cf. Ball,1972:109; BDB; RSV.

For the proposal that אי may mean "jackals" as in Isa 13:22, 34:14, Jer 50:39, and that "jackals" parallels "the gods of the earth," see Watts, 1975: 171.

Alternatively, one has to supply an implied "even," as in KJV: "even all the isles of the heathen."[533] This implied "even" is understandable because איים may refer to "the islands and coast of the Mediterranean Sea" which "are the most furthermost part of the Western world" (KBL[2], cf. KBL[3]).

(e) Zeph 2:11 stands in the middle of the sayings against the nations, after the units concerning Philistia, Ammon, and Moab, and before the sayings against Cush and Assyria. There is no doubt that Zeph 2:11 is only loosely connected to both the preceding and the following units. Although the pronominal suffix in עליהם at the beginning of the verse anchors Zeph 2:11 to the ongoing text, the contents of the verse go far beyond the described actions of YHWH against the Moabites and the Ammonites (the antecedent to which עליהם refers, see v. 10). Also the resumptive גם in v. 12 is only a stylistic device in order to keep the continuity of the text and does not point to an inner relations between v. 11 and v. 12.[534]

3.3.12. Zeph 2:12

(a) Cush in the OT generally means Nubia.[535] It has been suggested, and sometimes firmly proposed, that the announcement against Cush is actually an announcement against Egypt.[536] Although many times Cush and Egypt are mentioned together, which is understandable on historical and geographical grounds, there is no clear instance of Cush meaning Egypt in the OT. To the contrary, one may note that Cush cannot be

---

[533] See also Abrabanel; cf. Calvin who understands the verse as pointing to those "countries beyond the sea."

[534] According to Radak this גם means "even", so the meaning of the verse is "even (i.e., although you are far from Israel) you, Cushites . . . " That is geographical distances will not preempt God's judgment. Cf. Ball, 1972/1988: 140-41.

[535] It may mean a bedouin tribe somewhere South of Judah, see 2 Chr 21:6; cf. Hab 3:7. The context in Zeph 2:11 makes such identification unlikely.

[536] See, for instance, G. A. Smith: 63; J. M. P. Smith: 232; Hyatt, 1948:28; Elliger: 1951, 69-70; Krinetzki: 118-19; Boadt, 1982: 219; Renaud, 1986:14; Edler: 241-42.

understood as Egypt in many of its occurrences (e.g., Gen 10:6; Isa
20:3,4, 43:3; Ezek 29:10, 30:5). Moreover, the only Cushite king of
Egypt mentioned by name in the OT is called, "king of Cush" and not
"king of Egypt" (2 Kgs 19:9//Isa 37:9).[537] If so, why has the idea of
Cush as Egypt arisen? The answer is simply, if one understands the claim
of the superscription as pointing to a Josianic date and to the prophet
Zephaniah's authorship, and if one accepts this claim (at least concerning
Zeph 2:12), then insofar as one considers that the preaching of the prophet
must reflect contemporaneous events that are historically known, one
should conclude that Zephaniah could not have intended to announce
judgment over Cush but over Egypt. The extent to which such reasoning
is based on preconceptions instead of focusing in the text is self-
evident.[538] The text simply says Cush; moreover, the text has no
announcement against Egypt. These are basic data for the understanding
of the section containing the oracles against the nations in the Book of
Zephaniah as a unit, as well as for the Cushite oracle as a separate unit.[539]

(b) The expression חללי חרבי is sometimes emended to חרב ה'
חללי. Since the "sword" is YHWH's sword in any case, the difference
is in the identity of the speaker.[540] According to the MT, the speaker is
YHWH as in vv. 8-9 but unlike vv. 13-15; the emendation reverses the
data. The proposed emendation is technically likely and simple. An
abbreviation of YHWH written י may have been misunderstood by a
scribe and as a result חרב י turned out to be חרבי.[541] One may find

---

[537] Cf. with the Assyrian reluctance to call the rulers of the twenty-fifth (the Cushite)
dynasty: Pharaoh. Furthermore, Egypt was always distinguished from Cush in the
Assyrian sources. See Spalinger, 1973: 100; esp. n. 36 and the bibliography
mentioned there.

[538] In the general framework of exegesis of the Latter Prophets, there are several examples
of exegesis that introduces into the oracles against the nations a people, which does not
appear in the text but "should have been mentioned." For instance, and concerning
Zephaniah, Radak interpreted וים על הצפון as a reference to Babylon, and Luther took the
announcement against Assyria as an announcement against Babylon (Luther: 346).

[539] On the possible reason for including announcements against Philistia, Ammon, Moab,
Cush and Assyria and for the absence of announcements against Babylon, Egypt and
Edom that may have been expected, see the commentary section.

[540] See O'Connor: 253 and the bibliography mentioned there.

[541] Cf. G. R. Driver, 1960:119

some support for the emendation in the fact that the pronominal suffix in v. 12 is too remote from its antecedent in vv. 8-9. This objection to the text, however, may be removed either by considering vv. 10-11 a later addition or by pointing to the clear contextual meaning of the verse or by both (i.e., the contextual clarity of the verse made unnecessary a change in v. 12 at the time of the addition of vv. 10-11).

(c) The proposal that חרבי המה was the result of a corruption of 'ה חרב[542] is more unlikely, because the former expression is the more difficult reading.[543] The proposal itself, however, points to the difficulties that the word המה brings about. The pronoun המה is a third person masculine plural pronoun, but v. 12 opens with a second person plural pronoun. This "incongruency" has been explained in several ways, among them: (a) המה is a copula;[544] (b) המה means "look!;"[545] (c) similar abrupt changes from one grammatical person to the other occur several times in the OT, especially in poetry, and therefore, המה may be the third personal masculine pronoun;[546] and (d) חללי חרבי המה is a quotation of the divine speech made by the speaker who addressed the Cushites.[547]

The expression חללי חרב is well attested in the OT (e.g., Num 19:6; Isa 22:2; Jer 14:18; Ezek 31:18, 32:20, 21,25, 28,29,30, 31,32, 35:8; Lam 4:9) and the same holds for the figure of the "sword of YHWH" (e.g., Deut 32:42, Isa 34:5; Ezek 21:8, 9, 10, 32:10;1 Chr 21:30).

---

[542] E.g., Elliger (BHS); Kapelrud, 1975: 34.

[543] So, for instance, Edler: 19.

[544] E.g., O'Connor: 253.

[545] E.g., Sabottka: 94.

[546] See GKC § 144p; Gerleman, 1942: 41.

[547] For a discussion on these and other proposals see Irsigler, 1977: 124-25 and the bibliography there. For the proposal that the expression contains a rare and long form of the third person pronominal suffix, חרב(י)מה meaning "their (the remnant of my people's [v. 9]) sword," see Wernberg-Møller, 1957. Medieval commentators were well aware of the problem. Ibn Ezra and Radak pointed to the third approach among those mentioned above. They brought Job 17:10 as a clear example supporting their position. They also considered possible that there is a missing comparative כ before המה, and that המה refers to the Ammonites and Moabites. Calvin explicitly mentioned the latter possibility though he did not adopted it, and he implicitly rejected the first approach by saying: "But is seems to me that the sentence is irregular, *even ye Ethiopians*, and then *they shall be slain by my sword*" (Calvin:253).

(d) The announcement against the Cushites is unique among the announcements against the nations in the Book of Zephaniah because of its brevity, and because it is the only one that does not clearly point to future events and situations. To the contrary, it is likely that it refers to a present condition or even to a status that originated in the past.[548]

3.3.13. Zeph 2:13

The use of the jussive form (וְיֵט) instead of, and with the force of an imperfect, is a well attested feature in the OT.[549] The verbal form וְיֵט occurs more than twenty times in the OT (e.g., Gen 39:21; Exod 8:2,13; Isa 5:25). The expression נטה יד על occurs also in Zeph 1:4;[550] the root אבד (with YHWH as its subject) appears in the announcement of judgment against Philistia;[551] and Ashkelon will turn into שממה (Zeph 2:4) as Nineveh will do. The announcement in general recalls other prophetic announcements, such as Hos 2:5; Jer 51;43.

3.3.14. Zeph 2:14

The figure of "flocks" lying down (ורבצו) in the destroyed city occurs also in the oracle against Philistia.[552] A similar image of destruction is attested in Isa 13:21. The reference to ציים in the latter and the employment of the word ציה in Zeph 2:13 (cf. Jer 50:12) may point to a

---

[548] See, for instance, Exod 32:16; 2 Sam 21:2; 1 Kgs 9:20; Ezek 27:17; for a similar use of the feminine pronoun (הנה) see, for instance, Gen 41:26,27; Exod: 1:19; Lev 18:10; Judg 19:12; Ezek 42:13,14. Cf. Hyatt, 1948: 28.

[549] See GKC § 109 k.

[550] See notes on Zeph 1:4.

[551] Although there in its *hiphil* form.

[552] It is worth noting that Ashkelon, which will turned into שממה as Nineveh (Zeph 2:7,13), is singled out there.

pun on words in v. 13.[553] The pair קאת - קפד occurs in a similar context in Isa 34:11.

The *waw* ending of the nomens regens in the expression כל חיתו גוי points to poetry, or elevated prose.[554] The form X-חיתו occurs elsewhere in Gen 1:24; Isa 56:9; Ps 50:10, 79:2 104:11,20. In these occurrences X stands for שׂדי, יער, and ארץ. This feature leads to the expectation of another place-noun in Zeph 2:14, and this is the case, according to Barr. He proposed that גוי may mean "people, nation" but also may mean "field, land."[555] Other scholars point to the LXX and Tg. Neb. which instead of גוי have place-nouns (earth, field [i.e., ארץ and יער, respectively). But the question whether these translations point to a Hebrew text different from the MT or whether they have translated the expression dynamically remains open.[556] The MT, as it stands,[557] has been interpreted as "every beast of a (every) nation, i.e., "all kind of beasts in the world." [558] Alternatively, גוי may be understood metaphorically, as in Joel 1:6 where it means a "swarm of locust." If this is the case, one may translate "all the beasts living in flocks (or herds)."[559] This understanding of the text provides a heightening movement from one verset to the other in the first four versets of v. 14, and such a stylistic

---

[553] The term ציה may mean "wild beasts." Olivier suggests that ציה in Zeph 2:13 refers to "wild beasts/demons of the desert," accordingly he emends the text from ציה כמדבר to ציה במדבר. See Olivier, 1980: 95-97

[554] See GKC § 90 o.

[555] Thus, גו is included in the list of biblical homonyms. See Barr, 1968: 144, 324, n. 74.

[556] Cf. the "literal" approach of the Vg. The "dynamic" character of the rendering India (הודו) instead of Cush in Tg. Neb. Zeph 3:10 is self evident. In the LXX text of the Minor Prophets there is a tendency to free translation in problematic MT phrases (e.g., LXX Zeph 1:12; see, for instance Gerleman, 1942: 17). See, for instance, Ziegler, 1944. It is noteworthy that in Zeph 1:12 both the Tg. Neb. and LXX followed a free, or probably in their understanding, a dynamic translation, while the Vg. follows a literal one. This situation clearly resembles the one in Zeph 2:14.

[557] For different proposals of emendations, see, for instance, J. M. P. Smith: 233, 236-37 Rudolph, 1975: 278; Sabottka: 95-96 and the bibliography mentioned in these works.

[558] Cf. Rashi, Radak, Calvin, Ehrlich: 460; Ball, 1972/1988:109-10; O'Connor: 253; Edler: 10,19; NJPSV; and the Vg. and the Peshitta.

[559] E.g., Barthélemy, 1980: 378.

feature has been already noted in several occasions in Zephaniah, and is a well attested feature of biblical poetry.[560]

The last line in v. 14 is undoubtedly difficult. Textual corruption has been suggested for almost all the words in the line. Moreover, even in those cases in which seems to be a certain consensus about the original writing of a certain word, there is not such consensus about its meaning (e.g., קוֹל meaning "hark !" or "voice"). Nevertheless, the context makes the general meaning of the expression unquestionable: a picture of desolation.

The literal meaning of the expression has been a focus of scholarly discussion. If the MT is retained, the line can be translated as follows:

> A voice will sing in the window,
> desolation[561] in the threshold
> yea! her [Nineveh's] cedar (works)
> are laid bare.[562]

This reading suits the context and stands in accordance with both attested meanings of terms and usual Hebrew grammar. To be sure, the ancient versions provide different readings, and scholars have proposed textual emendations.[563] However, if the emendation or the ancient version provides a more simple and clear text, then the MT is the difficult reading. For instance, if one may compare the proposed translation with that of the RSV:

> the owl shall hoot in the window,
> the raven croak on the threshold;
> for her cedar work will be laid bare[564]

---

[560] See note on Zeph 1:7.

[561] Cf. Isa 61:4 (עָרֵי חָרְב) ; Jer 49:13 (לְחָרְב).

[562] One may compare this translation with those proposed by Gerleman, Ball, Barthélemy, Kapelrud,and House (see Gerleman, 1942: 71; Ball, 1972/1988: 112, 292; Kapelrud, 1975: 106; Barthélemy, 1980: 378-79; House: 123).

[563] See, for instance, J. M. Smith: 234, 237; Gerleman, 1942: 44-45, 71; Ball, 1972/1988: 112; Sabottka: 96-98, 144; Rudolph, 1975: 276,278 and the bibliography mentioned in these works.

[564] Similarly, NJPSV translates: "The great owl hoots in the window, and the raven (croaks) on the threshold. For he has stripped its cedarwork bare." The NRSV follows the RSV.

The main question is: Is it more likely that such a text (i.e., the Hebrew text that stands behind this translation) developed into the MT or vice versa?

Is it likely that a scribe simply confused the concrete terms employed in the hypothetical RSV Hebrew text, such as "owl" (Heb. כוס [the RSV text is based on Ps 102:7])[565] and "raven" (Heb. ערב [here, the RSV text follows the LXX and the Vg]) by abstract terms as "voice" and "desolation" (Heb. קול and חֹרֶב)? Could the scribe miss the concrete image but build the abstract one? But, if there was no scribal mistake, why should a scribe take a concrete, clear and relatively known image (cf. Isa 34:11) and rarify it?

The second alternative, i.e., that a quite uncommon and quite abstract image was turned into a more concrete one, which in addition recalls Isa 34:11 (MT as well as LXX), seems much more likely (cf. the LXX; OL and Tg. Neb. renderings of הקפאים על שמריהם in Zeph 1:12).

One of the few words in this line that is not under critical suspicion is ישורר. The occurrence of ישורר in v. 14 is worth noting. Words from the root שיר according to the *qal* pattern occur many times in the OT and across barriers of style and date (e.g., Exod 15:1; Judg 5:1; Isa 42:10; Jer 20:13; Ps 33:33, 101:1; 105:2 [//1 Chr 16:9]; Prov 25:20; Qoh 2:8). Words from the same root but according to the *polel* pattern show a different pattern of occurrence. They occur in Zeph 2:14, in Job 36:24 (שררו) and in the participial forms משררות or משררים in Ezra 2:65; Neh 7:67; 1 Chr 6:18; 2 Chr 29:28; and more than twenty additional times in 1-2 Chronicles, Ezra and Nehemiah in relation to the Levitical singers.

The only difference between the two is that the former reads "at the window" and "its cedar work" instead of "in the window" and "her cedar work."

565 The word כוס occurs only in Lev 11:17; Deut 14:6 and Ps 102:7.

3.3.15. Zeph 2:15

The first four versets of v. 15 occur almost word for word in Isa 47:8, which refers to Babylon. This is a clear example of how formal grounds for the judgment of nations may move from one people to the other. If this is the case, one has to conclude that the real stress of these units is not in the "historical" truth, namely that the people of Nineveh, or Babylon, actually thought in this way but on: (a) that such a way of thinking is utterly wrong, and this is a message clearly conveyed to the community for which and out which the book was written;[566] (b) that YHWH will judge the mentioned city.

The contrast between a previous situation of grandeur and the miserable situation thereafter is expressed many times in the OT by expressions opening with איך as in the third line of this verse (e.g., Ps 73:19 [לשמה איך היו] ; 2 Sam 1:19,25,7; Isa 14:17). The word מרבץ occurs in a similar context in the announcement of judgment against Ammon in Ezek 25:5.

The image and most of the language of the last line of v. 15 are attested in 1 Kgs 9:8; Jer 18:16,19:8, 49:17, 50:13 (cf. Lam 2:15).[567]

---

[566] See note on Zeph 1:12.
[567] Most if not all these passages are post-monarchic.

3.4 Notes on Zephaniah 3

3.4.1. Zeph 3:1

Chapter 3 opens with a הוי formula.[568] This formula typically occurs either as "הוי + noun,"[569] or as "הוי + participle/participial phrase."[570] In both cases the word or phrase that follows הוי identifies the person or group for whom the הוי is said. In most cases this identification also characterizes the group in such a way that explains the reasons for its punishment.[571]

Following הוי, Zeph 3:1 shows two participles pointing to the character of the bewailed city. The city is also described by an attributive adjective (העיר היונה). In addition, the further verses continue describing the character of the city. The description of the character of the city in Zeph 3:1 is a clear indictment. Moreover, certainty concerning its punishment may already be expressed by the הוי exclamation, provided that הוי in Zeph 3:1 is understood as expression of sorrow.

The description/indictment of the city in v. 1 is built around ironical puns on words:

(a) The word מֹרְאָה is probably a *qal* feminine participle of the root מרה, meaning "stubborn, refractory."[572] If this is the case, then מוראה will be another instance of a ל"ה verbal form that follows the paradigm of the ל"א verbs.[573] The main alternative proposal is to consider מֹרְאָה a

---

[568] See note on Zeph 2:5.

[569] E.g., Isa 1:4, 10:5, 29:1; cf. Jer 22:18.

[570] E..g. Isa 5:11, 18; Jer 23:13; Mic 2:1; Hab 2:12; Zech 11:17.

[571] See, for instance, Roberts, 1982: 296-300; Buss, 1978: 169 and the bibliography there; see also Hillers, 1983; cf. Gerstenberger, 1964, esp. 251-52.

[572] So, for instance, R. Yeshouah—mentioned by Ibn Ezra--; BDB, J. M. P. Smith: 244; Gerleman, 1942:47; Delekat, 1964: 296; Ball, 1972/1988: 150; Rudolph, 1975: 284-85; R. L. Smith: 137.

[573] Cf., for instance, רְצָאתֶ (Ezek 43:27); יִשְׁנָא (Lam 4:1); וַיֶּחֱלָא (2 Chr 16:12). See GKC 75 rr and the list of examples given there. The regular ל"ה masculine participle מֹרֶה, occurs in Deut 21:18,20; Jer 5:23; Ps 78:8; מֹרִים occurs in Num 20:10, but also the usual ל"ה perfect of רצה—see above—is well attested (e.g., Ps 44:4), as well as the usual ל"ה

hophal participle of a denominative verb from ראי (see Nah 3:6; Job 33:21), meaning either "filth, mud, excrement" or "spectacle."[574] The verb itself is not attested elsewhere. Moreover, the context, especially if v. 2 is taken into consideration, tends to support the meaning "stubborn, refractory."[575]

It is self-evident that the word מֹרְאָה sounds like מֹרָא (from the root ירא) that means "fear, reverence, or an awe-inspiring spectacle or deed" (see Deut 4:34, 26:8, 34:12; Jer 32:21), or even an epithet for YHWH (see Ps 76:12), a meaning not entirely impossible after הוי (cf. הוי חרב ה', Jer 47:6). If the verse is read aloud—as it certainly was—the audience hearing הוי מֹרְאָה is able to understand that a negative notice will follow (because of the הוי) but certainly wonders concerning the meaning of the ongoing saying. Thus, the audience needs and expects further information. One may conclude that this is another example of the use of intentional ambiguity in order to get and to channel the attention of the audience to the main point of the unit: the identity and indictment of the city.[576]

(b) The ambiguity goes further in the second participle: נגאלה. This participle not only sounds but is also written exactly as the נגאלה

---

imperfect form of שׁנה (e.g., 1 Sam 21:14; Prov 31:5), and compare Jer 52:33 with 2 Kgs 25:29.

[574] Ibn Ezra is already acquainted with this interpretation of מֹרְאה, Radak and Altschuler supported it, and among modern scholars who support this proposal one may mention Sellin. For a proposal of revocalization of מֹראה to מריאה, meaning "fat" and connoting "arrogance," see Sabottka, 102-03; O'Connor: 255.

[575] The ancient versions strongly differ in their understanding of the word מראה. For instance, the LXX, the OL (Tyconius; *inlustris*, i.e., "famous") and the Peshitta (perhaps depending on the LXX, see Gelston, 1987: 176-77) probably understood it as a *hophal* participle of ראה; the Vg. reads "*provocatrix*", which may have been the rendering if the word were from the root מרר (see Jongeling,1971:1; Rudolph, 1975: 285); Tg. Neb. translates מראה ונגאלה as דמוחיה ומתפרקא ("she who hurries to be redeemed)" and one wonders if the "author" of the Targum did not think of a word derived from the root מהר (see Jongeling, 1977: 1971:21; cf. Ribera Florit: 146, n.40 and the bibliography mentioned there.
For comparative summaries of the different renderings, see, for instance, Ball, 1972/1988: 150; Jongeling, 1971: 541; Rudolph, 1975: 285.

[576] Cf. Jongeling, 1971: 542. Some scholars (e.g., Hitzig) have proposed an additional play of words, מֹראה - מוריה. According to 2 Chr 3:1, the Temple hill is הר מוריה, and cf. the inscription of Khirbet Lei, המוריה אחה חנח נוה יה ה' which is also a post-exilic document (see Gibson, 1975: 57-58; Naveh differs concerning the dating).

meaning "redeemed." The homonym root גאל conveys the meaning of "defiled, polluted," and it is contextually obvious that this is the sense in which the term נגאלה was used in Zeph 3:1.[577] This contextual sense, however, would not be so obvious for an audience that heard only מִרְאָה הוֹי.[578]

It is noteworthy that words from this root—i.e., גאל meaning defiled, polluted—in the *niphal* pattern, such as נגאלה in Zeph 3:1, occur elsewhere in Isa 59:3 and Lam 4:14. Words from this root in other patterns, but with similar meanings occur in Isa 63:3; Mal 1:7,12; Ezra 2:68; Neh 7:64; Dan 1:8 (cf. Neh 13:29).[579] Significantly, all these occurrences are post-monarchic.

(c) The expression העיר היונה may be understood as "the oppressing city" (feminine *qal* participle of ינה; e.g., Jer 46:16, 50:16) or as "the dove city," i.e., connoting a sense of powerlessness (cf. Hos 7:11, 11:11; Jer 48:28).[580] Again, this is another clear case of ambiguity. As in the former instances, the contextual meaning—i.e., the "הוֹי formula," and especially vv. 2-4—clearly supports the rendering "the oppressing

---

[577] However, all the ancient versions interpreted נגאלה as "redeemed, ransomed." Such interpretation was in accordance with their understanding of מֹרְאָה and העיר היונה, as well as of the entire verse (see above and below). Jerome probably knew that נגאלה may mean polluted in Zeph 3:1, even though he translated "redeemed," perhaps because of theological reasons (see Jerome: 695; Gerleman: 1942, 48; cf. R. Moses HaCohen on Zeph 3:1—quoted by Ibn Ezra). The word נגאלה was obviously interpreted as "polluted" in the following saying attributed to R. Reuben in Lam. Rab. 31: "The word (מֹרְאָה) is Greek because they called a foolish woman 'morah'. Woe morah therefore means: woe on account of a foolish woman [Zion] 'And polluted' because they removed themselves from hearing words of Torah, she hath been polluted in the priesthood" (ET according to Soncino Edition, p. 57).

[578] On the the generally unusual use of homonyms in a confusing way, see Barr, 1968: 145-51, esp. 148. On the play on homonyms and double meanings as a stylistic device—e.g., Zeph 3:1, see Barr, 1968: 151-55.

[579] On Job 3:5 and on the general question of the two (homonym) roots גאל, see Blau,1956: 244-45.

[580] The image of the dove may connote further meanings (cf. Cant. 1:15, 2:14; and also cf. Isa 60:8) but the image of powerlessness stands in opposition to the oppressor image, and so does the attribute "redeemed" to "polluted, defiled." But cf. Jongelin, 1971: 541-43.

The LXX, the OL (Tyconius) and the Vg. render יונה as "dove." Tg. Neb. contains a paraphrastic expression that makes no reference to the "dove." The Peshitta understands יתה as a reference to the prophet Jonah, in spite of the definite article before יתה (cf. Lam. Rab. 31).

city."[581] Of course, if there is an oppressing city there are also oppressed people. If "Jerusalem" is the oppressor then the oppressed may theoretically be either other nations or "non-Jerusalem" Judeans, i.e., Judeans who are not represented by the term "Jerusalem." The context of the Book of Zephaniah clearly suggests the second option, for there is no reference in the book to the Judeans as oppressing other nations. If the oppressed are "non-Jerusalem" Judeans, then what does the term Jerusalem stand for? Does it refer to the Jerusalemites in general or only to the ruling elite, or to some other group? Verses 3-4 suggest an answer to these questions, but not before the chain of ambiguities of v. 1 is clarified in v. 2.

3.4.2. Zeph 3:2

In verse 2 the ambiguity of v. 1 begins to vanish and a straightforward indictment arises.

The four versets show a clearly parallel structure. For instance, the subject each is indicated by a perfect negated by לא,[582] and it is always "the city" mentioned above (i.e., Jerusalem);[583] שמעה בקול and מוסר לקחה are equivalents in the first two versets, and so are YHWH and "her God." There is also an evolving and heightening message that goes from verset to verset. The first two versets have קול and מוסר at their center;

---

[581] The Murabba'at text, the MT—see the *setumah* separating Zeph 2:15 from Zeph 1:3, the Vg. and Tg. Neb—pace Rudolph, 1975: 285; see Ribera Florit, 1982: 156 n. 40—connect Zeph 3:1 with Zeph 3:2 ff. and separate the former from Zeph 2:15. But the Peshitta connects Zeph 3:1 with Zeph 2:15. This may hold true for the LXX (see Gerleman, 1942: 47-48). The connectedness between Zeph 3:1 and Zeph 3:2 ff., is supported by the use of הוי, which marks some kind of break with the preceding verse and the beginning of a new unit (or subunit). Moreover, "the city" is the only possible antecedent for all the third person feminine singular references in vv. 2-5 (eleven times). Certainly, if vv. 2-5 follow v. 1, then there is no doubt concerning the identity of "the city, for it is said that YHWH is "her God. The city is Jerusalem.

[582] Or more exactly, and using B .P. Kittel's terms, the subject is indicated by the personal pronoun "affixed" to an "affix form" (i.e., "perfect") negated by לא.

[583] See footnote 14, above.

the last two YHWH and "her God." Even among these two, one can perceive the move from YHWH to the stressed "her God."[584]

The first two versets occur almost word for word in Jer 7:28. The main difference between the two is the prose style and the explicit wording קול ה' אלהיו in Jer 7:28.[585] Although two thirds of the occurrences of the term מוסר in the OT are in the Book of Proverbs,[586] the same does not hold true for the idiom לקח מוסר. It occurs in Jer 2:30, 5:3, 7:28, 17:23, 32:33, 35:13; Zeph 3:1,7; Prov 1:3, 8:10, 24:32. Furthermore, מוסר occurs in the Book of Jeremiah and in Zephaniah 3, only as an element in the idiom לקח מוסר. This idiom occur nowhere else in prophetic literature.

The expression בטח בה', "to trust in YHWH," occurs more than twenty times (Ps 9:11; 21:8; 22:5,6; 25:2; 26:1; 28:7; 32:10; 37:3; 40:4; 55:24; 56:5,12; 62:9; 84:13; 91:2; 112:7; 115:9,10,11; 125:1; 143:8). Elsewhere, it occurs in 2 Kgs 18:5, 19:10 [//Isa 37:10]; Isa 26:3,4; Jer 17:7; 39:18; Zeph 3:2; Prov 16:20, 29:25; 1 Chr 5:20. "To trust in YHWH" is a general statement, but in the vast majority of its occurrences it is explicitly related to a "blessing" that falls or is expected to fall upon those who trust YHWH.[587] Accordingly, בה' לא בטחה is not only an indictment but also a statement that Jerusalem does not do what leads to YHWH's blessing.

The expression קרב אל ה' occurs in the Book of Ezekiel, but there "to draw near to YHWH" is related with "to serve" (שרת) in the Temple (Ezek 40:46, 44:15, 45:4).[588] Since the expression is paired with a

---

[584] Also note the use of קרב.

[585] See the note on חללו קדש חמסו תורה in Zeph 3:4.

[586] It occurs there thirty times out of the fifty times it occurs in the entire OT.

[587] The "blessing" may be of different kinds. For instance, success in war (2 Kgs 19:10; 1 Chr 5:20; happiness (Prov 16:20); peace of mind and security (Jer 17:7); keeping your life (Jer 39:18), etc. Obviously, all the mentioned blessings are in this world.

[588] The expression קרב אל-X shows a variety of meanings in the OT, including sexual meanings (e.g., Gen 20:4; Lev 20:16; Deut 22:14; Isa 8:3). Although a feminine image is used for the city in Zeph 3:1, and God is usually referred in masculine terms, a sexual connotation is contextually impossible in Zeph 3:2. קרב אל-X, in which X stands for a sacred object (but not YHWH) occurs many times in P material (e.g., Lev 9: 7,8; Num 1:51, 18:4)

general בה' לא בטחה, and since there is no special stress on cultic services in the Temple neither in Zeph 3:2 nor Zeph 3:1-4, it seems unlikely that this is the meaning of the phrase in Zeph 3:2.[589]

The expression קרב אל ה'/אלהים occurs in 1 Sam 14:36, where the phrase is related to requesting God's oracle; and in Exod 22:7 (cf. Josh 7:14), where it is related to inquiries to God concerning the administration of justice.[590] This can hardly be the meaning of the phrase in Zeph 3:2.

Since the expression אל אלהיה לא קרבה is paired with a relatively popular expression in the Book of Psalms, בה בטח, it seems that the use of קרב אל ה' in Psalms may be suggestive concerning the meaning of the phrase in Zeph 3:2. The expression occurs in Ps 69:19.[591] The speaker asks God there "to draw near to" him in order to redeem him (cf. Lam 3:57). Although it seems that Zeph 3:2, as well as vv. 3-4, deals more with the actions of Jerusalem than the long-term consequences, it seems that the underlying logic of the text is the conception that if Jerusalem had drawn near to YHWH it would have not been indicted. Furthermore, the general connection (not only in Psalms) between בה' בטח and "blessing" supports such understanding.

However, it seems that the above mentioned understanding points only to one of the shades of meaning conveyed by the verset. The expression קרב אל occurs also in Deutero-Isaiah (Isa 48:16). In Isa 48:16, the people are called by God "to draw near to God " in order to hear God's words.[592] It seems enticing to understand the verse as containing a connotative ring of meaning, namely, "She (Jerusalem) hears no voice . . . she does not come near to her God (in order to hear her God's voice). The indeterminacy of the first "voice" is overcome, and the issue of the

---

[589] For the proposal that the texts means "come near to worship," see R. L. Smith: 138

[590] Cf. Exod 16:9, but the expression there is קרב לפני ה'.

[591] Psalm 69 is probably post-monarchic, see Anderson: 499; Fohrer, 1970: 289.

[592] Cf. Deut 5:24; Isa 34:1 but there the expression קרב אל ה' does not occur. There has been some scholarly discussion concerning the originality of the call "draw near" in Isa 48:16; but see, for instance, Whybray, 1981: 132.

rejection to hear the "voice" comes again to the forefront, connecting v. 2 with v. 3.[593]

3.4.3. Zeph 3:3-4

Four Jerusalemite groups are singled out for indictment in verses 3-4: שׂריה ("her officers"), שׁפטיה ("her judges"), נביאיה ("her prophets") and כהניה ("her priests"). The first two groups are described in metaphorical terms, in comparison with predatory animals. The last two are described in terms of their actions and character but not in metaphorical terms. The language of the unit clearly recalls Ezek 22:25-28, but there are also important differences between the two notes, especially between the two lists of indicted socio-political groups.[594] The list in Zeph 3:3-4 and the relationship between Zeph 3:3-4 and Ezek 22:25-28 are worthy of study but according to the methodology employed in this work, the investigation must begin with the study of the text in Zeph 3:3-4.

The first two versets in v. 3 present no real problem. In most ancient versions[595] an explicit comparative occurs before "lions." For instance, the Vg reads *quasi leones* and Tg. Neb. כאריון. Such a comparative does not occur before "wolves" in the third verset; it neither points to different Hebrew text nor changes the meaning of the unit, but to a certain tendency towards explicitness.

The text, and consequently, the meaning of the last two versets in v. 3, i.e., שׁפטיה זאבי ערב לא גרמו לבקר have been in dispute in modern scholarship. The understanding of the text depends to a large extent on the understanding of two words in it. The first is ערב. Already

---

[593] Cf. the present notes on these two last versets with Ball's discussion on the same issue, see Ball, 1972/1988: 205-08.

[594] Cf. Edler: 150-56; Fishbane, 1985: 461-63 and the bibliography mentioned there.

[595] So LXX, the Vg., Peshitta, and Tg. Neb.

the LXX and the OL (Tyconius)[596] understood the word as referring to
Arabia. On the other hand, the Vg., the Peshitta and Tg. Neb. support the
MT text which clearly means "evening" (עֶרֶב). Among modern scholars,
Elliger has strongly advocated the reading "steppe."[597] This interpretation
has enjoyed a certain acceptance.[598] Since "evening" stands as an
equivalent to "morning" in the verse,[599] those who reject the reading
"evening" tend also to reject the reading "morning." Accordingly,
different hypotheses have been put forward to explain the development of
the text from a supposedly original stage that did not include any reference
to "morning" to the present MT, which is supported in this respect by all
the ancient versions.[600]

The reading "morning," however, seems to be supported by Zeph 3:5
and by the fact that judging is related to morning in other places in the OT
(see 2 Sam 15:2-5; Jer 21:12; Ps 101:8; cf. Ps 37:6).[601] To be sure, one
may claim that these features explain how an original text with no

---

[596] The extant text of Zeph 3:1-5 according to the OL is from Tyconius; Zeph 3:8 from
Cyprian. Both are considered reliable renderings of an early OL text. See Oesterley,
1904: 76-77, 386.

[597] That is, עֶרֶב or עֲרָבָה or עֲרָבוֹת (cf. Jer 5: 6) instead of the MT עֶרֶב. See Elliger, 1950. Note
the title of Elliger's article: "Das Ende der "Abendwölfe" Zeph 3:3 Hab 1:8."

[598] See, for instance, Rimbach, 1972: 79, 98-99; Brockington, 1973: 263; Rudolph, 1975:
284-86; NJPSV; JB.
Nevertheless, the reading "evening" is supported by most modern scholars. See, for
instance, Stenzel, 1951; Dahood, 1968: II, 331; Sabottka: 104-05; Kapelrud,
1975:107; Watts, 1975: 175; Barthélemy, 1980: 380; O'Connor: 255; R.L. Smith:
137; Krinetzki: 130-31; Edler: 10,20; House 123, 131; RSV/ NRSV; Schöckel-Valverde
(Nueva Biblia Española).

[599] The pair בקר - ערב occurs also in Gen 49:27, Ps 65:9. Krasovec includes this pair in his
list of merisms (Krasovec,1977:87) and cf. Dahood, 1968, II: 113 and the bibliography
mentioned there. If this is the case, the pair "morning and evening" will point to the
entire light-time of the day, from dawn to dusk.

[600] For instance, Elliger proposes an original שֹׁפְטֶיהָ זְאֵבִים לֹא עָזְבוּ גֶּרֶם that was corrupted by a
copyist's mistake and eventually reached the MT sentence. See Elliger, 1951: 71 and
Elliger (BHS). Rudolph proposes an original text saying לֹא גָרוּ מהבֹּקֶר instead of MT לַבֹּקֶר
לֹא נֶרְמוּ. Accordingly, Rudolph translates: "die (auch) vor dem Großvieh keine Angst
haben" (i.e., נָרוּ from III גור. See Rudolph, 1975: 284, 285-86).

[601] Ball has noted that light has been used as one of the symbols for God's justice and that
Shamash, the sun-god, was the god of justice in Mesopotamia. See Ball, 1972/1988:
157 (cf. Anderson: 294). For justice and morning, see, for instance, Stenzel,1951: 303;
Jongelin, 1971: 544-45; Ball, 1972/1988: 156-57; Edler: 153-54, and the
bibliography cited there. Van der Toorn thinks of an ordeal procedure that took place
during the night. See van der Toorn, 1988, and esp. p. 436. No clear references to any
kind of ordeal occur in Zeph 3:3,5.

reference to "evening" or "morning" could become the present text. But the proposed original text is an unnecessary hypothesis and rightly rejected, if the present text is not proved to be either composite or inadequate in some respect.

The expression זאבי ערב occurs twice in the OT, in Zeph 3:3 and Hab 1:8. Since there is no reference to "morning" in Hab 1:8, one cannot explain the occurrence of this expression as a textual development from a previous עָרָבָה due to the influence of בֹּקֶר ; thus a new hypothesis seems to be necessary, such as influence of Zeph 3:3 on Hab 1:8. Certainly, this hypothesis is unnecessary if עֶרֶב carries its well attested meaning of "evening" (more than one hundred times in the OT) also in Hab 1:8. Moreover, in a third text, in Gen 49:27, the activity of the wolf is related to "evening" and "morning." Furthermore, there is an attested, and different, expression that clearly means "wolf of the steppe," namely, זאב עֲרָבוֹת (Jer 5:6).[602] Thus, one may tend to conclude that the most likely meaning is "evening wolf", that is, "wolves in the evening."[603]

However, the text most closely related to Zeph 3:3 is Ezek 22:27, and there one reads שָׂרֶיהָ בקרבה כזאבים טרפי טרף, i.e., זאבים instead of the expected זאבי ערב. But this is not the only difference between the two units. Insofar as it concerns the discussion here, one may note that in Ezekiel there is no reference to judges (שפטים). Taking into account the relation between judging and morning, one may wonder whether the reference to the judges in Zeph 3:3 is related to the image of זאבי ערב. Moreover, since the use of double entendre is clearly attested in Zeph 3:1, one cannot rule out beforehand the possibility of double meanings in Zeph 3:3. A simple analysis of the meaning of the noun עֶרֶב shows that it has three possible meanings in the OT: (a) evening (more than one hundred times); (b) land of steppe-dwellers, Arabia (see 1 Kgs

---

[602] Here the mention of the "steppe" is needed in order to conveyed a sense of entirety along with "forest" (יער) and "cities."

It is noteworthy that although the LXX reads "wolves of Arabia" in Zeph 3:3 and Hab 1:8, such a reading does not occur in Jer 5:6. See below.

[603] So Barthélemy, 1980: 380.

10:15; Jer 25:20,24, 50:37; Ezek 30:5);[604] and (c) heterogeneous body, mixed multitude—a quite derogatory term (Exod 12:38, Neh 13:3). Taking into account these meanings of עֶרֶב, one may ask which of the following alternatives the writer of Zeph 3:3 would prefer:

(a) to write simply זאב which connotes the idea of attacking especially the defenseless (cf. Isa 11:6; 65:25) in such a way that leaves almost no remains of them (Zeph 3:3), and whose actions may be described as related to morning and evening (Gen 49:27);

(b) to write זאב ערבות as in Jer 5:6, in which the wolf is paralleled to the lion, and perhaps its fierce character underlined;

(c) to write זאבי עֶרֶב that not only includes the meaning conveyed by the other two alternatives, but also allows the writer to bring to the forefront the otherwise (only) potential description of the wolf's acts in terms of evening and morning, and therefore to provide a new dimension to the comparison between the acts of the judges and those of the wolves,[605] and in addition, to stress the "pack" character of the wolf (or "wolf") in a quite derogatory way.

If the writer of Zeph 3:3 is the writer of Zeph 3:1, it seems that he/she would have preferred the third alternative.

The other problematic word in the line is גָּרְמוּ.[606] The noun, גֶּרֶם meaning "bones" is attested in Prov 17:22, 25:15; Job 40:18.[607] In a figurative way, the word occurs in 2 Kgs 9:13, meaning "self, bare"[608] and in Gen 49:14 meaning "strong." The figurative sense of Gen 49:19 and the contextual meaning of גרם in Prov 25:15 show that "bone" (גרם)

---

[604] Thus, the LXX reading "wolves of Arabia" does not necessarily point to a different Hebrew text but may point to a different choice among possible meanings of עֶרֶב. It should be noticed, however, that in the LXX version of 1 Kgs 10:15; Jer 25:20,24, 50:37 and Ezek 30:5 עֶרֶב is not translated as Arabia—but none of them occurs in Minor Prophets.

[605] See the discussion on גרמו, below.

[606] There have been several proposals of textual emendation concerning גָּרְמוּ. Stenzel proposes an original reading: שפטיה זאבים לערב נורים לבקר. There, נורים stand instead of גָּרְמוּ. See Stenzel, 1951.

[607] In biblical Aramaic a cognate form meaning "bone" is attested in Dan 6:25.

[608] גרם המעלות, "the bare steps."

had the connotation of "strength." If this is the case one may compare the range of meanings of גֶּרֶם, i.e., "bone" with the range of meanings of a second Hebrew word whose basic meaning is "bone", i.e., עֶצֶם (e.g., Gen 2:23; Exod 12:46; Ezek 37:3; Job 40:18).

Significantly, words from the root עצם may convey both the meaning "self" (e.g., Gen 7:13; Exod 24:10)[609] and the meaning of "strength," just as words from the root גרם. Moreover, the meaning "strength" is the only one that occurs in the *qal* pattern of the root עצם (e.g., Gen 26:16). In the *piel* pattern the only occurrence of a word from the root עצם is in Jer 50:17> There, it means "to break, to crush." Significantly, the denominative *piel* verbal form from גרם occurs in Num 24:8 and means "to crush," and the direct object there is bones (עצמתיהם).[610] The only occurrence of a word from the root גרם in the *qal* pattern is in Zeph 3:3. On the basis of the connoted meaning of "strength" attested for גרם, the parallelism of meanings between גרם and עצם, and the usual intransitive meaning of denominative verbs in the *qal* pattern, one may conclude that it is more likely that גרמו in Zeph 3:3 means to be strong than any other alternative.[611]

If this interpretation is correct then the writer is playing on the different meanings of words and images. The judges of Jerusalem are "fierce wolves" (worthy companions of a lion). These wolves attack in packs their defenseless preys, and since they do most of their work from dusk on, they are "evening wolves." Accordingly, they belong to the realm of the tenebrous. When it is light, at morning, these wolves are tired (have no strength), so how can the judges (i.e., wolves) do what was expected of them, namely, to bring justice (light) at morning (cf. Zeph 3:5).[612]

---

[609] See note in BDB, 782 a.

[610] It also occurs in Ezek 23:34, in a very difficult passage. See Zimmerli, 1979: 477 and the bibliography mentioned there.

[611] That the most likely meaning of לא גרמו is "not to have strength" has already been pointed out by Ball. See Ball, 1972/1988: 158-59.

[612] Cf. Jongeling, 1971.

It is noteworthy that by accepting the most probable meaning of the
words occurring in the line, the most sensible and sophisticated meaning
of the line is received; and conversely, the more complicated the suggested
textual process behind the present text of the line, the less sophisticated is
the proposed original text.[613] Certainly, Zeph 3:1 and many other pieces
in prophetic literature and elsewhere in the OT clearly show that the
existence of sophisticated writers cannot be automatically ruled out
anytime the text seems to be "too sophisticated."[614]

The word פחזים occurs only in Zeph 3:4 and Judg 9:4.[615] The
common meanings associated with the word are "insolent, loose,
unreliable."[616] Words from the root פחז occur elsewhere in Gen 49:4
and Jer 23:32. In Jer 23:32 the prophets are indicted because they
prophesy dreams that are false, narrate them and lead the people of
YHWH astray with their falsehoods and wild words (פחזותם).[617] The
exact shade of meaning of נביאיה פחזים may be under dispute, but the
general message is clear: They were unreliable prophets. The expression
אנשי בגדות[618] only stresses the point, for it means "men of treachery,
men of deceitfulness."[619] The term בגדות is a hapax; words from the
root בגד occur many times in the OT in general and in the prophetic
literature in particular (e.g., Exod 21:8; Judg 9:23; 1 Sam 14:33; Hos 6:7;
Hab 2:5; Mal 2:15; Prov 25:19; Job 6:15; Lam 1:2). As even a cursory

---

[613] See the proposals of emendation mentioned above.

[614] Cf. Ben Zvi, 1990:92.

[615] אנשים ריקים ופחזים, i.e., "worthless and reckless fellows" (RSV; NRSV).

[616] See, for instance, KBL³; Gerleman, 1942: 49. Cf. Radak on Zeph 3:4,
פחזים. קלים כלומר קלי דעת כמו אנשים ריקים. Calvin says, "the word פחזים means strictly men of
nought, and also the rash, and those who are void of judgment as well as of all
moderation (Calvin:267).
Sabottka and others propose "boaster", see Sabottka: 106 and the bibliography
mentioned there.

[617] See Mc Kane, 1986:588. For a discussion on the meaning of פחזות, and consequently on
the meaning of פחזים, see Mc Kane, 1986: 594-95.

[618] For a discussion on the way in which the LXX translates פחזים and אנשי בגדות (also cf. OL),
see Gerleman, 1942: 50; cf. Ball, 1972/1988:159, 161. Gerleman has suggested that
the translator of the LXX thought of Jonah in these verses.

[619] The word בגדות may be interpreted as a feminine plural name but it is contextually more
likely that it is an abstract noun. For abstract nouns ending in ות see GKC § 86 l.

reading of the mentioned verses shows, the nature of the mentioned "treachery, deceit, faithlessness" can be deduced only from the context in which the term is used; the Hebrew terms from the root בגד do not differ in this respect from their equivalent in English (such as "treason" and the like).

In the vast majority of the instances in which there is an explicit reference to their wrongdoing (e.g., Jer 5:31; Ezek 22:28; Mic 3:5; Zech 13:3; Lam 2:14), prophets are indicted because of their prophesies. Sometimes, there is a note explaining why they have delivered false prophecies, for instance, they may have prophesied by "baal" (Jer 2:8) or for "money" (Mic 3:11), but in any case the result is the same, they did what they were not supposed to do: to prophesy false prophecies. Therefore, it is reasonable to conclude that the most probable "treachery, deceitfulness" of the prophets in Zeph 3:4 is that they did not prophesy authentic prophecies from YHWH.[620]

The priests are indicted because they חללו קדש, "profaned what is holy" (i.e., the exact opposite of what they are supposed to do) and תורה חמסו, "did violence against the instruction" (cf. Jer 22:3; Prov 8:36; Lam 2:6). The priests are supposed to perform rituals according to certain rules which are called תורה in priestly material (e.g., Lev 6:2,7,18, 7:1,11, 11:46, 12:7, 13:59, 14:2,32,57,15:32; Num 5:9; Num 6:13). While prophets cannot fulfill their role in society if their do not prophesy true prophecies, the priests cannot fulfill their role if they lose their true knowledge of the ritual instructions (see Ezek 7:26, cf. Jer 18:18).[621] It is noteworthy that whereas a priest may profane the holy unintentionally, the kind of act and attitude expressed by חמסו is clearly intentionally.

The expression חלל קדש occurs elsewhere in Lev 19:8, 22:15; Num 18:32; Ezek 22:26; Mal 2:11. The expression חמסו תורה occurs

---

620 Against scholars who related this "treachery" with breaking the "covenant" on the basis of the assumption that the "office" of the prophet was to "guard" the "covenant." E.g., Ball, 1972/1988: 161. The (or a) covenant is not mentioned in most of the indictments against prophets and certainly not here. See also the discussion on the term לעד, below.

621 According to Hag 2:11; Mal 2:7; 2 Chr 15:3, the priest is also a teacher of "instruction" for the people.

elsewhere only in Ezek 22:26. As mentioned above, scholars have noticed the existence of similarities between Zeph 3:3-4 and Ezek 22:25-28. The latter is considered post-monarchic and coming from Ezekiel, or his disciples,[622] or even much later.[623] There is a relatively widespread agreement that the writer of Ezek 22:25-29 used the text of Zeph 3:3-4 as a basis for his/her writing,[624] perhaps along with other texts already existent in the Ezekielian tradition.[625] The following comparison[626] of the texts shows the degree of similarity and dissimilarity between the two,

שׂריה בקרבה	קשׂר נביאיה בתוכה
אריות שׂאגים	כארי שׂואג טרף טרף
	נפשׂ אכלו חסן ויקר יקחו
	אלמנותיה הרבו בתוכה
Zeph 3:3a	Ezek 22:25
	(LXX points to a Hebrew
	אשׂר נשׂיאיה instead of
	the MT קשׂר נביאיה)

שׂפטיה זאבי ערב	שׂריה בקרבה
	כזאבים טרפי טרף
לא גרמו לבקר	לשׂפך דם לאבד נפשׂות
	למען בצע בצע
Zeph 3:3b	Ezek 22:27

נביאיה פחזים	ונביאיה טחו להם תפל
אנשׂי בגדות	חזים שׂוא וקסמים להם כזב
	אמרים כה אמר אדני ה'

---

622 See Zimmerli, 1979: 466-67.

623 See Garscha, 1974: 51-53; 283-311.

624 E.g., Zimmerli, 1979: 466-67; Rudolph, 1975: 287; Edler:151-60; Fishbane, 1986: 462-63. For the opposite proposal, see Smith-Lacheman: 138.

625 Garscha, 1979, 51-53; cf. Fishbane, 1986: 462-63.

626 The comparative outline follows Fishbane, 1986: 462, with a major difference. Here, the MT text is presented without any emendations and in Hebrew, that is, independent of the interpretative analysis implied in the translation.

ו ה' לא דבר

Ezek 22:28

Zeph 3:4a

כהניה חללו קדש   כהניה חמסו תורתי

חמסו תורה   ויחללו קדשי

בין קדש לחל לא הבדילו

ובין הטמא לטהור לא הודיעו

ומשבתותי העלימו עיניהם

ואחל בתוכם

Zeph 3:4b   Ezek 22:26

עם הארץ עשקו עשק

וגזלו גזל

ועני ואביון הונו

ואת הגר עשקו בלא משפט

Ezek 22:29

Clearly, it is much more likely that the writer of Ezekiel elaborated the basic outline of Zeph 3:3-4, according to his/her own tradition and language, than that the writer of Zeph 3:3-4 took the relatively large unit from the Book of Ezekiel, trimmed all the Ezekielian language and condensed it into four pairs of versets. The question, however, is whether the two texts point to a certain common tradition that in both cases has been adapted to the message and language of their respective books or that the present text of Zeph 3:3-4 stood before the writer of Ezek 22:25-29.

The note concerning the priests in Ezek 22:26 clearly resembles the one in Zeph 3:4b. They share the language, חמסו תורה, חללו קדש, and the additional lines in Ezek 22:26 seem to be explanatory. Nevertheless, it should be noticed that while the text in Ezek 22:6 reads תורתי and קדשי, i.e., a pronominal possessive suffix that refers to YHWH has been attached to the nouns (the latter in the plural), the text in Zeph 3:4b reads תורה and קדש, i.e., the "bare" noun without any suffixes. This difference between the two texts is significant because a similar one is attested in another case of "parallelism" between the text in Zeph 3:2-4 and prophetic literature elsewhere, namely between Jer 7:28 and Zeph 3:2. While Jer 7:29 reads בקול ה' אלהיו, Zeph 3:2 simply reads בקול ה'. As Lacheman and Smith have already pointed out, it is more probable that the writer of Zeph 3:2-3 made the same change in two received texts than that the authors of Jer 7:28 and Ezek 22:6 altered in the same way a received text of Zeph 3:2-4.[627] Accordingly, one may wonder if the proposal that the writer of Ezek 22:25-29 wrote under the influence of Zeph 3:3-4, and quoted from it, is not too simplistic.

Insofar as it concerns the two notes on the prophets (Zeph 3:4a; Ezek 22:28), one cannot point to any common language between them, except the word נביאיה. The occurrence of expressions that do not occur elsewhere in the OT (אנשי בגדות) or rarely occur (פחזים) is consistent with the preference for rarely attested words and expressions in many parts of Zephaniah (e.g., מלח ,כרת ,רעים ,גרמו ,רזה ,לחמם מכרה ,חרול ,ממשק ,חרב ,מראה). On the other hand, the language in Ezek 22:28 is consistent with the Ezekielian tradition of writing and clearly resembles Ezek 13:6-7.

A metaphorical language that is not attested in the other notes characterizes the notes concerning her (Jerusalem's) officers and judges in Zeph 3:3, and those concerning either "her princes"[628] (נשיאיה) or "her gang (or conspiracy) of prophets"[629] and "her officers" in Ezek 22:25,27.[630] This metaphorical language comprises references to animals, in both cases to lions and wolves. Neither the simple occurrence

---

[627] See Smith-Lacheman: 138-39.

[628] Following the LXX because of the existence of another note concerning the prophets, see Zimmerli, 1979: 465; Fishbane, 1986: 462, and the similar image in Ezek 19:1-6. Moreover, all the elements of the comprehensive list "kings, officers, priests and prophets" (see Jer 2:26, 4:9, 32:32; Neh 9:32) occur in Ezek 22:25-28, provided that "king" stands for the Ezekelian נשיא (cf. Ezek 12:12; Ezek 19:1-14).

[629] On behalf of this reading one may mention that because of the note on the prophets in Ezek 22:8 and because of the list mentioned above, this reading is the most difficult one. Moreover, the order in which the different groups are mentioned (in both MT and the LXX) is very unusual if the first group are "kings" but understandable if they are "prophets" (see below).

[630] Does it suggest a different traditional history for the two halves of the unit, before the unit was composed?

of these animals together (cf. Jer 5:6) nor the common motif of a roaring lion (cf. Judg 14:5; Am 3:4; Ps 22:14; Job 4:10) provide the main link between Zeph 3:3 and Ezek 22:27,25. Instead, the occurrence of the expression שריה קרבה in both texts, and especially the metaphorical reference to separate members of the ruling elite as wolves and lions connect the two. Nevertheless, even a cursory reading of the texts shows that the metaphorically described members of the elite do not overlap. The case is self-evident in the MT, but it holds true even if one accepts the reading suggested by the LXX and reads נשיאים in Ezek 22:25, for one cannot but read שריה in the "parallel" text in Zeph 3:3.

Since the king is called נשיא (commonly translated as "prince") in the Book of Ezekiel, and since the book contains many references to the "prince," and "princes of Israel" (e.g., Ezek 19:1, 21:2,22:6), one may only expect that an Ezekelian list of the ruling elite will open with a reference to "the princes," and accordingly, in our case with a metaphorical reference to lions (i.e., kings), and not to wolves. In addition, it is noteworthy that the language in Ezek 22:25 that is not "paralleled" in Zeph 3:3 clearly resembles Ezek 19:1-6 which also refers to the kings (or in Ezekielian language, the "princes") Summing up, the note concerning the "princes" in Ezek 22:25 (according to the LXX) is consistent with the Ezekielian tradition in contents and language.

While the (human) king (or "prince") is mentioned numerous times in Ezekiel, he is not mentioned at all in the Book of Zephaniah. Accordingly, the lack of reference to the king in Zeph 3:3 is as coherent with the general approach of the book as its mention in Ezekiel.

If Ezek 22:25-29 contains a list of the ruling elite that opens with the "kings" then it is hardly surprising that the list includes a reference to the "officers" (see Jer 1:18, 2:26, 25:18, 32:32; Neh 9:32, cf. Jer 49:38; Hos 13:10). What is surprising in this text is the order in which the different groups are mentioned: namely, kings, priests, officers, prophets, and the people of the land. This order may suggest either an original text reading "prophets" instead of "kings" (but see above), or the existence of an ideal conception of the society in which the two main figures are the "king"

(נשׂיא) and the "priest." Such a society may be discerned in Ezek 40-48.[631]

Such an ideal society is not mentioned in the Book of Zephaniah. So, one can hardly expect the same order in Zeph 3:3-4. Moreover, since the list in Zephaniah opens with "officers," it cannot continue with "officers." Thus, a new group is needed if the images of "lions" and "wolves" are to be maintained and referred to separate groups. The context in Zephaniah, especially v. 5, suggests that the most suitable group will be "judges."

The specific contents and the language of the image of the "judges-wolves" in Zephaniah differ almost in any detail from those in the "parallel" text in Ezekiel, except for the common mention of "wolves."[632] Significantly, the image of these wolves and the language in which this image is conveyed in Zeph 3:3 are in clear correspondence with Zeph 3:5, just as the image and the language of the "parallel account" in Ezek 22:27 are consistent with Ezek 22:3,6,12,13.[633] Needless to say, the "wolves" in Ezekiel are not "judges" as in Zeph 3:3, but "officers." The lack of a reference to the "judges" in the Ezekielian elite in Ezek 22:25-29 is consistent with a general tendency in the Book of Ezekiel, for this book contains no reference at all to "judges," even if words from the root שׁפט occur tens of times.

Comparing the contents of the two lists of the ruling elite leads to further significant results. Ezek 22:25-28 (according to the LXX reading) presents a version of the common list: kings, officers, priests and prophets (see Jer 2:26, 4:9, 32:32; Neh 9:32).[634] These are also the main groups mentioned in Lamentations, along with הזקנים, "the elders" (see Lam 1:6,19; 2:2,9,14; 4:16,20; 5:12), and the active groups in the narrative

---

[631] See Garscha, 1979:52. Obviously, this consideration has its implications on the dating of the piece.

[632] The same holds true for the proposed emendations of the text in Zeph 3:3.

[633] On the relationship between the language of Ezekiel 22: 25-29 and the language of other units in the Book of Ezekiel, see Garscha, 1979: 51-53.

[634] If the MT text is accepted, the list will read as follows: prophets, priests; officers, prophets (for the first pair cf. 2 Kgs 23:2; Jer 2:8, 4:9, 5:31, 8:10, 18:18, 23:11,33; 26:7,8,11,16, 28:7; Mic 3:11; Zech 7:3; Lam 4:13; the second pair is very unusual but occurs in both the LXX and the MT version of Ezek 22: 27-28.

concerning the trial of Jeremiah (Jer 26:11,16). In the latter, also the "people"—probably some kind of representation of the Jerusalemites—is mentioned all along the report, and זקני הארץ in Jer 26:17. The זקנים are mentioned in 2 Kgs 23:1-2, and probably in Mic 3:11 (both lack the "officers"); the "people" are mentioned in Ezek 22:29 (the verse that has no parallel in Zeph 3:3-4) and in Jer 1:18 (which lacks the prophets). "Judges" (שפטים) are not mentioned in this kind of lists, except in Zeph 3:3.

The recurrent mention of "kings, officers, priests and prophets," and to a certain extent also "elders" and "the people," reflects the conception of the writers and it was acceptable to their public. This conception cannot be entirely disassociated from the reality of the monarchic period, especially because of the dating of the pieces and the social-cultural continuity of the society.

The list in Zeph 3:3-4 mentions four clearly separate groups: officers, judges, prophets and priests. Judges and officers, as two separate groups, do not tend to occur together in the OT. One of its few possible occurrences[635] is in Mic 7:3, if the text really points to two different groups. According to Melammed, the pair שר ושפט in Exod 2:14 is a clear instance of a stereotypical hendiadys. Sometimes the two members of a hendiadys are separated in order to achieve a stylistic effect, but this feature does not alter the meaning of the stereotypical pair. Accordingly, he proposes that Mic 7:3 really means, "the prince and the judge [i.e., the stereotypical phrase] ask for payment." That is, the two groups are actually one.[636] It seems that this hendiadic meaning has influenced Zeph 3:3-4 (see below), but unlike Mic 7:3, Zeph 3:3-4 is an ambiguous text that plays on two different conceptions of the pair (as two different groups and as one single group) at the same time.

---

[635] The pair שר and שפט occurs in Isa 3:2-3, but there the term שר shows a narrow meaning (שר חמשים). In other two instances, Ps 148:11 and Am 2:3, the word שפט conveys the meaning of "ruler" and not that of "judge" The meaning of שפט is unclear in Hos 7:5-7, 13:10, and perhaps the text too.

[636] See Melammed, 1961, esp. 131-32.

The animal imagery in v. 3 does not convey a clear sense that "her officers" and "her judges" are the same group, or that they point to the same people (contrast with Moses in Exod 2:14). To the contrary, it seems to stress that they are not the same, for "her officers" are "lions" and "her judges" are "wolves," and everyone knows that "wolves" are not "lions."[637] Moreover, since the following "pair" ("her prophets" and "her priests") does not comprise one single group but two clearly distinct groups, the structure of the text suggests that the same holds true for the first pair.

Thus, one may conclude that in Zeph 3:3-4, "her officers" and "her judges" are two different groups. Since neither the pair "judges and prophets" (see Isa 3:2) nor the triad "judges and prophets and priests" tend to occur in lists concerning the Jerusalemite (or Judean) elite, and since Isa 1:23 seems to imply that "officers" acted as "judges,"[638] one has to conclude that Zeph 3:3-4 presents a rare list in both comparative and historical terms. The explanation is at hand: The list in Zeph 3:3-4, and especially, the note concerning the "judges," is consistent with its literary context (see v. 5), where the emphasis on judging is clear, both thematically and stylistically (see the link connecting בקר and בבקר בבקר [v. 3 and v. 5]).

But the text also points to another link—בקרבה (v. 3) with בקרבה (v. 5), one between YHWH and "her officers." Thus, YHWH is not in equivalence only to the second rank "judges" ("the wolves;" see בקר and בבקר בבקר) but also to the "officers" ("the lions"). But, if YHWH is the judge and also the officer (cf. Exod 2:14) then שׂר and שׁפט have a hendiadic connotation, for both terms converge in one figure: YHWH. Of course, the obvious question is why YHWH is not compared (or better, contrasted) with the highest possible rank: the king. The question is even sharpened by the fact that the most common list of the elite groups is

---

[637] The parallel note in Ezekiel 22:25-27 also suggests that the "lions" and the "wolves" are not to be taken as a unit, for v. 26 separates them, and נשׂיא and שׂר are clearly not a case of hendiadys.

[638] Cf. Weinfeld, 1977.

"kings, officers, priests and prophets" (see above). Certainly, this double "requirement" for the presence of the king in the text indicates that his absence is probably not accidental. The answer seems at hand: as mentioned above, there is no reference to a human king in Zephaniah 3 or in the entire Book of Zephaniah.[639] The lack of any reference to the king in Zeph 3:3-4 is consistent with the general trend of the book.

To sum up: Zeph 3:3-4 and Ezek 25-29 show similarities that point to a common textual tradition, but they also show important dissimilarities. Among the similarities one may mention the use of the expressions קדש חלל and חמס תורה concerning the priests, the animal images of lions and wolves, and the fact that both texts offer a relatively comprehensive list of the main groups in the described ruling Jerusalemite elite. The lists, however, are similar but far from being identical. The animal images do not correspond to the same referent, and the prophetic units share no language at all. The text in Zeph 3:3-4 is much shorter than the text in Ezek 22:25-29, but it is not less consistent with attested features occurring elsewhere in the Book of Zephaniah than Ezek 22:25-29 is in accordance with the Ezekielian literary tradition. Even the differences in the exact wording of חלל קדש and חמס תורה do not seem to be accidental but to reflect a certain tendency in Zeph 3:2-4 (see above). Consequently, one may conclude that the same type of compositional or redactional forces that shaped one of the pericopes shaped the other but in different ways. If this is the case, it is noteworthy that most of the features that cause Zeph 3:3-4 to be closely related to Zephanic material[640] do not occur in Ezek 22:25-

---

[639] For Zeph 1:8 see the note on this verse. Zeph 1:8 stands in a different unit that contains a different list of list of elite members, and that accuses them of different wrongdoings. Also the language of Zeph 3:3-5 does not resemble the one in Zeph 1:8-9 (except for the presence of the common word שר).

[640] Such as the absence of a reference to a human king, the reference to the judges, the presence of the phrase זאבי ערב לא גרמו לבקר in the note concerning the "judges," the occurrence of קדש and תורה instead of קדש and תורתי, and, probably, also the use of the expression אנשי בגדות. Certainly, one cannot infer from these observations that all the material found in Zephaniah is homogeneous from either a linguistic or a thematic point of view, or both. For instance, the differences between Zeph 1:4-5,8-9 on one hand and Zeph 3: 3-4 on the other are self-evident in both aspects. Significantly, there is no polemics against the Judean/Israelite worship of foreign gods in Zeph 3:3-4 (or in the

29.[641] Similarly, the features that cause Ezek 11:25-29 to be Ezekielian (see above) do not occur in Zeph 3:3-4.[642] These data can be easily explained by assuming that the writers of Zeph 3:3-4 and Ezek 22:25-29 shaped a common textual tradition, each on his/her own way. Alternatively one has to suggest that the writer of Ezek 22:25-29 took the present text of Zeph 3:3-4, removed its Zephanic features, changed the entire unit concerning the prophets and developed the rest according his/her own (Ezekielian) approach. This alternative, although possible, seems less likely.[643]

Zeph 3:3-4 is important not only because of the explicit conveyed message but also because of the implicit message. Since the officers, judges, prophets and priests are condemned because of their actions, the community reading the text is indirectly taught that they were capable of acting in that way. The officers and judges were capable of doing so because there were other, simple people, whom they oppressed. There is no oppressor without an oppressed. The prophets were unreliable and they prophesied the wrong prophecies, but this is possible in a society in which people are attentive to prophecies. Zeph 3:3-5 contains no indictment against people for listening to the prophet; that is exactly what they are supposed to do. The point in Zeph 3:3-5 is not that the people are

---

entire third chapter of Zephaniah), although it could be easily mentioned in a unit that refers entirely to the misbehavior of the Jerusalemite elite.

[641] The exception is the expression בקרבה in Zeph 3:3 (cf. Zeph 3:5) and Ezek 22:27. But בקרבה is a relatively common expression in this general context (cf. Jer 6:6, 29:8, 46:21; Hos 5:4, Am 3:9; Lam 4:13; Ps 55:11,12). If there was a common textual tradition to these two units (see below), one should assume that the expression בקרבה was already in this tradition, along with חמס תורה and חלל קדש. If this is the case, the idiom בקרבה was important for the composition of the unit, and used again in Zeph 3:5 because of its common association with some sort of the presence of God or of godly elements (cf. Jer 14:9; 31:33; Ezek 36:26; Mic 3:11; Ps 46:6). The expressions חמס תורה and חלל קדש, which point to issues that were not developed in the Book of Zephaniah, or any of its possible levels, were not employed as compositional or redactional devices.

[642] See the discussion of each of the separate notes.

[643] One may compare the situation here with the discussion concerning Isa 7:1 and 2 Kgs 16:5 (see Ben Zvi, 1986: 35-39, 63; cf. Thompson, 1982: 81-83).
The Book of Zephaniah, itself, contains a similar case, namely, Zeph 2:15 and Isa 47:8,10. There the language of the two texts is very close, and significantly, none of them seems to contain midrashic expansions or to depend on the other. See note on Zeph 2:15.

faithless, but that the prophets were faithless, and therefore the society influenced by them went astray. The same applies to the priests; the Jerusalemite priests are not accused of worshiping foreign gods (the contrast with Zeph 1:4-6 is self-evident) but they are accused of performing their duties in a way that did violence to their instructions concerning these matters. But since one can profane an offering only if there is an offering, one has to assume that the text implies that there were people who supported and felt dependent on the Yhwistic priests and their services. They cannot be condemned by doing so since it is exactly what they were supposed to do, but the priests behaved wrongly, and therefore, the society went astray.[644]

Finally, it is worth noting that the four groups mentioned —officers, judges, priests and prophets—are characterized by occupations in the service sector of the society, in what can be loosely defined as administration. There is no reference, for instance, to insatiable landlords (cf. Isa 5:8-10), or to cheating merchants (Am 8:5). Obviously, this does not mean that the writer[645] presumes that there were not such figures, nor that he/she presumes that the mentioned members of the elite would not take a field by violence or cheat in commerce. But the fact remains that the four groups are characterized by their function as members of the administration, by their roles in the service sector.

3.4.4. Zeph 3:5

While verses 3-4 explicitly characterize the ruling elite and its behavior, v. 5 characterizes a different kind of ruler: YHWH. The expression צדיק ה' in the first sentence and the closely related צדיק ה' are well attested in

---

[644] This socio-religious picture of the society sharply differs from the one in Zeph 1:4-6, as even a cursory reading of the text clearly shows.

[645] Strictly speaking, the implied author of this unit. But it seems unlikely that the writer thought significantly different from the implied authoritative author of this unit. For methodological issued concerning the social location of the implied author, see Robbins, 1989.

the Book of Psalms. The first occurs in Ps 129:4 (cf. Ps 116:5) and the second in Ps 11:7, 119:137, 145:17 (most if not all post-exilic).[646] In all cases but Ps 119:137, these expressions of praise provide the grounds for an explicit expectation of YHWH's action against wrongdoers, or in favor of the afflicted, or both, or if the action is explicitly described as something done in the past, they provide a kind of explanation for it, or a comment on it (Ps 129:4).

The phrase in Zeph 3:5 fulfills the same role. It is connected to the preceding verses in its contents as well as its grammar.[647] Not only that the contrast between YHWH's way of ruling, and especially of judging, and the ways of the groups mentioned in the preceding verses (esp. v. 3) is self-evident, but it is also underscored by the use of the language בקרבה and בקר in both v. 3 and v. 5. Thus, while the preceding verses provide the negative picture, the expression צדיק ה' provide the grounds for the expectation of change. The immediately following phrases in v. 5 develop such expectation.

The expression צדיק ה' occurs also in a similar context in Dan 9:14. Different is the case in Lam 1:18, 2 Chr 12:6 and probably Ezra 9:15. There, "Israel" is in distress because of its wrongdoing and these expressions state the awareness of the wrongdoers that they were wrong and that YHWH, who brought the distress upon Israel, is right (cf. Exod 9:27; Deut 32:4; Neh 9:32-33). The general formula צדיק אתה in judicial contexts states the innocence of the accused (see Prov 24:24) and may also be put in the mouth of the accuser (e.g., 1 Sam 24:18; cf. Josh 22:31).[648] Certainly, if YHWH is the accused, the formula will be ה'

---

[646] Psalms 116,119, 129, 145 are post-exilic. See, for instance, Anderson: 790, 805-07, 871-72, 935-36. Anderson considers that Ps 11 may be pre-exilic but see his own reservations on this point; see Anderson: 123; cf. Kraus: 826.
Ball suggests a potential difference of meaning between צדיק ה' and ה' צדיק, and that while the former should be translated "YHWH, the Righteous"(i.e., as an apposition, the latter may mean "YHWH is righteous." See Ball, 1972/1988: 221-22, and the bibliography mentioned there. Cf. GKC § 131c but also 132b.

[647] Note the third person feminine singular pronominal suffix in בקרבה. It is another ring in the chain of pronominal suffixes that extends from v. 5 to the city mentioned in v. 1.

[648] See Ramsey, 1977: 52. For the judicial connotations of צדיק see, for instance, Gen 18:23,25; 1 Kgs 8:32; Ezek 18:9; Qoh 3:17.

צדיק or צדיק אתה ה' (cf. Jer 12:1; Ps 119:137; Ezra 9:15; Neh 9:8). Consequently, one may understand texts such as Lam 1:18 and 2 Chr 12:6 as implying the rejection of the accusation against YHWH made by a group under distressful circumstances. In these texts, however, the accusation is rejected by the accuser, who acknowledges that YHWH is not to be blamed for the misfortune, and confesses the wrongdoing that caused the distress. Also a text such as Jer 12:1 becomes clear against this judicial background. If this is the case in all these instances, one can hardly assume that the writers and the public addressed by Ps 11:7; 116:5; 119:137; 129:4; and 145:17 were unaware of the judicial connotations of the formula, and the same holds true for Zeph 3:5. The emphasis on judgment (משפט) in Zeph 3:5 as well as the theme of punishing the wrongdoers and saving the oppressed or wrongly persecuted in the mentioned Psalms only confirms this understanding.[649]

Accordingly, a paraphrastic translation of the first line of Zeph 3:5 will read as follows: "YHWH who is not to be held responsible for the wrongdoing stated above is in its [Jerusalem's] midst. YHWH does[650] no wrong."

The issue addressed in the line is now clear: The predatory officers, along with the wolves-judges, the unreliable and unfaithful prophets and the priests who are doing the opposite of what they are supposed to do,[651] all are in Jerusalem but so is YHWH, who does no wrong. The recurrent use of the term בקרבה is a stylistic device that sharpens the point: YHWH stands at one side and the ruling elite at the other. Who is prevailing? The situation described seems to imply that the officers and their companions prevail. Why does evil prevail in a city in which

---

[649] Certainly, this understanding of צדיק ה' does not preempt the existence of other possible meanings and connotations for word צדיק, especially when non-judicial imagery is used.

[650] The imperfect form יעשה is used with the sense of "habitual, always done." Cf. Prov 15:20; Job 1:5.

[651] The presence of the three latter groups is implied in the text.

YHWH, who does no wrong, is also present ? The issue of theodicy emerges again (cf. Zeph 1:12).[652]

One may notice that the idiom עשׂה עולה, in the second part of this line occurs in Zeph 3:5,13 and elsewhere in the OT in Ps 37:1.[653] Significantly, Ps 37 is one of the *anwim* psalms. It deals with the problem of theodicy. It instructs the "righteous ones" not to be envious of the wicked (because they are doing well), reassures the "righteous ones" that they will be saved (in this world) from the hands of the "wicked," that the latter will be cut off (v. 9), and that at that time the righteous will inherit the land (v. 9, note the verbs יכרתון, יירשׁו).[654] These topics are present in Zephaniah.

The imperfect form יתן can be understood as pointing to a future action or to a continuous behavior.[655] The second alternative seems more appropriate because the only other imperfect in the verse indicates perpetual behavior (and not a future action), and besides a verbless clause, the other clauses contain participles. The use of the adverbial form בבקר בבקר is congruent with such an understanding. Besides Zeph 3:5, this form occurs in Exod 16:21, 30:7, 36:3; Lev 6:5; 2 Sam 13:4; Isa 28:19, 50:4; Ezek 46:13,14,15; 1 Chr 23:30; 2 Chr 13:11. In these occurrences בבקר בבקר means "every morning."[656] In contrast to the wolves-judges who are unable (and perhaps have no desire) to judge in the morning (see above), YHWH issues his judgment every morning. The

---

[652] See notes on Zeph 1:12.

[653] The similar idiom פעל עולה occurs in Ps 119:3 and Job 36:23. See note on Zeph 2:3.

[654] This psalm shows also several wisdom features. Most scholars consider it post-exilic. On Ps 37, see Anderson: 292-301; Gerstenberger, 1988: 157-60. Concerning the intention of this psalm, Gerstenberger writes: "to admonish the faithful to keep on the right path in spite of all the irritation and provocation from the wicked ones, and to revive and sustain hope for a fundamental change for the better (Gerstenberger, 1988: 160)."

[655] O'Connor considers יתן a *qal* passive, separates the two בבקר and sees עולה as the subject of the sentence. Accordingly, he translates: "The evil one does not act in the morning." See O'Connor: 256. For a critical approach to O'Connor's position, see Cathcart, 1984.

[656] For repetition of one or more words in order to express the idea of "all" or "every," see GKC § 123 c.

expression נתן משפט is unusual; it occurs elsewhere in Job 36:6 (יתן רשע ומשפט עניים יחיה (לא[657] and in Ezek 23:24.[658]

The MT, the LXX, and the Vg.[659] relate משפטו יתן to לָאוֹר (cf. Hos 6:5) and so do, for instance, Rashi, Luther and Calvin, as well as several modern scholars.[660] In modern scholarship, however, there is a tendency to relate לאור to the following phrase.[661] On behalf of the first approach, besides the fact that it is the unemended MT and that it is supported by other ancient versions, one may point to Hos 6:5 and suggest therefore that there is an implied ויוציא in Zeph 3:5.[662] The general comparison between משפט ("justice") and אור ("light") in Isa 51:4 (cf. Ps 37:6), as well as the text of the Peshitta, led several scholars to the proposal that the original Hebrew text read כאור instead of לאור. This אור may be understood as "light" or "sun."[663] In any case this understanding of the text leaves לא נעדר without a temporal modifier and rejects an almost self-evident relation between בבקר בבקר and לאור. [664]

The basic meaning of the word אור is "light," as opposed to "darkness," (e.g., Gen 1:3-4; Isa 42:16, 45:7, 59:9; Job 38:19). Like the English word "light" the Hebrew אור appears in a relatively large number of derived uses and meanings.[665] Already in Gen 1:5 "the light" (האור)

---

657 From Elihu's speech.

658 Cf. Krinetzki: 132-33.

659 Tg. Neb. to Zeph 3:5 is far from being a literal translation.

660 See, for instance, Sabottka, 1972: 107-08; Krinetzki: 21; House: 124. Cf. KJV.

661 E.g., J. M. P. Smith: 241; Gerleman, 1942: 51; Bic: 65; Ball, 1972/1988: 161-62; Cathcart, 1984; R. L. Smith: 137; Kapelrud, 1975: 107; Edler:10, 95; O'Connor: 256; van Grol: 189; cf. RSV; NRSV; Schöckel-Valverde (Nueva Biblia Española).

662 See, for instance, Bula.

663 See, for instance, Rudolph, 1975: 284, 286; Elliger (BHS). According to Ribera Florit, Tg. Neb. also supports the emendation (Ribera Florit: 147) but see Cathcart, 1984: 36. Concerning the Peshitta, see Cathcart, ibid.

664 See, for instance, Gerleman, 1942: 51. In addition to the topical link between אור and בקר, the two words tend to occur together in the phrase אור הבקר/אור בקר (see, Gen 44:3; Judg 16:2; 1 Sam 14:36, 25:34,36; 2 Sam 17:22, 23:24; 1 Kgs 7:9; Mic 2:1). If this is the case, Zeph 3:5 presents another instance of breaking up common phrases for stylistic purposes (cf. אש להבות [Ps 105:32] and אש להבות [Ps 29:7] with Isa 10:17; Num 21:28) See Melammed, 1961; cf. Berlin, 1985: 76.

665 BDB mentions eleven different special uses of אור.

is called "day" (יום). In Judg 19:26 האור conveys the sense of "the first light," and clearly means "dawn" in Neh 8:3.[666]

If "the light" (האור) is interpreted as "dawn,"[667] or "daylight," the phrases בבקר בבקר משפטו יתן and לאור לא נעדר show a parallel structure. Both begin with a modifier of time (thematically related to v. 3), have the verb at the end, and communicate the identity of the subject of the phrase (YHWH) by the verbal form.[668] Moreover, in that case, these two versets seem equivalent to the first two in the verse, and the movement from the affirmative verbal form to the negative in both pairs of versets formally stresses the correspondence between the two. Furthermore, in that case, the four versets develop a clear ongoing message:

(1) In Jerusalem's midst is YHWH, who is not to be blamed for the wrongdoing.

(2) YHWH does no wrong (a negative assertion that leads to the question: Can YHWH do right?).

(3) YHWH issues his/her judgment every morning (so YHWH can do right).

(4) YHWH does not fail[669] at (every) daybreak (so YHWH not only can do right but also cannot but do his/her judgment).

If one strips the four versets from the adverbial modifiers that relate the text to vv. 3-4, one finds the sequence:

ה' צדיק - לא יעשה עולה - משפטו יתן - לא נעדר

This sequence clearly supports the above mentioned understanding of the text.[670]

---

[666] Perhaps it means "dawn" also in Job 24:14.

[667] Or daylight, see Ball, 1972/1988: 162. It has been suggested that אור means "evening" in Job 24:14. This meaning is attested in Mishnaic Hebrew (e.g., m. Pes. 1.1) and cf. the Aramaic אורתא (see Jastrow).

[668] In the third verset also by the pronominal suffix in משפטו.

[669] See, for instance, BDB III עדר, Ball, 1972/1988: 162-63; Cathcart, 1984: 37.

[670] The same holds true if אור means "evening" as it may occur in Mishnaic Hebrew. In that case, בבקר בבקר and אור will be a merism, equivalent to בקר and ערב (e.g., Gen 1:5). However, אור meaning "evening" is not clearly attested in the OT. The same meaning is achieved if one proposes a simple haplography in an original text reading לא לאור (cf. Job 12:25; see Sabottka: 108, n.27 and the bibliography mentioned there). Although such scribal error is technically possible, and the suggestion leads to a very plausible

The crucial question concerning the last portion of the verse, עַוָּל בֹּשֶׁת
וְלֹא יוֹדֵעַ, concerns the identity of the subject of the sentence.
Apparently the answer is simply: YHWH, as in all the other sentences in
this verse. If this is the case, the sentence says: "YHWH does not 'know'
X," where X stands for עול בֹשֶׁת. The term עול בֹשֶׁת is certainly
negative; therefore, the use of "not to know"[671] is expected if one
compares Zeph 3:5 with Nah 1:7 ("YHWH is mindful [יָדֵעַ] of those who
seek refuge in him." The same kind of divine attitude is mentioned in
other biblical pieces in which the wicked are described as enjoying
prosperity (e.g., Prov 24:19; Ps 37:12-20; Ps 94:23). The main objection
against this approach is that עול בֹשֶׁת does not occur elsewhere. The
word עַוָּל, meaning "wicked," occurs elsewhere in Job 18:21, 27:7,
29:17, 31:3, but עַוָּל occurs nowhere else in the OT as *nomen regens*.
Moreover, the noun בֹשֶׁת means "shame" in the vast majority of its
occurrences.[672] But the expression "wicked of shame" seems unusual
indeed. A simple emendation from בֹשֶׁת to בֹשֵׁם may solve the objection
(cf. Exod 33:12),[673] or alternatively one may consider בֹשֶׁת to be a late
addition, due to an erroneous understanding of עול as the subject of the
sentence.[674]

Neither the MT nor any of the versions understood the text in such a
way. The existence of a copulative *waw* at its beginning set the clause
apart from the other sentences in v. 5 (and from the rest of Zeph 3:1-5 as
well). Thus, the third person singular in יוֹדֵעַ (i.e., the subject) is not
necessarily YHWH. The MT, the Vg and Tg. Neb. consider עול the

---

original text; yet it remains an unnecessary hypothesis if the text can be explained
without proposing emendations.

[671] Perhaps, it should be translated: "not to be mindful." Cf. Nah 1:7 (NJPSV).

[672] In Hos 9:10; Jer 3:24, 11:13 בֹשֶׁת stands instead for "Baal," and in 2 Sam 2:8, 11: 21, בֹשֶׁת
stands for the theophoric element "Baal" in the names ירבעל (cf. Judg 6:32); אשבעל (cf. 1
Chr 8:33).

[673] Cf. Ball, 1972/1988: 164.

[674] Ball suggests that בֹשֶׁת stands for Baal (see Ball, 1972/1988: 164-65), but this is neither
the most common use of בֹשֶׁת nor is the ruling elite mentioned in vv. 3-4 accused of
worshiping Baal. Sabottka, who interprets the verse differently, also thinks that בֹשֶׁת
refers to Baal (see Sabottka: 108-09). For a critical approach to Sabottka's proposals,
see, for instance, del Olmo Lete: 301 and Kapelrud, 1975: 36.

subject. The phrase reads, therefore: "and the wicked knows no shame."[675] This is not only a change of subject but an entire change in orientation. Instead of focusing on theodicy, the phrase focuses on the culpability of the wicked (human beings), and the underlying question turns out to be: why the wicked do evil in spite of the presence and actions of God? The answer given is clear: because they know no shame. If this is the case, the cumulative weight of the change in the general outlook, the change in the subject, the interpretative character of the phrase, and the use of the copulative *waw* to anchor the phrase to the text,[676] suggest that the phrase is due to reflective activity on the text (cf. Hos 14:10).[677]

3.4.5. Zeph 3:6

Unlike the situation in the preceding verses, YHWH is the first person singular in v. 6. The verse describes YHWH's actions against the "peoples" (גוים)[678] and their results.

Concerning the word פנות, see note on Zeph 1:16. The rest of the verse,

החרבתי חוצותם מבלי עובר

נצדו עריהם מבלי איש מאין יושב

clearly recalls the following phrases,[679]

(Jer 2:15) עריו נצתה מבלי ישב

---

[675] For different proposals of emendation leading to different understandings, see, for instance, Cathcart, 1984 and the bibliography mentioned there.

[676] The phrase also seems to disrupt the structure of two pairs of two versets and stands after, and unrelated to, the climax of this structure. For an analysis based on metrics that leads to similar conclusions, see van Grol: 189

[677] For the position that the phrase is secondary, see, for instance, J. M. P. Smith : 241; Irsigler, 1977:164, 188; Bic:67; Brockington: 263; Edler: 108. Some scholars waver (see Kapelrud, 1975: 36) and others reject this proposal (e.g., Ball, House).

[678] The LXX probably read נאים instead of גוים. This reading provides a smooth transition from vv. 3-5 to v. 7, and is therefore suspicious. Moreover, the references to עריהם and חוצותם clearly point to the reading גוים. This reading is attested in the MT, the Vg., Tg. Neb. and the Peshitta.

[679] See, Krinetzki: 139.

(Jer 4:7) עריך תצינה מאין יושב

(Jer 9:11) נצתה כמדבר מבלי עֹבֵר

(Jer 26:9) העיר הזאת תחרב מאין יושב

The expression מבלי איש occurs nowhere else in the OT but עֹבֵר
מבלי איש occurs in Jer 9:9.[680] The expression מבלי יושב occurs in
Jer 9:10 but nowhere else.[681]

The similarities between the texts only sharpen the main difference.
Jeremiah shows a verbal form from II נצה ("fall in ruins");[682] Zeph 3:6
reads נצדו from II צדה ("lay waste"). Words from the root II צדה do
not occur elsewhere in the OT, but the cognate Aramaic צדי is common
(cf. Tg. Neb. Zeph 3:6).[683]

3.4.6. Zeph 3:7

The verb אמרתי does not necessarily mean "I said (with my mouth),"
but may mean "I said (in my mind), i.e., "I thought" (e..g. Gen 20:11,
26:9; Exod 2:14; Num 24:11; Josh 22:33; 1 Sam 20:26; 2 Sam 12:22,
21:16; 1 Kgs 5:19; 2 Kgs 5:11; Ruth 4:4; 2 Chr 13:8, 28:10,13, 32:1
[without parallel in 1-2 Kgs]).[684] Accordingly, one may understand

---

[680] מאין איש occurs nowhere in the OT.

[681] It is noteworthy that the expression מאין יושב is attested in eleven times in Jeremiah (Jer
4:7, 26:9, 33:10, 34:22, 44:22; 46:19, 48:9. 51: 29, 37) but elsewhere only in Isa 5:9,
6:11; Zeph 2:5, 3:6. The only other occurrence of מבלי עובר besides Zeph 3:6 and Jer
9:9,11 is in Ezek 14:15.

[682] See KBL3, entry II נצה (cf. BDB, III נצה). Concerning Jer 2:15, see also KBL3, entry יצת
(the qere in Jer 2:15 reads נצתו instead of נִצְּתָה, i.e., from יצת. On the נצה - יצת controversy
in Jer 2:15, see Mc Kane, 1986: 36.

[683] Rudolph suggests that נצדו is an Aramaism. See Rudolph, 1975: 286. Certainly, this
means neither that the word is not a Hebrew word (and therefore that it is not governed
by the rules of Hebrew grammar) nor that is an imitation of Aramaic, but that there is a
certain pattern of occurrence for this word, and that this pattern may point to linguistic
influence. On the general issue of Aramaism, see Barr, 1968: 121-24.

[684] The meaning "to think" is sometimes explicitly stressed by the addition of a modifier
such as בלבבך (e.g., Deut 8:17; Isa 14:13, 47:8,10; Zeph 1:12, 2:15; Ps 14:1; Qoh
2:1,15). As the examples mentioned in the text, the addition of this modifier is not a
necessary condition for conveying the meaning "to think."

YHWH's saying in v. 7 as a quotation of YHWH's previous thought[685] and then, the second person feminine (תיראי, תקחי), although it refers to Jerusalem does not turn Jerusalem into the addressee of the entire speech of YHWH (note the third person singular suffix in מעונה and עליה, v. 7). Moreover, it is worth noting that in that case Jerusalem will be only the formal addressee of the linguistic form in which a thought was expressed. Thus, the text does not claim that Jerusalem is the actual addressee but claims that YHWH, while addressing an unidentified audience (not Jerusalem, see above), "incidentally" indicates that in his/her own thinking, YHWH referred to the wicked Jerusalem (before its punishment) as it were his/her addressee,[686] and that at that time YHWH was hoping that the punishment would never take place, that Jerusalem "will learn the lesson" (תקחי מוסר)[687].

The text in Zeph 3:7 claims that according to YHWH the most fundamental lack in Jerusalem is the lack of יראת ה'.[688] Such centrality of יראת ה' is clearly stated in Prov 1:7, 9:10[689] and Ps 110:10, whose language recalls the language of Prov 1:7, 9:10.[690]

---

[685] See, for instance, Abrabanel; Eiselen: 540; Watts, 1975: 177; Sabottka: 111; Rudolph, 1975: 284; cf. NJPSV; NJB.

[686] The change from the third person to the second person, and vice versa, while referring to the same person, is a well attested stylistic device, mainly in poetry (see Berlin, 1985: 40-41 and the bibliography mentioned there; cf. Gevirtz 1972: 170-71). Sometimes, it is used to emphasize the closeness between the speaker and the referred person (e.g., Cant 1: 2-4; cf. Zeph 3:7).

[687] Concerning לקח מוסר see note on Zeph 3:2.

[688] The word אך in Zeph 3:7 has a restrictive meaning which includes an element of contrast with the preceding thought (i.e., "only"; cf. Gen 27:13; Judg 10:15; 1 Sam 18:17; 1 Kgs 17:13; Isa 45:14; cf. Snaith, 1964). For this understanding of אך in Zeph 3:7, see, for instance, del Olmo Lete: 302; Watts, 1975: 177; Bic: 65; R. L. Smith: 139; Krinetzki: 21; cf. Schöckel-Valverde (Nueva Biblia Española).
In other cases, the sense of "on the contrary" has led to a conveyed meaning of "nothing else than," which is translated by "surely" (e.g., Gen 44:28; see R. J. Williams: 65 § 389. Many scholars understand אך as "surely" also in Zeph 3:7. See, for instance, J. M. P. Smith:242; Ball, 1972/1988: 293; House: 124; cf. RSV; NRSV. Sabottka considers אך a defective writing for איך, "how," see Sabottka:111. For a critical response, see del Olmo Lete: 302.

[689] Cf. Prov 2:5, 8:13, 10:27,14:26,27, 15:33, 23:17. For Prov 22:4, see note on Zeph 2:3.

[690] The importance of the motif יראת ה' is stressed in other Psalms (e.g., Ps 19:10, 25:12, 34:12-15, 128), and it certainly does not occur only there (e.g., Gen 20:11; Job 28:28; Isa 11:2,3, 50:10). It is noteworthy that the concept יראת ה' tends to be associated with

What will happen if Jerusalem learns the lesson? The answer is in the phrase ולא יכרת מעונה כל אשר פקדתי עליה. The two halves of the phrase have been interpreted in different ways. The LXX, as well as the Peshitta, understood מעיניה instead of מעונה; Tg Neb. understood פקדתי עליה in a positive way,[691] unlike the Vg. and the LXX. Jerome understood the phrase to mean, "and her dwelling place will not vanish because of all which I punish upon her."[692] More recently, many scholars have preferred the LXX reading מעיניה.[693] In addition there is a tendency to understand פקד על according to its meaning in Job 36:23; 2 Chron 36:23//Ezra 1:2, instead of its more common meaning "to visit, to reach for punishment, to punish" (cf. Zeph 1:8)[694] This tendency leads to translations of the second part of the phrase such as "anything I have laid upon her."[695]

An analysis of the first part of the phrase shows that it is a relatively simple Hebrew expression. The *waw* means not only "and" but also "so" (cf. 1 Sam 15:23). As אך opens the protasis, *waw* opens the apodosis.[696] The verbal form יכרת in Zeph 3:7 is clearly related to הכרתי in v. 6. Contrasting different patterns of the same root is a well-attested stylistic device.[697] A similar change, but the other way around (i.e., from *niphal* to *hiphil*) occurs, in Gen 6:12. In Gen 6:12, the change to *hiphil* underscores the active role of "all flesh;" while the opposite move (i.e., from *hiphil* to *niphal*) in Zeph 3:6-7 seems an effort to withdraw the image of YHWH as the active figure in the unit. The expression מעון

---

ethical (or moral) behavior (e.g., Gen 20:11; Ps 34:12-15; Prov 16:6; Job 28:28 [interpreted as another instance of a breaking up of a stereotypical formula, see above] and cf. Neh 5:15)

691 Cf. Rashi; Grotius (mentioned by Owen in Calvin:279); Ball, 1972/1988: 169-70.

692 The ET of the Vg. according to Ball, 1972/1988: 168. Radak and Calvin understood the verse in a very similar way.

693 E.g., G. A. Smith: 68; Ehrlich: 461; J. M. P. Smith: 242; Elliger, 1951: 72; Rudolph, 1975: 286; House: 132; Edler: 21; RSV; NRSV; cf. NJB.

694 See note on Zeph 1:8.

695 J. M. P. Smith: 242.

696 See del Olmo Lete: 302; R. J. Williams: 72 § 440; cf. GKC § 493 c.

697 See Berlin, 1985: 36-40 and the bibliography mentioned there.

698.החרבתי חוצותם מבלי עובר is unique but is equivalent to כרת
The use of here מעונה points to an interesting development of the
metaphorical personification of Jerusalem: She (Jerusalem) may fear
YHWH, may learn the lesson, so she is a person. As a person she has a
dwelling place. What is her dwelling place? Of course, Jerusalem.

The second part of the phrase, כל אשר פקדתי עליה[699] stands either
as a parallel (perhaps, a heightening parallel) to יכרת מעונה or as an
explanatory note (appositional clause)[700] to, or more probably, a parallel
to מעונה. The latter approach is followed by Rashi, Grotius and Ball; the
former by the Vg., Radak and KJV.

Although the verbal form פקדתי על occurs in several meanings, it
generally conveys a negative sense, such as " to reach for punishment, to
punish."[701] Contextually, one may notice that the first part of the phrase
concerns punishment and that the entire meaning of the apodosis is that
upon certain conditions the expected punishment will not take place. In
addition, the description in v. 6—which is the prototype of the destruction
potentially cancelled in v. 7—is not focused on the city or its battlements
but conveys a sense of general destruction, desolation. Taking into
consideration all these elements, one may conclude that the most likely
understanding of כל אשר פקדתי עליה is the one conveying a sense of
"punishment." The range of possible meanings for V- כל אשר (where V
stands for "verb") is restricted to possible accusatives of V. For instance
"all that God had made" (כל אשר עשה) in Gen 1:31 can refer only to
objects that can be "done by God," and according to Exod 18:24,
"(Moses) did all that he (Jethro) said" (ויעש כל אשר אמר). Of course,
the question is what did Jethro say to Moses? The meaning of this אשר
כל is to derived from the preceding verses. Thus, in our case, פקדתי

---

698 Significantly, there is no equivalent to הכרתי גוים (i.e., something such as הכרתי ישראל).

699 O'Connor separates כל from אשר פקדתי עליה, and accordingly translates, "Nothing (כל)
    shall be cut off from her dwelling, when I take notice of her" (O'Connor: 257). It is
    worth noting that the expression כל אשר occurs more than two hundred times in the OT.

700 . . . כל אשר introduces a clause that stands for a noun, see below.

701 See note on Zeph 1:8.

כל אשר refers to "objects" that are possible accusatives of עליה פקדתי, whose meaning is to inferred from the preceding verse, and that conveys a negative message. Therefore, the meaning of פקדתי עליה here must be in range of " lay upon as a charge (BDB), imposed," and one understands the nature of what has been imposed by the preceding words: the destruction of Jerusalem.

Thus, the phrase can be understood as: (a) "her dwelling will not be cut off and all (punishment) I have imposed on her (will not be);" or (b) "her dwelling will not be cut off (as, i.e., according to) all I have imposed on her."[702] The first proposal implies an elliptic negation of the second phrase. Certainly, the context makes an affirmative understanding of the phrase absurd. The second proposal implies the existence of a non-written comparative כ before כל. That comparisons between the main elements of two subsequent versets can be expressed without a written כ is clear already from Zeph 3:3-4.[703] It is noteworthy that according to both readings the verbal form פקדתי על has indeed the meaning attested in Job 36:23; 2 Chron 36:23 (// Ezra 1:2) but conveys the meaning of punishment, as usually conveyed by the expression פקדתי על. Moreover, such an understanding provides another example of ongoing heightening in the apodosis. First, the reference to "cut off," and then "to all I have imposed on her."

The word אכן introduces the note concerning the response of the people of Jerusalem to the "if . . . then" proposal made by YHWH. אכן not only introduces the response but already points to circumstances that are the opposite of what was expected or hoped (i.e., "but;" e.g., Isa 49:4; 53:4; Jer 3:20; Ps 82:7).[704]

The verbal form השכימו in השכימו השחיתו has an adverbial meaning, "eagerly, ardently." Such a construction is well attested in the

---

[702] Cf. the Vg.

[703] See Bula. Sometimes, the comparison is contextually implied (i.e., elliptic) even in the absence of a parallel structure, cf. Jer 3:20, where אכן means "but" (see below).

[704] See BDB.

OT (e.g., Hos 9:9)[705] but the exact pair does not occur elsewhere, as it is the case in many of these pairs. The use of עלילות in notes of indictment (or in references to a past shameful behavior) along with a pronominal suffix pointing to the indicted is attested in the Book of Ezekiel (Ezek 20:43,44, 21:29, 24:14, 36:17,19)[706] but occurs nowhere else in Latter Prophets but in Zeph 3:7,11.[707] In Ezekiel עלילות is usually paired with דרכים[708] but this is not the case in Zeph 3:7, which in this sense recalls the use of עלילה in Ps 14:1, 99:8.[709]

3.4.7. Zeph 3:8[710]

The verbal expression חכו לי is in the imperative. The addressees, in the second person plural,[711] seem to be those referred to by the third person plural pronominal suffix in the preceding אכן clause, i.e., the Jerusalemites. This interpretation is consistent with the context, for the Jerusalemites have rejected the divine offer and the following לכן ("therefore") clause is one of judgment. However, the verbal expression חכה ל -X, "waiting for X," occurs elsewhere with X standing for desirable objects (e.g., Isa 8:17, 64:3; Hab 2:3; Ps 33:20; 106:13; Job 3:21; cf. Isa 30:18). This feature has led some interpreters to suggests that the addressees are not those who are to be punished in that day but someone else, someone who is longing for the day in which YHWH will

---

[705] See GKC § 120 g.

[706] Cf. its use in Ezek 14: 22, 23,

[707] The word עלילה itself occurs elsewhere in these books only in Isa 12:4 (the exact expression occurs in Ps 105:1 and 1 Chr 16:8; cf. Ps 9:12) but there refers to the deeds of God. Cf. Jer 32:19, which also refers to God's deeds.

[708] See, Zimmerli, 1979: 316.

[709] But not in the parallel version of the psalm, in Ps 53:2. Both Ps 14 and Ps 53 are probably post-monarchic, see Gerstenberger, 1988: 218-21. Ps 99 is one of the YHWH *malak* Psalms (Psalms celebrating the kingship of YHWH).

[710] As a curiosity, it is worthy of mention that this is the only verse in the Hebrew Bible that contains all the letters of the Hebrew alphabet (ש stands for both שׂ and שׁ), including one representative of each final letter.

[711] The LXX reads second person singular feminine, namely, "the city." The same holds true for the Peshitta.

act against the "wicked," not only in Jerusalem but all over the "world."[712] Moreover, nowhere else in Zeph 3:6-8 (or Zeph 3:1-8) there is a clear reference to someone in the second person, except in v. 7 when YHWH quotes a previous thought. One may conclude that Zeph 3:8, as well as Zeph 3:1-8, makes no attempt to clarify the identity of the addressees, and consequently it remains ambiguous.

The expression חכו . . . ליום קומי points to a patient waiting for "the day" that surely will come. It does not convey the sense that the "day" is near. In this respect, Zeph 3:8 is clearly different from Zeph 1:14.[713]

The most disputed term in the verse is לעד. The three main approaches to this term are already represented by the MT (in its literal sense, see below), by the LXX and by the Vg. While לעד is vocalized in the MT לְעַד, i.e., meaning "for the booty" (cf. Gen 49:17; Isa 33:23), the LXX[714] points to a Hebrew reading לְעֵד, i.e., "as an accuser, as a witness, (cf. Mic 1:2; Mal 3:5; Ps 50:7). Finally, the Vg. suggests a Hebrew reading לָעַד, i.e., "forever, everlasting."[715]

The MT reading, "for the booty," is contextually appropriate, for YHWH's decision has been already made (כי משפטי לאסף גוים . . .) on the basis of the mentioned acts in the last line of v. 7 (see לכן,

---

[712] This timeless hope is not unique to prophetic literature (see, for instance, Pss 37, 94; Prov 24:19). The literary figure of the righteous asking YHWH to arise (קום) in order to act against the wicked (and rescue the righteous), or of YHWH doing so, occurs many times in the Book of Psalms (e.g., Ps 3:8; 44:24-27; 68:2-4; 74:21-23; 76:10; 82:8).

[713] The image of YHWH arising (קום) to execute judgment occurs elsewhere in the OT (e.g., Ps 12:6; 76:10; Isa 28:21; 33:10; cf. Am 7:9; Ps 3:8; 12:6; 44:24-27; 68:2-4; 74:21-23; 82:8; 102:13-14; 132:8-9). It is noteworthy that this image in Ps 12:6 and 76:10—which are the closest to Zeph 3:8—is explicitly related to rescuing ענוים or עניים (cf. Zeph 2:3).

[714] Also the Peshitta, which follows the LXX in this case, and probably Tg. Neb. (see Ribera Florit: 156).

[715] A fourth approach to the question is Sabottka's proposal to understand לעד as "vom Throne" (see also Watts, 1975:118), i.e., to understand the preposition ל as "from" (see Pardee's response; Pardee, 1974) and עד as "throne," following Dahood. See Sabottka, 113-14. Also there have been proposals for emendations of the consonantal text (e.g., Ehrlich proposes an original לָעֵץ instead of לעד, see Ehrlich: 462.

"therefore" at the beginning of v. 8).[716] The metaphorical image of the verse is not a "judge" (because "judging' has already been taken place) but a "warrior," or even "executor."

The LXX reading suggests the image of a court in which YHWH is the judge and the accuser (cf. Jer 29:23;[717] Mic 1:2; Mal 3:5; Ps 50:7). Since the nature of the expected verdict is self-evident, such an understanding of the verse is consistent with the reference to YHWH's prior decision to punish the peoples. Thus, the statement that YHWH will testify is to be understood as a different way of saying that the accused is already doomed. Without entering into the scholarly discussion concerning the existence and main features of the "prophetic lawsuit" genre,[718] there is no doubt that Zeph 3:8 strongly differs from the main pieces that have been assigned to this genre (Isa 1:2-3, 18-20 [or 10-20]; Jer 2:4-13 [or 2-37]; Mic 6:1-8; Hos 4:1-3; cf. Deut 32:1-25; Ps 50).[719] Moreover, there is no mention of specific judicial procedures in Zeph 3:8, except for this proposed reading. Instead the text points to the ubiquitous and entirely general concept that YHWH will act against those who deserve it, or that YHWH's deeds against them are nothing but judgment. Certainly, this concept is not inconsistent with a metaphorical reference to YHWH—who is considered omniscient—as the most reliable witness. Thus, YHWH's true and condemning testimony together with YHWH's words in the

---

[716] Cf. Radak; Calvin; Altschuler; KJV. Concerning modern research, see Gerleman, 1942: 55; Barthélemy, 1980: 382; cf. Ball, 1972/1988: 172, 231-32, 294.

[717] There is a special need for YHWH's testimony in Jer 29:23, for the issues at stake are adultery made in secrecy and the matter that YHWH order the prophets to prophesy. See Carroll, 1986: 555. Such a necessity does not fulfill a significant role in the other instances.

[718] See, for instance, Daniels, 1987, and the bibliography mentioned there.

[719] In Zeph 3:8, the solemn preamble is missing; there is no appeal for attention; the judge/plaintiff does not address the accused in an interrogatory form, to the contrary it is questionable if YHWH address the accused at all; there is no mention of YHWH's previous deeds in favor of the accused (YHWH's thought that Jerusalem would be saved if it will learn the lesson is not equivalent to the "historical" accounts in Jer 2:6-7, Mic 6: 4-5, for instance). Also the important appeal to heaven and earth, whose occurrence in some of these pieces supposedly supports the idea that this genre is related to "covenant," is not in Zeph 3:8; the concept of "covenant" or its breakdown is not mentioned at all in Zeph 3:8, (or Zeph 3: 1-8). Also Zeph 3:8 contains neither the characteristic term ריב (e.g., Jer 2:9; Hos 4:1,4; Mic 6:1,2) nor the common reference to the futility of the cultic deeds of the addressees (see Isa 1:11-15; Mic 6:6-7; Ps 50:8-14).

second part of the verse (i.e., . . . כי משפטי לאסף גוים) point to the
two parts of a double inference statement, namely a) the condemned have
behaved wrongly, therefore (b) the already decided action of YHWH is
necessarily judgment; and (a.1) YHWH's decision to punish is judgment,
therefore (b.1) the condemned must have behaved wrongly. To sum up,
although the LXX reading does not turn Zeph 3:8 into a unit that could be
considered belonging to a lawsuit genre,[720] the LXX is consistent with the
text, and provides a certain shade of images that enriches it.[721]

The Vg. points to a Hebrew לָעַד, and accordingly, the text would say,
YHWH will arise "forever."[722] The patient expectation for "the day" (and
for YHWH), as well as the extent of the punishment (see the following
lines in v. 8) are consistent with such understanding. Moreover, if v. 9-
10 are also taken into account the received image will be that of the ideal
future.

To sum up, the three main readings point to well attested meanings, all
are contextually possible, and to some extent even suggested by the text.
Moreover, none of them contradicts the other but complements it.
Furthermore, while, sometimes the text itself provides ways for
overcoming ambiguity,[723] the contrary occurs in Zeph 3:8. There, the
context protects the ambiguity. It is almost self-evident that the existence
of multiple possible meanings is the main stylistic feature of the phrase.[724]

---

[720] And even less a covenantal suit.

[721] The LXX reading is preferred by the vast majority of modern scholars. See, for instance,
Eiselen: 541; G. A. Smith:69; J. M. P. Smith: 247; Elliger, 1951: 73; Brockington,
1973: 263; Rudolph, 1975: 286-87; O'Connor: 257; Kapelrud, 1975: 65, 108; R. L.
Smith: 139; Krinetzki: 22, 261; Edler: 21; House: 132; Schöckel-Valverde (Nueva
Biblia Española) and so for instance, RSV; NRSV; NJPSV; NJB.

[722] The Vg. translates "in die resurrectionis meae in futurum." For a Christological
interpretation of Zeph 3:8, see, for instance, Luther: 355. The "eschatological"
understanding of the verse is by no means restricted to a Christological exegesis. For
instance, Jerome says that he is dependent on his Hebrew teacher for his interpretation
of לְעַד; Abrabanel thinks of קימה נצחית, i.e., interpreting לעד as "forever;" cf. Ibn Ezra.
Exod. R. considers Zeph 3:8 as a prophecy to the "time to come," i.e., the Messianic
period (see Exod R. 17.4; Soncino ET, p. 214).

[723] On disambiguation and ambiguity, see Berlin, 1985: 96-99.

[724] Each of these meanings is based on attested Biblical Hebrew idioms (לְעַד, לְעַד, and לְעַד)
and even if one conjectures that the writer was more lucky than skilful, one can hardly
conjectures that the audience would be unaware of the meaning of these three idioms.
Besides, the existence of double meanings in the Book of Zephaniah has already been

If metaphors function many times as a practical shortcut allowing the description of an object, or situation, by analogy, especially when the same description by other ways is practically impossible, or stylistically undesirable,[725] then a double (or triple) metaphor is a double (or even triple) condensed way of expressing something. The Hebrew text interpreted as a communicative message contains all these shades of meanings, whether they are explicitly stressed by a certain vocalization or conveyed by connotations suggested by close similarity of the words (only slight changes in the vocalization separate the different meanings) and supported by the context.[726]

To conclude, the communicative meaning of the phrase is not exhausted by the translation "for the booty", "as a witness, as an accuser" or "forever", but embraces all of these meanings. This is not only a condensed way of expressing ideas, but also another case in which ambiguity draws attention to the described divine actions on the future day in which YHWH will arise. According to Zeph 3:8, these actions are characterized as: (a) victory over the wicked (whose power, and whose wealth, will be brought to nigh as the plunder image suggests), (b) justice (because the plundered are wicked and their faults will be proved beyond any doubt by the testimony of the omniscient YHWH); and (c) a turning point in human life all over the world (לאסף גוים לקבצי ממלכות כי משפטי).

The pair קבץ-אסף is well attested in the OT (e.g., Isa 43:9; Ezek 29:5; Joel 2:16; Mic 2:12; Hab 2:5). The pair ממלכות-גוים is attested in Jer

---

noticed. Moreover, this is not an unique feature of this book, see, for instance, Alonso Schöckel,1988: 160-61).

[725] Cf. Ecco: 196-97.

[726] This is the reason that some traditional commentators who followed the "booty" reading, nevertheless added some "eschatological" dimension to their interpretation. Radak, for instance, strongly supports the "booty" reading, however, he also thinks in terms of Og and Magog. Calvin, who supports the "booty" reading and criticized the "forever" understanding, writes "God . . . does here denounce *final* destruction on the wicked" (Calvin: 281; the emphasis is mine). Yalkut Shimoni, on the other hand, points to the "witness" interpretation, but most likely its author had the MT text. These "conflated" interpretations reflect the communicative message of the phrase.

1:10 (cf. Ps 102:23; Isa 14:16), [727] and the expression לקבצי ממלכות
לאסף גוים resembles Hab 2:5, although in the latter the gatherer is not
YHWH. The expression שפך זעם occurs elsewhere in Ps 69:25,[728] and
Ezek 21:36; 22:31.[729] The word זעם occurs in parallelism to חרון אף in
Zeph 3:8 and Ps 69:25, in both cases as the first member of the pair.

  The expression באש קנאתי תאכל כל הארץ occurs in Zeph
1:18.[730] The explicit reference to the "nations" and "kingdoms" makes
unambiguous the meaning of כל הארץ in Zeph 3:8, namely "all the
earth."[731]

3.4.8. Zeph 3:9[732]

The expression אל עמים (the Murabba'at text reads על העמים)
clearly points to the "peoples." There is no textual reason to emend it to
אל עמי, and therefore to restrict the scope of the announcement in v. 9.
Moreover, the occurrence of the terms גוים, ממלכות (i.e., "nations,"
"kingdoms") and the third person pronominal suffix, which refers to
them, in v. 8 are consistent with the attested על העמים/אל עמים.[733] In

---

[727] Also cf. Isa 13:4; Hag 2:22; 2 Chr 20:6.

[728] Probably post-exilic, see Anderson: 499.

[729] Relevant to the discussion is also the expression שפך חרון אפי in Lam 4:11. For the
expression חרה אף, see Rabin, 1961: 390-91. For X-שפך in which X stands for other
terms meaning "anger" see Isa 42:25 (חמה אפו), Jer 6:10 (חמת ה'), 10:25//Ps 79:6 (חמתך),
Hos 5:10 (עברתי), and Ezek 7: 8, 9:8, 14:19, 20: 8, 13, 31, 22:22, 36:18 (חמתי/חמתך),
21:36, 22:31 (זעמי), cf. Ezek 20:33, 34 (חמה שפוכה).

[730] For comparative notes see note on Zeph 1:18.

[731] According to several scholars, this expression is a later addition to the text, see for
instance, Rudolph, 1975: 290, Elliger (BHS), Edler:109, van Grol: 190 (on stylistic
grounds). For the contrary opinion, on the basis that the phrase is the climax of the
punishment, see J. M. P. Smith: 248. Also see Kapelrud, 1975: 36, House:132.

[732] Zephaniah 3: 9-10 is considered a late addition by many scholars (e.g., G. A. Smith: 69;
J. M. P. Smith: 248; Edler: 57-60. For the contrary position, see, for instance,
Rudolph, 1975: 295.

[733] See also כל הארץ (i.e., "all the earth") in v. 8. Of course, one may propose a double
emendation: עליכם to עליהם and עמים to עמי. See, for instance, Elliger (BHS). There is
neither textual support for such a proposal nor is the text incomprehensible, but it
simply says what one may not be ready to accept.

addition, if the Murabba'at text is preferred then one needs to drop the *mem* of עמים and also the article.

The expression שפה ברורה occurs only in Zeph 3:9. Certainly, the word שפה does not mean "one lip," here. The usual Hebrew word for "lips" is שפתים.[734] If the writer of the text would like to say "pure lips" he/she would have written either שפתים ברורים or שפתות ברורות (see Prov 26:23; Ps 12:4; cf. Isa 6:4,5,7) but not שפה ברורה. Consequently, the meaning of Zeph 3:9 cannot be derived from Isa 6:1-7, and the proposal that ברורה means "pure" in a cultic sense is to be rejected. Accordingly, one has also to reject the interpretation of the text as saying that the lips of the peoples should be purified in order to worship YHWH because they had prayed to and swore by other gods.[735]

The word שפה meaning "speech, language" is well attested in the OT (e.g., Gen 11:1, 6,7,9; Isa 19:8, 28:11, 33:19; Ezek 3:5-6, 36:3; Ps 12:3, 81:6, 120:2; Prov 12:19, 17:4,7). שפה ברורה, "pure, sincere speech," stands as the opposite of expressions such as שפת חלקות (Ps 12:3) and שפת שקר (Prov 17:7). One may compare שפה ברורה to ברור מללו ודעת שפתי ("what my lips know they speak sincerely" [RSV, NRSV]) in Elihu's speech, in Job 33:3.[736] The emphasis on the importance of a "pure, sincere" language in Zeph 3:9 is consistent with the clear stress on

---

For an entirely different proposal of emendation and a reassessment of the generally accepted meaning of the unemended words, see Seybold, 1985: 60-61. Seybold translates the first part of v. 9 as follows: "Denn dann stürze ich den Pfeiler am Leute-Tor; die Schwelle wird freigelegt."

[734] It is attested more than one hundred times in the OT. שפה meaning "lip" occurs only a rare expression in Ps 22:8 (and in the *qere* of Prov 16:27).

[735] Since the use of the word "lip" with the meaning "lips" is unattested, the theoretically possible meaning of the phrase is "a pure lip." But, from a cultic perspective, "one pure lip" is close to nonsense. For a different approach to the entire question, see, for instance, Davidson: 132; J. M. Smith: 248; Kapelrud, 1975: 69; Edler:59.

[736] It has been proposed that Zeph 3:9a is related to Gen 11:1-9 as a reversal (e.g., Watts, 1975: 178-79). But, according to the narrative there, before the construction of the Tower of Babel, there was only one language and only one people. Zeph 3:9a explicitly speaks of "peoples" (in plural) and does not mention one language (שפה אחת) for all humanity. Insofar as it concerns the language of the two pericopes, one may notice that they share no common language. Only two significant words occur in both: שפה and שם. The former occurs elsewhere many times (see above), and the latter do not convey the same meaning in Zeph 3:9 (בשם ה'. . .לקרא) and in Gen 11:4 (לנו שם פן נפוץ על פני כל הארץ ונעשה). Moreover, it occurs hundreds of times in the OT. If there is any relation between the accounts, it can only be a very loose one, built around free associations.

the same topic in Zeph 3:12, and comparable to Ps 15:2-3. Ps 15 reflects the (ideal) requirements for entering the community in Jewish congregations in the post-monarchic period.[737]

The expression 'לקרא בשם ה occurs several times in Genesis (Gen 4:26, 12:8, 13:4, 21:33, 26:25), but only twice in Exodus (Exod 33:19, 34:5) and elsewhere only in 2 Kgs 5:11 (cf. 1 Kgs 18:24);[738] Joel 3:5; Zeph 3:9 and Ps 116:4,13,17.[739] In 1 Kgs 18:24; 2 Kgs 5:11; Joel 3:5 and Ps 116:4 the expression has a clear connotation of making a request from YHWH in stressful situations.

Thus, Zeph 3:9 can be translated: "Yea,[740] at that time, I [YHWH] will change the speech of the peoples to a sincere one, so they may call on the name of YHWH, to serve him in one accord[741] (cf. RSV)."

Several scholars have compared Zeph 3:9 to Isa 45:20-25,[742] however, it is questionable if Isa 45:20-25 is so universalistic.[743] The theme of the peoples accepting YHWH occurs in Zeph 2:11, and especially in the "YHWH malak" Psalms (see, Ps 47; 96:10; 97:7; 99:2).[744]

---

[737] See Gerstenberger, 1988: 86-89. Also Ps 12, one of the עניים/ענוים Psalms, reflects the importance of "language, speech."

[738] Both in the Elijah-Elisha cycle.

[739] See Even-Shoshan: 1026-28. Ps 116 is probably post-exilic, see Anderson: 790 and the bibliography mentioned there.

[740] Perhaps as an adversative כי, namely, "but, nevertheless;" also כי או may mean "then," (e.g., 2 Sam 19:27).

[741] The expression שכם אחד, "in one accord" (lit. "with one shoulder"), occurs nowhere else in the OT (שכם אחד in Gen 48:22 has an entirely different meaning). Although the word שכם may connote a sense of " oppressive burden" (e.g., Isa 10:27; 14:25) it also may connote the closely related sense of "responsibility," in a very positive sense (Isa 9:5, 22:22). Certainly, the image of the oppressive burden is contextually impossible in Zeph 3:9. To some extent the expression שכם אחד in Zeph 3:9 is comparable to לב אחד in Jer 32:39 and Ezek 11:19, but there לב אחד connotes the concept of "one people." לב אחד occurs also in 1 Chr 12:38 and 2 Chr 30:12.

[742] E.g., Kapelrud, 1975:69

[743] See Whybray, 1981: 111-113.

[744] See note on Zeph 2:11. Also cf. Mal 1:11, but the meaning of this verse is highly disputed.

3.4.9. Zeph 3:10

The key expression for the understanding of the verse is בת פוצי
עתרי. Two main approaches to this question can be discerned.

According to one of them, עתרי and בת פוצי are proper names. More
specifically, the names, or the supposed names, of two remote peoples
(see the third person plural form יוֹבְלוּן). According to this approach,
these otherwise unknown peoples are mentioned in order to stress the
point that even the most remote peoples will send their offerings to
YHWH.[745] The explicit mention of "from beyond the rivers of Cush"
supports such an understanding,[746] for the Southern edge of biblical
geography, as well as of the historical ancient Near East, was Cush (i.e.,
Nubia).[747] If this is the case Zeph 3:9-10 is a variant of the general image
of the peoples' pilgrimage to Zion/Jerusalem in a distant ideal future (e.g.,
Isa 2:1-4; Joel 3:5; Mic 4:1-4; Zech 14:16) and similar to Isa 18:7.
Moreover, the sense of "strange" people that Isa 18:7 conveys by its
language may have its parallel in Zeph 3:10 in the use of unknown names.
The fact that these names seem to allude to the fate of these peoples, one
עתרי, i.e., "my suppliants, my worshipers," and the other בת פוצי,
"Fair 'my dispersed',"[748] suggests that these may have literary names for
remote people and not real names. In any case, this understanding of
בת פוצי is consistent with the common use of idiom X בת where X
stands for a geographical name, or related concepts (e.g., בת ירושלם,

---

[745] Cf. Ibn Ezra, Radak, Abrabanel, Altschuler.

[746] Tg. Neb. changes from Cush to India in order to provide the same sense of remoteness
(note that Tg. Neb. does not change from Cush to India in Zeph 2:12. Also the
possibility that the Targumist understood Cush as standing in Mesopotamia (see Gen
10:8) cannot be ruled out. For the proposal that Cush in Zeph 3:10 refers to the land of
the Kassites, see Ball, 1972/1988: 244-52.

[747] Cf. Esth 1:1, 8:9.

[748] The peoples may be considered YHWH's dispersed. It is obvious that if there was a
general accepted belief that YHWH created one man and one woman, then in order to
reconcile this conception with reality, a proposal concerning some event that brought
about dispersion was a must (cf. Gen 11:8). Since it is totally unlikely that Israelites
thought that the event that brought about the present social and political order of the
earth was not due to YHWH's actions, one should conclude that "the peoples" could have
been considered "my dispersed." In addition, such a reference would be a nice stylistic
way of pointing to the largest populated geographical territory.

צִיוֹן, בת יהודה, בת בבל, בת צידון, בת אדום, בת מצרים
(בת)[749] Although X must not necessarily be a proper noun (see כשדים
בת in Isa 47:1,5) it is a proper name in most instances. The most
conspicuous exception is בת עמי, "Fair 'my people' "(Isa 22:4; Jer 4:11,
6:26, 8:11,19,21,22,23, 9:6, 14:17; Lam 2:11, 3:48, 4:3,6,10).

This exception, along with the meaning of פוצי (i.e., "my dispersed"),
suggests a second approach, namely, בת פוצי and עתרי are not proper
names but an expression saying, "my suppliants, (the daughter of) my
dispersed," namely, "Israel in the dispersion."[750] Such an understanding
is consistent with biblical Hebrew, requires no textual emendation,[751] but
it certainly requires interpretation, for the text can be read in two different
ways: (a) "from beyond the rivers of Cush, my suppliants, my dispersed
(people), will bring my offering"[752] or (b) "from beyond the rivers of
Cush, my suppliants, my dispersed people will be brought as my
offering." The second alternative takes the third person plural of יובלון
as impersonal, the first one as related to the proposed subject, "my
suppliants." Both are possible, but clearly the most common use of
מנחה is not the metaphorical one (also cf. Isa 18:7). Nevertheless,
because of the general image of the ideal time in the OT contains the
element of "gathering the dispersed Israel" (e.g., Am 9:14; Zeph 3:20; Isa
56:8), and because of Isa 66:20, which explicitly says that the peoples
when they will turn to YHWH will bring the dispersed as מנחה לה', one
cannot rule out the second alternative interpretation.[753]

---

[749] See, for instance, 2 Kgs 19:21 (//Isa 37:22); Isa 23:12, 47:1; Jer 4:31, 46:11; Zeph
3:14; Lam 2:2, 4:21.

[750] Most of the ancient versions support this approach (the phrase is missing in the
Peshitta and not always present in the LXX). For a comparative summary of the readings
of the ancient versions see Ball, 1972/1988: 175. See also Gerleman, 1942: 57-58.
Unlike other Medieval Jewish commentators (see above), Rashi supported this
approach. Calvin explicitly rejects the idea that עתרי בת פוצי refers to proper names, for
him עתרי בת פוצי points to Jews in the exile (286-88).

[751] See Gerleman, 1942: 57-58.

[752] See, for instance, Ball, 1972/1988: 252-54, 294; O'Connor: 258; House:125

[753] This is basically the way in which Tg. Neb. interprets the verse, cf. Davidson:132-33;
Ball, 1972/1988:176-77.

In addition to these interpretations, one may propose to separate עתרי
from בת פוצי, i.e., to propose only a change of accents in the MT. If
this is the case, then the verse will turn into two versets: "from beyond the
rivers of Cush (shall be) my suppliants/the daughter of my dispersed shall
bring my offering" (Owen's translation).[754] This reading is not only
consistent with the contents of v. 9 but even seems to be a loose parallel of
it, for עתרי may be related to לקרא בשם ה' and לעבדו to מנחה
יובלון. The meaning conveyed by כֻלם in the first verset of v. 9 also
seems to have a parallel remark in v. 10 in the form of לנהרי כוש
מעבר, i.e., "(even) from beyond the rivers of Cush." If this is the case,
v. 10 refers to the peoples and not to Israel. Thus, this interpretation
corresponds to a large extent with the first approach mentioned above.[755]

Since several alternatives are textually correct, contextually possible and
similar in contents (and to a certain extent in language, cf. Isa 66:20) to
ideas expressed elsewhere in the Latter Prophets, one may face another
case of ambiguity. Significantly, this case seems, at least on the surface,
slightly different from the others mentioned above. This is so because if
the meaning of עתרי בת פוצי is at the center of the ambiguity, then the
main question to be explained in the following verses would be: Who are
עתרי בת פוצי? However, the focus in v. 11 is on Jerusalem (or "Fair
Jerusalem", or "Fair Zion") which cannot be the answer to the question
mentioned above, but seems to be the answer to the question: where are

---

[754] See Owen's note in Calvin: 287. Cf. Davidson 133.

[755] Without changing the consonantal text, Sabottka has proposed to understand בת פוצי as it
were בדי בוץ (on the basis of 2 Kgs 23:7, and a b to p change); he is supported in this
point by Kapelrud (see Sabottka: 119-21; Kapelrud: 108). But בת-X is a very common
expression in the OT and it is not used elsewhere in the sense of "clothes made of X."
The word פוץ meaning בוץ is also unattested in the OT. It is noteworthy that although
there are several possible meanings for the phrase as it stands in the MT (or with slight
changes in the accents), and all of them are consistent with biblical Hebrew and with the
contents of other biblical texts, there have been proposals for comprehensive textual
emendations of the consonantal text (e.g., to read עד ירכתי צפון instead of עתרי בת פוצי, see
Elliger [BHS]). In order to accept such an emendation one must accept that the most
simple reading has turned into the most difficult reading, which is quite unlikely.
Moreover, these emendations have no support in ancient versions, and it seems that the
main "evidence" supporting them is that they can be reconciled with the idea that their
proposers have concerning what the text "must have been."

the offerings brought to?[756] Accordingly, it seems that the other questions
are considered either resolved or irrelevant to the main point of the passage
here.[757] If this is the case, then the quest for meaning of עתרי בת פוצי
can only be be resolved on the basis of v. 9, and therefore, it is likely, that
עתרי בת פוצי points to "the peoples" and not to Israel. But what is
their מנחה ? One may assume that they are normal "offerings" as the term
is usually used. But the response presented by Isa 66:20 cannot be ruled
out, especially since it points to a clear ideal age in which all the peoples
will accept YHWH, and since the rest of Zephaniah 3 deals with the life of
the new and ideal community of the remnant of Israel living in Jerusalem.
Moreover, if the text is post-monarchic, one can hardly assume that Israel
in the dispersion is envisaged as automatically excluded from the new ideal
community. Thus, the return of exiled Israel is implied in the text. If this
is so, either exiled Israel is already "poor and oppressed" and therefore
acceptable members of the new community, or they have to come to
Jerusalem before YHWH will take away from it all the "haughty," that is,
before the divine actions mentioned in v. 11 take place.[758]

3.4.10. Zeph 3:11-12

Verses 11-12 open with ביום ההוא. This phrase is used many times
in the OT as a compositional or redactional device for introducing a new
theme.[759] The sense of discontinuity with the preceding verses is

---

[756] Only if one considers vv. 11-12 an insertion and relates v. 10 to v. 13, then one may
have an answer to the question: The remnant of Israel, which includes those who have
come back to Jerusalem. Even if this is the case, the ambiguity remains, are they those
who bring the offering? or are they the offering that is brought by other peoples?

[757] The stress in the statement is in the "here." For the general question, in terms of the
Book of Zephaniah, see chapter 4.5.

[758] This interpretation is obviously based on context. Therefore, it does not rule out the
possibility that in a different textual context the phrase may have meant something
else. However, one cannot propose first a contextual meaning and later the context on
the basis of the contextual meaning, without falling into circular thinking.

[759] E.g., Isa 17:7; 28:5; Am 9:11; Mic 2:4; Obad 1:8; Zech 3:10, 13:1. Cf. the related
language והיה ביום ההוא (e.g., Jer 4:9; Ezek 38:10; Hos 2:23; Joel 4:18).

underscored in Zeph 3:11-12 by a move to direct speech to the personified Jerusalem (second person feminine singular).

Verse 11 opens with לא תבושי and v. 12 ends with a חסו בשם ה'. Whether redactional or compositional, this form breaks up and reverses a syntagmatic pair attested in Ps 25:20, 31:2, 71:1 (cf. Ps 22:6, 25:2; Job 6:20). (The expression חסה בה' means to rely on YHWH for protection[760] [e.g., Ps 7:2, 11:1, 141:9]). Ps 25:20, for instance, reads: "let me not be put to shame, for I take refuge in thee" (RSV); the other mentioned verses in the show similar contents. Zephaniah 3:11-12 inverts the order; that is, Jerusalem may have reasons to feel shame for her past deeds, but in a future that according to YHWH has already to influence her behavior (לא תבושי), the poor and humble people whom YHWH will leave in (the new) Jerusalem will rely on YHWH. Accordingly the present Jerusalem to whom YHWH addresses the speech is not to be ashamed. Significantly, according to Isa 57:13, those who rely on YHWH (כי החוסה)—cf. Zeph 3:12—will inherit the land (ינחל ארץ) and possess YHWH's sacred mountain (ויירש הר קדשי)—cf. Zeph 3:11.

However, unlike the cases in the mentioned Psalms and Isa 57:13, the expression in Zeph 3:12 is חסו בשם ה'. Although חסה בה' occurs about thirty times in the OT (e.g., 2 Sam 22:31; Nah 1:7; Ps 2:12, 7:2, 118:8,9; Prov 30:5), חסה בשם ה' occurs only in Zeph 3:12.[761] It is noteworthy that the idiom בטח בשם ה' (instead of בטח בה') occurs in Isa 50:10 and in Ps 33:21 (cf. Ps 124:8).[762] Perhaps, also the presence of לקרא בשם ה' in Zeph 3:9 is related to this departure from the regular expression.

Concerning עלילתיך see the note on Zeph 3:7. The idiom גאוה עליזי occurs only in Zeph 3:11 and in the oracle against Babylon in Isa

---

[760] Literally, "to take refuge in YHWH."

[761] The expression means, "to take refuge in the name of YHWH" (i.e., a hypostatic meaning). It does not mean "to take refuge by the name of YHWH, saying the name of YHWH." See Gerleman, 1942: 60 and the bibliography mentioned there.

[762] Pss 33 and 124 are probably post-monarchic. See Anderson: 260, 859; Gerstenberger, 1988: 142-46; Fohrer, 1970: 287,292 and the bibliography mentioned there.

13:3,[763] where it probably refers to YHWH's warriors, those who will carry out the divine judgment against Babylon. The use of the expression in Isa 13:3 and especially the contrast between מקרבך עליזי גאותך אסיר (v. 11) and והשארתי בקרבך עם עני ודל (v. 12) suggests that עליזי גאותך stands for the ruling elite of Jerusalem, the polar opposite of עם עני ודל.[764] If this holds true then לגבהה (עוד) בהר קדשי (v. 11) stands as an opposite to 'ה חסו בשם. Accordingly, since 'ה חסו בשם means to rely on YHWH, לגבהה conveys not only, or even mainly, the meaning of "proud" but also of "rely on your own," in this case in the own power of the ruling Jerusalemite elite (cf. Ezek 28:2,5; 2 Chr 26:16, 32:25).[765] To a large extent, this is only a variant of the general idea that "human pride" is mutually exclusive with "hearing the word of YHWH," or behaving in accordance to YHWH's will (e.g., Jer 13:15; Ezek 16:50).[766]

The idiom X-הר קדש, in which X stands for a pronominal suffix referring to YHWH, occurs mainly in the Book of Psalms and in Trito-Isaiah.[767]

The occurrence of the expression עם עני ודל in Zeph 3:12 is worthy of notice. The idiom עם עני occurs in 2 Sam 22:28//Ps 18:28, and דל

---

[763] Cf. Ginsberg, 1953: 258-59. According to Ginsberg there are many other similarities between Isaiah 13 and the Book of Zephaniah. Consequently, Ginsberg claims that the writer of the Book of Zephaniah knew the text of Isaiah 13 (the other way around is more difficult, see Ginsberg's list). Since Ginsberg considers the Book of Zephaniah Zephanic, he concludes that Isa 13 was written before the days of Josiah and Zephaniah (the prophet) . This conclusion supports his view that Isaiah 13 is Isaianic. Obviously, if the question at stake is the date of the Book of Zephaniah, and if one accepts the most common approach concerning the date of Isaiah 13, namely post-monarchic (e.g., Clements, 1982: 132) then Ginsberg's list of comparisons can only suggest a post-monarchic dating for the Book of Zephaniah.

[764] For a different understanding of the expression see Ball, 1972/1988: 177-8, 294. He proposes an abstract meaning for עליזי גאותך, i.e., "the exultations of your pride." Ball's understanding of the expression is similar to the one in the LXX and the Vg.

[765] The expression there is נבה לב.

[766] Ezek 16:49-50 recalls to a certain extent Zeph 3:11-12: אסיר with YHWH in the first person occurs in both; תגבהינה in Ezekiel, לגבהה in Zephaniah; גאון in Ezekiel, עליזי גאותך in Zephaniah. According to Ezek 16:49, Sodom and her daughters had abundance of food and a prosperous ease, but did not aid the poor and needy. This was one of its major sins. For the theme of the poor and needy, see below.

[767] It occurs in Isa 11:9 (//Isa 65:25), 56:7, 57:13, 65:11, 25, 66:20; Ezek 20:40; Joel 2:1,4:17, Obad 1:16; Zeph 3:11; Ps 2:6, 3:5,15:1, 43:3, 48:2, 79:9; Dan 9:16.

עם in Prov 28:15. The expression עם עני ודל occurs nowhere in the OT but in Zeph 3:12. Nevertheless, דל and עני occur several times as equivalent terms in parallel structures (e.g., Isa 10:2, 26:6; Prov 22:25; Job 34:28; cf. Ps 82:3).[768] The general meaning conveyed by the pair עני and דל in these expressions, as well as in many (or even most) of their separate occurrences, is not just "poor" as a matter of fact, but as someone who because he/she is "poor, afflicted; powerless" should receive special protection in human society, and above all one whose rights are especially protected by YHWH (e.g., Lev 19:15; Am 4:1-3; Ps 72:12-13, 82:3, 113:7).[769] Consequently, עני ודל (and in many occasions עני and דל separately) does not stands in opposition to "wealthy" (עשיר) *per se* but to "oppressor."[770] If YHWH is the defender of the oppressed then the oppressors must be either ignorant—which is certainly not the claim of these texts[771]—or "haughty, boastful" who rely on their own power against YHWH, or believe that YHWH will do nothing or can do nothing (cf. Zeph 1:12). Accordingly, עני or דל or both stand also as an opposite of גאה, and therefore, connote "humble, lowly" (cf. Prov 3:34; Ps 18:28//2 Sam 22:28; Zech 9:9). In Zeph 3:11, both, גאותך and לגבהה connote an opposite meaning to the "humble" element in עם עני ודל and in חסו בשם ה' (v. 12).

To sum up: The inhabitants of Jerusalem in the ideal time envisaged in v. 12 will be poor and humble, they have a past experience of oppression, they are entitled to the protection of YHWH, rely on YHWH, and they will stand.

---

[768] The most attested paired word of עני is אביון (see, Deut 15:11, 24:14; Isa 41:17; Jer 22:16; Ezek 16:49, 18:12, 22:29; Ps 12:6, 35:10, 37:14, 40:18, 70:6, 74:21, 86:1, 109:16,22; Prov 31:9; Job 24:14).

[769] In general terms, the underlying issue in many (or even most) of the notes concerning people described as either דל or עני (or אביון) is the claim that the worldly balance of power according to which the powerful can do whatever they want with the powerless is entirely misleading. This is so because no human being or social group overpowers YHWH, and YHWH will defend the cause of the oppressed powerless (e.g., Prov 14:31; 22:22-23). In other words, the "powerless" is not "helpless."

[770] Obviously, the oppressor is likely to be wealthy.

[771] Cf. Jer 5:4-5, there the poor (דלים) are assumed to be unlearned in the "way of YHWH" but knowledge (obviously not acceptance) of this way is assumed for "the great" (גדולים).

3.4.11. Zeph 3:13

In the Book of Zephaniah, from Zeph 1:1 through Zeph 3:13, Israel is mentioned only once in the idiom נאם ה' צבאות אלהי ישראל (Zeph 2:9).[772] Although the expression שארית-X occurs elsewhere (Zeph 2:7, 9), there X stands for "the House of Judah" and "my (YHWH's) people." Since not only the "literal meanings" of שארית בית יהודה and ישראל שארית differ but also their pattern of occurrence,[773] one has to conclude that they are not interchangeable. In Zeph 3:13, שארית ישראל clearly refers to the humble and poor people that will be in Jerusalem.[774] Thus Israel there is obviously not the Northern Kingdom, a term that stands opposite to Judah, but a religious, ideological concept that includes both the children of the North and those of the South. The perspective of Zeph 2:7 is entirely different. Zeph 2:7 does not refer to a group of poor and humble living in Jerusalem but to the House of Judah inheriting the land of the Philistines. Moreover, this remnant of the House of Judah is explicitly described as pastoral people, not urban.[775] Consequently, Zeph 3:13 and Zeph 2:7 present different images of the future and different images of the remnant.

The behavior of the remnant of Israel is characterized in v. 13 by three short sentences, each of which opens with the negation of an imperfect. Taking into consideration that the text claims to be the word of YHWH, these three sentences express what ought not to be done in the ideal Jerusalem.

---

[772] On this phrase see note on Zeph 2:9.

[773] For the pattern of occurrence of שארית בית יהודה and שארית יהודה, see note on Zeph 2:7. The expression שארית ישראל occurs in Jer 6:9, 31:7; Ezek 9:8, 11:13; Mic 2:12; Zeph 3:13; 1 Chr 12:38 [שרית]; 2 Chr 34:9; cf. Isa 46:3. The expression שאר ישראל occurs in Isa 10:20 and Neh 11:20.

[774] The LXX connects שארית ישראל to the preceding verse; i.e., as the subject of חמו. Whether this reading is accepted or rejected, Zeph 3:12-13 refers to one group and not to two. That is, the "poor and humble" people are the remnant of Israel, and they will do no wrong, utter no lies, and have no deceitful tongue.

[775] From the perspective of Zeph 2:6-7, the cities have no value for the House of Judah, the remnant will not rebuild them, certainly not to use their ports. They only will be shepherds taking care of their flocks among the ruined houses.

The first sentence, לֹא יַעֲשׂוּ עַוְלָה repeats word for word the first sentence characterizing YHWH's behavior in the midst of the wrongheaded Jerusalem (Zeph 3:5). Although restricted to a certain sphere, this is a kind of *imitatio Dei*.

Obviously, since only the remnant of Israel will live in the ideal Jerusalem, and "they will do no wrong," there will be no "wrongdoing" at all in the ideal Jerusalem. Whatever idea the writer has about what "do wrong" means, he/she certainly implies that there is a clear and direct relationship between "doing wrong" and belonging to a certain socio-political group. YHWH has only to remove the proud and haughty from Jerusalem, to leave the poor and humble who rely on him, and none will do wrong in Jerusalem; wrong will be no more. This utopian (and simplistic) thought may well be compatible with the self-identification of a social group which has no access to what is conceived by the group as the ruling elite.[776]

While to do wrong is a very general category of behavior, the behavior that is negated in the next two sentences is much more explicit: "(they shall) utter no lies, nor shall be found in their mouth a deceitful tongue" (RSV). That is, among all the plausible images in prophetic literature of what YHWH thinks ought not to be in the ideal society (e.g., killing, stealing, adultery, idolatry, indifference to the poor and needy), the image that comes to the forefront in Zeph 3:13, and the only one explicitly singled out, is deceitful tongue. Since such a choice can hardly be the result of blind chance and cannot be considered a requirement of the genre,[777] one has to conclude that the stress on deceitful tongue reflects a

---

[776] Significantly, the idiom עשׂה עולה occurs a third time in the OT, in Ps 37:1, and there it refers the wrong deeds of the prosperous wicked. See note on Zeph 2:5. Caution is needed in relating ideas to social groups, or better, social location. Quoting Robbins, "it is not that certain experiences produce certain beliefs, but that given certain experiences a limited range of beliefs should be plausible options for most of those who share the social location" (Robbins, forthcoming). For methodological issues concerning social location, see Robbins, forthcoming.

[777] Obviously, this choice cannot be explained in terms of specific cultic ritual against "slandering" or "false testimony." Cf. Gerstenberger on Ps 12 (see Gerstenberger, 1988: 80-83).

certain perspective of the writer.[778] After all, he/she is the one who claims that YHWH chose to emphasize deceitful language above any other wrong behavior in the short list of what ought not to be in the ideal Jerusalem (and in the ideal world?; cf. Zeph 3:9).

It seems that this quite distinct perspective of the writer is more plausible in certain social locations than others. One may note, for instance, that in a community in which leadership relies mainly on its social acceptance, leadership is extremely dependent on a socially accepted assumption that the leaders are trustworthy.

Concerning prophetic literature, it is self-evident that the legitimacy of a transmitted prophetic book relies upon the socially-accepted conception that it contains truthful speech.[779] But, what is at stake eventually is not the prophetic book but a specific kind of education, of thinking and of behaving, for a prophetic book was transmitted in order to be read for instruction, and the goal of this learning was to educate the readers[780] — either the community or some special group within the community— according to certain norms (cf. Hos 14:10). Education by means of reading, learning and reflecting on prophetic books implies communal teaching and teachers. In this respect one may notice that teaching is an impossible endeavor unless the members of the community consider their teacher a reliable speaker.[781]

---

[778] Strictly speaking, the implied author, see note on Zeph 3:3-4.

[779] This does not mean that the prophetic book was considered literally true, in the most simplistic sense of the word literal. If that were the case almost no prophecy in the Latter Prophets could have been considered fulfilled. See the hyperbolic character of many prophetic announcements. Certainly, they did not consider false all the prophecies against Samaria or Babylon because they were not literally destroyed by the Assyrians and Cyrus respectively.

[780] The word "readers" does not necessarily imply the image of silent people reading alone. Reading the text may be (and it was, probably in the majority of the cases) a group or a communal experience. In such cases it is likely that one was reading the text aloud and the others listening.

[781] The study of the role of the teacher of prophetic traditions in the transmission, redaction and perhaps composition of the received prophetic books has been largely neglected.

Significantly, a similar stress on reliable language occurs in Ps 15, which mentions the (ideal) requirements for being a member of the social-religious community.[782]

It is worthy of notice that the stress on language occurs in a prophetic book that shows a sophisticated use of language in the form of ambiguities, connotations, puns on words, and similar features, and in which the topic of language is clearly underscored in a note referring to all the peoples (Zeph 2:9).

Concerning the language of text here, the idiom דבר כזב occurs in Ps 5:7; 58:4; Dan 11:27, and דבר כזבים in Hos 7:13; Judg 16:10,13. In Psalms 5 and 58, those who speak lies are the wicked ones who stand against the speaker of the Psalm.[783] The word כזב either in plural or singular occurs also in Isa 28:15,17; Ezek 13:6,7,8,19, 21:34, 22:28; Hos 12:2; Am 2:4; Ps 5:7, 40:5, 62:5 and Prov 6:19, 14:5, 25,19:5, 9, 22, 30:8, 31:28. The idiom לשון תרמית occurs only in Zeph 3:13. Unlike, כזב which frequently occurs in the Book of Proverbs, the word תרמית never occurs in the Book of Proverbs, or in wisdom material in general, but is attested elsewhere only in Jer 8:5, 14:14, 23:26 and the relatively late Ps 119:118.[784] Significantly, neither the noun כזב nor verbal forms from the root כזב occur in the Book of Jeremiah.

The first part of the last phrase in v. 13 (i.e., כי המה ירעו ורבצו) clearly resembles Zeph 2:7.[785] As mentioned above, Zeph 2:7 presents a different image of the ideal future and of the remnant than the one described in Zeph 3:13. In this respect it seems that use of an expression in Zeph 3:13 that recalls Zeph 2:7 is a mild attempt to bridge between the two notes. If this is the case, then the difference between the two expressions is worthy of notice. The location of the "pasturing" is not mentioned in Zeph 3:13. Perhaps this is so because an explicit mention of

---

[782] See Ps 15:2-3; on Ps 15 see note on Zeph 3:10.

[783] Both Psalms are probably post-monarchic (cf. Gerstenberger, 1988:60-61,234-35; Anderson: 81,429).

[784] Ps 119 is post-monarchic and contains allusions to the Book of Deuteronomy, Proverbs, Isaiah and Jeremiah. See, for instance, Anderson: 805-07.

[785] For this expression, see note on Zeph 2:7.

Jerusalem as a place for pasturing would have had a connotation of destruction (cf. Zeph 2:7) but also because such a mention would have made impossible any bridging between the two notes.

The second part, namely, ואין מחריד, is a common expression for undisturbed peace (see, Lev 26:6, Jer 30:10//46:27; Ezek 34:28, 39:26; Mic 4:4; Job 11:19).[786]

3.4.12. Zeph 3:14-15

Verse 14 contains four imperatives summoning to rejoice; v. 15 provides the reasons for the joy, i.e., both salvific acts of YHWH and YHWH's presence in Jerusalem. The joy of Israel is therefore a hymn of praise and thanksgiving to YHWH. The structure of vv. 14-15 and its contents points to a well attested genre: call to praise YHWH (e.g., Exod 15:21; Jer 20:13; Ps 9:12-13; 106:1; 107:1; 117:1-2; 118:1; 136:1).[787] One of the characteristics of the genre is that the actions of YHWH are not described by verbal forms in the imperfect. The use of the perfect in Zeph 3:15 is therefore in complete accordance with the genre of the unit.

The reasons given for the rejoicing in v. 15 are of different sorts. Two finite actions of YHWH are described with verbs in the perfect, the continuous situation of YHWH's presence in the midst of Jerusalem and YHWH's kingship by a verbless clause, and the consequences of these new circumstances for Jerusalem by a verbal form in the imperfect, explicitly open to an unending future.

As mentioned above, the imperfect is not used for indicating the acts of God that are the reasons for the summons to praise YHWH. This feature does not necessarily mean that the writer or his/her community considered that the acts described by verbs in the perfect have actually happened in the

---

[786] Cf. Deut 28:26; Isa 17:2; Jer 7:33; Nah 2:12.

[787] See Gerstenberger, 1988: 16-19; 245. The main difference between Zeph 3:14-15 and the units mentioned above is that the word כי is implied in the former but explicitly written in the latter.

past (cf. Isa 43:3; Num 17:27, 24:17).[788] Moreover, in Psalmody, especially in the complaints of the individual, the mention of the actions of YHWH in the perfect in close relation to the petition is certainly not to be taken as literal descriptions of past deeds of YHWH concerning the speaker but as an expression of praise to YHWH, as well as reassurance to the speaker (cf. Ps 3:8; 55:19).

The four imperatives in v. 14 are a *qal* form from the root רנן, a *hiphil* form from רוע, and *qal* forms from שמח and עלז. Although both the genre and the contents recall Psalms, it is worthy of notice that there is only one occurrence of a verbal form from רנן in the *qal* pattern in the Book of Psalms (Ps 35:27), but there are twenty-one occurrences of *piel* verbal forms in Psalms.[789] One can hardly dismiss such numbers as mere coincidence. Moreover, *qal* forms of רנן, meaning to give a cry in joy, are well attested in post-monarchic prophetic literature, and especially in the Book of Isaiah (see Isa 12:6, 24:14, 35:6, 44:23 [//רוע in the *hiphil*], 49:13, 54:1; Jer 31:7, Zech 2:14 [//שמח]).[790] The pair עלז-שמח (both in the *qal*) occurs in Zeph 3:14 and elsewhere in another post-monarchic prophetic piece, in Jer 50:11.[791]

The addressee of the imperatives summoning for joy is called בת ציון in Zech 2:14, 9:9 and בת ירושלם[792] in Zech 9:9 but nowhere else in the OT, but Zeph 3:14.[793] Moreover, Zeph 3:14-15 and Zech 2:14, 9:9 show

---

[788] See GKC § 106 n,m; Meyer III:52; R. J. Williams: 30 § 165.

[789] Ps 5:12, 20:6, 26:19, 33:1, 51:16, 59:17, 63:8, 67:5, 71:23, 84:3, 88:8, 89:13, 90:14, 92:5, 95:1, 96:12, 98:4, 132:9,16, 145:7, 149:5.

[790] For the references to Isa 1-39, see, for instance, Clements, 1982: 127-29, 196-200, 203-04, 275-77, and the bibliography cited there. For Jer 31:7 see Carroll, 1986: 590-93.

[791] See Carroll, 1986: 823-25.

[792] The feminine personification of the city in these pericopes is an important argument in Crüseman's proposal concerning the existence of a prophetic genre: *Aufruf zur Freude* whose original setting was in fertility cults. See Crüseman, 1969: 55-65.

[793] Ihromi has pointed out that the combination of verbal forms that occurs in Zeph 3:14 occurs nowhere else in the prophetic literature. He also stressed that these verbal forms tend to occur in what is generally considered "secondary" material in Jeremiah (רנן in Jer 31:6; רוע in Jer 50:15 ; שמח in Jer 31:13, 43:13, 50:11 [qere]; עלז in Jer 11:15, 50:11 [qere]), "secondary" material in Isa 1-39 (רנן in Isa 12:6, 24:14, 35:6; רוע Isa 15:4; שמח Isa 14:8, 25:9, 39:2; עלז Isa 23:12), and in Deutero and Trito-Isaiah (רנן in Isa 41:7,

a second common feature, namely that they deviate from the common call to praise YHWH in the same way, by turning from the third person feminine singular in the summons clause to the second person feminine singular in the reason clause.[794]

The pair סור in the *hiphil* and פנה in the *piel* occurs only in Zeph 3:15. Verbal forms from פנה in the *piel* occur elsewhere in the Latter Prophets in Isa 40:3, 57:14, 62:10; Mal 3:1 and always with דרך as a direct object.[795]

All the main MSS of the MT read אֹיְבֵךְ,the Murabba'at text reads איבך, the LXX, and the Peshitta and Tg. Neb. support a plural reading. Radak and Altschuler understood the MT as referring to "enemies" (in plural) but one expects that "your (feminine, singular) enemies" will be written either אֹיְבַיִךְ (cf., Isa 62:8; Nah 3:13; Lam 2:16) or probably אֹיְבָיִךְ, i.e., a pausal form because of the 'atnah (cf. Mic 4:10). Thus, since the pronominal suffix has to refer to a second person feminine singular (cf. תיראי, בְּקִרְבֵּךְ, מִשְׁפָּטַיִךְ)[796] then the MT, as it stands, points to a noun that is grammatically singular.

Since, it is unlikely that Jerusalem had only one enemy, and since most of the ancient versions point to a plural meaning, many scholars have proposed to emend the MT to איביך, i.e., to prefer the Murabba'at text.[797] Undoubtedly, the proposed interpretation of the text as pointing to enemies in plural is correct because if this interpretation is rejected it would mean that the verse points to either a kind of "transcendental" enemy of Jerusalem or *one* foreign king. Since there is no reference in the

---

55:14; שמח Isa 65:13, 66:10; רוע Isa 42:13, 44:23) and that while שמח is attested in Trito-Isaiah but not in Deutero-Isaiah, the opposite is true concerning רוע. See Ihromi, 1983.

[794] Zeph 3:15 and Zech 9:9 also omit the כי before the reason clause. See above.

[795] פנה in the *piel* occurs also in Gen 24:31; Lev 14:36 and Ps 80:10.

[796] If the pronominal suffix were masculine singular, at least theoretically one may propose to read "your enemies" for אֹיִבְךָ, that is, to propose a defective spelling, which even though statistically rare occurs several times in the OT (see Andersen-Forbes: 136-38 but cf. GKC 257§ k)

[797] E.g., J. M. P. Smith: 261-62; Elliger (BHS); Rudolph, 1975: 293; Krinetzki: 158; Edler:23.

text to "the enemy" of Jerusalem, either earthly or transcendental, that interpretation is contextually impossible.[798]

However, it should be noticed that from the understanding of איבך as "enemies" it does not necessarily follows that the text should be emended, for איבך may stand for a "poetic" singular, i.e., a collective noun with a plural sense.[799] For instance, סוס ורכבו רמה בים in Exod 15:1 certainly does not mean that only one horse and one driver were thrown into the sea.[800] In this sense the emendation to איביך may be a "vulgarization" of the text.[801]

Who are these enemies? Two interpretations are possible: (a) the enemies are the foreign forces that have attacked Jerusalem; and (b) the enemies of Jerusalem are those who brought, or may bring judgment upon Jerusalem. The most probable answer to this question depends on the question whether Zeph 3:14-15 is to be read along with Zeph 3:11-13 or not.

Zeph 3:11-13 and Zeph 3:14-15 are not only adjacent units but they contain several similarities in their language. One may compare מקרבך and אסיר in v. 11 with בקרבך and הסיר in v. 15; עליזי in v. 11 with עלזי in v. 14 and Israel in v. 13 with Israel in vv. 14,15 (the only occurrences of the term Israel, in the Book of Zephaniah, except for Zeph 2:9).[802] Since these similarities can hardly be explained as the result of blind chance, one has to conclude that, at least in the compositional level

---

[798] For a different approach, see Sabottka: 127-28; Watts, 1975:182. Sabottka suggests that the enemy is Baal (he also understands מלך in this verse as a reference to Baal, and in doing so he detaches מלך from ישראל and both from YHWH; for a critical approach to Sabottka's proposal, see del Olmo Lete: 302). According to Watts, the enemy "may be the arch-enemy who incorporates all chaotic powers or it may be a collective term for all collaborators with the Assyrian power and worship." It is worth noting that neither the Assyrians—or Assyrian worship—nor Baal—or Baal's worship—are mentioned in Zeph 3:14-15. Moreover, they are not mentioned in the entire Zephaniah 3. Furthermore, the entire topos of "foreign worship" is not attested in the third chapter of Zephaniah .
Pace Watts, 1975: 182, there is no reference in the text to the 'foe of God,' the enemy, or enemies is never called YHWH's enemy/ies but "your (the city's) enemy/ies."

[799] See GKC § 126 m, and the examples mentioned there.

[800] For this position, see Owen's note in Calvin: 300; Bula; Ball, 1972/1988: 181

[801] One may compare this emendation with Radak's quotation of the MT in his commentary: איביך; Altschuler quotes אויביך.

[802] See note on Zeph 3: 13.

of Zeph 3:11-15, the two units have been related one to other, and that the writer quite explicitly underscored the relationship between them by the use of similar language.

In Zeph 3:11-13, no foreign enemies of Jerusalem are mentioned. But, according to Zeph 3:11-13, Jerusalem will stand when the only group that can bring disaster upon Jerusalem, עליזי גאותך, will not be in her midst (see notes above). The same line of thinking leaves no room for questioning the identity of the real enemy of the jubilant Jerusalem, the only one capable of bringing distress to Jerusalem is no other than גאותך עליזי. Certainly, this understanding of the identity of the foe of Jerusalem is not unique to the Book of Zephaniah, but is rather the overwhelming OT response to the question concerning the responsibility for the disasters that fell upon Jerusalem. For instance, the main reason for the destruction of Jerusalem and the Temple has always been considered internal, namely the behavior of the Judeans (e.g., Jer 7:1-15; Lam 1:18), or of Manasseh (e.g., Jer 15:4).

The word מִשְׁפָּטַיִךְ (v. 15) means "your sentence, judgment;" i.e., "the judgments against you." The Vg. supports the MT reading but Tg. Neb. reads שׁקרא דייני as if it were translating a Hebrew text reading שׁפטיך[803] or perhaps משׁפטיך (cf. Job 9:15; Ps 109:31).[804]

It has been proposed to emend the text to משׂפטיך and to interpret it as "your adversaries, your opponents."[805] However, the MT as it stands contains a well attested word,[806] unlike the proposed emendation that rarely occurs. Moreover, the word משפט occurs in the plural and with a strong negative implication—as in Zeph 3:15—in Ezek 5:8. Furthermore, הסיר משפט occurs in Job 27:2, 34:5. There it means to take away Job's right. This shade of meaning of משפט leads in Zeph 3:15 to a

---

[803] See Ribera Florit: 157. Cf. b. San. 98a and b. Sabb. 139a.

[804] The LXX reads here, " your iniquities, your errors."

[805] E.g., J. M. P. Smith: 256,261; Crüseman, 1969: 57; Brockington,1973: 263; Elliger (BHS); Kapelrud, 1975: 90-91, 108; Krinetzki: 158; Schöckel-Valverde (Nueva Biblia Española). See also the bibliography mentioned in J. M. P. Smith: 261.

[806] E.g., Jer 48:47; Ezek 5:8, 39:21; Zeph 3:8; 1 Kgs 20:40; and tens of times with the same or related meanings.

sense of "removing what Jerusalem deserves; i.e., her punishment;" which may only underscore a meaning already existing in "taking away the judgments against you" (cf. Ezek 5:8). In addition, the existent parallelism with איבך does not necessarily imply that משפטיך should be a concrete term referring to persons. The line may well be considered either another case of ongoing heightening message, namely, not only that the judgment is over but also that there will be no potential for a future judgment (cf. הסיר v. 15 with אסיר v. 11) or it may refer to a "natural" flow of events, i.e., the sentence is revoked, then the enemies are taken away.[807] To sum up, there is no compelling reason for emending the MT.[808]

It is noteworthy that an unemended MT provides no support for the idea that Zeph 3:15 directly refers to the image of YHWH as a divine warrior[809] who vanquishes his enemies and becomes king.[810] To the contrary, it makes that proposal quite impossible by proposing an image of YHWH as the one who has brought judgment upon Jerusalem and then removed his judgment.[811] In this sense the image of YHWH is similar to the one in Deutero-Isaiah (e.g., Isa 40:2, 44:21-23). Significantly, the enemies are always referred to as Jerusalem's enemies, never YHWH's foes, and they are not mythological but a certain group of Jerusalemites. The image of YHWH removing the wicked from Jerusalem, so that Jerusalem will not fear again to be smitten by YHWH (the only one who

---

[807] For instance, the parallelism in Isa 16:5, 40:9 clearly refers to the natural flow of events. Cf. Berlin, 1985:90-91; Kugel, 1981: 4-5.

[808] For the position that the MT is not to be emended, see, for instance, Davidson: 134-35; Ball, 1980:180; Rudolph, 1975: 292-93; Edler: 23; Barthélemy, 1980: 383; del Olmo Lete: 302.

[809] For the image of YHWH as a divine warrior, in general, see P. D. Miller; cf. Kang, 1989: 197-204. To the extent that one holds that "to speak about the judgment of God in the Old Testament is to be confronted again with the imagery of the divine warrior" (P. D. Miller: 174), Zeph 3:15 along with the lion's share of the prophetic literature refers to this image. The following discussion concerns only the specific image of a warrior who defeats his enemies and becomes king; or in other words, of a king whose legitimacy relies on his attested capability to bring victory to his people.

[810] For a different approach concerning Zeph 3:15, see Gaster, 1969: 684; Watts, 1985: 172; Kapelrud, 1975: 70.

[811] YHWH certainly does not become the king only when he removes judgment; YHWH is a king also when he executes judgment.

can declare and execute judgment over it), that is, the image of YHWH eliminating the potential for future distress is equivalent to the image of YHWH in Jer 31:31-34, among others. This image is quite distinct from the one of the victorious hero.

The form תירא (i.e., from the root ירא) is attested in both the Aleppo Codex and the Leningrad Codex (B 19ᴬ). It is also supported by the note on Isa 60:5 in the Masorah Parva (Mp). The idiom ירא רע occurs elsewhere in Ps 23:4. On the other hand, the "Second Rabbinic Bible (Ben Chayim)" reads תראי, suggesting a verb from the root ראה.[812] The expression ראה רע also occurs in the OT, in Hab 1:13. The first approach leads to an English translation: "shall fear evil no more" (e.g., RSV) and is supported by both the Vg. and Tg. Neb., while the second approach leads to: "shall experience (lit. see) evil no more" and is supported by the LXX and the Peshitta.

It is worth noting that the author did not write the common expression אל תירא (cf. Zeph 3:16)[813] but one conveying a double sense. Moreover, the two meanings are not mutually exclusive but complementary, each of them providing a certain shade to one picture of the ideal future. Certainly, this ambiguity could not escape the readers/hearers of the verse (cf. note on Zeph 3:8).

The idea that YHWH is the king of Israel, or of the entire world, occurs many times in the OT and especially in Psalms.[814] The apposition ה' מלך ישראל in Zeph 3:15 occurs, in the inverse order, in Isa 44:6 (cf. Isa 41:21). The motif of YHWH in the midst (בקרב) of the city occurs

---

[812] So Abrabanel understood the verse. Also cf. *Minhat Shai* on Zeph 3:15.

[813] See, Gen 15:1, 21:17, 26:24, 35:17, 43:23, 50:19,21; Exod 14:13, 20:20; Josh 8:1, 10:25; Deut 1:21, 20:3, 31:6, Judg 4:18, 6:23; 1 Sam 4:20, 12:20, 22:23, 23:17, 28:13; 2 Sam 9:7, 13:28; 1 Kgs 17:13; 2 Kgs 6:16; Isa 7:4, 35:4, 40:9, 41:10,13,14, 43:1,5, 44:2, 54:4; Jer 30:10, 46:27,28; Joel 2:21,22; Zeph 3:16; Hag 2:5; Zech 8:13,15; Ps 49:17; Ruth 3:11; Lam 3:57; Dan 10: 12,19; 1 Chr 22:13, 28:20; 2 Chr 20:17. Cf. Zakir inscription l. 13.

[814] See, for instance, 1 Sam 12:12; Deut 33:5; Isa 6:5, 41:21, 43:15, 44:6; Jer 10:10; Obad 1:21; Mal 1:14; Ps 5:3, 10:16, 29:10, 44:5, 48:3, 68:25, 74:12, 84:4, 145:1, 149:2.

also in Zeph 3:5. The motif of being in (or being removed from) the midst (בקרב) of the city occurs in Zeph 3:3,5,11,12,15,17.[815]

3.4.13. Zeph 3:16

The idiom יֵאָמֵר ל-X , where X stands for the addressee of the announcement, follows a temporal phrase such as ביום ההוא in the introduction of the unit.[816] This kind of introduction ("on that day it shall be said to Jerusalem;" RSV, NRSV) not only projects the announcement into an undetermined future but also adds to the vagueness of the picture by using a passive verbal form that points to the identity of the addressee, Jerusalem, but leaves entirely undefined the identity of the future speaker or speakers.

While Zeph 3:14-15 claims to be the word of the prophet, Zeph 3:16-17 claims that the prophet prophesied concerning a similar message to his own that will be delivered to Jerusalem in the future by an unspecified agent. The irrelevance of the identity of this agent, in spite of the fact that his or her words will be similar to those of the prophet, is only underscored by the use of the passive voice. From the perspective of people living in the putative future of the prophet it means that a contemporaneous message of salvation is accepted as legitimate on the basis of the authority of a similar saying of a prophet in the past, rather

---

[815] On the basis of the LXX reading according to several MSS, and especially on the basis of the Lucianic recension, as well as on the basis of metric considerations, some scholars have proposed to read ימלך instead of מלך ישראל (e.g., Elliger [BHS]; Irsigler, 1977:191). But see, for instance, Ball, 1972/1988: 181-82; Rudolph, 1975: 293; del Olmo Lete: 302; O'Connor: 260; van Grol; Edler: 23; House: 133; Barthélemy, 1980: 383; cf. J. M. P. Smith: 256; Sabottka: 128.

[816] Cf. Jer 4:11. The expression "on that day" (ביום ההוא) and similar expressions introduces words of salvation, as well as announcements of judgment, elsewhere in the Latter Prophets (e.g., Isa 27:12,13; Jer 4:11, 30:8; Hos 2:8; Am 9:11; Zeph 3:20). On ההוא ביום see note on Zeph 3:10.

than on the basis of the authority of the one who is actually saying these words, in the present time.[817]

The similarity of the prophet's saying and the later saying (vv. 16-17) concerning contents is stressed by the occurrence of similar words. But the difference between them is underscored by the language of these two units, for there is no exact repetition of idioms. For instance, one may compare בת ציון - בת ירושלם (v. 14) with ירושלם - ציון (v. 16); שמחי . . . רני (v. 14) with בשמחה עליך ישיש . . . ברנה עליך גבור יושיע (v. 15) with ה' מלך ישראל ה' בקרבך יגיל (v. 17); תיראי (v. 15) with לא תיראי רע עוד (v. 17); ה' אלהיך בקרבך אל (v. 16).

It is worth noting that the linkage between vv. 14-15 and vv. 16-17 defines the character of Zeph 3:14-15 as a prophecy concerning an undefined future. This is so because if the claim of the text is that the prophet spoke concerning his own time in vv. 14-15, it would imply either that these words were false prophecy or that there was a reversal of the situation between the time of the prophet and the time of the second saying, for an announcement of salvation opening with "on that day, it shall be said to Jerusalem: Do not fear" can hardly be reconciled with the existence of constantly ideal situation from the days of the prophet through the days of the second saying. Since, neither text claims that the prophet was a false prophet nor mentions any reversal, one may conclude that the claim is that the prophet spoke concerning a future in which the second saying will be said.[818]

Promises of salvation containing an address to Israel in the second person singular, the expression אל תירא X, and the announcement of future events are attested in Deutero-Isaiah (Isa 41:14-16; 44:1-5) and in

---

[817] This approach to authority leads either to reinterpretation of received tradition in order to make it supportive of the points of view of the interpreter and related to the needs of his or her community, or to pseudepigrapha, or both. Biblical interpretation and pseudepigrapha flourished during the Second Temple period.

[818] If Zeph 3:16-17 is later than Zeph 3:14-15 then the former will introduce a necessary interpretative key for the latter, for those who considered that the ideal situation reflected in Zeph 3:14-15 was not yet fulfilled.

exilic or later Jeremiah (Jer 30:10-11//46:27-28; cf. Joel 2:21-22).[819]
Expressions like אל תירא occur many times in the OT,[820] but in the
Latter Prophets they occur in Isa 7:4, 35:4, 40:9, 41:10,13,14, 43:1,5,
44:2, 54:4; Jer 30:10, 46:27,28; Joel 2:21,22; Zeph 3:16; Hag 2:5; Zech
8:13,15. The expression רפה ידים occurs in 2 Sam 4:1; Isa 13:7; Jer
6:24, 50:43; Ezek 7:17, 21:12; Neh 6:9; introduced by the negation, as in
Zeph 3:16, it occurs in 2 Chr 15:7 (אל ירפו ידיכם).[821]

3.4.14. Zeph 3:17

The role of the expression ה' אלהיך בקרבך גבור יושיע in v. 17 is
similar to the role of מלך ישראל ה' בקרבך in v. 15. The main
difference between the two is that גבור יושיע stands instead of ישראל
מלך.[822]

The word גבור may mean both "warrior" and "mighty, powerful." To
be sure, the two meanings may and do converge in many cases. But,
although one may assume that any "warrior" called גבור in the OT is
considered a "mighty warrior" (e.g., 2 Sam 23:8), and obviously this is
true when the imagery of the "warrior" refers to YHWH (e.g., Ps 24:8;
Isa 42:13; Zeph 1:14); one cannot assume that every "mighty one" was
"mighty in war" (see Gen 10:9; Isa 5:22; Prov 30:30) or only "mighty in
war," (with reference to YHWH, see, for instance, Jer 14:9; cf. Deut
10:17; Neh 9:32). Thus, although גבור conveys military connotations,
these connotations do not always stand at the center of the communicative
meaning of the word in a specific literary context.[823]

---

[819] See Carroll, 1986: 577-79, 772-74. For the general issue of words of salvation, see
Rendtorff, 1986: 120-22 and the bibliography mentioned there.

[820] See above.

[821] ירפו, as in Zeph 3:16 and 2 Sam 4:1, and not תרפנה as in Isa 13:7; Ezek 7:17. See GKC §
145 p.

[822] In addition, the MT has a disjunctive accent between בקרבך and , גבור יושיע; but cf. the Vg.

[823] Significantly, the same situation holds true for the closely related word גבורה. See, for
instance BDB.

The commonly accepted understanding of גבור יושיע claims that there is an implied אשר between גבור and יושיע, or in other words, that יושיע is a relative (or better attributive) clause introduced by simple juxtaposition (e.g., Jer 13:20; Isa 40:20).[824] Relative clauses conveying an adjectival sense tend to occur in this way. For instance, and focusing on phrases composed of a non-determined (i.e., without the definite article) noun in juxtaposition with a verb in the imperfect as גבור יושיע, one may mention זאב יטרף in Gen 49:27, "a ravenous wolf," and ימות מאנוש in Isa 51:12, "of a mortal person."[825] The idiom גבור יושיע, which is similar to them, basically means "a saving hero, a saving mighty one."[826]

The phrase ה' אלהיך בקרבך גבור יושיע in v. 17 follows the expression אל תיראי in v. 16. Since אל תיראי is a typical response to someone in distress,[827] vv. 16-17 as a unit are also a response to someone in distress. The contents of v. 17 and אל ירפו ידיך in v. 16 support this understanding. To be sure, the existence of a response implies the existence of an implicit (or explicit) request for it, a plea for the divine help in time of distress. The phrase בקרבך גבור יושיע ה' אלהיך recalls, almost word for word, the context of a plea in Jer 14:9. There the text says,

---

[824] See, for instance, Rashi; Radak; J. M. P. Smith: 256-57, 262; Ball, 1972/1988: 183-84; Rudolph, 1975: 293. For the grammatical issues, see GKC § 155f; Meyer, III: 96-97; R. J. Williams § 540.

[825] See GKC 155f.

[826] Not unlike the English expression, the Hebrew "saving hero," (גבור יושיע) has several connotations depending on the communicative value of both "saving" and "hero." Modern English translations, unlike KJV, tend to provide a restrictive meaning of the phrase, such as "a warrior who brings triumph" (NJPSV) or "a warrior who gives victory" (RSV/NRSV). This meaning is based on a contextual understanding of the phrase, namely, on an interpretative position according to which the image of YHWH as a victorious warrior (see above) is central to the unit. This position is based either on the supposed occurrence of this image in v. 15 (but see above) or on the conception that the text refers to the day of YHWH and that the day of YHWH concerns YHWH's manifestation as a victorious king destroying his enemies or both. Cf. Kapelrud,1975: 91-92; Edler: 65; J. M. P. Smith: 143-44.

[827] Not necessarily distress related to war. See, for instance, Gen 35:17; 1 Sam 4:20; 2 Sam 9:7; 1 Kgs 17:13; Joel 2: 21,21; Ruth 3:11; 1 Chr 28:20. Accordingly, only contextually one can understand the nature of the distress. On the use of the phrase תירא אל, see Lande, 1949: 92-95.

למה תהיה כאיש נדהם כגבור לא יוכל להושיע

ואתה בקרבנו ה' ושמך עלינו נקרא אל תַּנִּחֵנוּ

The reason for the plea is the extreme distress brought by drought, and not by a military foe. In Jer 14:7-9 the people address YHWH, confess their faults, proclaim that their hope is in YHWH, but they are not confident that YHWH will save them; they can only entreat YHWH. While the following verses in Jeremiah 14 claim that the entreaty of the people was rejected by YHWH, Zeph 3:17 seems to be an announcement of acceptance, saying "YHWH, your God, is in your midst a saving hero."

Significantly, Jer 14:9 points to the conception that the presence of YHWH in the midst of the city, or the people, is not synonymous with salvation (cf. Zeph 3:5), for salvation is dependent on the attitude of YHWH, and YHWH may act as a hero who cannot —or do not— save. The same perspective is probably implied in Zeph 3:15,17, for a clarifying phrase is added in both cases to the statement concerning the presence of YHWH in Jerusalem (i.e., לא תיראי רע עוד and גבור יושיע).

The non-military circumstances of Jer 14:1-10 cautions against overstressing the existent military connotations of the term גבור. YHWH is conceived as savior, who may save in war but certainly not only in war (cf. Jer 14:8). Taking into account that v. 15 does not refer to YHWH's victories against his enemies, but to the removal of YHWH's judgment upon Jerusalem and to the removal of the wrongdoers from Jerusalem, i.e., "her enemies," so that she will not suffer judgment again, one may conclude that the military connotations of the phrase גבור יושיע are not necessarily the main element in the communicative message of יושיע גבור in Zeph 3:17.

The expression יחריש באהבתו is emended sometimes to באהבתו יחדש,[828] i.e., according to the reading suggested by the LXX and the

---

[828] Although חדש ב occurs nowhere in the OT, some scholars propose this reading because of the parallel בשמחה and ברינה; see J. M. P. Smith: 262. A literal translation of this reading is: "He (YHWH) will renew his love."

Peshitta,[829] and sometimes to יַרְחֵשׁ בְּאַהֲבָתוֹ, "stir up in his love."[830] The main claim behind these proposals is that the MT, which is supported by the Vg. and in a paraphrastic way by Tg Neb (see below), is contextually incomprehensible, or at least very unlikely.

Although those who propose to emend the MT generally agree that the MT יַחֲרִישׁ בְּאַהֲבָתוֹ means "he will be silent in his love," or perhaps "he will rest in his love," there is no such an unanimity concerning the meaning of the MT יַחֲרִישׁ בְּאַהֲבָתוֹ among those who reject the proposed emendations. The basic source for the main differences of opinion is that words from the roots[831] חרשׁ may convey a basic sense of " ploughing" (e.g., 1 Sam 8:12 Am 9:13; Mic 3:12; Job 1:14), of "engraving, doing skillful artisan work" (e.g., Gen 4:22; 2 Sam 5:11; 2 Kgs 24:14; Jer 17:1; and metaphorically, "plotting, devising" (e.g., 1 Sam 23:9, Prov 3:9, 6:14, 12:20, 14:22), and also of "being silent, being dumb" (e.g., Gen 24:21; 2 Kgs 18:36; Mic 7:16; Neh 5:8).

It has been proposed, for instance, mainly on the basis of Ugaritic, that חרשׁ means not only "to do artisan work, engrave, work metal" but also may mean "to devise artfully, to compose songs,"[832] and accordingly the phrase has been translated either "he will compose a song in his love" or in free translation "he will sing a song in his love."[833] Since there is no clear occurrence of יַחֲרִישׁ meaning singing or composing a song in the OT, but there are many with the general sense of "be silent," proposals made on the basis of the basic meaning "be silent" must be preferred, provided they are contextually possible.[834]

---

[829] See for instance, Owen in Calvin: 304; Elliger (BHS); J. M. P. Smith: 257, 262; G. A. Smith: 73; Brockington, 1973: 273; Loretz, 1973: 226; House: 133; cf. RSV; NRSV; NJB; NEB.

[830] Cf. Ps 45:2; see Rudolph, 1975: 293; Krinetzki: 262, Edler: 23; and the bibliography mentioned in Ball, 1972/1988:184.

[831] It seems that two independent roots have converge into the Hebrew חרשׁ. See Loewenstamm, 1959; Dahood, 1965: 58; KBL[3].

[832] See Dahood: I, 270; Sabottka: 132-34.

[833] Cf. Sabottka: 132-34; Kapelrud, 1975: 109; O'Connor: 261; Watts, 1975: 183.

[834] The meaning "ploughing" is highly unlikely because of contextual reasons. For "devising," see below.

The same holds true for Ehrlich's proposal. On the basis of the meaning "plotting, devising," Ehrlich proposes that the text says that YHWH will devise good schemes for Jerusalem in his love.[835] But חרש meaning "devising" in both *qal* and *hiphil* forms always has an explicit direct object (e.g., Prov 3:29; 6:18; 1 Sam 23:9) and this direct object does not occur in Zeph 3:17.

Three main interpretative approaches have arisen around the "be silent" understanding of חרש.[836] According to the first, the love of God "will be too tender and strong for expression;"[837] according to the second, God will be at rest (lit. silent), i.e., God will be satisfied;[838] according to the third, God will be silent concerning the sins of the people.[839]

An analysis of *hiphil* verbal forms from the root חרש ("be silent") in the OT shows that many of them actually convey the meaning of refraining from reacting to the deeds of someone else (e.g., Gen 34:5; Num 30:5; 8,12,15; 1 Sam 10:27; Isa 42:14; Hab 1:13; Ps 50:2; Esth 4:141). Moreover, they clearly convey the sense of refraining from executing judgment in Gen 34:5; 1 Sam 10:27; Hab 1:13; Ps 50:21.[840] If one considers that vv. 16-17 contain the image of a positive response to an implied entreaty made by the people to God, asking God to deliver them from their present distress, then the meaning of יחריש באהבתו becomes clear. The people have already confessed their wicked behavior, i.e., the reason for the distress (cf. Jer 14:7; Ps 41:5, 51:5-7); the divine

---

[835] ה' באהבתו יחשוב מחשבות להשיב לך. See Ehrlich: 462.

[836] In addition to them one may mention Gaster's proposal to read יחריש באהבתו as a concessive clause. Accordingly, he translates the verse: "Though now He be keeping silent about His love, He will then joy over thee in a burst of song." See Gaster, 1967: 267.

[837] See Davidson: 135. For bibliographical references concerning this approach, see J. M. P. Smith: 257. The quotation from Eiselen: 545. Eiselen rejects this understanding and proposes to read יחריש "overflowing" (cf. Ps. 45:2).

[838] See, Calvin:304; cf. R. L. Smith: 143.

[839] Cf. Tg. Neb.; Rashi; Ibn Ezra; Yosef Kara; Radak; Abrabanel; Altschuler; Ball, 1972/1988: 184-87.

[840] Cf. Ball, 1972/1988: 185-86. *Qal* forms conveying a similar sense occur in Ps 35:22, 50:3, 83:2, 109:1; see Ball, 1972/1988: 186.

answer is that God will refrain from executing the judgment because of love for the people.[841]

The self-evident contrast between יחריש באהבתו, which also conveys the meaning of being silent (see above), and יגיל ברינה and ישיש בשמחה reinforces the contrast between the divine restraint (insofar as it concerns judgment against Jerusalem) and the divine hectic activity (insofar as it concerns rejoicing over Jerusalem).

3.4.15. Zeph 3:18

It seems that already the ancient versions had considerable difficulties in interpreting this verse. The LXX, the Vg, Tg. Neb.; and the Peshitta render the verse each in its own way, and none of them can be easily reconciled with the MT. Significantly, the same holds true for modern translations.[842] Certainly, this is not the result of two millennia of incompetent reading but of an intrinsic difficulty in the verse: Too many words may have different meanings that may be clarified only contextually.[843] The obvious result is that too many combinations of meanings are possible. But, strangely enough, none of them provides a smooth rendering of the Hebrew text. Alternatively, one may recur to the versions. But also the versions strongly differ among themselves. Moreover, the MT is clearly a *lectio difficilior* and the comprehensible rendering of the version may point to the conjecture of the translator rather than to a different Hebrew *Vorlage*.[844] The strong divergence among the versions seems to suggest that this is the case. Furthermore, even if one accepts the need for some kind of textual emendation in the OT, the extent

---

[841] Cf. Mic 7:18-19.

[842] "Among modern translators and commentators, of over thirty translations checked, no two were exactly the same" (Ball, 1972/1988: 188).

[843] For instance, נוגי, ממועד, אספתי, ממך, משאת, עליה. For a list of theoretically possible understandings, see Ball, 1972/1988:188.

[844] See Gerleman, 1942: 64.

of the needed emendation is dependent on a set of interpretative decisions concerning the meaning of the unemended words.

This situation leads to one main conclusion: No proposal concerning the meaning of the verse can be compelling to any significant extent. No solid foundations for the understanding of the Book of Zephaniah, or any of its units, can be laid upon any of the existent conjectural readings.

A possible reading of the verse, but by no means more than a simple conjecture among others, may be based on the following considerations:

(1) נוגי is a *niphal* participle from יגה, it may be translated as "those who grieved, who are afflicted" (cf. Lam 1:4).

(2) מועד may mean "festival" (cf. Lam 1:4).

(3) Therefore, נוגי ממועד may mean "those who are afflicted because they are deprived of the festivals."[845]

(4) אספתי may mean "I (YHWH) have gathered" (e.g., Ezek 11:17).

(5) ממך היו may mean "they were from you."

(6) מַשְׂאֵת may mean "sign, signal" (see Jer 6:1, הכרם שאו מַשְׂאֵת על בית).

(7) עליה may mean "on Jerusalem," even if Jerusalem was referred to in the second person feminine before (cf. Cant. 1:2).[846] If this is the case, this is a transition from a textual claim of being an address to the claim of being a statement.

(8) חרפה may mean "a reproach, a mockery" (see, for instance, נתתיך חרפה לגוים וקלסה לכל הארצות in Ezek 22:4).

(9) Therefore, the entire verse may be understood as saying: "Those who are afflicted because they are deprived of the festivals, I (YHWH) have gathered, they were from you, (they were) a sign on her, (they were) a (source of) mockery."

This rendering assumes the existence of an implied verb in the last two clauses.[847] Perhaps the expression may be explained by an attempt to

---

[845] Cf. Barthélemy, 1980: 384-85.

[846] See GKC § 144 p. Several MSS of the MT read עליך and the Peshitta supports this reading

[847] For examples of elliptic verbs, see, for instance, Isa 2:3; Ps 79:4.

stand as close as possible to the idiom לשאת על-X חרפה, "to bear reproach because of X, for the sake of X" (see Jer 15:15; Ps 69:8). Accordingly, the verse points also to the meaning " . . . they [those who have been deprived of the festivals] have borne mockery because of her, for her sake [Jerusalem]." It is worth noting that the identification of משאת with נוגי ממועד and with חרפה implies that אספתי refers also to חרפה; that is, recalling the idiom אסף חרפה (see Gen 30:23, Isa 4:1).[848]

One may compare this conjectural reading with readings such as:

> "Those grieved for the festivals have I gathered from thee//they were a burden on thee, a reproach."[849]

> "Those who grieved in the assembly I will gather from you//They were a burden upon it, a reproach."[850]

One may contrast this reading with other proposed renderings such as:

> "Mourners from the place of assembly//I will remove far away from you//they were a burden//upon her and a reproach."[851]

> "Those who went away from me//I swept away from the festival gathering//they are away from me/having heaped insults upon her."[852]

> "He will exult over you with a shout of joy as in days long ago (vv. 17+ 18a)//I will take your cries of woe away from you and you shall no longer endure reproach for her."[853]

---

848 It is noticeably that reproach (חרפה) is taken away (אסף) or is asked to be taken away from women, or a feminine personification.

849 Suggested by Owen in Calvin 308. Cf. "those driven away from festivity have I gathered//from thee they are- a burden on her is reproach." (Marckius, quoted by Owen in Calvin:308).

850 O'Connor, 1980: 261.

851 Ball, 1972/1988: 295.

852 Kapelrud, 1975: 109; cf. R. L. Smith:143

853 NEB; see Brockington, 1973: 263.

3.4.16. Zeph 3:19

Verse 19 contains the second among three successive units that are anchored to the ongoing text by a temporal phrase (i.e., vv. 16-18, v. 19 and v. 20). The temporal phrase in v. 19 is בעת ההיא as in v. 20. But unlike Zeph 3:20, and many other units announcing future deeds of YHWH (e.g., Isa 18:7; Jer 3:17, 4:11; cf. Isa 27:1; Zeph 3:16; Am 9:11),[854] Zeph 3:19 does not open with בעת ההיא + a verb in the imperfect.

Temporal phrases may occur in the second position, following the first verbal clause (or even interrupting it).[855] But the form הנני + participle, although very common in the Latter Prophets for divine speech, does not directly follow or precedes there a temporal clause, such as בעת ההיא or ביום ההוא.[856] Moreover, none of the regular literary surroundings of this form (e.g., לכן . . . כה אמר ה') occur in v. 19.[857]

The main interpretative problem concerning the meaning of כל מעניך הנני עשה את is that the indeterminacy of עֹשֶׂה. Since מְעַנַּיִךְ[858] means "those who oppress or afflict you," it seems likely that עֹשֶׂה points to judgment, to punishment. The Vg. and Tg. Neb. consider that there is

---

[854] Also compare, for instance, with Isa 3:18, 17:7,9, 19:16,18, 19,23, 28:5; Am 8:13; Mic 2:4; Zech 14:20.

[855] E.g., Isa 4:1, 5:30, 12:1,4; Ezek 45:22; Hos 2:20; Zech 14:4.

[856] See, Isa 13:17, 28:16, 37:7, 38:8, 43:19, 65:17,18; 66:12; Jer 1:15, 2:35, 5:14,15, 6:21, 8:17, 9:6,14, 10:18, 11:22, 12:14, 13:13, 16:9,16,21, 19:3,15, 20:4, 21:4,8, 23:2,15, 25:9, 28:16, 29:17,21,32, 30:10, 31:8, 32:3,28,37, 33:6, 34:2,17,22, 35:17, 39:16, 43:10, 44:11,27,30, 45:5, 46:25,27, 49:5,35, 50:18, 51:1,36; Ezek 4:16, 16:37, 21:3, 22:19, 23:22,28, 24:16,21, 25:4,9,16, 26:7, 28:7, 29:8,19, 34:17; Hos 2:8; Joel 2:19, 4:7; Am 6:14, 7:8; Mic 2:3; Hab 1:6; Zech 2:13,14, 3:8,9, 8:7; Mal 2:3, 3:1.

[857] Sabottka suggested that בעת ההיא is the opening clause of the next unit, in other words that בעת ההיא must be separated from הנני עשה את כל מעניך (which will turn into the last phrase of the unit containing vv. 16-18) and attached to the following phrase rendering בעת ההיא והושעתי את הצלעה... . See Sabottka: 138.

There have been suggestions that the temporal clause is a textual insertion, e.g., Elliger (BHS). Several scholars reject this proposal on the basis of the idea that the expression בעת ההיא points to an eschatological future, or directly to the day of YHWH. See, for instance. J. M. P. Smith: 259; Edler: 24.

[858] The word מְעַנַּיִךְ occurs elsewhere in Isa 60:14.

an implied כלה after עשה.[859] Accordingly, the phrase means: "At that time I will make [an end] of all who afflicted you" (NJPSV).

Alternatively, it has been proposed that עשה alone conveys the meaning of a punitive action. One way of doing so is turning to alternative roots,[860] but Ezek 22:14 and Ezek 23:25 are two clear instances of the use of את-X עשה, meaning "to deal with X, to take action concerning X,"[861] in an obviously negative sense, i.e., "to take action against X."[862]

Certainly, the text is vague concerning what YHWH will do with the "afflictors," the expectations of the readers through the ages have restrained this vagueness by stating that YHWH will act against them. The text is not so vague when it deals with the group that stands in contrast to the "afflictors," namely, "the lame" (הצלעה) and the "dispersed, outcast"[863] (הנדחה). They will be rescued, gathered and made famous.

Zeph 3:19, from והושעתי through בכל הארץ בשתם contains four versets. The first and second clearly resemble Mic 4:6,[864]

אספה הצלעה		והושעתי את הצלעה	
והנדחה אקבצה		והנדחה אקבץ	
Mic 4:6		Zeph 3:19	

---

[859] Of course, one may propose that they had a Hebrew text that contained the word כלה (see Ribera Florit: 158, cf. Rudolph, 1975: 294, but see the reservations expressed in Ball, 1972/1988: 193-94). It is worth noting that the proposed reading is not supported by the MT, the LXX, or the Peshitta. The LXX and the Peshitta either interpret the verse each in its own way, or—and unlikely—each of them had its own Hebrew Vorlage, which was different from the MT, the Vg. and Tg. Neb. The LXX suggests a Hebrew reading הני עשה אתך למענך and the Peshitta הני עשה את כלם עניך. See, for instance, Gerleman, 1942: 65.

[860] For instance, Moses HaCohen (quoted by Ibn Ezra, who proposed that there is an implied כלה) and Radak thought in terms of עשה, meaning "to press, to squeeze" (see Ezek 23: 3,8,21). Rashi and Yosef Kara (לשן רמיסה ברגלים הוא) related עשה to ועסותם רשעים ("you shall tread down the wicked," RSV; NRSV) in Mal 3:21.

[861] Cf. Gen 32:11; Jer 21:2; Ezek 20:44, 22:14; Ps 109:21. Although the expression עשה את may occur in a clear negative sense (see text), it also may occur in an obviously positive sense (see Jer 21:2; Ps 109:21).

[862] Sabottka proposes that עשה in Zeph 3:19 means "*vernichte*." He points to Ugaritic evidence and to Jer 9:6. See Sabottka: 137.

[863] See below.

[864] Mic 4:6-7/8 is generally considered post-monarchic. See, for instance, R. L. Smith: 39; Mays,1976: 99-101; Renaud,1977: 181-90.

... וְשַׂמְתִּי ...　　　　　　　... וְשַׂמְתִּים ...

Mic 4:7　　　　　　　　　　　　Zeph 3:19

The word צלעה occurs elsewhere in Mic 4:6,7, and צלע occurs in Gen
32:32. The use of a feminine form in Zeph 3:19, Mic 4:6,7 is probably
due to the collective sense.[865] The substantival form הַנִּדָּחָה [866] occurs
twice in the OT, in Zeph 3:19 and Mic 4:6.[867] Words from the root נדח
in the *niphal* pattern together with verbal forms from the root קבץ occur
elsewhere in Deut 30:4; Isa 56:8; Jer 49:5; Neh 1:9.[868] In addition, they
appear also with verbal forms from other roots whose meaning is close to
קבץ, e.g., with verbal forms from אסף (Isa 11:12)[869] and from כנס (Ps
147:2).[870] In all these cases the word from the root נדח in the *niphal*
pattern refers to exile. Accordingly, unless one sustains a prior conception
that Zeph 3:19 is pre-exilic and therefore cannot refer to the exile, one can
hardly dismiss the idea that the phrase refers to Israel, or the people of
Zion, who are in exile.[871] Significantly, Deut 30:4; Isa 11:12, 56:8; Mic
4:6-8; Ps 147:2 and Neh 1:9, which refer to Israel as Zeph 3:19 does, are
post-monarchic texts.[872]

---

[865] See GKC § 122s; Meyer, II: 44.

[866] That is, a definite noun composed by the feminine participle from נדח in the *niphal*
pattern and the definite article.

[867] The alternative form הַנִּדַּחַת occurs in Ezek 34:4,16. נִדְּחָה occurs also in Jer 30:17. There it
refers to Zion.

[868] All of those who refer to Israel (Deut 30:4; Isa 56:8; Neh 1:9) are post-monarchic.
Concerning Deut 30:4, see Levenson, 1975; Mayes, 1981: 367-70 and the
bibliography mentioned in these works.

[869] Isa 11:2 is also post-monarchic. See for instance, Clements, 1982: 125.

[870] Ps 147 is post-exilic. See, for instance, Anderson: 944.

[871] Cf. Tg. Neb. that translates הצלעה and הנדחה as מחלתליא and מבדריא (i.e., "the exiled, the
scattered").

[872] See footnotes above. Of course, this does not mean that the image of the deity or the
king gathering the dispersed was an innovation of post-monarchic Jewish communities.
This image antecedes the destruction of Jerusalem and the Temple by hundreds of years
(for instance, Hammurabi is "the gatherer of the scattered people of Isin"), and certainly
the literary expressions of this image always contain references to "scattering,
dispersing" and "gathering (see Widengren, 1984). The issue, however, is that in the
OT material are references to Israel's exile that share certain language and that occur
mainly in clearly post-monarchic material (e.g., Deutero-Isaiah; Nehemiah) or very
likely post-monarchic material (e.g., Deut 30; Ps 147).

Certainly, the existence of the meaning "dispersed, in exile" for הנדחה does not imply that other connotations of the word have to be ruled out. For instance, the word in its present context probably conveys also a sense of "outcast" (cf. Jer 30:17), and in accordance with the metaphor of the sheep and the shepherd also a sense of "strayed" (cf. Ezek 34:16; Deut 22:1).

Mic 4:7 concludes ושמתי את הצלעה לשארית. In Zeph 3:19, a plausible word pair of שארית, namely, שם (see 2 Sam 14:7; cf. Isa 14:22, Zeph 1:4)[873] appears instead of שארית. But the word שם receives a different set of connotations in Zeph 3:19 because it occurs there along with another of its attested pair words, namely in the form ולשם לתהלה (cf. Deut 26:19; Jer 13:11, 33:9; Zeph 3:20). The similarities between the expressions in v. 19 (ושמתים לתהלה ולשם) and v. 20 (כי אתן אתכם לשם ולתהלה) are self-evident.

Several proposals have been made concerning בכל הארץ בשתם. Among them, the main options are:

(a) to read as it were written לתהלה ולשם בכל ארץ בשתם ושמתים, i.e., to drop the definite article ה from ארץ. This approach is supported by the Vg. and Tg. Neb., by most traditional interpreters[874] and several modern commentators, who generally propose to emend the text.[875] If this approach is correct then the text can be translated, " I will get them praise and fame in every land where they have been put to shame" (KJV).[876] If this is the case, the entire expression ארץ בשתם ולתהלה בכל עמי הארץ ושמתים לתהלה ולשם בכל parallels בכל ארץ בשתם and אתן אתכם לשם in particular parallels הארץ בכל עמי. Moreover, since the occurrence of כל before a noun has led to the "mechanical" addition of the definite article in places where it was not supposed to be (see Jos 8:11; 1 Kgs 14:24; Jer 25:26, 31:40; Ezek

---

[873] See note on Zeph 1:4.

[874] E.g., Rashi, Radak, Calvin; see KJV.

[875] See Ehrlich:463; Köhler: 234; Edler:12; cf. Rudolph, 1975: 294.

[876] Cf. NEB; House: 126; Schöckel-Valverde (Nueva Biblia Española).

45:16),[877] the occurrence of the definite article in בכל הארץ (v. 19) may be explained as due to either the influence of כל or of the well attested expression בכל הארץ[878] or both.

(b) To consider בשתם the object of the verb (i.e., ושמתים) either by considering the מ enclictic or by dropping it out. If this is the case, one may translate "I will change their shame into praise and renown in all the earth" (RSV, NRSV).[879] A variant of this approach consists in proposing an elliptic verb in the second clause, and translating, therefore, " I will transform them into a praise, and their shame into a name in all the earth."[880]

In addition some proposals concerning the redactional history of the piece may shed light onto the meaning of the text. For instance, the suggestion that בכל הארץ has been added to an already existing text may lead to a translation, "I will transform them into praise, and their shame (in all the earth) into a name,"where the words in parentheses are an explanatory, locative gloss that may have been triggered by עמי הארץ בכל which stands immediately after ולתהלה לשם in v. 20.[881]

Although both options are plausible, taking into account that the unexpected occurrence of the definite article is attested in several places in the OT, and especially after כל, and since the expression in v. 19 parallels in many other aspects the one in v. 20, it seems that renderings like "I will get them praise and fame in every land where they have been put to shame" are to be preferred.

---

[877] See GKC § 127 g. Cf. Josh 3:17.

[878] E.g., Gen 41:57, 47:13; Exod 9:14,16, 34:10; Josh 6:27; 1 Sam 13:3; 2 Sam 24:8; 2 Kgs 5:15, 17:5; Isa 12:5; Zech 4: 10; 5:6; 13:8; Ps 8:2,10; 19:15, 45:17, 105:7; Job 42:15; 1 Chr 16:14; 2 Chr 16:9.

[879] See, for instance, Sabottka: 139; O'Connor: 262; Kapelrud, 1975: 109.

[880] See Ball, 1972/1988: 196, 295; cf. Gerleman, 1942: 66.

[881] Cf. Gerleman, 1942: 66. The alternative option that בשמם has been added to an already existing text has been proposed (cf. J. M. P. Smith: 260). This is less likely because it seems hardly to explain why it was added there. In addition, it is worthy of noting that since Wellhausen several scholars consider בשמם either a corruption or abbreviation of בשובי את שבותם (e.g., Elliger (BHS); NJB). On abbreviations in the OT, see Driver, 1960, 1964. Driver does not mention this proposal and the list of Driver's suggestions contain no similar case to the one proposed here.

3.4.17. Zeph 3:20

Unlike בעת ההיא in v. 19, בעת ההיא in v. 20 opens the sentence and is followed by a verb in the imperfect. This is in accordance with the common use of this expression (see above).

The LXX seems to suggest a Hebrew אָטִיב instead of אביא. This reading has been preferred by several scholars.[882] But the pair בוא in the *hiphil* pattern and קבץ in the *piel*, occurs in a very similar way in Isa 43:5, Jer 31:8 (cf. Isa 48:14-15; 56:7-8; 60:4-9; Neh 1:9).[883]

The general issue of שוב שבות has been discussed in the note concerning Zeph 2:7. The occurrence of the expressions אביא אתכם and בעת קבצי אתכם in verse 20 clearly indicates that even if לעיניכם בשובי את שבותיכם is understood as "restore their fortunes," the restoration announced in v. 20 includes the image of gathering the people out of the exile, and by no means excludes it. Since the image of YHWH gathering the dispersed, returning the exiles, clearly conveys a meaning of restoring the fortunes of the people, the difference between the understanding of the verse underlying a translation such as "when I turn back your captivity"[884] and the one underlying a translation such as "when I restore your fortunes"[885] is hardly significant.[886]

---

[882] See, J. M. P. Smith: 260, 263 and the bibliography mentioned there.

[883] Compare also with the redactional or compositional relation between Jer 23:3 and Jer 23:8. One may also compare with Ezek 34:13.

[884] The quotation from KJV, cf. the LXX, the Vg., Tg. Neb.; see also J. M. P. Smith: 220, 260

[885] E.g., O'Connor: 263; R. L. Smith :143; Kapelrud: 109; Sabottka: 147; House: 126; RSV; NRSV; NJPSV; NEB; REB; NJB; Schöckel-Valverde (Nueva Biblia Española).

[886] The clear reference to the exile, along with (a) the idea that Zephaniah—the seventh century prophet—could not have prophesied about the gathering of those who have been dispersed because of the fall of monarchic Judah, and (b) the idea that—at least—main parts of the Book of Zephaniah are literally Zephanic (on the basis of a certain understanding of the superscription) have led many scholars to the idea that the verse is a late addition to the text, or that it refers to the exile of the Northern Kingdom (e.g., Ball, 1972/1988: 198). Most modern scholars agree that at least some parts of vv. 14-20 are a late addition, and some consider the entire section a late addition. See the summary of modern research in Edler: 263. Concerning v. 20, even Kapelrud tends to consider it a late addition, but he (following Keller) bases his position on the prose character of the verse. See Kapelrud, 1975: 40. Also the "eschatological character" of Zeph 3:20 has been referred to as a reason for considering the verse late. For Zeph 3:20 as late addition, see, for instance, Gerleman, 1942: 66; Rudolph, 1975: 299-300.

A comparison between the concluding note in the Book of Amos and Zeph 3:20 shows that both point to an ideal future in which YHWH will bring back the exiles and will change their fortune for the best. Significantly, both notes include the key-phrase שוב שבות (Am 9:14) and both conclude with the legitimating, and authoritative, statement ה' אמר.[887] It is noteworthy that these are the only two prophetic books that conclude with such a statement.[888]

---

[887] In Am 9:14, אמר ה' אלהיך.

[888] To a certain extent, one may compare them with כי ה' דבר in Obad 1: 18. It is unclear whether the expression נאם ה' צבאות in Hag 2:23 refers to Hag 2:23 or to the entire book, or both.

4. Commentary

4.1 Preliminary remarks

While the goal of the textual, linguistic and comparative notes is to establish and examine the evidence concerning the meaning of words and expressions in the Book of Zephaniah, as well as their pattern of occurrence in the Old Testament, the goal of the commentary section is to analyze the Book of Zephaniah, its units, and the traditions embedded in it from a historical-critical perspective according to the approach described in the Introduction of this work and especially in the "Methodological Guidelines" section.[1]

The first and perhaps the most decisive stage in a historical-critical analysis is the demarcation of the different units, that is, the demarcation of the object to be studied. Certainly, if the objects of study are different, the conclusions drawn of their analysis can hardly be the same.

The Book of Zephaniah is readable; that is, one is able to read the book as unit. But there is no need to review the entire history of biblical criticism to sustain the idea that the meaningfulness of a text does not preclude the existence of pre-text components, such as, sources, traditions, and coined figures of speech, or subsequent additions. For instance, if one reads

עם קשה ערף הוא ועתה הניחה לי ויחר אפי

בהם ואכלם ואעשה אותך לגוי גדול ובאהרון

---

[1] Chapter 1.2. See also 3.1.

התאנף ה' מאד להשמידו ויתפלל משה בעד

אהרון ויחל משה את פני ה' אלהיו

instead of the MT Exod 32:10-11a, one is still reading a meaningful text.
But, the text is the result of the addition of the MT Deut 9:20 to Exod
32:10.[2] The Book of Chronicles is obviously a readable book but all
modern scholars agree that the author was dependent on a certain *Vorlage*
of the books of Samuel and Kings.[3]

However, it is true that the Book of Zephaniah—as many other biblical
books—not only can be read as a unit but to a large extent also calls for
such a reading. This is so not only because of the claim of the superscription (see below) but also because of stylistic devices. One of the most
conspicuous features in the Book of Zephaniah is the repetitive use of several words and expressions, even if they sometimes carry different meanings. In the words of Rendtorff,

> the often and varied mention of the day of YHWH (1.7,14); day
> of wrath (of YHWH) (1.15,18; 2:3); day of distress, of oppres-
> sion, of darkness, and so on (1.14-16); day of sacrifice (1.8);
> day in which YHWH raises himself up (3.8) or simply 'that
> day' (1.9,15; in the introductory formulae 1.8,10; 3.11,16; cf.
> "at that time' 1.12; 3.19,20). Then there is what happens 'in
> the midst' of Jerusalem (3.3,5,11,12,1,17); 'seeking YHWH'
> (1.6; 2.3); 'accepting instruction' (3.2,7); 'worshipping; (1.5;
> 2.11; cf. 3.9f.); 'fearing; (3.7, 15,16); 'visiting'
> (1.8,9,12;2,7; 3.7); 'raising hand' (1.4; 2.13); "gathering
> (*'asap, kibbez*) in different contexts (1.2; 3.8,19,20); 'leaving
> a remnant' (2.7,9; 3.12,13); cf. 1.4b; 'turning the captivity'

---

2   The reading above follows 4QpaleoExod^m and the Samaritan Exodus. See P. W. Skehan,
    "Exodus in the Samaritan Recension from Qumran, *JBL* 74 (1955) 182-87, and J. E.
    Anderson, *An Exodus Scroll from Qumran. 4QPaleoExod^m and the Samaritan Tradition*
    (HSS 30, Atlanta: Scholars Press, 1986), esp. 208-09, 266-71. A "classical" example of
    a meaningful text in the Samaritan Pentateuch that is the result of the introduction of
    sentences from Deuteronomy into the the text of Exodus is the reading
    וישמע משה לקול חתנו ויעש ככל אשר אמר ויאמר משה אל העם . . . לא אוכל אנוכי לבדי שאת אתכם
    (Sam.Exod 18:24-25). This reading has been analyzed by J. H. Tigay ("An empirical
    Basis for the Documentary Hypothesis," *JBL* 94 (1975) 329-42, esp. 333-35; Tigay,
    1985: 61-68, 90-91). See also Sanderson, *An Exodus Scroll*, 207-08, 267-68.

3   It is worth noting that also modern, clearly understandable texts are sometimes the result
    of a redactional process. For instance, the well known Pledge of Alliance to the Flag of
    the United States originally had "my flag" instead of present phrase "the flag of the
    United States of America;" more important insofar as it concern with contents was the
    addition of the words "under God," in 1954.

(2.7; 3:20), the city (2.15; 3.1); the 'arrogant' (2.15; 3.11);
mispat ('right,' etc.) with various meanings (2.3; 3.5,8,15).[4]

What historical-critical conclusions follow from such impressive evidence?

Since one cannot explain this evidence as the result of chance, the first conclusion is that the repetition of words and expressions in the Book of Zephaniah is either a compositional or a redactional device.[5] To be sure, this feature is not unique to this book. For instance, no one fails to recognize the recurrent theme of כבוד ה', or the recurrent use of the formula ויהי דבר ה' אלי לאמר or the address בן אדם in the Book of Ezekiel.[6] Similarly, the recurrent use of expression קדוש ישראל, of the word צדקה (with different meanings and connotations)[7] and the existence of cross references to blindness and deafness are easily noticed in the Book of Isaiah (Isaiah 1-66).[8]

If the existence of a general pattern of repetition, allusions, and cross references throughout a biblical book were a solid argument for single authorship then the first step in a historical-critical analysis of a book would be to find the latest datable reference in the book, and to date the book accordingly, for the writer could have been aware of past events and old language but could not have been aware of future developments.[9] However, the existence of such a pattern is not a solid argument for single authorship, out of nothing. If it were the case, one would have to conclude, for instance, that all the material in the Book of Isaiah was created, out of nothing, by a single author at a specific place and time. But, this position

---

4 Rendtorff, 1986: 236-37.
5 Cf. Amit, 1988.
6 See, for instance, Rendtorff, 1986: 208.
7 See, Rendtorff, 1986: 199-200, 208.
8 See, Clements,1985. On the redactional unity of Isaiah, see Sweeney, 1988: 1-25.
9 That is, the writer did not have the ability to see directly into the future. One of the basic assumptions of the historical-critical method is that there is a basic uniformity through the ages. Since there is no reliable evidence of people directly aware of future developments in present days, one concludes that the same holds true concerning people who lived in the past.

has received almost no support in modern scholarship and with good reason.[10]

Repetitions, cross references, and allusions do not rule out the possible existence of (a) received traditions and sources before the compositional level;[11] (b) units attached to a pre-existent text by means of these stylistic devices;[12] (c) units of variable size that have been triggered by the use of certain words and expressions;[13] and (d) a redactional layer of interpretation of a received text.[14] Certainly, this conclusion holds true even if one may discern structural, stylistic devices. For instance, after the reading of the Torah in the synagogue, when the scroll of Torah is brought back to the ark, the congregation says:

וּבְנֻחֹה יֹאמַר:

שׁוּבָה ה' רבבות אלפי ישראל :קומה ה' למנוחתך אתה וארון

עֻזֶּךָ: כהניך ילבשו צדק וחסידיך ירננו :בעבור דוד עבדך

אל תשב פני משיחך :כי לקח טוב נתתי לכם תורתי

אל תעזבו: עץ חיים היא למחזיקים בה ותומכיה מאושר :

---

[10] See, for instance, Clements, 1982: 3-8, 21-23; Rendtorff, 1986: 190-200 and the bibliography mentioned in these works.

[11] For instance, cf.1-2 Chronicles. See also

אשרי יושבי ביתך   עוד יהללוך סלה

אשרי העם שככה לו   אשרי העם שה' אלהיו

This short poem that is a part of the morning service in the Synagogue consists of Ps 84:5 and 144:15 —see below. Undoubtedly, the use of אשרי links the two lines together but from this fact does not follow that the two lines come from one single source.

[12] For instance, cf. the additions to the MT Book of Exodus in the Samaritan Exodus (and 4QpaleoEx), and the additions to the Book of Esther.

[13] Cf. the concept of "generation" or "triggering" in Mc Kane, 1986: lxxii-lxxxiii. See the examples given there. It is worth noting that poetry not only may generate prose (see Mc Kane, 1986: lxxii-lxxxiii) but poetry may also generate poetry. Almost any child knows that he use of a word in a "received text" may lead to the use the same word with a complementary or opposite sense in the "transformed text," that one verset may induce another verset, that one stanza may trigger another stanza, and one strophe may trigger another strophe. This is true not only concerning children's puns of words and songs but also is a well attested feature in popular singing, and in any literature in which the "received text" shows some sort of fluidity. The addition of several lines to the popular Israeli song "Jerusalem of Gold" immediately after the Six Days War is a clear, modern example of how a change in the historical-political circumstances may lead to the addition of new strophes to an existing text.

[14] See, for instance, the occurrence of the expression כל רשיעי ארעא in Tg. Neb. Zeph 1:18, 3:8. There the two related notes restrict the divine punishment to those who deserve it.

דרכיה דרכי נועם וכל נתיבותיה שלום ‏:השיבנו ה' אליך
ונשובה חדש ימינו כקדם

Even after a simple reading of the unit that follows the introductory
phrase ובנחה יאמר, one becomes aware of the chiastic structure of the
unit (see שובה and נשובה, with different meanings), of the central position of the Torah (לקח טוב) in it, of the movement from the theme of
the relationship between YHWH and Israel to the theme of Torah and back
to the relationship between YHWH and Israel at the end; and of the
movement of the cultic theme from the old form of cultic activities, which
are expected to be re-established, to the "Torah" centered service (cf. עוז
למנוחתך אתה וארון ה' קומה with the real act of bringing back the
scroll of the Torah to the ark), and finally to the hope of restoration of the
past. Significantly, this liturgical piece is a composite text. It is composed
of Num 10:36; Ps 132:8-10; Prov 4:2, 3:18,17 and Lam 5:21. Moreover,
the fact that the piece is composed of scriptural passages is certainly not irrelevant to its value as a communicative message for a synagogal congregation. Furthermore, at least concerning the quotation from Num 10:36
even the scriptural location of the cited verse is relevant, for the immediately preceding verse in the Book of Numbers (Num 10:35) opens the
passage that the congregation says when the ark is opened at the beginning
of the "Reading of the Torah" service.[15] Of course, it is not a simple coincidence that the service opens with a passage whose first verse is Num
10:35 and ends with one whose first verse is Num 10:36.

The short poem that the congregation says after the ark is closed provides another example,

אשרי יושבי ביתך   עוד יהללוך סלה
אשרי העם שככה לו   אשרי העם שה' אלהיו

The repetition of אשרי, among other stylistic features shapes this poem
as a literary unit. But it is a composite unit. This poem is composed of Ps
84:5 and 144:15. Both the author of the poem and the community that in-

---

[15] The passage continues with Isa 2:3b // Mic 3:2b. That is, it also begins with a reference
to the ark and immediately moves to the Torah.

troduced the poem into the liturgy were certainly aware of the original place of the two lines, and of the authority connoted by quoting scripture. Thus, one has to conclude that one cannot fully understand this poem as a communicative message, in historical-critical terms, if one does not know that it is composed of two verses already existing in the Book of Psalms.

To sum up: Repetitions of words, cross references, and stylistic devices shaping the structure of the unit do not prove that the text has no "history." They do not preclude: (a) the existence of separate textual units and traditions underlying the text (i.e., a pre-compositional history); and (b) the existence of post-compositional additions, interpretations, reinterpretations, and the like; or in other words, of a redactional history. Moreover, the existence of pre-compositional history is certainly relevant to the historical-critical understanding of the unit at its compositional level (see above).[16] In addition, it goes without saying that no study of the compositional level of a particular text can be carried out before a certain text is ascribed to this compositional level. In order to do so, one has to separate the redactional from the compositional.

Since the repetition of words, cross references, etc., are signs of compositional and redactional activity but not compelling evidence concerning the authorial unity of a given text, then the possible existence of different units reflecting different periods must be analyzed. This will be done according to the approach mentioned in the Methodological Guidelines section, in the Introduction of this work.

Authorial unity is certainly not the only possible sort of unity capable of keeping together a prophetic text, as the Book of Isaiah clearly shows. Also stylistic devices *per se*, despite their importance, are probably not the main unifying factor. For instance, although one can explain the recurrent use of the formula ויהי דבר ה' אלי לאמר, or the address בן אדם in the Book of Ezekiel in terms of stylistic devices that any redactor with a minimum sense of style could have used in order to anchor a new unit into

---

[16] Obviously, units reflecting a social, political, and religious background different from the one reflected in the compositional level may shed light into their own original circumstances as well.

the text, one cannot explain the absence of the term Zion in the entire Book of Ezekiel in terms of style alone. Similarly, the fact that the Book of Zephaniah contains no reference to a human king or to human, ideal (Messianic) king but refers to YHWH as the king, without any intermediaries (note the contrast with Isa 11:1-10 for instance) cannot be considered strictly a matter of style. One must assume, therefore, that there were constraints, and not only stylistic constraints, in the process that led from prophetic traditions to the present prophetic books. In other words, the tradents were not free to write their own thoughts in a prophetic text, even if they were able to write them in the right style.

This conclusion is to be expected, for prophetic traditions (including texts) were transmitted from generation to generation because they had (and probably have today) some sort of authority or, at the very least, relevancy. This authority (or relevancy) cannot but reflect a certain corpus of traditions. In other words, a text was not considered a part of the divine word (matter) that came to Isaiah, Zephaniah, or any other prophet according to the whim of a writer or according to his or her ability to write in the style of, but in accordance with the perceived meaning of the divine word that came to the specific prophet. Thus, each prophetic tradition shows a kind of unity that is not dependent on the exact wording of a text, for in such a case one expects a "frozen" text, but on the sense of a conceived meaning. Moreover, the conception that each prophetic tradition has its own message is perhaps one of the main reason that preempted prophetic traditions from collapsing one into the other despite the fact that communities received, learned, interpreted, and passed on more than one prophetic tradition.

The following discussion concerning the units composing the Book of Zephaniah, and the traditions reflected in them, will be sensitive to the Zephanic character of the units and traditions as they occur in the book, including the claim of the superscription that the following text is the divine word that came to Zephaniah at certain time, in the days of Josiah.

The Book of Zephaniah, as any other book, is a communicative object composed in order to present a message, to make sense to its public. Of course, a meaningful message cannot exist independently of forms or structures. Especially for historical-critical studies, the dialogue between the meaning suggested by the chosen structure of the book and the text of the book is worthy of study, for it provides a glimpse into the underlying thought that serves as the conceptual background against which the book as a communicative object—coming up from a certain community and for a certain community—is comprehensible. For methodological reasons, this issue will be discussed in a separate section, "The structure of the Book of Zephaniah and its message."[17]

4.2 Commentary. Zephaniah 1

4.2.1. Zeph 1:1

The superscription (Zeph 1:1) is a clearly delimited unit. It opens with the common דבר ה' אשר היה אל and concludes with a note identifying the historical time in which the "word" of YHWH came to Zephaniah. The unit claims to be neither divine speech nor the words of the prophet, for both are mentioned in the third person. The meaning of the superscription has been discussed in the Notes section.

In its present form, because of the long genealogical list, Zeph 1:1 resembles relatively late superscriptions (see notes). The basic formula of the superscription in Zeph 1:1 (i.e, "the word of YHWH that came to X", in which X stands for the name of the prophet) occurs in the superscriptions of the books of Hosea, Joel, Micah, and Jeremiah (LXX). Since a superscription cannot antedate the following text, or at the very least a kernel of it, but may postdate it, then Joel 1:1 will be clear evidence

---

[17] Chapter 4.5.

for the use of this superscriptional formula in the post-monarchic period, provided the Book of Joel or its kernel are post-monarchic—as commonly proposed.[18] Obviously, the use of such a formula in the post-monarchic period does not rule out the possibility that it was used also in the monarchic period, but certainly, does not prove it either.

The original unity of the long genealogical list is questionable but even if the present genealogical list is the result of interpretative activity, the existence of an underlying tradition (not necessarily in the written form of Zeph 1:1, or pre-Zeph 1:1) according to which Zephaniah was the son of Cushi can only be reaffirmed by this redactional activity, for the long genealogical list removes a possible suspicion concerning the origin of Zephaniah that may have been derived from the occurrence of the name Cushi.

It is worth noting that nothing in Zeph 1:2-3:20 may have led an ancient scribe, or an ancient community, to the conclusion that Zeph 1:2-3:20 is to be related to Zephaniah, son of Cushi. Moreover, the putative date (i.e., in the days of Josiah) can hardly be derived from the text of the book alone. Therefore, one has to assume the existence of traditional knowledge that ascribed Zeph 1:2-3:20 to the figure of the prophet Zephaniah, or at the very least, some traditional knowledge concerning a prophet Zephaniah, who lived in monarchic times. Moreover, the same holds true even if Zeph 1:2-3:30 is considered a pseudepigraphic work, written by a single author, independently of any sources or traditions, for even in that case the fact that the work was ascribed to Zephaniah presumes that he was a known figure. (It is so because such the pseudepigraphic claim would be made to legitimate a contemporaneous work by assuming the authorship of a known person from the past.)

Neither the social location nor the personal background of Zephaniah (or better, those assumed to be of Zephaniah) can be derived from the superscription (see note on Zeph 1:1).

---

[18] See, Wolff,1977:4-6; J.A.Thompson, 1974 and the bibliography mentioned there.

The question whether the date claimed in the superscription provides a relatively external framework to Zeph 1:2-3:20 or whether it was one of the shaping factors in the composition of the work will be discussed later, especially in the section concerning the announcements of judgment against the nations.

4.2.2. Zeph 1:2-3

The limits of the unit are marked by the end of the superscription and by the second נְאֻם ה'. The first נְאֻם ה' divides the unit into two subunits: Zeph 1:2 and Zeph 1:3. The two subunits are linked together by several features, including:

1) The use of the expression מעל פני האדמה נאם ה' as the conclusion of both subunits.

2) The repetitive use of אסף.

3) עוף השמים ודגי הים and אדם ובהמה (ובהמה) in v. 3 explains the general כל in v. 2 (see below).

4) The speaker is YHWH in both.

5) The addressees are not identified in either subunit.

6) The theme of both subunits is an announcement of a total but not necessarily universal destruction.

As a unit, Zeph 1:2-3 shows a clear repetitive pattern of words and sounds (e.g., אדם occurs twice, אדמה twice; אֹסֵף three times and אסֹף one), and perhaps a pun on words concerning the "fish of the sea" (cf. the pun on words concerning gathering grapes in Jer 8:13).

In the present text of the Book of Zephaniah, it is likely that the basic, attested meaning of אסף (i.e.,"gathering") provides a link between Zeph 1:2-3 at the beginning of the book and Zeph 3:18-20 at its end, forming an inclusio.[19] This inclusio is based upon the theoretically possible, positive

---

[19] E.g., Ball, 1972/1988: 281-82.

connotation of אָסֹף אָסֵף and its close relationship with קבץ (see Zeph
3:19,20), that is, as אסֹף אסף occurs in the likely post-exilic Mic 2:12.

Although there is no parallel to Zeph 1:2-3 in the OT, similar expressions
to those found in Zeph 1:2-3 occur elsewhere in the OT. The short divine
utterance followed by ה' נאם may reflect a certain form of oracle, but
even if this is correct it cannot be related to a specific time or even literature. Concerning other expressions, one may mention that ה' נאם ...
אָסֹף אָסֵף recalls Jer 8:13 and והכרתי את האדם, which occurs just
before the concluding phrase of v. 3, resembles Ezekielian language. The
degree of similarity between the latter phrase and Ezekielian language is
reinforced by the fact that והכרתי את האדם stands not only before על
ונטיתי ידי but also (at least in the present form of the text) in the same
chain of "waw + perfect" verbs that follows the imperfect אָסֵף, and formally ends in v. 6. This chain holds together Zeph 1:2-3 and Zeph 1:4-6
and includes another והכרתי (v. 4).

It is worth noting that according to Zeph 1:3, "everything" (see כל in v.
2) means animals. The destruction of "everything" is nothing but the destruction of "animals." The destruction of the sky, the sea, stars, and the
like, seems to be beyond the horizon of Zeph 1:3. Also there is no reference to destruction in the plant kingdom (despite the obvious connotations
of אסף, cf. Exod 23:10; Lev 25:3; Deut 11:14).[20] The author of Zeph
1:3 obviously knew that there are plants in the world but the implied perspective in his or her writing is of a tripartite (land, water, air) world that
is mainly a habitat for animals. Such perspective is perhaps more plausible in a herding group than in an agrarian group, but much more plausible
in an urban, elite group, quite removed from both, for a shepherd's perspective includes pasture land. In addition, the abstract, idealistic, and
non-economic character of the world's perspective in Zeph 1:3 (one can
hardly assume that hunting birds and fishing were main economic activi-

---

[20] Contrast, for instance, with Jer 12:4, ותאבל הארץ וישב כל השדה יבש ירבש מרעת ישבי בה ספתה בהמות ועוף
עד מתי. See also Hos 4:3, "For that, the earth is withered: Everything that dwells on it
languishes—Beasts of the field and the birds of the sky—Even the fish of the sea perish"
(NJPSV).

ties) seems to support the plausibility of an elite perspective. In simple terms, if what the biblical writer "sees" when he/she looks upon the world is land animals, birds and fish, it seems more plausible that he/she reflects the perspective of an urban elite than that he/she reflects the perspective of actual shepherds, agrarian workers, or of common people living in close relationship with them. If this is the case, the reference to animals and not to plants may be a constraint due to the ideal tripartite image of the world along with a sense of stylistic symmetry (there are no flying plants) and perhaps it may also reflect an ideal, and removed from actual life, preference for herding, animals, and pastoral life over the agrarian activities in which most of the population was involved (cf. Gen 4:3-4; Isa 7:21-22;[21] Zeph 2:6-7; and the patriarchal stories).[22]

The expression והמכשלות את הרשעים may have been added in a post-compositional stage to the book but not necessarily, or even more likely, at very late date such as second century BCE, or even later (see notes). The expression adds an ethical dimension to the divine announcement of destruction, or perhaps makes explicit the implied idea that the announced destruction is a kind of judgment. This note stresses the theological conception that punishment which is not an execution of judgment against those who deserve it is not godly. Obviously, this conception is not unique to the author of the note and his or her group (e.g., Gen 18:23-33; cf. Tg. Neb. Zeph 1:18, 3:8). A comparable note occurs in Zeph 1:17.

---

[21] Cf. Mc Kane, 1967: 217-18.

[22] Most of the people in ancient Israel and Judah worked in agriculture. The society was an agrarian society with some enclosed herding. See, for instance, Borowski, 1987; esp. 3-14. Concerning enclosed herding, see See, Rowton M.B., "Autonomy and Nomadism in Western Asia," *Or.* 42 (1973): 247-258; "Urban Autonomy in a Nomadic Environment," *JNES* 32 (1973): 201-15; "Enclosed Nomadism," *Journal of the Economic and Social History of the Orient* 17 (1974):1-30; "Dimorphic Structure and Topology," *Or Ant* 15 (1976): 17-31.

4.2.3. Zeph 1:4-6

The limits of the unit are marked by the closing נאם ה' in the preceding unit and by the interjection הס! that opens the following unit. The unit is held together by a chain of two verbs in the perfect preceded by *waw* (a series that goes back to אסף in v. 2 and links the two units, see above) followed by a series of participial phrases opening with ואת ה-X, where X stands for the participle, and by the common theme of judgment against those who engaged in illegitimate cultic activities. Although those who are to be punished are identified according to their deeds, the addressees of the unit are not identified.

The general conception that underlies the reference to the "illegitimate worship" in Zeph 1:4-5, as well as its polemic terms, are characteristic of the deuteronomic/ deuteronomistic literature. But the language of the text does not show heavy influence of the typical deuteronomic/ deuteronomistic phraseology, although some of the key terms occur in the account of Josiah's reform in 2 Kgs 23.[23] It is highly significant that most of the key terms in the unit (e.g., Baal, malkam, priestlings [כמרים], host of heaven) are not mentioned again in the Book of Zephaniah and that the topos of "illegitimate/alien worship" does not occur elsewhere in the Book of Zephaniah, even in places where one may have expected a reference, (e.g., Zeph 3:3-4). In sharp contrast, the concluding phrase of the unit points to Zeph 2:3 (cf. with the linkage function of . . . והכרתי את האדם in Zeph 1:3), and, because of this connection, to the topos of the ענוים and ענוה and to the topos of צדק (cf. Zeph 2:5; 3:5,10).

The opening expression נטיתי ידי על X-ל as it occurs in Zeph 1:4 appears mainly in the Book of Ezekiel (cf. the closing verbal phrase of the preceding unit), and once in a clearly post-monarchic section of the Book of Jeremiah (Jer 51:25). The expression נטיתי ידי על X-ל followed by a

---

[23] In addition, one may notice that the expression השתחוה לצבא שמים occurs in Deut 4:19, 17:3; 2 Kgs 17:16, 21:3 (// 2 Chr 33:3); Jer 8:2 and Zeph 1:5.

phrase opening with כרת in the *hiphil* is also characteristic of the Book of
Ezekiel, but elsewhere in the unit one finds no characteristically Ezekielian
language. Quite to the contrary, one finds expressions that do not occur at
all in the Ezekielian tradition. For instance, the expressions המקום הזה
and יהודה // יושבי ירושלם show a very definite pattern of occurrence
in the Latter Prophets: Most of their occurrences are in the Book of
Jeremiah, and a few later. Significantly, the last verse (v. 6) contains language that occurs neither in Jeremiah nor Ezekiel, but whose closer parallels occur in post-exilic literature. It is worth noting that Ezekielian and
Jeremianic (as well as Isaianic) expressions that do not occur together in
the Book of Ezekiel, Jeremiah and Isaiah, do occur along with one another
in the Book of Zephaniah, already in these first verses. Accordingly, it
seems that Zephaniah does not align itself according to the specific patterns, and to a large extent exclusive language, of any one of these books.

The dichotomy between כמרים and כהנים seems to point to late textual activity in the Book of Zephaniah (see notes), but probably not to a
very late compositional stage. The relationship between the language that
links the different units one another, and to the rest of the book, seems to
suggest a post-monarchic dating but the issue should be discussed in terms
of the entire composition.

Can the previously mentioned data (and those in the notes section) provide the necessary information for discerning different written sources,
and for proposing a series of different texts from the first proto-Zeph 1:4-6
(or proto Zeph 1:2-6) to the received Zeph 1:4-6 or Zeph 1:2-6?[24]

If one presupposes that the text is basically Zephanic and underwent
redactional additions through time then one may be tempted to answer in
an affirmative way. For in this case, one looks for phrases or words that
cannot be considered Zephanic, and after trimming them away what remains is nothing but the Zephanic text. The secondary material, consisting
mainly of separate notes, glosses, and half verses, is related to different

---

[24] Cf. Irsigler, 1977: 171; Edler: 74-80, 100-03, 113-23.

periods. If one only arranges them according to the axis of time one receives an ongoing text of the Book of Zephaniah.

But a different perspective is received if the point of departure for the analysis is the existing literary text and if Zeph 1:1 is not considered a compelling reason for accepting that at the very least large parts of the Book of Zephaniah were written by Zephaniah or closely follow his oral sayings in contents, style, and time. If this methodological perspective is accepted, as in this work, one studies first the compositional level, that is the way in which units are linked together, the recurrent themes and the like. Then, one looks for elements that do not seem to be fully integrated in the compositional work, for they present themes, topoi that are not followed in the book and contain terms and expressions that are not linked to expressions and terms found elsewhere in the book. It is more likely that the presence of these themes and topoi is due to a received tradition concerning the "word of God that came to Zephaniah" that constraints the freedom of the the compositor of the book than the result of his or her own free choice. Moreover, the existence of terms and expressions that are used nowhere else in the book suggests footprints of written traditions. If both the theme and the language converge in their singling out a certain element in the book, one may conclude that it is likely that it reflects traditional, received material. In this respect, it is worth recalling that the previous discussion in "preliminary remarks" pointed out that the existence of traditional material assumed to be related to the prophet and constraining the compositor of the book is only to be expected.

The reference to the illegitimate, alien cult in Zeph 1:4-5, as well as the use of the terms Baal, host of heaven, priestlings, etc., points to what may be considered a literary and traditional constraint that shaped the work of the compositor of the Book of Zephaniah. Moreover, this tradition may be roughly located in time, for it resembles texts and traditions from about the time of the Josianic reform through the early post-monarchic period, and especially those in the deuteronomistic history and in the Book of Jeremiah, but they are not attested in Trito-Isaiah, Zechariah 1-8, Haggai, Malachi, Ezra, Nehemiah. Certainly, the existence of this material in the

Zephanic tradition together with its secondary role in the book as whole suggests a changing focus in the Zephanic tradition.

The conceptual and methodological difference between pointing to the existence of received traditions at the time of the composition of the book and presenting a list of different textual forms from the Zephaniah's words to the received text is self-evident.

4.2.4. Zeph 1:7

The limits of the unit are marked by the interjectional הס and by the opening formula in v. 8. The putative speaker is the prophet; neither the addressees of the speech not those to whom the הס is said are identified. Moreover, there is no reference to a specific place, unlike the other occurrences of הס מפני ה'.

The verse presupposes an audience that knows what יום ה' is but does not know that it is at hand. The main point in the unit is to stress the imminence of the day.

The main stylistic feature is ambiguity, and especially in the last verset. In the present context, this ambiguity calls the attention of the reader/hearer to questions of identity that are resolved in the following unit. Thus, v. 7 leads to vv. 8-9. But the language and style of vv. 8-9 are clearly different from those of v. 7. The only expression linking the two units is the phrase that stands between the two (i.e., והיה ביום זבח ה'), and one may compare this with the way in which Zeph 1:2-3 is linked to Zeph 1:4-5.

The linking expression in v. 8 is the first of several temporal phrases linking different units to the ongoing text of Zephaniah (cf. Zeph 1:10,12, 3:16, 20). These connecting phrases not only connect units but also convey the sense that what is announced in the following unit will take place in an undefined future. It is noteworthy that the phrase in v. 8 removes (or at the very least strongly tempers) the sense of imminence that v. 7 brings to the text. A similar function is performed by ביום ההוא in

Zeph 1:15. Significantly, there is a very emphatic stress on, and awareness of, the temporal dimension of events and the announcements of
events in Zeph 1:7- 2:3 and Zeph 3:8-20 (Zeph 1:7,8,9,10,12,14,15,16,
18, 2:2,3, 3:8,9,11,16, 19,20). In other words, these literary blocks
express a sharp awareness that events not only occur but occur on a certain
day, at this or that time, and some at least must occur before time runs out.
Taking into account this temporal awareness in Zeph 1:7- 2:3 and Zeph
3:8-20, one may assume that the removal of the sense of the imminence of
the day of YHWH (in Zeph 1:8,15) is not without reason. It has already
been pointed out in the notes on Zeph 1:8 that if a post-monarchic
community interpreted the putative sayings of Zephaniah concerning the
day of YHWH in Zeph 1:7-18 as prophecies concerning the destruction of
Jerusalem and the Temple, then the temporal awareness, along with a
minimum of historical knowledge,[25] leads to the conclusion that
Zephaniah must have prophesied about a future not too distant from his
days but by no means imminent, if his prophecies were fulfilled. One may
compare the influence of temporal awareness and historical knowledge on
these units with its influence in the shaping of the section of the oracles
against the nations (see 4.3.2. below).

The sacrificial term *zebach* occurs as a more-or-less technical term in relation to YHWH's punishment elsewhere in the OT in post-monarchic literature. It is noteworthy that the image of *zebach* occurs nowhere else in
the Book of Zephaniah, even if there are other notes describing the day of
YHWH (Zeph 1:14-16).

4.2.5. Zeph 1:8-9

The unit is set off from the foregoing and from the following unit by
temporal connecting phrases. The speaker is YHWH and the unit is an

---

[25] See the commentary section on the announcements of judgment against the nations (Zeph
2:4-15), as a section (chapter 4.3.2.).

announcement of judgment against a clearly defined public. The unit holds together not only by affinities of contents but also by a similar structure and language.

The language is unique, containing expressions and themes that do not occur elsewhere in the OT, such as the characterization על המפתן כל הדולג and the expression מלבוש נכרי. The announcement of judgment is against the officers, the royal family (in its broad sense), those who dress in expensive alien clothes, and every servant/officer, whatever his rank and social circle, who enters the royal palace and brings into it wealth gained by violence and fraud, falsehood and lawlessness. That is, this is an announcement of judgment against the monarchic elite (except the king who is not mentioned) and those officers/servants serving this elite, i.e., the royal administration. The description of the Judean elite here does not resemble the one in Zeph 3:3-4. Moreover, there is no other reference to the royal palace in the Book of Zephaniah.

The negative reference to "alien, foreign" raiments has no parallel in the OT. The obvious inference from this note is that it describes a society in which there were differences between the Judean clothes and the foreign raiment and there was commerce between Judah and the "foreigners." It also implies that the ruling elite prefers the foreign garments over the Judean, i.e., they had a normative cultural point of reference, at least on clothes, outside Judah. However, the idea that this phenomenon was restricted only to clothes seems improbable. This social-cultural phenomenon is not referred to in any other unit in the Book of Zephaniah.

The unit concludes with a note containing the pair חמס-מרמה. This pair occur elsewhere in the OT in Isa 53:9. The pair points simultaneously to the social sphere (cf. Zeph 2:3, 3:12) and to the wrong use of "language, words" (cf. Zeph 3:9,13). The two themes occur together in Zeph 3:12-13. Thus, unlike the indirect reference to the king and the foreign clothes, the closing idiom of the unit (חמס ומרמה) seems to point to other units in the Book of Zephaniah. Moreover, as seen in the notes section, polysemy is a recurrent feature in the Book of Zephaniah.

If Zeph 1:8-9 reflects traditions that precede the compositional level of the Book of Zephaniah, what social groups and socio-political circumstances may underlie them?

Many scholars have considered the absence of a direct reference to the king a clear allusion to the days when king Josiah was a child and had no real power (and therefore could not be held responsible of the behavior of the royal palace).[26] This proposal seems likely provided that the text must be understood as written in the days of Josiah, and provided that it must truthfully reflect the historical circumstances and the actual responsibilities of the different members of the elite at the time when it was uttered.[27] If these premises are correct then if there was a king when the prophet Zephaniah uttered the divine (or claimed to be divine) announcement, Zephaniah should have mentioned the king and his guilt. However, the absence of any mention of the king in a condemnatory note concerning the ruling elite is not unique to Zeph 1:8-9, but a common feature in the Latter Prophets, especially in notes referring to social violence, oppression of the weak, lawlessness and the like, as is the case in Zeph 1:8-9 (e.g., Isa 1:21-26, 5:8-11, 20-23; Am 4:1, 5:7, 6:3-6, 8:4-6; Mic 2:1-2). Moreover, the absence of a condemnatory reference to the king in Zeph 1:8-9 may be explained in many different ways. For instance: (a) it may reflect the common royal idea, as well as a commonplace in royal propaganda through the ages, that "the king is above his officers," (i.e., although there are evildoers in the royal administration the king is pure and pious [e.g., 2 Sam 3:26-39; Lam 4:6,13, 20)]; (b) it may be a result of the image of Josiah, the pious king who reigned at the time of Zephaniah according to

---

[26] E.g., J. M. P. Smith: 196; Bic 42; Langhor, 1976:2-3; 1976a: 51.

[27] Some traditional interpreters who considered the prophecy as pointing to the future proposed also literal understandings of בני המלך, for instance Yoseph Kara thought of Jehoiakim, Jeoiachin and Zedekiah; Owen wrote: "This was a prophecy: though the king Josiah had no children at this time, yet he had some afterwards; and they proved themselves deserving of the judgment here announces, and it was inflicted on them. Henderson's objection, that as Josiah had then no children, the prophecy could not apply to them personally, seems wholly inadmissible: it was a *prophecy* [the emphasis is in Owen's note] " (see Calvin: 207); Radak related it to the execution of the sons of Zedekiah, and officers at Riblah (see 2 Kgs 25: 6-7, 19-20).

Zeph 1:1; (c) it may be the result of an intentional omission of any reference to a king flesh and blood in the Book of Zephaniah; (d) it may reflect
the historical circumstances of either the days of king Josiah's childhood,
when the king had no real power, or the days of king Zedekiah, who was
not considered a legitimate king, or not a king at all, by certain sectors in
the Judean elite;[28] and (e) if Zeph 1:8-9 was interpreted at the compositional level of the Book of Zephaniah as pointing to the destruction of
Jerusalem and the Temple, then even a minimal historical knowledge preempts a claim that Zephaniah announced that YHWH would "visit" king
Josiah when YHWH will destroy Jerusalem. Therefore, one can hardly
base an analysis of the social groups and socio-political circumstances that
underlie a pre-compositional tradition reflected in Zeph 1:8-9 on the absence of a condemnatory note concerning the king.

As indicated above, the conception and terms that shape the reference to
the "illegitimate worship," which is another theme in Zeph 1:4-5 that is
presented in a short unit but not developed through the Book of
Zephaniah, is characteristic of the deuteronomic/deuteronomistic literature.
Thus, it seems that the possibility of a certain amount of correspondence
between the image given in Zeph 1:8-9 and the deuteronomic/
deuteronomistic literature is worthy of analysis.

According to Deuteronomy, the king's wealth is limited by law (Deut
17:15-17,20), and his image is closer to that of a constitutional monarch
than to the absolute king (see Deut 17:19).[29] The term שׂרים/שׂר occurs
in Deuteronomy only in Deut 1:15 (dtr.) and Deut 20:9. In both occurrences, their role is limited to a military one. According to Deut 20:9 even
the right to draft people for the army was not in their hands. Even if the
picture of the Book of Deuteronomy is clearly not a mirror of the historical
situation of the monarchy in Judah, it remains a mirror of the ideas of the

---

[28] The dates in the Book of Ezekiel never refer to the regnal years of Zedekiah; cf. 2 Kgs
25:27.

[29] Contrast with 1 Sam 8: 10-18 and the narratives concerning the behavior of David,
Solomon, Jehoiakim. Certainly, they resembled much more the king of 1 Sam 8: 10-18
than the learning, humble king of Deut 17: 15-20.

writers concerning the ideal status of the king and the שׂרים. Moreover, since in the real world, the king and his officers enjoyed much more power than that allowed in Deuteronomy, one may conclude that Deuteronomy contains both a critique of the existent social-political system and also a "constitutional" proposal limiting the wealth and power of the king and his officers. The negative image of the royal administration in Zeph 1:8-9 seems coherent with the approach of Deuteronomy, but nothing beyond that can be asserted.

The implied reference to commerce and especially the negative attitude towards "alien, foreign" clothes and, implicitly, towards the acceptance of foreign points of reference for social behavior seem congruent with the ideology of the deuteronomic movement and with the politico-economical circumstances around the time when the movement exerted a large influence in the Judean palace, in the days of Josiah.[30]

These congruencies may suggest common social, political, economical, or cultural circumstances (defined in a very general way) for the pre-compositional tradition that underlies Zeph 1:8-9, but certainly are not compelling reasons for such a conclusion. Moreover, it should be noted that the language of Zeph 1:8-9 does not resemble the deuteronomic/deuteronomistic language.

---

[30] The existence of a politico-commercial Aramaic-Assyrian zone across the ancient Near East from the days of Tiglath Pilesser III until the eclipse of the Assyrian Empire is well attested. Judah was among the countries which belonged to this geopolitical entity. The political aspect is so well known that it does not require further discussion. The commercial aspects are attested archaeologically and epigraphically. One of the most informative and striking findings concerning Judean participation in this commerce is that in the year 660, at least once, grains were sold in Nineveh according to Judean measures (see Amiram, הקרמיקה הקדומה של א"י (1971):350).

Surely, the existence of the politico-commercial Aramaic-Assyrian zone also had a cultural impact upon the different societies that compounded it, and a sometimes tense bipolarity between particularism and distinctiveness on the one hand and Aramaic-Assyrian cultural ecumenism on the other consequently developed. Nationalist elements clearly appear in the Book of Deuteronomy (e.g., Deut 26:18-19). Moreover, the diatribe against the foreign cult, even if it actually refers to a popular Judean cult, implies a negative approach to real or assumed foreignness (Cf. Weinfeld, הלאומית בישׂראל במאה השׁביעית התעוררות החודעה, Oz l'David, Jerusalem,1964, pp 376 ff.).

4.2.6. Zeph 1:10-11

The unit is delimited by two temporal, linking expressions. The identity of the speaker cannot be deduced from the body of the unit, but the first temporal linking expression provides the way in which the piece has to be understood, i.e., as YHWH's words. The only cross-reference to other units in the Book of Zephaniah occurs in the last phrase (see עם כנען כל, cf. Zeph 2:5; in both cases כנען means merchants).

The unit is centered on the people of Jerusalem, who are going to be punished. The sense of Jerusalem as a whole is conveyed by references to different places in it. This stylistic device is attested in several places in the Latter Prophets, but the specific language used in Zeph 1:10-11 resembles the language in several units of the Book of Jeremiah that are commonly considered either late monarchic or early post-monarchic.[31] Whatever the specific location of these quarters of the city would be,[32] it is completely clear that the Jerusalem described here had expanded far beyond the hill of the City of David and the Temple Mount. From the archaeological point of view, it is the expanded city from the seventh century until its destruction.[33]

Zeph 1:11 mentions the merchants. In a big city there is less place or none at all for the self-sufficient family. In other words, there are people who buy from someone else what they need and there are people who produce surpluses to be sold. In addition, there is a need for some system

---

[31] See notes on Zeph 1:10-11.

[32] Mishneh probably refers to the Western Hill, or to all the area between Avigad's wall and the City of David's Wall. Machtesh may be the Tyropoeon area or another valley. "Hills" is obviously a general term, but cf. Jer 31:38 (N.W. area outside the walls?). A topographic discussion of Jerusalem is beyond the scope of this work.

[33] Jerusalem developed from a core of about thirty acres to about 125 acres and from an estimated population of about 5,000 in the Solomonic period to 25,000 inhabitants in the late monarchic period (see Broshi 1975;1978; and Shilo, 1980). Jerusalem was a huge city in Judean terms (cf. Lachish, at its apex, about thirty-five acres, Azeka little more than fifteen acres, Beth Shemesh about ten acres, Beer Sheba less than three [but, cf. Nineveh about 1,700 acres, Calah about 900, and Babylon about 500]). Among the extensive bibliography on Jerusalem from the seventh century until its destruction, see Avigad, *IEJ* 25 (1975):260 f.; Broshi, *IEJ* 24 (1974): 21-26; Geva, *IEJ* 29 (1979): 84 ff.; Tushingam, *ZDPD* 95 (1979):39 ff; Shilo, *Excavations at the City of David* (Qedem 19, Jerusalem,1980).

for the the exchange of commodities, and for merchants. Although probably post-monarchic, the image of the industrious wife in Prov 31:10-31
reflects the economic circumstances of at least some relatively prosperous
(see v. 20) urban families (see, especially, vv. 19, 24). According to
Prov 31:24, the capable wife delivers girdles to the merchant (כנעני).
These merchants are not members of the Jerusalemite elite[34] and do not
deal with the major products of the agrarian society (e.g., oil, wine,
grain). It is no accident that Prov 31:10-31 that values so highly the home
production of goods for sale, conceives the merchant a necessary element
in the economic system. On the other hand, merchants are singled out for
condemnation, either explicit or implicit, in some biblical texts (e.g., Zech
14:21; cf. Nah 3:16) including, the Book of Zephaniah. Obviously, this
feature does not provides a clue for dating the Book of Zephaniah, or even
of the core of Zeph 1:10-11 (if the "canaanite phrase" belongs to the language of the pre-compositional traditions that stand behind Zeph 1:10-
11[35]), but it suggests an underlying negative attitude towards the social
and economic world so praised in Prov 31:10-31 (cf. notes on Zeph 3:3-
4). It is worth noting that none of the terms כנעני (meaning merchant),
סחר, and רכל occurs in Deuteronomy.

Concerning the system of commodities of exchange, one may notice that
Zeph 1:11 does not mention coins. The negative archaeological evidence
supports the idea that this commerce was carried on without coins and

---

[34] See the ironical remark in Isa 23:8. Cf. Neh. 3:31-32.

[35] Although it seems very likely that pre-compositional traditions stand behind the present
text of Zeph 1:10-11, caution is advisable insofar it concerns specific language. The
"canaanite phrase" occurs at the end of the unit and contain a cross-reference to another
unit in the book. A similar feature has been already noticed in Zeph 1:6 and 1:9. Also, it
is noteworthy that out of the three clear references to places in Jerusalem in Zeph 1:10-
11, one (מכתש) is not mentioned elsewhere in the OT; other (המשנה) is mentioned elsewhere
in 2 Kgs 22:14 (// 2 Chr 34:22) and it refers to one of the quarters of Jerusalem in the
monarchic period; but another (שער הדגים) is mentioned elsewhere in Nehemiah and in
Chronicles when it does not parallel the deuteronomistic history (Neh 3:3, 121:39; 2 Chr
33:14).

without coin-like pre-weighted silver pieces in the monarchic and early
post-monarchic period.[36]

4.2.7. Zeph 1:12-13

The unit is set off from the foregoing one by a temporal linking phrase
and by the occurrence of the verb in the imperfect as the opening ring of a
new verbal chain. The unit clearly differs thematically and stylistically
from the following, DOY unit (vv. 16-17). The speaker in vv. 12-13 is
YHWH and the audience is not specified.

The condemned people are characterized clearly and they are not the entire people of Jerusalem. The trend of narrowing the group about to suffer
the divine judgment occurs again. One can hardly propose that it is by
chance that, at the compositional level, one finds narrowing after narrowing. The first narrowing moves from the total extermination of all human
beings, along with all the animals of an ambiguous "land" (vv. 2-3), to the
Judeans in general (either Jerusalemites or inhabitants of the countryside;
v. 4a), and finally to those who commit certain specific misdeeds (vv. 4-
6). The second narrowing is from a very ambiguous v. 7, which brings
attention to the issue of the identity of those who will be punished, to the
ruling elite of Jerusalem and those who serve it (v. 8). The third narrowing is from the entire population of Jerusalem (v. 10-11) to those wealthy
people who think that YHWH can do nothing. Eventually, the announcement of judgment in Zephaniah 1 closes with a "minor"[37] inclusio that
goes back to the general image (vv. 14-18). The existence of an inclusio
that marks the limits of the announcement of judgment, its hyperbolic
character that calls for attention, and especially the recurrent pattern of nar-

---

[36] The first coins of the area appear in the Persian period. Around the fourth century there
was probably a mint in Jerusalem (see Betlyon, 1986 and the bibliography there). Darics,
a Persian coin minted by Darius I, is referred to in 1 Chr 29:7).

[37] Minor in the sense that it does not include the whole text of Zephaniah, as the inclusio of
Zeph 1:2-3, 3:19-20 does. Cf. Alonso Schöckel, 1988: 78.

rowing in the announcement, demonstrate that the author/s of Zeph 1:2-18
wanted to indicate that the divine punishment is indeed the execution of
judgment against the persons who deserve it (Zeph 2:3).

To be sure, the existence of a compositional meaning does not imply
authorial creation out of nothing. Moreover, the very different characterization of the different condemned groups, in contents as well as in language, suggests, at the very least, the existence of footprints of pre-compositional Zephanic traditions in some of the units.

As mentioned in the notes, the image of wealthy people who think that
YHWH (or God, אלהים) will (or can) do nothing occurs in two likely to
be post-monarchic Psalms (Ps 10, 14// 53). The main point of these
pieces is not to reform the mentioned wrongdoers or wrongthinkers but to
stress that what is said in the saying is not to thought or believed by the
community to whom the literary piece is addressed (cf. Mal 3:13-18). The
implied perspective of such a community is one in which the wicked enjoy
well being, power and wealth and the pious (those who are rightful members of the community) are being oppressed, live in poverty and hope for
the reversal of the situation, i.e., for the time when God will accomplish
the divine judgment against the wrongdoers. This perspective is shared by
many of the communal *anwim* Psalms (e.g., Psalms 10, 22, 34, 37).[38]

Verse 13 refers to plundering. Obviously, if there is a plundering, there
are plunderers, but they are not identified in the unit and their role is only
circumstantial. Moreover, since the unit explicitly stresses that not only
the wealth of the indicted is to be destroyed but also their that efforts to
restore it will be in vain, it points to a continuous situation and not to a
destructive but short-time looting, such as after a military defeat.

A noteworthy feature concerning the language of this unit is that except
for the opening image אחפש את ירושלם בנרות, the rest of the unit is
built around images, phrases and expressions that occur elsewhere in the
OT (cf. Jer 48:11; Jer 10:5; Isa 41:23; Am 5:11; and see notes).

---

[38] See notes on Zeph 2:3.

4.2.8. Zeph 1:14-16

The unit is set off from the foregoing one by language, structure and contents. The first two mentioned criteria suggest that, at least heuristically, Zeph 1:14-16 should be separated from Zeph 1:17-18, although there is a clear relationship of contents between the two units.

Zeph 1:14-16 describes the DOY. The unit opens with a very common expression in DOY literature (קרוב יום ה'). In the Book of Zephaniah, the phrase is a clear cross reference to Zeph 1:7, where the image of DOY was used to call attention to an announcement of judgment against the royal elite and its servants. Moreover, just as in Zeph 1:7, the theme of the imminence of the day does not remain circumscribed to the first expression but is stressed by the following verset/s, in order to be eventually mitigated in the next verse (v. 8 'והיה ביום זבח ה ; v. 15 ההוא יום עברה היום). The last two versets of v. 14 contain a cross reference to Zeph 3:17. The image of YHWH as גבור who punishes (Zeph 1:14) but eventually saves (Zeph 3:17), unites them.[39] The language of these two versets does not occur elsewhere in DOY literature, but resembles, partially, Isa 42:13, which is a part of a hymn of praise (Isa 42:10-13).

Verses 15-16 are a poem describing DOY, characterized by the emphatic use of the word יום (seven times) and by a similar structure that concludes with the two ועל phrases. Although the contents of vv. 15-16 are coherent with general images elaborated in DOY literature, the expressions that appear in these verses do not tend to occur in DOY literature (except for יום חשך ואפלה יום ענן וערפל that occur word for word in Joel 2:2). At least some of the expressions occurring in vv. 15-16 or similar to them appear in wisdom literature (mainly in the Book of Job) and in probably post-monarchic Psalms. In addition one may notice that the use of פנה as fortification is attested elsewhere in the Book of Chronicles and

---

[39] See commentary on Zeph 3:17. Also the absence of any reference to a human גבור units them.

Nehemiah. The specific motifs introduced in these verses are not elaborated further in the Book of Zephaniah, and the unit contains no cross references with other units in the book, except those in the last two versets,
where פנה occurs (cf. Zeph 3:6). Accordingly, one may conclude that
vv. 14-16 are a specific literary elaboration of the theme of DOY characterized by language that points to a certain influence of wisdom literature, and
a post-monarchic date is more probable than a monarchic one. One may
conclude also that it seems likely that at least the core of vv. 14-16 reflects
pre-compositional material. If this is the case then the pre-compositional
level presumes a general concept of DOY, and the compositional level presumes not only a concept of DOY but also the existence of a specific literary elaboration of it. These conclusions are coherent with the previous
analysis of Zeph 1:7,14 that showed that these verses presume an implied
audience that is acquainted with the concept of DOY and considers it an
extremely threatening event.

An analysis of this concept in OT literature is beyond the scope of this
work. In the Book of Zephaniah, the pre-compositional images that go
along with the concept of DOY point to a "day" of utterly unusual and destructive acts of YHWH, which are described either in cultic imagery or
war imagery or both and also contain elements of traditional epiphanic imagery.

In different forms, these images appear in many places in the ancient
Near East and to some extent continue to appear in the present, expressing
the idea that the world will not follow the usual sequence of events forever; that the constraints of the general order that "guides" the world, as it
exists, will be overcome by a divine action; that there will a rupture in the
uniformity of the world.

The image rupture of the constraints of the regular order may certainly
lead to images of utter destruction but also to ideal, utopian images. Both
images have influenced the compositional level of the Book of
Zephaniah,[40] for the DOY imagery in Zeph 1:14-16—along with vv. 16-

---

[40] Cf. Isa 2:12-21.

18—serves together with Zeph 1:2-3 as a minor inclusio to the block of material that deals with the punishment of Jerusalem (or more specifically, the Jerusalemite elite), but Zeph 1:2-3 together with Zeph 3:19-20 builds a large inclusio to the entire book. This inclusio stresses the change of the divine attitude from punishment to salvation just as does the cross reference between Zeph 1:14 and Zeph 3:17.

It is noteworthy that in the OT, the term DOY, or related terms, or the imagery of DOY tends to be employed as a literary device to describe past or future acts of divine judgment.[41] It appears, for instance, in the execution of the judgment against Babylon (see Isaiah 13), against Edom (see Isaiah 34), against Egypt and Cush (Ezek 30:3-5), against Jerusalem/Israel/Judah or their respective elites (e.g., Ezek 13:5; Am 5:18-20; Lam 2:22), or against "all the peoples" (e.g., Obad 1:15). One may conclude therefore, that these terms and images convey a clear sense of heavy destruction but they are not unequivocally related to a specific set of historical circumstances. Consequently, readers or hearers of a DOY unit may be moved by the forceful description (e.g., Zeph 1:14-16), but the DOY unit alone does not provide them with the necessary information for the understanding of the communicative message. They need to know who was, is, or will be punished. In the Book of Zephaniah this information appears in the section that is surrounded by the minor inclusio. As mentioned above this section contains a set of temporal linking phrases that keep all the relevant units together (including the DOY units) and explicitly refer their contents to one time in the future. The message of the section is clear: The people that are to be punished are the Jerusalemites, or specific groups among them. It is worth noting that this message does not exist independently of the compositional level. If the compositional level is post-monarchic then one cannot but assume that the DOY description, i.e., the judgment against Jerusalem, was conceived as already accomplished. The message of Zephaniah 1 is therefore: There was prophet

---

[41] In Joel 1-2 repentance and a ritual of repentance preempt the complete execution of the judgment; see also Mal 3:23.

in the days of Josiah to whom a divine word came. The divine word included (among other issues, see Zephaniah chapters 2 and 3) an announcement of judgment against Jerusalem. This announcement came true.

4.2.9. Zeph 1:17-18a

The unit continues the theme elaborated in the foregoing unit but with different language. It is separated from v. 18b-c by the linking as well as interpretative phrase ביום עברת ה'. The speaker of the unit is YHWH, except for the ethical note כי לה' חטאו (cf. Zeph 1:3, see notes and commentary). The audience is not specified.

While a universal understanding of the unit cannot derived from the text, a social characterization of the people who are to be punished is implied: They are the wealthy. This characterization is in accordance with Zeph 1:6,13; 3:11-12. In addition, it is plausible that Zeph 18a stands in dialogue with Zeph 1:6,13; 3:2,11-12,19. It is noteworthy that the phrase that concludes the unit contains cross-references to other units in the Book of Zephaniah, just as in Zeph 1:3,6,9,10,16.[42] In this unit also the first phrase points to another unit in the book, to Zeph 1:3 (see אדם).

The language and themes present in the unit are diverse, only some of them tend to occur in DOY literature.

4.2.10. Zeph1:18b-c

The unit is an important element of the minor inclusio mentioned above. Most of the issues concerning it have been discussed, either in the notes section or the commentary section.

---

[42] Perhaps the reference to the houses in Zeph 1:13 contains a reference to Zeph 3:7 but the case is dubious.

The occurrence of נבהלה may suggest a post-monarchic date but this is not a decisive argument. The use of an expression (באש קנאת ה') that occurs elsewhere in the Latter Prophets in the Book of Ezekiel—to be more precise, in widely accepted post-monarchic material in Ezekiel[43]— is noteworthy since it recalls the existence of Ezekielian features in the opening verses of the chapter (Zeph 1:3-4a). One may notice that most Ezekielian features in Zephaniah 1 occur mainly in units and sentences that fulfill an important compositional role in the Book of Zephaniah.[44]

In addition to the compositional value of Zeph 1:18b-c already mentioned, one cannot but notice that the expression תאכל כל הארץ באש קנאתו occurs almost word for word in the conclusion of the second section of announcements of judgment against Judah and the nations (Zeph 3:1-8). While the first unit containing the expression כל הארץ באש קנאתו תאכל leads to a call to seek righteousness and humility so perhaps the (putative) hearers may be saved on the day of the "wrath of YHWH," the second unit containing the expression opens the announcement of the establishment of the ideal world, in which a poor and humble people will live in Jerusalem (also cf. אף ה' in Zeph 2:3 with חרון אפי כל in Zeph 3:8).

4.2.11. Do the units reflecting pre-compositional material, or some of them, constitute one Zephanic source?

The previous analysis has shown that one must expect that at least certain Zephanic traditions precede the Book of Zephaniah (i.e., the prophetic

---

[43] Concerning Ezek 36:5 see, for instance, Zimmerli, 1983: 283. A comparable expression occurs in Ezek 38:19 that also is dated to the post-monarchic period (see Zimmerli, 1983: 302-04).

[44] To a certain extent, these considerations call into question the widely accepted idea that נם כספם גם זהבם... in Ezek 7:19 is a gloss taken from Zeph 1:18. See also the notes on יום עברת ה'.

book concerning the word of YHWH that came to Zephaniah).[45] The
previous analysis has also shown that there are units in Zephaniah 1 that
reflect pre-compositional material. What is the relationship between these
units? Do they, or some of them, constitute *one* source, already related by
tradition to Zephaniah, or even an oracle of the prophet?[46]

The search for an answer must begin with the discussion of some
methodological issues. If the point of departure of the analysis is that certain units in the Book of Zephaniah, or Zephaniah 1, reflect materials already existent at the time of the composition of the Book of Zephaniah,
and whose inclusion in a book concerning the word of YHWH that came
to Zephaniah was likely to be a traditional constraint, then the hypothesis
that the mentioned units, or some of them, constituted *one* source that was
fragmented and dislocated at the compositional level of the Book of
Zephaniah seems to be, at the very least, an unnecessary hypothesis.
Accordingly, this hypothesis is to be rejected unless it explains certain
features of the text better than a simpler hypothesis that does not assume
that the referred texts, or some of them, existed in the form of *one* single
source.[47]

If one assumes that there was a single original source, and one attempts
to reconstruct this source, one has to assume that the text of the Book of
Zephaniah contains a quite literal quotation, even if dislocated and fragmented, of the original source. However, a biblical author who relied on,
or quoted, received materials did not have to quote them word for word—
this would assume that the text is considered unalterable either because of
its sacredness or because of some other social or cultural constraints.
Moreover, he or she did not have to mark any deviation from the received

---

[45] It is worth noting that although there are numerous oracles that contain only judgment
(e.g., 1 Kgs 16:1-4; Am 7:16-17) there is no prophetic book in the OT that contains only
judgment. Accordingly, neither Zephaniah 1 in its entirety nor any combination of its
units can be considered a prophetic book, if this term means a specific literary genre.

[46] Cf., for instance, Sandmel, 1963:106-10; Pfeiffer: 600; Edler.

[47] One should not multiply the assumptions without necessity. If both hypotheses provide
an equally plausible explanation for the origin of the present text, but one presupposes
that there was one single source, and that this source was fragmented and dislocated and
the other does not assume that, the latter is to be preferred.

material with a "strange" language. Furthermore, a late author may use characteristic language of older material (the contrary, is obviously false, since an early author can hardly use characteristic language of a late period) and in many occasions he or she would tend to use the existent language of the received text even when he or she introduces his or her own ideas into the text (e.g., המקום אשר יבחר [MT Deut 12:5,11] is rendered המקום אשר בחר in Sam. Deut 12:5,11). There are many attested cases of a heavy and clear reliance on existent materials that do not contain an exact quotation word for word. For instance:

רגליהם לרע ירוצו וימהרו לשפך דם נקי

Isa 59:7

כי רגליהם לרע ירוצו ומהרו לשפך דם

Prov 1:16

אמרת ה' צרופה מגן הוא לכל החסים בו

Ps 18:31//2 Sam 22:31

כל אמרת אלוה צרופה מגן הוא לכל החסים בו

Prov 30:5

וצלפחד בן חפר בן גלעד בן מכיר בן מנשה

לא היו לו בנים כי אם בנות

ואלה שמות בנותיו מחלה ונעה חגלה מלכה

ותרצה ותקרבנה לפני אלעזר הכהן

ולפני יהושע בן נון ולפני הנשיאים לאמר

Josh 17:3-4

וצלפחד בן חפר לא היו לו בנים כי אם בנות

ושם בנות צלפחד מחלה ונעה חגלה מלכה

ותרצה ותעמדנה לפני משה ולפני אלעזר הכהן

ולפני הנשיאים וכל העדה פתח אהל מועד לאמר

Num 26:33+27:2

In all these cases, either one of texts is a quotation from the other, or both are quotations from a common text. Accordingly, at least one of the preceding pairs is heavily dependent on a previous text that is quoted almost word for word. But the emphasis in the last sentence must be in the word "almost," for the differences are not meaningless. Of course, not every case of textual reliance on existent material must be so literal as in the cases mentioned above.[48] One must conclude therefore, that even if one assumes that a specific text in Zephaniah 1 does not only reflect a received tradition but is heavily dependent on a received text, it does not mean that every word or expression there corresponds exactly with every word or expression in the received text. As a result, the reconstruction of a text behind each of the units that seems to contain pre-compositional material is to a certain extent hypothetical. If the main criteria for determining the compositional nature of a work is the existence of cross references, doubts concerning the original reading of a very few words may be significant, especially since the mentioned units occur in the context of the Book of Zephaniah, and one may expect that changes in the wording providing some kind of cross references are more likely to occur than those which eliminate previous cross references.

There are no cross references between the texts that reflect, and may have quoted, previous sources,[49] and none of them presumes the other or further elaborates the specific themes of the other. Since this is the case, what can be a compelling reason for considering these units, or some of them, one original unit?

Some of these units are an explicit or implicit announcement of judgment against Judah, Jerusalem, or specific social group (see, Zeph 1:4-6, 8-9, 10-11). But, obviously, the fact that two or more units contain an announcement of judgment against the same public is not a solid support for the idea that the units should have been parts of one original work, and neither is the fact that in their present form they occur in the same

---

[48] The more distant are the texts, the more difficult it is to prove the textual reliance. Accordingly, the results of the critical analysis concerning textual dependence are strongly biased insofar as it concerns the relative weight of the texts showing closely quotations. But compare Prov 22:1 with Prov 29:13; or even Ps 68:8-9 with Judg 5: 4-5. See, for instance, the discussion in notes concerning Zeph 3: 3-4. It seems likely that most quotations were not close quotations.

[49] See commentary and notes, especially concerning Zeph 1:4-6, 7, 8-9, 10-11; 14-16, and see below.

prophetic book. Both features can be explained without resorting to the idea of one source. Moreover, these features cannot be considered sufficient evidence for claiming the existence of one single source, for if they were consistently considered so in the Latter Prophets they would have led to utterly unlikely proposals.

An obvious exception to the absence of cross references and common specific themes among the different units that reflect pre-compositional material in Zeph 1 concerns the reference to DOY (Zeph 1:7 and Zeph 1:14-16) and the phrase קרוב יום ה' in v. 7 and v. 14, but even there the reference to *zebach* in v. 7 is not elaborated in vv. 14-16. Moreover, the phrase קרוב יום ה' is relatively common in DOY literature and it also may point to the compositional level of the Book of Zephaniah. Furthermore, the influence of wisdom material in vv. 14-16 is not attested in v. 7. One may conclude that there is no solid basis for the idea that v. 7 should have been the opening verse of a unit concerning DOY which contained also vv. 14-16.[50]

Summing up: The hypothesis that the units reflecting pre-compositional material, or some of them, constitute one Zephanic source is to be rejected.

4.3 Commentary. Zephaniah 2

4.3.1. A summons to repentance: Zeph 2:1-3

The unit is be identified as a prophetic summons to repentance, or more precisely, a report of a prophetic summons to repentance. Prophetic summons to repentance may follow an announcement of judgment, even if the announcement employs the imagery of DOY (see Joel 2:12-14). The summons to repentance in Zeph 3:1 opens with a call for gathering.

---

[50] As proposed, for instance, in Scharbert, 1982.

Similar calls for gathering occur in the context of "on the eve of the judgment" several times in the OT, and their probable background is a ritual of penitence (see notes). The conception that calling the people to repent is a prophetic task is well attested in the OT (e.g., 2 Kgs 17:13; Jer 35:15; Zech 1:2-6; Mal 3:23-24; 2 Chr 12:5-6; cf. Jer 18:12, 26:12-13; Ezek 14:6-11, 18:30-32; Am 5:14-15), as is the closely related "historical image" of prophets calling for repentance, before the execution of the main judgment against Judah and Jerusalem, i.e., the destruction of Jerusalem and the Temple (e.g., Jer 35:15; Zech 1:2-6; cf. Jer 26:12-13). The claim of the text in Zeph 2:1-3, namely, that Zephaniah also called for repentance fits well in this general "historical picture." Thus, Zephaniah not only announced a judgment against Judah and Jerusalem that would be fulfilled with the fall of the monarchy (Zeph 1:2-18) but also called to repentance, as a prophet is expected to do.

The unit is delimited by the closing words of Zeph 1:18 and by the opening of a series of oracles against the nations in Zeph 2:4. The addressees in Zeph 2:1-3 are the condemned people, who are referred to in the third person in vv. 1 and 3 but in the second person in v. 2. Since YHWH is addressed in the third person in vv. 2 and 3, and because of the character of the pericope, one may conclude that the speaker is the narrator, the prophet. This conclusion is supported by the emphasis on the possible, but not necessary, character of any specific divine response to human behavior (see אולי in v. 3) that occurs only in units in which the prophet is the speaker (e.g., Exod 32:30; 2 Kgs 19:4 // Isa 37:4; Am 5:15) but not in those where YHWH is the speaker (e.g., Jer 3:12-15; 4:1-2). Significantly, summons to repentance, in which the speaker is human may contain an explicit note stressing the freedom of YHWH, and conversely those in which the speaker is YHWH may contain an explicit note stressing human freedom (e.g., Jer 36:3). Concerning summons to repentance, one must conclude that there was a clear awareness of the difference between literary pieces which claim to be direct divine speech and units which claim to be human speech. Thus, the communicative message of these units is not independent of the identity of the putative speaker.

Although the presence of a summons to repentance in the Book of Zephaniah, its position in the book, and its general structure point to common features occurring elsewhere in the OT, the same does not hold true concerning the language of Zeph 2:1-3, and to some extent concerning the ideas expressed there.

A relatively large number of expressions that either occur nowhere else or occur only rarely in the OT appear in these three verses (see ענוה ח ק, התקוששו וקושו, לא נכסף, בטרם לא בקשו, צדק ב קשו, משפט פעל, לדת). As mentioned in the notes,[51] one of the characteristic features of the Book of Zephaniah is the presence of numerous expressions that either occur nowhere else or occur rarely in the OT.

Another characteristic feature of the Book of Zephaniah, namely, the use of expressions that convey ambiguous meanings (e.g., העיר היונה) is represented in Zeph 2:1-3 by לא נכסף.

Just as in other units in the Book of Zephaniah, the last expression of Zeph 2:1-3, יום אף ה', is a clear cross reference to another unit in the Book of Zephaniah, namely, to Zeph 3:8. By means of these cross references, the day of YHWH's wrath (see חרון אף ה' in v. 2; יום אף ה' in v. 2 and ביום אף ה' in v. 3) from which the people are warned in Zeph 2:1-3 is compared with the day of judgment against all the nations. Moreover, because of the relation between Zeph 3:8 and Zeph 1:18, Zeph 2:1-3 is indirectly related back to Zeph 1:2-18.

Certain words in the unit, such as משפט, צדק and especially ענוה are key terms in the system of cross references that holds the book together (e.g., Zeph 3:5, 12). One may conclude, therefore, that Zeph 2:1-3 is an integral part of the compositional level, and that even if it is possible that some of its elements reflect pre-compositional traditions, one can hardly point to them with any amount of confidence, except for the common expression בקשו את ה'.

The interpretation given to the general בקשו את ה' in terms of צדק בקשו ענוה בקשו and the occurrence of the expression ענוי הארץ

---

[51] See, for instance, notes on Zeph 3:3-4.

כל point to similarities in language as well as in thought with wisdom literature, and especially with the *anwim* and related post-monarchic psalms (see notes on Zeph 3:3). The occurrence of אשר משפטו פעלו in v. 3 is consistent with this conclusion (see notes).

4.3.2. The announcements of judgment against the nations: Zeph 2:4-15, as a section

The Book of Zephaniah follows in general terms the tripartite organization: (a) a message of judgment against Judah/Israel, (b) announcements of judgment against the nations (or as commonly called "oracles against the nations," hereafter, OAN), and (c) message of salvation.[52]

Before one analyzes the announcements of judgment against the individual nations, and their specific background, attention must be drawn to the fact that these announcements do not occur alone but constitute the OAN section of a prophetic book that claims to be to the word of YHWH that came to the prophet Zephaniah at a very specific period in Judean history, i.e., in the days of Josiah, king of Judah (639-609 BCE,[53] or perhaps 641-610 BCE[54]).

The main elements in the OAN sections are announcements of judgment against the super-powers of the region (i.e., Assyria, Babylonia, Egypt; in Zephaniah, they are represented by Assyria and Cush) and announcements of judgment against neighboring nations. In the Book of Zephaniah, in addition to the two super-powers, three neighboring nations are mentioned: Philistia, Ammon and Moab. Announcements against Philistia, Ammon, and Moab occur in close textual vicinity one to the other not only in Zeph 2:4-10 but also in Jer 47:1-49:6 (cf. Jer 25:20-21); Ezek 25:1-

---

[52] The dialogue between the meaning suggested by the chosen structure of the book and the text of the book as well as the message that this dialogue elaborates will be discussed in a separate chapter, namely, "The structure of the Book of Zephaniah and its message."

[53] See, for instance, Miller-Hayes, 1986:391-92.

[54] See Hayes-Hooker, 1988: 84-89.

11,15-17 and Am 1:6-8,13-15, 2:1-3. Certainly, the fact that the same nations are mentioned in entirely different (putative) circumstances suggests that the criteria for their inclusion in the OAN section are not directly related to specific historical events that occurred in each of the putative circumstances.[55]

It is noteworthy that except for the OAN section in the Book of Zephaniah, the judgment against Edom is always mentioned whenever Philistia, Ammon and Moab are mentioned in closely textual vicinity (see Jer 25:21, 49:7-22; Ezek 25:12-14; Am 1:11-13). Of course, one may ask, why is there no announcement of judgment against Edom in the Book of Zephaniah, as expected from the comparison with other prophetic books?

It seems that while the references to neighboring countries are a common feature shared by prophetic books assigned to different periods, references to the super-powers tend to be more specific. For instance, although it is likely that the Book of Amos underwent some editorial reworking in the post-monarchic period, no redactor added an announcement of judgment against Assyria, Babylon or Egypt to Am 1:3-2:16. Similarly, the OAN sections of the Book of Ezekiel and of the Book of Jeremiah do not con-

---

[55] Concerning the putative time of the oracles in Zephaniah, the days of Josiah:

(a) There is no historical evidence pointing to a special tension between Josiah and the Transjordanian nations.

(b) There is no clear evidence supporting the idea that Josiah conquered Philistine territories. The evidence of the Mesad Hashavyahu ostracon has sometimes been interpreted as pointing to Josiah's rule over the place. For instance, Naveh proposes that sometime after the fortress was established by Greek mercenaries of Psammetichus I (ca. 630-25 BCE), Josiah conquered the place, which was eventually abandoned in 609 (see, Naveh, 1962: 97-99). However, the text of the ostracon does not point to Josiah's control of the area, and not even to Judean conquest of the area. Moreover, one can hardly assume actual Judean domination of the sea-coast from 616 BCE through 610/09 (Josiah's last year), for the Egyptian army would not have campaigned in Northern Syria when the coastal area, i.e., their military highway to Egypt, was in alien hands. See, for instance, Spalinger, 1978:52; Miller-Hayes: 388-89; Na'aman. 1986: 13-14.

(c) There is no evidence supporting the hypothesis that Josiah ever revolted (or intended to revolt) against Assyria. Moreover, when the Assyrian rule collapsed, Josiah became an Egyptian vassal.

(d) The only clear action outside the borders of Judah that can be attributed to Josiah is the destruction of Beth-El and perhaps some cultic shrines in Samaria.

On these issues, see, for instance, Miller-Hayes, 1986: 383-91; Na'aman,1986, esp. 13-14 and the bibliography in these works. For the opposite opinion, see, for instance, Christensen, 1984.

tain oracles against Assyria. One has to conclude that historical knowledge was an important criterion for inclusion or exclusion of certain super-
powers from the OAN section of a prophetic book,[56] both at the compositional and at the redactional levels.[57]

If this is the case, a reference to Assyria is to be expected in the Book of
Zephaniah, for Judah was an Assyrian vassal during most of the days of
Josiah. The reference to Cush, on the other hand, is entirely unexpected,
for at that time the Southern power was not Cush but Egypt. Already in
664 BCE, the last attempt to restore the rule of the Cushite dynasty over
Egypt ended in a complete defeat when Tanwetamani, king of Cush, and
his Egyptian allies were crushed by the Assyrians. By 656 BCE, Egypt
was unified under the rule of the Saitic dynasty, in 655-54 Psammetichus I
defeated the Libyans, and his influence on Syro-Palestine affairs grew
steadily during the following decades, particularly as the Assyrian control
over the Levant begun to decrease from the late 630's and especially from
627 BCE. Sometime between the end of the 630's and the two following
decades, the Egyptian influence turned into direct military and political intervention that became actual hegemony in the area during the 610's, especially after the encounter with the Scythians sometime around 622-
617.[58] Moreover, Egypt and Assyria were not enemies (as Cush and
Assyria were) but allies,[59] so one cannot explain the existence of an announcement of judgment against Assyria along with a loud silence concerning Egypt by proposing that the Zephanic tradition contained a clear
preference for one historically existent political side (the Egyptian against

---

[56] Perhaps the reference to Babylon in Isaiah chapter 13 is to be considered an exception to
this rule, especially if one thinks in terms of Isa 1-33 (or Isa 1-35), but the present book
of Isaiah contains sixty-six chapters.

[57] To be sure, this was not the only criteria, as the different treatment that Egypt and
Babylon received in the Book of Ezekiel clearly shows.

[58] See, Spalinger, 1978. For a general picture of the Egyptian history of the period, see, for
instance, Spalinger, 1974, 1974 a, 1976, 1977, 1978, 1978 a, 1978 b, and the
bibliography there.

[59] Saitic Egypt never rebelled against Assyria, to the contrary it kept a "friendly" attitude
towards Assyria until its very end. See, for instance Spalinger, 1976, 1978 and 1978a; cf.
Grayson, 1975: 91, 95, 96 (Babylonian Chronicle 3 lines 10-11, 61, 66-69. The
Assyrian series of civil wars begun in 627 BCE; see Reade, 1970.

the Assyrian), as it is the case in the Book of Ezekiel (there the preference
is for the Babylonian side over the Egyptian). Why is Egypt not mentioned in the OAN section of the Book of Zephaniah but Cush?

It is noteworthy that on the one hand the lack of any reference to Egypt
undermines the idea that actual historical conditions of the time of Josiah
are reflected in the criteria for inclusion and exclusion in the OAN section,
and on the other hand, the lack of reference to Edom undermines the idea
that post-monarchic enmities shaped these criteria, for at that time there
was a tendency to single out Edom for judgment (cf. Isa 34:1-17; Ezek
35:1-15; Obad 1:1-21; Lam 4:22).

To be sure, the OAN section is not an independent unit but an important
part of a prophetic book whose meaning, structure and, to a very significant extent, wording is dependent on the compositional level.
Accordingly, it seems that the preferable point of departure for an historical-critical study of the OAN section, as a section, is the compositional
level of the book.

The compositional level claims that the book is to be understood as the
word of YHWH that came to Zephaniah at a specific historical time, during the reign of Josiah. Of course, if the author(s) and the book's public
had not have conceived this period different—at least in certain respects—
from any other historical period, including their own, they would not
claim that the text is to be understood in the specific terms of the Josianic
period. This implies that the community in which the book was composed, read, and studied for instruction had a set of historical images. In
addition, the recurrent mention of geographical places points out that the
community had also a relatively vast geographical knowledge of its own
area. In this respect one may mention that biblical geography is generally
correct, and certainly no biblical account ever presented Nineveh as if it
were an Egyptian city, or Tyre as it were in Mesopotamia, as some modern students do. The general accuracy of the biblical geography is also attested in what today may be called political and social geography. No biblical writer ever failed to recognize, for instance, the singular social and
political system of the Philistines, namely, city-states instead of a unified

kingdom. Accordingly one cannot find a biblical reference to the "king of Philistia," but one finds references to the "king of Moab." Of course, the numerous historical references, either explicit or implicit in the text, that occur in many prophetic books (e.g., Isa 7:1; Isa 36-39; Jer 46:1-2, 47:1; Ezek 19:1-9, 33:21; Hos 12:1; Am 7:10-17), as well as the mentioned pattern of exclusion and inclusion in the OAN sections, as well as many of the prophetic superscription, point to a relatively high degree of historical awareness, and also to a very significant extent of historical knowledge, for there is no major historical gaffe either in the Latter Prophets or in 1-2 Kings, especially insofar as the late monarchic period is concerned. Moreover, since none of these books was written mainly for the sake of the description of the events themselves, but in order to convey specific messages to certain communities, in order to instruct them, the existence of a clear historical framework that admits no main deviation, is even more remarkable, and obviously points to the importance of both historical awareness and historical knowledge in such communities.

People with a certain degree of historical and geographical awareness could easily understand that the announcements against the nations employ hyperbolic language (see notes to Zeph 3:13). But the nations were not hyperbolic concepts for them. They had some historical and geographical knowledge about them. Assuming that their knowledge reflects in general terms the historical events, one finds the following striking picture concerning the nations mentioned in the OAN section of the Book of Zephaniah:

(a) Assyria is a nation whose power vanished during the days of Josiah, especially in his last two decades. Nineveh fell in 612 and the last Assyrian king, Ashuruballit, is not mentioned after 609.[60] Thus, to claim that Zephaniah prophesied (note the language pointing to events in the future in Zeph 2:13-15 and elsewhere in Zeph 2:4-15 except Zeph 2:12) the fall of Nineveh, and of Assyria in general, is to claim that Zephaniah delivered an announcement of judgment that was clearly fulfilled.

---

[60] See, Grayson, 1975: 96; Babylonian Chronicle 3, l. 66.

(b) Zephaniah also prophesied against Philistia. All the mentioned cities (Ashdod, Ashkelon, Ekron, Gaza) suffered conquest and some amount of destruction during the last two (perhaps, three) decades of the seventh century, when first Egypt and later Babylon became the hegemonic power in the area.

The situation in Ekron is clarified by the Adon letter found at Saqqara[61] and by the archaeological data pointing to a clear level of destruction that is likely to be related to the Babylonian campaign, either in the last years of the seventh century or the first years of the sixth.[62] Necho II crushed Gaza, either in 609 BCE or 601/0 BCE.[63] The settlement Ha-za-tu, in the Nippur area, was probably founded by people from Gaza—as its name suggests—in the days of Nebuchadrezzar.[64] The capture of Ashkelon by the Babylonians (around 604/3 BCE) is probably referred to in the Babylonian Chronicle number 5 line 18;[65] in any case Aga', king of Ashkelon, was held captive in Babylonia along with his sons (cf. the fate of Jehoiachin [2 Kgs 24:12]; ANET 308b).[66] According to Herodotus, Ashdod was conquered by Psammetichus I after twenty-nine years of siege.[67] In any case, the conquest of Ashdod would have preceded the Egyptian campaign to Gablini in 616 BCE.[68] Dothan points to two levels

---

[61] See, Porten, 1981 and the bibliography there.

[62] See, for instance, Gittin, 1987. On the general issue of the campaigns of Nebuchadrezzar II to the West before the first capture of Jerusalem (597 BCE), see Wiseman, 1985, 21-31 and the bibliography there. For the Egyptian side of the events, see Spalinger, 1977 and 1978, and the bibliography there.

[63] See Herodotus ii, 159. See Spalinger, 1977: 230; Freedy-Redford: 475 n. 57. Cf. Jer 47:1; on this verse see Carroll, 1986: 774-75 and the bibliography there. For the Babylonian conquest of the area in 601, see Wiseman, 1985: 29 and the bibliography there.

[64] Zadok, 1978: 61.

[65] See, Grayson, 1975: 100; cf. Spalinger, 1977: 230.

[66] See, for instance, Wiseman, 1985: 25, 83 and the bibliography there. The name of the settlement Isqallunu, by the Sin-Magir canal at Nippur, suggests that it was founded by a group of Ashkelonian exiles (see, Zadok, 1978: 61; Wiseman, 1985: 77).

[67] Herodotus ii, 157; see Spalinger, 1978: 50-51 and the bibliography there.

[68] See, Grayson, 1975: 91; Babylonian Chronicle 3, 1. 10. On Gaza, Ashkelon and Ashdod and their fate during this period, see Spalinger, 1977:229 and especially the bibliography in note 24.

of destruction (of stratum VI, and VII) and relates the first of them to Psammetichus I, and the second to the Babylonians.[69]

One must conclude that if Zephaniah delivered an announcement of judgment against Philistia in the days of Josiah, as claimed in the Book of Zephaniah, his prophecy can be considered fulfilled.

(c) According to the OAN section of the Book of Zephaniah, the prophet announced a divine judgment against Moab and Ammon. According to Josephus (*Ant.* 10.9.7 § 181), Nebuchadrezzar made war against the Ammonites and the Moabites in his 23rd year, i.e., 582/1 BCE.[70] According to Jer 52:30, in the 23rd year of Nebuchadrezzar, Nabuzaradan deported 745 Judeans. The two events are probably related, and perhaps both of them are related to Gedaliah's assassination (see Jer 40:14, 41:10,15,17-18).[71] In any case, from the perspective of a post-monarchic community, the prophecy against Ammon and Moab was certainly fulfilled.

(d) The OAN section of the Book of Zephaniah also contains a reference to Cush. As mentioned above, Cush as an imperial power was crushed in 664 BCE, i.e., before the putative time of the announcement of Zephaniah. But the Cushite unit is unique among the OAN units because of its brevity, but also and more important for the present case, because it is the only one that does not clearly point to future events. To the contrary, it seems likely that it refers to a present condition or even to a status that originated in the past. If this is the case, then the author was very sensitive to the historical data. It is noteworthy that such an author described YHWH, or the prophet when he communicated the divine speech, as supporting a claim concerning the future by a reference to something known.[72] This is certainly a common rhetorical element but certainly a

---

[69] See, for instance, M. Dothan, "Tel Ashdod," *IEJ* (1972): 243-44; *EAEHL* I, 116, and the bibliography there.

[70] See, for instance, Parker-Dubberstein: 28.

[71] See, for instance, Miller-Hayes: 425.

[72] An alternative understanding of the unit can be based on the assumption that also the Cushite unit points to future events, and that the prophecy was fulfilled by the successful

significant one in a book that contains not only a series of prophecies that are considered as fulfilled (the announcement against Jerusalem in Zephaniah 1 and the announcements against Assyria, Philistia, Ammon and Moab in Zeph 2), but also prophecies yet not fulfilled, such as Zeph 3:9-20.

The previous analysis has suggested that the mention of Assyria, Philistia, Ammon and Moab in the OAN section is not an accident but a conscious attempt to show that what Zephaniah announced has been fulfilled. Does this hypothesis explain the absence of a unit against Egypt and another one against Edom? It seems that the answer concerning Egypt is positive, for neither Nebuchadrezzar nor any other Babylonian king conquered Egypt, as Cambyses did in 525 BCE.[73]

Edom is not mentioned in the OAN section of the Book of Zephaniah. Significantly, while Josephus explicitly says that Nebuchadrezzar made war against the Ammonites and the Moabites in his 23rd year (*Ant.* 10.9.7 § 181), he says nothing about a campaign against Edom. Moreover, there is no biblical or Babylonian text which claims that Nebuchadrezzar attacked Edom.[74] Archaeological evidence from Tawilan shows that the place declined only from 539 BCE on (the death of Nabonaid and Cyrus' capture of Babylon),[75] and with Bartlett one has to conclude that the most likely assumption is that the kingdom of Edom came to an end when Nabonaid moved to Teima (ca. 553 BCE).[76] Later, Mal 1:2-5 clearly implies that Edom is in ruins.

---

and well "broadcasted" campaign of Psammetichus II against Cush in 593/92 BCE (cf. Herodotus ii, 161). On this campaign see Spalinger, 1978b, 21-23.

[73] It is possible that Nebuchadrezzar invaded Egypt during the days of Apries, but there is no real support for the idea that he conquered Egypt, or deposed her king. The struggle between the two powers continued during the days of Amasis. On this issue, see Spalinger, 1977: 236-44, Wiseman, 1985: 39-41.

[74] For a different position, including the proposal that Nebuchadnezzar conquered Edom either in 560 or 567 BCE, see Vogelstein M., "Nebuchadnezzar's Reconquest of Phoenicia and Palestine and the Oracles of Ezekiel," *HUCA* (1950/1) 23: 197-220.

[75] See Bennet, 1984. In a previous work Bennet mentions a superstructure in mudbrick at Buseirah that was destroyed by fire, "probably during an attack by the neo-Babylonians" (see Bennet, 1982: 15).

[76] Bartlett, 1989: 157-61.

To conclude: If the OAN section of the Book of Zephaniah would have
an announcement against Edom, or Egypt, or for that matter, against
Babylon, it could not have been seen as fulfilled by a community living in
the early post-monarchic period (i.e., in the Babylonian period). Since the
announcements against the nations in the OAN section of the Book of
Zephaniah seem to be selected according to the criterion of fulfillment in a
certain span of time (from late monarchic to the early post-monarchic period) it is only to be expected according to this criterion that oracles against
Egypt, Edom, or Babylon will be entirely absent, as they are. These data,
therefore, suggest an early post-monarchic date for the composition of the
OAN section of the Book of Zephaniah.

4.3.3. The announcements against the nations (individual units)

4.3.3.1 Against Philistia (Zeph 2:4-7)

The announcement contains two units: (a) Zeph 2:4 and (b) Zeph 2:5-7.
The first unit is delimited by the opening כי and by the presence of another opening, namely הוי, in v. 5. The unit consists of four versets
closely related in style and contents. Stylistic features, such as alliteration,
paronomasia, and connotative double meaning provide much of the flavor
of unit. The latter feature occurs several times in the Book of Zephaniah,
including the following verse, Zeph 2:5 (see חבל הים, גוי כרתים).
The speaker is indefinite, just are the addressees. The message is: destruction all over Philistia. The question whether this short "poem" existed before the compositional level of the Book of Zephaniah, or was
composed at that time and for that purpose cannot receive a clear-cut answer. The use of pre-existent material cannot be ruled out (cf. notes on
Zeph 2:15). Moreover, the stress on Ekron—which is the climactic point
of the heightening trend in the poem—is not elaborated in the book, and
neither is the image of עזובה, or the pun on words and meanings with

אשדוד בצהרים יגרשוה and עקרון תעקר. Thus, the suggestion that there was a pre-compositional poem seems perhaps more likely than not.

The limits of the second unit are marked by the opening הוי and by the introduction of a new theme in v. 8: judgment against Ammon and Moab. The kernel of the unit is the divine speech that goes from והאבדתיך (v. 5) to ירבצון (v. 7) and is bracketed by and introduction and a concluding note that claims to be the words of the prophet that communicate the divine speech to a human audience.

The divine speech has been analyzed in the notes. One may only emphasize that it implies a conception that the destruction of the cities bring the advance of pastoralism, and that the Judeans who will take control of Philistia will not rebuild the cities, and certainly not work in commerce, although three out of the four cities had ports and were important commercial centers.[77] This image is certainly not identical with that in Zeph 3:12-13 of the ideal society of the "poor and humble" living in Jerusalem. Significantly, at the compositional level the two images are related by a system of cross references based on רבץ-רעה. A similar situation occurs with שארית ישראל (Zeph 3:13) and שארית בית יהודה (Zeph 2:7). These two terms are obviously joined together by the system of cross references embracing Zeph 2:5-7 and Zeph 3:12-13, and by the use of the word שארית. But the two terms have a different pattern of occurrence. As mentioned in the notes, שארית יהודה occurs only in the Book of Jeremiah, and only in reference to Gedaliah's community. The reference to שארית יהודה in Zeph 2:7[78] is highly suggestive in this respect. Whether it refers to Gedaliah's community, or to what remained from it after the assassination of Gedaliah, that is, Judeans living in Judah during the Babylonian period, or to any other group of post-monarchic Judeans, it does not connote the theological, comprehensive meaning conveyed by the term "Israel."

---

[77] Cf. notes on Zeph 3:3-4.

[78] שארית בית יהודה in Zeph 2:7 is a variant of שארית יהודה (cf. Isa 46:3), and see notes.

To sum up: The horizon of the ideal future envisaged in the divine speech in vv. 6-7, as well as the explicit images of this future, are different from those found in Zeph 3:12-14. Nevertheless, or probably because of that, an emphatic system of cross references (see above and below) relates the two texts at the compositional level. But, this relationship is not one of equals. Zeph 3:12-14 occurs after Zeph 2:6-7, and certainly in a much more climactic position. For the reader or hearer of the Book of Zephaniah, Zeph 3:12-14 becomes the interpretative key for Zeph 2:6-7, but not the other way around. It is noteworthy that interpreting Zeph 2:6-7 in the light of Zeph 3:12-14 actually means that a reference to Judah (either the actual Judah or an ideal Judah including Ashkelon) can be interpreted in terms of "Jerusalem," and that the terms "House of Judah" and "Israel" are considered different communicative codes for one single referent. The referent is certainly not a physical object or objects, but a comprehensive, cultural and theological conception,[79] as Zeph 3:12-14 clearly shows.[80] The concept of שארית יהודה in its other occurrences and in Zeph 2:7 (when it is interpreted only in the context of the divine speech in Zeph 2:5-7) points to a cultural, social, and political concept that was not considered as overlapping the concept of שארית ישראל, as the differential pattern of occurrence and the contextual meaning—in narrow sense—of the two terms clearly shows.

Summing up: Taking into account that the divine speeches in Zeph 2:5-7 and Zeph 3:12-14 contain different images concerning the ideal future, different terms and concepts, and especially taking into account the interpretive effort, at the compositional level, to read Zeph 2:5-7 in the light of Zeph 3:12-14, one may conclude that the divine speech in Zeph 2:5-7 probably reflects a pre-compositional tradition. The reference to יהודה שארית may suggest that this tradition is somehow related to Gedaliah's

---

[79] Obviously, not unrelated to the social experience of those who carry the concept.

[80] The conception of "Israel" in the compositional level will be analyzed in the chapter "The structure of the Book of Zephaniah and its message."

community, or much more probably to a Judean community, or communities, in the years that followed Gedaliah's assassination.[81]

The introduction to the divine speech contains a title that occurs elsewhere in Zech 12:1. Its role as a prefixed interpretative note to a following text suggests a written literary enterprise (see notes). The introduction also contains a note connoting a negative evaluation for the "merchants" (כנעני)[82] that is also a cross reference to Zeph 1:11. The conclusion attached to the divine speech employs a verbal form of פקד that refers to the salvific action of YHWH. Significantly, Zeph 1:8,9 refers to the punishing actions of YHWH by using the verbal form פקד על. If the compositional level of the Book of Zephaniah is post-monarchic, then the phrase שב שבותם includes both the idea of return from exile and of reversal of judgment (for instance, cf. Jer 48:47, 49:6; see notes). The phrase contains a cross reference to Zeph 3:20. Thus, one may conclude that not only that the conclusion of this unit contains cross references to other units in the Book of Zephaniah—as in other cases, but also that the divine speech includes cross references and is bracketed by an introduction and a conclusion that also contain cross references.

4.3.3.2 Against Ammon and Moab (Zeph 2:8-10)

The unit is set off from the foregoing unit by the conclusion of Zeph 2:5-7 and from the following unit by the clear change of topic. This announcement contains two subunits: (a) Zeph 2:8-9 and (b) Zeph 2:10. The beginning of a new subunit is marked by the new opening זאת and by the change of speaker.

The subunit contains stereotypical images of Ammon and Moab,[83] several words and expressions that occur nowhere in the OT, and employs

---

[81] One may also hypothesize about the relation between the picture of destroyed Ashkelon as a herding place and the fate of monarchic Jerusalem.

[82] See notes on Zeph 1:11, 2:5 and and commentary on Zeph 1:11.

[83] A stereotypical image can hold some kernel of historical truth. For instance, the recurrent motif of the Ammonite encroachment of Israel's territory suggests an Israelite claim concerning disputed areas (cf. Judg 11:12-28; Jer 49:1). I wrote elsewhere that the list of

double entendre as well as ongoing heightening from verset to verset. These stylistic features occur many times in the Book of Zephaniah. As in other units in the book, the concluding phrase of this unit—more precisely subunit—attaches the specific unit to a system of cross references that shapes the book. The concluding reference to שארית עמי clearly recalls Zeph 2:7 and Zeph 3:12-13. Moreover, since on the one hand it stands closer to the שארית ישראל in Zeph 3:12-13 than to בית יהודה שארית in Zeph 2:7—because the pronominal suffix in שארית עמי refers to ה' צבאות אלהי ישראל, but on the other hand, it has in common with Zeph 2:7 the idea of inheriting (foreign) people/s that does not occur in Zeph 3:12-13, it provides a kind of link between the two. It is noteworthy that this compositional role relies in part on the use of a unique variation of the common formula חי אני נאם ה'.

The pattern of occurrence of several words and expressions in Zeph 2:8-10 points to closer affinities with commonly accepted post-monarchic literature than with commonly accepted pre-monarchic literature (see notes).

Ammon and Moab are the only peoples in the OAN section that are punished because of their actions against the Judeans. Especially taking into account the results of the study of the OAN section as a section, this feature perhaps also reflects the events of 582/1 BCE, and the Ammonite and (and likely to be the Moabite as well) attitude concerning the assassination of Gedaliah (see Jer 40:14, 41:10,15).[84] If this is the case, these events would be a *terminus a quo* for the unit.[85]

The second subunit, Zeph 2:10, is an interpretative note that does not claim to be YHWH's speech but human speech. It employs the language

---

the Transjordanian cities of asylum (Deut 4:43; Josh 20:8) reflects this tendency as well (Ben Zvi, "The List of the Levitical Cities," *JSOT* [forthcoming]). The recurrent appearance of this motif in post-monarchic literature may suggest the existence of tensions and conflicts in Transjordan between Israelites/Judeans and Ammonites. The references to Tobiah, the Ammonite, in the Book of Nehemiah (e.g., Neh 2:10, 19; 3:36, 13:4,8) suggests that Israelites lived in this area in the Persian period. The issue and its historical implications are worthy of study but this stands beyond the limits of the present work.

[84] See above.

[85] This does not mean that the unit contains no reference to traditions that may precede that time (e.g., the reference to Sodom and Gomorrah).

and motifs of the first subunit but turns the ויגדילו על גבולם in v. 8
to ויגדלו על עם ה׳ צבאות. Significantly, the expression צבאות ה׳
occurs in the Book of Zephaniah only in v. 9 (first subunit) and in v. 10.
Since the potential use of ה׳ צבאות is not limited to these two verses but
the actual use of ה׳ צבאות is limited to them, one may conclude that the
text of these two subunits was probably influenced by a tendency that did
not affect the text of other units in the book.[86]

4.3.3.3 Against Cush (Zeph 2:12)

The short reference to Cush can hardly be considered an announcement
of judgment. It is embedded in the text and by itself it cannot be an announcement, and probably—as mentioned above—is a statement about the
status of the Cushites.[87]

4.3.3.4 Against Assyria (Zeph 2:13-15)

The announcement against Assyria stands between the note on the
Cushites and a הוי unit referring to Jerusalem. This announcement contains two subunits: (a) Zeph 2:13-14 and (b) Zeph 2:15. The beginning of
a new subunit is marked by the new opening (זאת העיר . . .) in v. 15.
The speaker in vv. 13-14 is YHWH, but is undefined in Zeph 2:15.

The verbal forms in Zeph 2:13-14, or forms similar to them, occur elsewhere in the Book of Zephaniah. The subunit contains several stylistic
features, such as heightening of the message from verset to verset, a probable pun on words (ציה - מדבר), and alliteration with some extent of
repetition (גם קאת גם קפד), that occur elsewhere in the Book of
Zephaniah. One may also notice the existence of several words and ex-

---

[86] One may suggest, for instance, that if v. 10 is a redactional addition to a text that already
included the expression נאם ה׳ ׳ אלהי ישׂראל in v. 9 then under the influence of ה׳ צבאות in v.
10 and facilitated by the existence of the common expression נאם ה׳ צבאות, the word צבאות
was added to v. 9.

[87] The unit has been discussed in the notes and in the general commentary on the section.

pressions that occur nowhere else in the OT, i.e., another feature of the Book of Zephaniah. Of course, it does not follow from these considerations that the subunit must not reflect any pre-compositional material. The pattern of occurrence of several words and expressions occurring in Zeph 2:13-14 points to closer affinities with commonly accepted post-monarchic literature than with commonly accepted pre-monarchic literature (see notes).

The first four versets of Zeph 2:15 occur word for word in Isa 47:8, the rest of the verse is similar in language and images to other units in the OT, most if not all of them post-monarchic. The city mentioned in Zeph 2:15 can be identified only on contextual grounds as Nineveh (in the parallel to the first four versets of Zeph 2:15, in Isa 47:8, the city is Babylon). Therefore, Zeph 2:15 could not have existed as an independent unit in the OAN section of the Book of Zephaniah, for the announcements of judgement in the OAN section are directed to identifiable nations.[88]

It is noteworthy that forms from רבץ occur in Zeph 2:15 and Zeph 2:14 (i.e., the previous subunit), as well as in Zeph 2:7. The word שממה appears in Zeph 2:4 (in relation to Ashkelon), Zeph 2:9 (Ammon and Moab), Zeph 2:13 (Assyria) and cf. שמה in Zeph 2:15. The announcements in the OAN section, although different, one from the other, are interrelated by common language and insofar as it concerns רבץ, to some extent by a common imagery as well.

4.3.4. YHWH is superior to all the gods of the earth and all the peoples will bow to YHWH (Zeph 2:11)

Just in the middle of the announcements of judgement against the nations one finds a "strange" verse. Although the unit is anchored to the text by the pronominal suffix in עליהם at the beginning of the verse and by the resumptive גם that opens v. 12, there is no doubt that the verse is only

---

[88] The communicative significance of the quotation has been discussed in the notes section.

loosely connected to the other units in the OAN section, and that the statement that YHWH is superior to all the gods of the earth and all the peoples will bow to YHWH certainly goes beyond the contents of an announcement of judgement against Moab and Ammon.

The study of the verse in the notes section has shown similarities between Zeph 2:11 and Psalms celebrating the kingship of YHWH. In these Psalms, notes concerning either the superiority of YHWH over other gods, or the theme of the nations accepting YHWH, or both are integral elements in hymns that include calls to praise YHWH with joy and singing (see Pss 95, 96, 97). Indeed, the hymnic element that one may expect in relation to a verse such as Zeph 2:11, if it were not closely bracketed by and anchored to announcements against the nations, occurs in the Book of Zephaniah, but later on in Zeph 3:14-17. There it follows announcements of salvation concerning the ideal future and including another reference to the theme of the peoples accepting YHWH (Zeph 3:9), and provides the hymnic response for the announced divine actions. This location for hymnic response is much more suitable in terms of context and style than the middle of the OAN section.

What is the function of Zeph 2:11 in the OAN section? It it is an explanatory note concerning the announcement of judgment. Leaving aside for the moment the hymnic language, the issue is clear: YHWH's purpose is not to destroy nation after nation—as the series of announcements of judgment may suggest—but to bring them to bow to YHWH.[89]

---

[89] On the function of the announcements of judgment in the structure and their meaning in the Book of Zephaniah as a unit, see the chapter "The structure of the Book of Zephaniah and its message."

4.4. Commentary. Zephaniah 3

4.4.1. A different announcement of judgment (Zeph 3:1-8)

The first chapter in the Book of Zephaniah contains a message of judgment
against Judah, the second chapter a message of judgment against the nations, therefore, according to the general tripartite organization of most of
the prophetic books that contain an OAN section,[90] one expects that
thethird chapter of the Book of Zephaniah will contain a message of salvation. Indeed, the chapter contains a message of salvation, but it does not
begin with this message but opens with a lengthy and uncommon announcement of judgment. This announcement opens with a denunciation
that contains two elaborated invectives (Zeph 3:1-5, 3:6-7). The first of
them is against Jerusalem or its leaders or both, and the second, although
against Jerusalem, contains nonetheless a reference to previous judgments
against the nations. The denunciation leads to the announcement of a day
of justice and punishment against the nations of the earth,[91] of a day that
will be a turning point in the relationship between YHWH and the human
beings (note the different connotations of לעד). This day is not described
as at hand, but instead the divine speech contains a request (or command)
to the addressees (i.e., the community to whom the address is delivered)
to wait patiently for YHWH, for the day when YHWH will execute
universal judgment will surely come (v. 8).

As the previous summary clearly shows, Zeph 3:1-8 is not the rehearsal
of a theme already developed in the first two chapters. It differs from the

---

[90] Such as the books of Ezekiel, Isaiah and Jeremiah (LXX).

[91] The concepts and issues that underlie and explain the existence of an announcement of
judgment against the nations that is preceded by an invective against Jerusalem and the
note claiming that YHWH hoped that Jerusalem would learn the appropriate lesson from
the divine punishment of the nations that took place before her own punishment (Zeph
3:7) are strongly related to issues such as the relationship between Israel and YHWH and
their respective relationship with Jerusalem, the relationship between YHWH and the
nations, the relationship between the nations and Israel. These issues will be discussed
in the chapter, "The structure of the Book of Zephaniah and its message."

units in both chapters in their invective section, and strongly differs in its
announcement concerning the future.

Since the announcements concerning the future in chapter one point to
the destruction of Jerusalem and the Temple and were considered fulfilled
by a post-monarchic community, and those in chapter two were also considered fulfilled, then the compositional work could have taken two approaches:

(a) to introduce immediately after the second chapter a message of salvation. In this case the message conveyed by the text to a post-monarchic
community would be that the era of punishment is over and the ideal future
will come out of their present situation, and perhaps soon.

(b) to introduce a new announcement of judgment pointing to the future
and only thereafter a message of salvation. In this case, the era of punishment is seen as not over but yet to come. Only after the world is
changed by YHWH's judgment and only thereafter the ideal world will
come to be.

For reasons that will be explained in the chapter "The structure of the
Book of Zephaniah and its message," the second approach was actually
preferred, as the text of the Book of Zephaniah clearly shows. It is worth
noting that this implies that the main function of the fulfilled prophecies
claimed to be delivered by Zephaniah in the days of Josiah and arranged in
the Book of Zephaniah is persuasive. That is, since these prophecies have
been fulfilled Zephaniah was a true prophet; accordingly, unfulfilled
prophecies also claimed to be his will come true in the future.[92] This way
of legitimating the message, and the putative deliverer of the message as
well, is well attested in the OT (cf. Deut 18:22; 1 Sam 10:1-16; Zech 1:4).

4.4.1.1 The first invective (Zeph 3:1-5)

The unit opens with a הוי subunit (Zeph 3:1-2). This subunit is deeply
related to next one, namely, the condemnation of the Jerusalemite elite in

---

92 Cf. commentary on Zeph 2:12.

Zeph 3:3-4, by a system of feminine pronominal suffixes that embraces both and goes back to העיר היונה in v. 1, and by the recurrent motif of בקרבה. The same motif is central to the next subunit: the note concerning theodicy in v. 5. Moreover, the recurrent use of לבקר (v. 3) and בבקר בבקר (v. 5) and the references to "justice" (note שפטיה in v. 3, צדיק and משפטו in v. 5) clearly attach the subunits one to the other.

The first subunit (Zeph 3:1-2) is characterized by stylistic devices that occur elsewhere in the Book of Zephaniah, especially the use of ambiguity for calling attention to the issue that is elaborated immediately thereafter, and the heightening of the message from verset to verset (e.g., Zeph 1:7). Although the recurrent use of certain stylistic devices does not point necessarily to authorial unity, and certainly does not rule out the possible existence of diverse traditions behind the present text, it clearly points to the existence of a coherence throughout the book that can hardly be accidental.

Certain expressions in the subunit recall Jeremianic expressions that contain at least wisdom flavor, others point to language and ideas found in Psalms. In general terms, the pattern of occurrence of words and expressions occurring in Zeph 3:1-2 points to closer affinities with commonly accepted post-monarchic literature than commonly accepted pre-monarchic literature (e.g., נגאלה).

The nature of the traditions behind Zeph 3:3-4, their probable social location, the relationship between Zeph 3:3-4 and Ezek 22:25-28, the occurrence of Zephanic (i.e., related or belonging to the Book of Zephaniah) characteristics in Zeph 3:3-4, and the noteworthy difference between Zeph 3:3-4 and Zeph 1:4-6 have been discussed in the notes on Zeph 3:3-4

The elements in common between the concluding note of the unit (Zeph 3:5) and Zeph 3:3-4 have been mentioned above. Again the last note of the unit contains cross-references, in this case לא יעשה עולה in v. 5 occurs word for word in Zeph 3:13. Since the expression עשה עולה occurs elsewhere in the OT in Ps 37:1 it is significant that the characterization of these עשי עולה in Ps 37:1-2 recalls the concluding phrase in Zeph 3:1-2, and that from the perspective of Ps 37:1 the description of YHWH in Zeph 3:5 stands in direct contrast with the description of Jerusalem in

Zeph 3:2, just as the description of YHWH stands in contrast with the description of the Jerusalemite elite, from the perspective of Zeph 3:3-5 alone. Ps 37, one of the *anwim* psalms, shows additional expressions and ideas that are reflected elsewhere in the Book of Zephaniah, and is probably post-monarchic.[93]

The last phrase in v. 5 (לא ידע עול בשׁת) is an important testimony concerning one of the ways in which communities—whose *terminus ad quem* is the time of the fixation of the text of the Book of Zephaniah—thought concerning the problem of theodicy. Awareness of the problem is clearly reflected in Zeph 1:12 and Zeph 3:5. The methodological claim of the last phrase in Zeph 3:5 is that religious thinking on this problem should not be disassociated from religious thinking on the question of why human beings do wrong. If the phrase is a later addition—as suggested in the notes—then it will point to a kind of reflective theological thinking that was developed in direct response to a received, but not yet fixed, prophetic text.[94] On the surface one may compare this note with the ethical notes: והמכשׁלות את הרשׁעים in Zeph 1:3 and כי לה' חאטו in Zeph 1:17. But it should be observed that the note in Zeph 3:5 goes beyond an affirmation of the righteousness of YHWH,[95] either directly or indirectly as in Zeph 1:3 and Zeph 1:17, and suggests a community which answered the question of theodicy by suggesting a different (and additional) set of questions (see notes).

---

[93] See notes on Zeph 3:5.

[94] A similar procedure, i.e., adding short notes to the prophetic verse in order to express the theological response of the reading community to the problems presented by the prophetic text, by then already fixed as MT, is well attested in Tg. Neb. (e.g., Tg. Neb. 3:8 [the addition there, כל רשׁיעי ארעא]).

[95] Perhaps in spite of the experienced reality and not because of it. That is, as a leap of faith by people in distress, or under real or conceived oppression, who will remain entirely hopeless unless they reassure themselves that God is, in spite of all, righteous.

4.4.1.2 The second invective (Zeph 3:6-7)

The second invective claims to be divine speech. It opens with verbal forms that in this context indicate that YHWH is the speaker; it is delimited by the לכן that opens the punishment clause.

As Zeph 3:2, Zeph 3:6 contains language that recalls the Jeremianic tradition. On the other hand, the word עלילות (v. 7) occurs nowhere else in the Latter Prophets except in the Book of Ezekiel and Zeph 3:11, but the use of עלילות in Zephaniah is closer to its use in Ps 14:1 and 99:8. The latter is one of the YHWH *malak* Psalms that have been mentioned in reference to Zeph 2:11. The centrality of the concept of יראת ה' (v. 7) may reflect priorities expressed in wisdom and wisdom-influenced literature. Several words and expressions occurring in this unit suggest that a post-monarchic date is more likely than a pre-monarchic date.[96]

Perhaps Zeph 3:6 and Zeph 1:16 allude one to the other. Besides the very common reference to "cities," they also share a very unusual term in the Latter Prophets: פנה.[97] The expression תקחי מוסר (v. 7) is an evident cross reference to Zeph 3:2, just as עלילותם (v. 7) to Zeph 3:11. Both are in the last verse of this subunit.

4.4.1.3 The announcement of the divine punishment (Zeph 3:8)

The announcement opens with לכן, as in numerous announcements of punishment in the OT, and concludes with the phrase תאכל כל הארץ כי באש קנאתי.

Certainly, Zeph 3:8 and Zeph 3:9 describe the future turning point from the existent situation to the ideal situation.[98] First comes the divine punishment against the nations, and later the divine transformation of the nations. Taking into account the importance of the message, one can hardly

---

[96] See notes.

[97] Similarly, one may mention that מבלי איש, מבלי יושב, and מבלי עובר recall מאין יושב in Zeph 2:5.

[98] See, the section "The structure of the Book of Zephaniah and its message."

consider it accidental that these two verses show a clear concentration of cross-references. At the compositional level cross-references may be used as stylistic device to stress the difference between two seemingly similar descriptions, and this is the case in Zeph 3:8.

The phrase כי באש קנאתי תאכל כל הארץ is a self-evident cross reference to Zeph 1:18. The phrase in Zeph 1:18 stands at the end of the fulfilled announcement of judgment against Jerusalem and the Judeans, and there the term ארץ was intentionally ambiguous. In sharp contrast, the announcement of judgment in Zeph 3:18 was not yet fulfilled, and the ambiguous ארץ is explicitly clarified by the preceding phrases גוים לאסף and לקבצי ממלכות. These two expressions convey the sense of punishment in Zeph 3:8. In Zeph 3:19-20 a similar image points to the reversal of a previous punishment. In Zeph 3:8 those who are "gathered" are the nations, but Israel is "gathered" in Zeph 3:19-20. The expression כל חרון אפי in Zeph 3:8 refers to the punishment against the nations. In Zeph 2:2 it refers to the punishment of the Judeans. In Zeph 2:2 it occurs before a call to repentance that included the possibility (אולי) that repentant people would find refuge at that time; in Zeph 3:8, the phrase occurs before כי באש קנאתי תאכל כל הארץ. The word משפטי in Zeph 3:8 points to משפטו in Zeph 3:5. In the latter the claim of the text is that YHWH issues the divine judgment every daybreak, but this judgment does not seem to end the reign of the wicked—and therefore the problem of theodicy arises. The contrary is implied in Zeph 3:8 and in Zeph 3:9.

This system of cross-reference shows therefore that the divine action envisaged in Zeph 3:8 is different from the daily judgment of YHWH and different from YHWH's previous judgment of Judah/Israel.[99]

What does remain outside the system of cross references in Zeph 3:8? The pair גוים - ממלכות and the first expression in the announcement: חכו לי—נאם ה'— ליום קומי לעד. All the main ideas of the verse

---

[99] It also suggests (cf. Zeph 3:19-20) that Israel is singled out among the nations, this issue will be discussed in the section "The structure of the Book of Zephaniah and its message."

are concentrated in this phrase. The day is characterized by לעד with its different connotations. The day is not described as if it were at hand, but instead, there is a request (or command) to the addressees (i.e., the community to whom the address is delivered) to wait patiently for YHWH (לי חכו), i.e., for YHWH's transformation of the world (see v. 9). The pair גוים - ממלכות explains the scope of this day.

4.4.2. A message of salvation (Zeph 3:9-20)

The second part of chapter three is a message of salvation, conveyed by means of announcements of salvation in which YHWH is the speaker, and of summons to rejoice in which the putative speaker is either undefined or is "the prophet." The unit contains two announcements of salvation (Zeph 3:9-13 and Zeph 3:18-19), which are separated by two different but related summons to rejoice (Zeph 3:14-15 and Zeph 3:18-19), and ends with the concluding unit of the Book of Zephaniah (Zeph 3:20).

4.4.2.1 The first announcement of salvation (Zeph 3:9-13)

The first announcement of salvation contains two different units, Zeph 3:9-10 and Zeph 3:11-13. The second subunit is set off from the foregoing one by a temporal linking phrase (ביום ההוא), by the references to Jerusalem in the second person—which occurs only in the second unit— and by the move from the theme of the nations to the theme of Jerusalem and its community in the ideal period.

The first unit (Zeph 3:9-10) is linked to the concluding phrase of the preceding announcement of judgment by the similar and recurrent use of כי and by the explicit אז, "then, at that time." As a result, the universal announcement of judgment in Zeph 3:8 turns out to be the first act of the divine action that leads to universal salvation.[100]

---

[100] See, the section "The structure of the Book of Zephaniah and its message."

Most of the issues in Zeph 3:9-10 have been discussed in the notes section. One may only recall that the theme of the peoples accepting YHWH occurs also in Zeph 2:11 and in the *malak* psalms. Similarities between these psalms and Zeph 3:14-17 have already been mentioned. The stress on "sincere speech" occurs also in Zeph 3:13. A similar emphasis is attested in some pieces of wisdom literature and especially in the probably post-monarchic, congregational Ps 15:2.[101]

Those who understand the verse as saying that the nations will bring Israel out of its dispersion to Jerusalem as an offering (cf. Isa 66:20) are likely to conclude that a post-monarchic date is very probable. The same holds true if one proposes an ambiguous meaning that includes the one mentioned above.[102]

While the first unit deals with the divine actions concerning the nations and their outcome, the second one (Zeph 3:11-13) concerns with the divine actions concerning Jerusalem and its people and especially with their result: The ideal community of Jerusalem. The main issues in this unit have been discussed in the notes section. The language of the unit supports more a post-monarchic dating than a monarchic dating (see notes).

It is worth noting that Zeph 3:11-13, that is, the unit that provides a characterization of the ideal Jerusalemite community,[103] contains a relatively large number of clear cross-references to other units in the Book of Zephaniah.[104] A similar concentration of cross-references has been noticed in another crucial verse, Zeph 3:8. One may conclude that Zeph 3:11-13, as well as Zeph 3:8, reflect the compositional level.[105]

---

[101] See notes on Zeph 3:13.

[102] Although not compelling, the pattern of occurrence of the key idiom לקרא כלם בשם ה׳ (v. 9) in the Latter Prophets and in Psalms seems to suggest that a post-monarchic date is more probable than a monarchic date. The image of the nations' pilgrimage to Zion/Jerusalem is, at least, consistent with a post-monarchic dating

[103] See notes.

[104] E.g., עליליותיך (v. 11) and cf. Zeph 3:7; מקרבך (vv. 11, 12) and cf. Zeph 3:3-5, 15, 17; עשה עולה (v. 13) and Zeph 3:5; המה ירעו ורבצו (v. 13) and cf. Zeph 2:7; שארית ישראל (v. 13) and cf. Zeph 2:7,9. Issues concerning these cross-references have already been discussed in the commentary section.

[105] It is noteworthy that Zeph 3:11-13 contains words or expressions whose pattern of occurrence shows a clear concentration either in wisdom literature, or in the Jeremianic

4.4.2.2 The two summons to rejoice (Zeph 3:14-15 and Zeph 3:16-17)

The first summons to rejoice is set off from the preceding announcement
of salvation by the first in a series of four imperatives summoning to rejoice. The second summons to rejoice is connected to (and set off from)
the first one by a temporal linking phrase (ביום ההוא), just as the first
announcement of salvation (Zeph 3:9-10) is linked to (and set off from)
the second (Zeph 3:11-13).

Despite the formal similarities between the two temporal linking phrases,
they point to different points in time, and convey a different message.
From context one learns that the temporal linkage between the two announcements of salvation (Zeph 3:9-10 and Zeph 3:11-13) and between
both of them and the announcement of judgment in Zeph 3:8 points to a
specific time in the future in which the series of announced events will take
place. The same does not hold true for the two summons to rejoice. The
temporal phrase in Zeph 3:16 does not relate the two summons to one time
(either as simultaneous or in sequence). To the contrary, the temporal
phrase claims that the second summons will be proclaimed at an undefined
future time from the temporal perspective of the first summons to rejoice.

Significantly, the ideal situation stands in the future from the perspective
of the putative prophet—as well as from the perspective of the community
in which the book was composed—but this future is not without some
continuity with the "present" of the putative prophet, for the future summons to rejoice is only a variation of the original summons to rejoice proclaimed by the prophet. Accordingly, the text suggests a kind of continuity between the expressions, and implicitly the conceptions, of the pious in
a non-ideal situation (i.e., that of the putative prophet) and what will be

---

tradition, or in likely post-monarchic Psalms, or in late Isaianic material, or any
combination of the the literary corpora mentioned above, as well as unique uses of words
and expressions. See, for instance, the patterns of occurrence—see notes—of עשׂה עולה,
תרמית, עליזי נאותך, עולה, בסח בשם ה', הר קדשׁ, לשׁון תרמית, עם עני ודל. Cf. כזב and לבהה pointing
to pride. To a large extent, these features characterize the entire Book of Zephaniah, but
their concentration in this unit may suggest that there is little, if at all, of a pre-
compositional text in Zeph 3:11-13.

generally accepted in the ideal future. In this respect, it is worthy of recalling that the future, ideal community of Jerusalem in Zeph 3:11-13 is described in terms similar to those describing the requirements that a person
has to fulfill in order to deserve to be a legitimate member of the community in Ps 15.[106]

As already pointed out in the notes, the fact that the second summons to
rejoice is a rephrasing of the first suggests that from the perspective of
people living in the putative future of the "prophet," a contemporaneous
message of salvation is accepted as legitimate on the basis of the authority
of a similar saying of a prophet in the past, rather than on the basis of the
authority of the one who is actually saying these words, in the present
time.

Both summons to rejoice are linked to themes and language occurring
elsewhere in the text of Zephaniah (e.g., גבור יושיע in v. 17, which is,
to some extent, a reversal of Zeph 1:14, see notes) and especially in
Zephaniah chapter 3. For instance, the use of בקרבך (vv. 15, 17) continues to develop a theme already present in Zeph 3:3-5,11-12, and
משפטיך (v. 15) one elaborated in Zeph 3:5, 8. The discussion in the
notes section also pointed out that הסיר ה' משפטיך פנה איבך is
probably related to אסיר מקרבך עליזי גאותך in Zeph 3:11.

The material in these two summons to rejoice that is not clearly related to
other units in the Book of Zephaniah consists mainly of variations of
common themes and language of summons to rejoice in the OT. But the
variation is probably not accidental, for it shows tendencies to ambiguity
and a certain preference for unique expressions that have been found elsewhere in the Book of Zephaniah. In addition, it seems that the language of
the text stands closer to language attested in the Latter Prophets—mainly in
post-monarchic pieces—than to similar and potentially alternative language
occurring in the Book of Psalms.

---

[106] Cf. Ps 24:1-6. See notes on Zeph 2:3.

4.4.2.3 The second announcement of salvation (Zeph 3:18-19)

The limits of the unit are marked by the change of speaker from the putative prophet to YHWH in v. 18 and by the temporal linking phrase that
opens the concluding unit of the Book of Zephaniah. Although one cannot
be sure of the exact meaning of most of the announcement (v. 18-19a), the
context clearly shows that it is an announcement of salvation. The last part
of the announcement elaborates the theme of the reversal of a punishment
described in terms of dispersion, exile. The pattern of occurrence of the
language, the imagery, and the theme of this part of the announcement indicate that a post-monarchic date is more likely than a monarchic one (see
notes).

The emphasis on the theme of "gathering the dispersed" as well as the
use of אספתי point to the other announcement of "gathering" in the
book, i.e., Zeph 1:2-3a. The two units build an inclusio including almost
all the Book of Zephaniah. This inclusio represents one of the main transformations in the book, i.e., from "divine gathering" in order to punish to
"divine gathering" to save, to bring to the ideal status.

4.4.2.4 The concluding unit of the Book of Zephaniah (Zeph 3:20)

No prophetic book ends with an announcement of judgment against
Judah, Israel, or Jerusalem, or any combination of them (i.e., against any
concept that may represent the community of the readers of the text, or
their ancestors). Prophetic books generally end with a unit conveying a
clear message of salvation.[107]

The Book of Zephaniah is no exception. It concludes with an announcement of salvation. This announcement is closely related to the
concluding part of the preceding announcement in both language and con-

---

[107] In some cases, this message of salvation includes, or even consists of, a message of
doom for those who are conceived as deserving the divine punishment (e.g., Joel 4:18-
21; Am 9:13-15; Obad 1:19-21; Hag 2:23; Zech 14:20-21; Mal 3:23-24).

tents and exhibits similarities with the concluding unit of the Book of Amos.

Zeph 3:20 explicitly refers to the future gathering of those who have been dispersed, in exile. In post-monarchic days—which are much more likely to be the time of this note, as well as of the compositional level of the book, than the monarchic period—such a reference certainly points to the fall of Jerusalem, the Temple, and the monarchy. The people will not only be gathered together but be made praised among the nations. The theme of the relationship between Israel and the nations in the ideal world reappears in this closing note. This theme will be discussed in a separate section, on the basis of the dialogue between the message of the structure of the entire Book of Zephaniah and the message of the text.

4.5 The structure of the book of Zephaniah and its message

The books of Isaiah, Jeremiah (LXX), Ezekiel and Zephaniah have in common a general tripartite organization: (a) a section that concerns mainly with announcements of judgment against Judah/Israel and whose general message is judgment, (b) oracles against the "nations" (OAN) in medial position, and (c) a section that concerns mainly with announcements of salvation and whose general message is salvation. Of course, the existence of this general structure does not obliterate their differences in style and content; nor the fact that each of them underwent a separate redactional process; nor that there are units that do not conform to the pattern. Nevertheless, despite all these differences, a similar general structure can be discerned in at least four different books.[108] This evidence cannot be explained by assuming a series of random coincidences, and certainly not as the result of the idiosyncratic character of a certain prophet, or of the

---

[108] It seems implied in Obadiah.

author/redactor of a certain prophetic book, or of the tradents of a particular prophetic tradition.

It is reasonable to assume that a common structure conveys a common message, the one conveyed by this structure. Of course, this message may be supported, subverted (totally or partially) or reinterpreted by the texts themselves. But, if this is the case, then the message conveyed by each of these books may be understood in terms of a dialogue between the explicit and implicit messages of the general structure on one hand, and the specific claims of each text on the other. Of course, such possibilities can be tested only after the common "structural" meaning is elucidated.[109]

The tripartite division mentioned above provides a clear trajectory. Judah/Israel[110] always starts from a status of a sinner who is about to be punished (hereafter, status A). This is the putative situation of the monarchic society. After the punishment, Judah/Israel is in a status of not-being about to be punished (hereafter, status non-A). Since, according to the text, the punishment against Judah/Israel is nothing but the execution of judgment against it, then the status of not-being about to be punished implies a status of not- being indicted.

This trajectory from A to non-A, does not occur by itself, but there is an active agent involved: YHWH. Thus, one may express this trajectory as a performance in which YHWH is the agent who acts on Judah/Israel and brings it from a state of conjunction with X to a state of disjunction from X (X= "to be punished," but also—according to the claim of the text—indicted of serious sinning). That is, in formal terms: $Y(Is) \longrightarrow [(Is \wedge X) \longrightarrow (Is \vee X)]$.

Undoubtedly, the situation of "not going to be punished" is far from the ideal status, as described in the prophetic books (hereafter, status B).

---

[109] For obvious reasons, this study is restricted to the book of Zephaniah but its conclusions shed a certain light on the general issue.

[110] From an historical point of view the references are to Judah, or to post-monarchic groups composed mainly or exclusively by Judeans. However, from a conceptual point of view they may be called Israel. In order to express the maximum degree of generalization, the terms Judah/Israel and Israel/Judah will be used in this chapter.

However, it should be noticed: the first step, and a necessary one, for reaching B from the point of departure of A has already taken place.[111]

Since the sentence "no Judah/Israel who is about to be punished (as in Zeph 1:2-18) is in the ideal status (as described in Zeph 3:9 ff.)," or in its equivalent form: "all/any Israel/Judah who is in the ideal status is not about to be punished,"[112] are clearly true in the context of the book of Zephaniah—as well as in other prophetic books—then one can legitimately consider A and B as contraries. By definition, A and B are logical contraries if both can be false but both cannot be true. In other words, Judah/Israel cannot be simultaneously on the eve of the judgment mentioned in Zeph 1:2-18 and in the ideal situation described in Zeph 3:9 ff. However, it is noteworthy that both statements can be false simultaneously, i.e.; Judah/Israel can be far from the ideal situation, yet this does not mean that Judah/Israel would necessarily be in a situation in which a divine judgment similar to Zeph 1:2-18 is expected.[113] If A and B are contraries one may draw the logic square, and consider its implications:

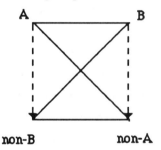

---

[111] There is no possible trajectory from A to B that does not include a sub-trajectory from A to non-A. This is so because A and B are logical contraries, see below.

[112] Turning a '(P)E(Q)' proposition (i.e.,"no P is Q;" E stands here for the universal negative) into a '(P)A(non-Q)' proposition (i.e., all P is non-Q) is always a valid procedure. This procedure involves two stages: (a) conversion: '(P)E(Q)' -> '(Q)E(P),' which is valid for E propositions; and (b) '(Q) E (P)' -> '(Q) A (non-P), i.e., obversion which is always valid.

[113] It should be noticed that this logic holds because the Judah/Israel who is to be punished and Israel/Judah in the ideal situations are considered well defined groups that are existent or potentially existent. If there were eternal empty classes, this logic would turn out to be meaningless.

In this square, non-A and non-B are subcontraries, i.e., both can be true but both cannot be false. For the case that both are true, see above. If both were false this would imply that A and B can be true simultaneously and that cannot be so because they are contraries.

A and non-B are sub-alternates, i.e., if A is true then non-B is true but one cannot legitimately deduce that if non-B is true then A is also true. In biblical terms, if Judah/Israel are about to be punished because of their sins then, it is true that they are not in the ideal status; however, the fact that they are not living in these ideal status does not mean that they are about to be punished as in Zeph 1:2-18.

B and non-A are sub-alternates, i.e., if B is true then non-A is true but one cannot infer from a true-value for non-A that B is also true. That is, if Israel/Judah are in the ideal status (e.g., Zeph 3:9 ff.) then they are not about to be punished. For the second case, see above.

A and non-A, as well as B and non-B, are contradictories. Both cannot be true and both cannot be false.

As mentioned above, the first part of the tripartite structure of these prophetic books ends with the first step in the trajectory from A to B, i.e., A to non-A. Before the next step in this trajectory is accomplished, the text enters into the second part of the tripartite pattern: the oracles against the nations (OAN). Since there is a resting point in the "narrative," and not just a resting point, but a resting point for the addressees of the prophetic book, one should ask: What are the socio-historical groups in Judah/Israel that could identify themselves with people living in status non-A and hoping to reach status B? Taking into account the occurrence of the tripartite pattern in three indisputably post-monarchic books (i.e., Ezekiel, Jeremiah [LXX] and Isaiah) and the preceding analysis of the compositional level of the Book of Zephaniah, it seems that the best candidates are post-monarchic communities, These tripartite prophetic books come up as communicative objects from these communities and for them.[114] These communities are not only the actual addressees of these books, but it is obvious that: (a) they considered themselves as living after the execution of the divine punishment against monarchic Judah/Israel; and (b) they did not (and could not) consider themselves as living in the ideal situation described in the announcements of salvation. That is, they saw themselves as living in a non-A situation. This being the case, one of the most relevant questions[115] for them—in general, and as readers of these prophetic books in particular— was: If and how can the movement from non-A to B be realized? That is, if and how Israel/Judah that are now in the status of not-being about to be punished (non-A) would reach the ideal status (B).

Accordingly, one may expect the prophetic book to go forward and to lead Israel/Judah from the post-punishment and not about to be punished situation to the ideal one. Indeed one may find numerous cases in which announcements of judgment against monarchic Israel/Judah are followed by announcements of salvation describing an ideal future. But, while this is a very common pattern, it does not characterize the large structure of the tripartite books, for their second section consists (mainly) of announcements against the nations.

In the second section of these books, the focus of the text is on the "nations." Their initial situation contrast sharply with the situation of Judah/Israel. The "nations" always enter the OAN section in good shape. They are described as boasting because of their power (or their wealth, or both), rejoicing in the fall of Judah, having taken profit from it and the like. At the very least, the nations have not suffered the awesome punishment that Judah/Israel has suffered. From the point of view of post-monarchic communities, this is the basic reality of their days, namely, the nations (i.e., non-Yahwistic peoples) are in a better situation than the

---

[114]Independently of any position taken on issues like prophet and prophetic book, authorship, etc, the tripartite structure is an attribute of the books. As an attribute of the books it expressed and dialogued with the position of the communities in which this books were written, read and interpreted.

[115] For further and related questions that may have troubled them, see below.

Yahwistic communities. This being "reality" the relevant question is: what does this reality mean?

If a debased earthly situation points to a people who has angered God, then a good situation suggests a people who has not angered God, or perhaps has even pleased God. Moreover, this suggestion is supported by the widespread doctrine that a person, or a people, cannot succeed without divine help. (This doctrine, needless to say, was shared by all the peoples in the ancient Near East.) Since a good (earthly) situation suggests divine blessing, the question turns out to be whether the two are equivalents, that is, if one implies the other. In other words, whether the following statements are valid: (a) "if there is divine blessing then there is a good earthly stand"; and (b) "if there is a good earthly stand then there is a divine blessing."

To be sure, the issue was not an academic one for Israel/Judah, but one of far reaching consequences concerning their own self understanding. If the double implication stands, this means for a post-monarchic community that the nations have behaved substantially better than Israel/Judah. Accordingly the relevant question to be asked by a post-monarchic community would be: what can we learn from the nations' behavior in order to improve ours? But this was not the prophetic message of the books of Isaiah, Jeremiah (LXX), Ezekiel, or Zephaniah. To the contrary, their message stands against such a proposal.[116] Therefore, it was imperative for these books to show that there is no valid double implication, even if it sounds at odds with the widespread "common sense" doctrine mentioned above.[117]

---

[116] Although, the issue is so well-known that there is no real need of mentioning examples one cannot but recall the poem in Jer 10:2 ff.

[117] To be sure, there is clear logical gap in the line of reasoning represented by the double implications mentioned above. Basic logic tells us that from the "fact" that Israel/Judah is in bad shape because it has angered God, one cannot validly deduce that everyone who is in good shape has not angered God. But this is a very common fallacy, and people at all ages tend to be trapped by its persuasive appeal. The best way to convince an audience that this is a fallacy is to bring clear examples that negate it. In fact, this is exactly what the tripartite prophetic books do. See below.

The foundations for the negation of the double implication are in the section that contains the judgments against Judah/Israel. This section claims, this time in accordance with the widespread doctrine, that the debased situation of Judah/Israel is the result of divine anger, and consequently that a debased situation is an earthly sign of the 'after the divine punishment' situation, i.e., of non-A. Conversely, the relative opulence of the former period serves as an earthly sign for the A situation. As a result, on the basis of this section, one should conclude that a good worldly situation may serve as an earthly sign of divine approval (a B-like situation), but also as an earthly sign of the status of "about to be punished" (i.e., of A). If the second option is the relevant one, then relative opulence means exactly the opposite of what it would mean according to an unsophisticated use of the common sense doctrine. In practical terms this means that Israel/Judah *may* look to the nations as sinners whose behavior is to be regarded as an example of what ought not to be done.

The section containing the judgments against Judah/Israel opens the way for the rejection of the double implication mentioned above, but this section leaves the main question undecided: are the nations enjoying the divine blessing because of their behavior (i.e., an A-like status), or are they about to be punished because of their misdeeds (i.e., a B-like status)? In the first case they would provide a positive example to Israel, in the second, an example of what Israel ought not to do. To decide the question a complementary section is called for: the OAN section.

The OAN section tells its audience that the nations are going to be punished, that they are going to be moved from their present status (hereafter, A1) to a status non-A1. Eventually, the nations will reach the ideal status (B1)—to be sure, ideal from the standpoint of the different groups in Israel/Judah who were responsible for the diverse ideal pictures described in the prophetic books mentioned above. This second stage of the trajectory is related to the trajectory of Judah/Israel to B (e.g., Zeph 3:9-10,

Isa:56:3-7). Since, A1 and B1 are logical contraries,[118] the logical square
for the OAN section is as follows:

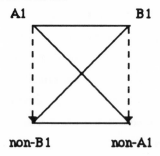

Since the logical inferences made above concerning A, B, non-A, and
non-B are dependent on the fact that A and B are logical contraries but independent of the specific content of A and B, then one may substitute A1
for A and B1 for B in the list of inferences made above. The resulting
statements will be equally valid. Thus, for instance, if the nations are
about to be punished because of their sins then it is true that they are not in
the ideal status (i.e., if A1 is true then B1 cannot be true for A1 and B1 are
contraries); however, the fact that they are not in the ideal status does not
necessarily mean that they are about to be punished (i.e., non-B1 is true
does not imply that A1 must be true, for non-B1 and non-A1 are sub-con-
traries, and therefore, both can be true but both cannot be false, accordingly non-A1 may be true or false, in the first case A1 must be false and in
the second one, A1 must be true).

In terms of performance, one can describe the OAN section in terms
taken from our previous analysis of the section of judgments against
Judah/Israel, substituting, obviously, the name of the previous subject
with the name of the new one. Thus, the OAN section reflects an action in
which YHWH is the agent who brings the nations from a state of conjunction with X to a state of disjunction with X (X means, here, "to be punished" but also means to be indicted, see below). In formal terms this performance can be written: $Y(N) \longrightarrow [(N \wedge X) \longrightarrow (N \vee X)]$.

---

[118] Cf. the discussion on A and B, above.

In spite of these valid substitutions of Israel/Judah by the nations in the performance formula and in the logical square, there is no doubt that the prophetic texts, and Zephaniah among them, do not assume the equation: Israel = nations, but reject it. Thus, while the structure of the text suggests similarity, the role of the texts themselves is to point out that there are differences, to show the limits of the likeness. As a result, one of the main issues in the OAN section concerns the differences between A and A1,[119] and between the related states non-A and non-A1.

Since the two A's mean "indicted," and accordingly "about to be punished," the main differences are to be found in the so-called small details of each indictment, such as, indicted for doing what? Israel/Judah are always indicted for forsaking YHWH, and for doing so in manifold ways. Moreover, although different announcements of judgment have different emphases, all of them share a main and basic concept that reflects the basic tenet of the writers and their publics, namely, doing wrong is forsaking YHWH and forsaking YHWH is doing wrong. But, can the nations be indicted according to these lines?

Obviously, any answer to this question should be derived from the prophetic books themselves, and according to the limits of the present study, we shall only look for those answers that may be inferred from the book of Zephaniah. The OAN section in Zephaniah is a composite text, so no uniform reading of the entire section can be made without losing sight of the individual points of view of each unit. The announcement against the Philistines (Zeph 2:4-7*) does not mention any grounds for the expected punishment. However, an additional note in v. 7 refers to a post-punishment situation in which their land will be for the "remnant of Judah." Accordingly, the main explicit difference between Judah and the Philistines is that after the punishment of both, a remnant of Judah will settle in the Philistine land but no remnant of the Philistines will settle in Judah. The reference to such a future may also suggest that the legitimacy

---

[119] Because of the same reasons, one of the main issues in the salvation section is what is the difference between B and B1.

of the Philistine possession of the land, or part of it, is questioned, but legitimacy of Judah's possession of its land is unquestioned.

The announcement against Moab and Ammon (Zeph 2:8-11*) contains a reference to territorial encroachment of Judah/Israel and to their taunting the people of YHWH. The first theme leads to a reversal, after the punishment (v. 9b). So far the expression of the difference between Judah/Israel and Moab and Ammon is similar to that mentioned above (Zeph 2:7), but there is one difference: the remnant of Judah is explicitly called the remnant of the people of YHWH. The second theme, the taunting of YHWH's people, leads to a harsh punishment: total desolation.[120] This can be explained on the grounds that Ammon and Moab did not taunt any people, but the people of YHWH. Of course, neither the writer nor his/her audience could have thought that the fatal mistake of the Ammonites and the Moabites was that they did not know that the Israelites were the people of YHWH. Such a claim would be historically impossible. Significantly, nowhere in the book of Zephaniah, or in the OT in general, one finds the claim that the nations do not know that Israel worships YHWH. This being the case, from the standpoint of the writer and his/her audience, the real source of trouble for the Ammonites and Moabites can only be that they failed to recognize that YHWH is not a god but God. Therefore they could not but fail to take into account the logical inference from the "fact" that YHWH = God of Israel = God, and consequently they dared to taunt Israel, and by implication, no other than God.[121] In other words, their basic error and the cause of their eventual

---

[120] Obviously, there is a tension between total desolation and Israelite settlement, see the discussion on this unit.

[121] The idea that boasting and taunting is inherently wrong was widely accepted in ancient Near East (e.g., Wiseman, 1985:63), but the Ammonites and Moabites are not condemned because of boasting and taunting in general, but because they did so against the people of YHWH (see חרפו וינדלו על עם ה' צבאות in v. 8 and אשר חרפו את עמי וינדילו על נבולם in v. 9). It is noteworthy that the Moabites and the Ammonites are the only two groups that are explicitly condemned because of their actions against Israel/Judah. This singularity certainly emphasizes the main point: Ammon and Moab are not indicted of taunting in general, but of taunting "*my* people."

punishment is that they had and respected their own gods and did not acknowledge that the real God is YHWH.

This underlying issue comes to the forefront in the note in v. 11, making
the implicit explicit and deriving the logical consequences. Thus, verse 11
explicitly states that YHWH will diminish the other gods; the peoples, recognizing that, will bow to YHWH, each of them in its own place. Thus,
the real reason for the peoples' misbehavior will be removed. What about
the similarities and differences between Israel and the nations at that time?
No special role is assigned to Israel or Zion in v. 11. Verses 8-10, however, emphasize that Judah/Israel are the people of YHWH, and consequently, that recognizing YHWH as God implies a recognition of a special
status for Israel/Judah.

The only sin of Assyria mentioned in Zeph 2: 13-15 is a boasting
thought in its heart (v. 15). The text tells its audience that Assyria thought
in this way because of its secure dwelling. But what should Assyria have
done in such circumstances? To acknowledge that its secure dwelling is
not (only?) due to its own acts but to the divine will (as well ?). But if this
is the case, what should they have done? to praise Assur, and the other
Assyrian gods (as they actually did)? Since the nations are not accused in
the Old Testament of being unfaithful to their gods, but quite the contrary,
of being faithful to gods that are not worthy of faithfulness, one may ven-
ture that the answer mentioned above is not the right one. But if Assyria
should not relate its secure dwelling to its worldly power, nor to the power
and mighty deeds of the Assyrian gods, what Assyria ought to do? The
obvious answer is to acknowledge that its power comes from the real
source of power, from YHWH. Therefore, the underlying thought in this
unit leads to the idea that Assyria's source of misbehavior is that Assyria
does not recognize YHWH. To sum up, the announcements against
Assyria, Moab and Ammon in the book of Zephaniah convey a clear
meaning to the community: the common source of the misbehavior of the
nations is that they do not recognize that YHWH is God.

According to the general pattern of the tripartite division mentioned at the
beginning of this section, one expects that Zeph 3:1 would be the opening

of the salvation section. Instead, Zeph 3:1 goes back to judgment against
Judah/Israel, and further references to the judgment of the nations are
made. With regard to the present issue, the thought expressed in Zeph 3:7
is extremely interesting. According to Zeph 3:7, the nations have been
punished before Judah/Israel. The divine hope, according to this verse, is
that Israel/Judah will learn the lesson and accordingly will amend its ways,
so the expected punishment would be tempered, or even avoided. The
point is not that the divine hope turned out to be in vain but that the starting
point of the putative speaker, no other than YHWH, is that Judah/Israel
could have learned the lesson. How? Only if there is a basic uniformity in
YHWH's treatment of the nations and of Israel/Judah. Only if there are
general rules that apply to all, could Judah/Israel have understood that the
nations are being punished by YHWH because of their deeds and that they
are the next nation in line unless the amend their ways. Similarity, uniformity, but nevertheless; even here, there is a detail that subverts this uniformity: YHWH began with the peoples hoping that Judah/Israel would
learn, and not the other way around.

The tension between similarity, even close similarity (as expressed by
several aspects of the structure underlying the tripartite division and by the
underlying notions behind certain texts [e.g., Zeph 3:7]), and differentiation characterizes the entire book (see below) and reflects the ambiguity of
the community/ies in which the book of Zephaniah was written and interpreted. The conspicuous occurrence of this tension suggests that these
communities were not able to develop a self-image of Israel except in
terms of a general framework including both Israel and the nations. The
reason that the conception of Israel was understood by means of similarities and differences with the nations is that this concept was grounded in
the relationship between YHWH and Israel. Yet, YHWH is a universal
God who deals with all the nations. Thus, the question of the relationship
between YHWH and the nations is deeply related to the question of Israel

and the nations. The nations are not supposed to worship[122] YHWH before the establishment of totally new circumstances that are dependent on a specific action of YHWH (Zeph 3:9 ff.). Yet, the nations are condemned because of a behavior that is rooted in their failure to recognize YHWH. It is worth noting that this tension is unavoidable if one takes into account the accepted concept that in regards to Israel, it is true that forsaking YHWH is wrongdoing and wrongdoing is forsaking YHWH. Although the first part of the sentence can be considered irrelevant concerning the nations, the second cannot be considered irrelevant unless YHWH is devoid of universal attributes, and this would have been unthinkable in groups that accepted the message of the prophetic literature. The tensions cannot find a solution in the first two sections of the book of Zephaniah. A third section is needed, the one containing the announcements of salvation.

At this point and before the analysis of the third section, it seems useful to approach the message of the tripartite prophetic books in general, and of the book of Zephaniah in particular, from a different perspective.

One may be able to analyze the issues mentioned above from a different angle with the help of the following veridiction diagram:[123]

---

[122] Since worship is one of the expressions of the recognition of YHWH, one should assume that they are not supposed to recognize YHWH as God. This recognition is not explicitly demanded from any nation in the OT but from Israel. The idea that all the nations *will* serve YHWH occurs many times in the OT and in several forms (e.g., Zeph 3:9; Isa 2:2-4; Mic 4:2-4 [but cf. Mic 4:5]) the idea that the nations (except Israel) *are* commanded to serve YHWH occurs nowhere.

[123] On veridiction diagrams, see for instance, CADIR, Rudiments d'analyse narrative IV; Calloud, 1979: 81-83.

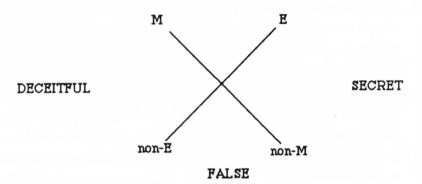

E= long term will of YHWH.
M= manifestation of YHWH's will, i.e., the historical situation.

For people living in the post-monarchic period the basic features of the manifestation were clear. They knew their historical situation. They knew that non-Yahwistic peoples, i.e., "the nations," were in better shape than Judah/Israel and that no substantial change was to be expected if things continued to go as usual.[124] The issue for them was whether this particular manifestation of the will of YHWH reflected the long term will of YHWH, or not. If the first option is chosen then the world, as it is, points to the long term will of YHWH, i.e., the (message of the) world stands at the "true" position in the veridiction diagram. Moreover, since the world reflects the long term will of YHWH no change is expected in the fu-

---

[124] In monarchic times there may have been groups or individuals who thought in this way, but the destruction of the social, cultural, political and religious center of Jerusalem made such understanding of the manifestation unavoidable. This was not so until the tradition according to which Zion was inexpugnable was not falsified by the historical events. For instance, from the standpoint of the account of Hezekiah's deliverance in 701 BCE (2 Kgs 18:17- 19:37*), the manifestation is clearly not that Assyria is more powerful than Jerusalem. Any Judean reader who was influenced by this kind of literature would probably reached the same conclusion (cf. Jer 7:4, which is very critical of such position). The present writer thinks that much of this literature is from the days of Zedekiah but in any case, after the destruction of Jerusalem and the Temple there was no question whether they can be destroyed or not.

ture.[125] Was this the option of the prophetic books mentioned above and of the book of Zephaniah in particular? Certainly not.

The books of Isaiah, Jeremiah, Ezekiel, and Zephaniah do not stand for the acceptance of the world as it is and forever, but convey a clear expectation that there will be an essential change in the world. Thus, only one option remains for the prophetic books: to claim that the manifestation of the will of YHWH, as expressed by the world, does not reflect the long term will of YHWH. Accordingly, a glimpse at the events in the world would only provide a deceitful image (see the veridiction diagram). Where, then, is the truth?

According to their own logic, the prophetic books claim that in the long run, the truth will be known to all, because the long term will of YHWH will be implemented, and consequently there will be no difference between the manifestation of the divine will and the will itself. However, neither the authors/redactors of the prophetic books nor their audiences lived in such glorious days. Thus, the truth cannot be derived validly from any publicly known data (manifestation), or the truth even contradicts what seems to be valid inferences from these data. The truth, therefore, can only be a secret knowledge of someone who is acquainted with more data than any one human could manage to have. Thus, it becomes clear why the prophetic book claims that YHWH has given secret knowledge to the prophet. There is simply no other option for the legitimation of the secret knowledge claimed in the book. That is something like: we certainly know that this is the long term will of YHWH because YHWH, him/herself said so. This legitimation is crucial because the basic aim of the prophetic book is to reveal its secret to the community, and to convince the community that the truth is in the secret and not in what the manifestations of YHWH's actions in the world seem to indicate.

---

[125] This is not a totally theoretical option. Certainly it is hard to believe that any people or community will cling to a hopeless alternative. But the manifestation mentioned above can be interpreted in a positive way. Something like, although the nations who do not acknowledge (and serve) YHWH are in better material shape than Israel, the latter are the uplifted ones because they do serve YHWH and live according YHWH's commandments.

What is the content of the secret that the book of Zephaniah seeks to reveal? The secret is that the historical situation, the fact that the nations are
in a better situation than Judah/Israel, is indeed a manifestation of
YHWH's will but not of YHWH's special blessing over the nations because of their deeds. Instead the historical situation points to the "fact"
that the nations have not been punished, yet. Moreover, neither the punishment of Judah/Israel nor the expected punishment of the nations reflects
the real long term will of YHWH, so all these manifestations, both in the
past and in the future, are deceitful. The long term will of YHWH, as expressed in the tripartite prophetic books (as well as others) is the creation
of a totally new historical situation (see Zeph 3:9 ff.): the ideal situation
described in the third section of these prophetic books.

The message of the section containing the announcements of salvation is
clear: The ideal status B and B1 will be reached, and then the manifestation
of the will of YHWH will reflect YHWH's true, long term will. The deceitfulness of the world will then disappear. Since the message of the
world (= the manifestation of YHWH's attitude to Israel and the nations)
can be either deceitful or true but not both at the same time, then one may
draw a logical square in which A2 represents deceitfulness and B2
truth.[126] Therefore, the trajectory from A2 to B2 necessarily passes
through non-A2, namely, the stage after the punishment and before the
reconciliation. Accordingly, one may conclude that the agent YHWH
moved the world (or the message of the world) from a state of conjunction
with deceitfulness into one of disjunction, and eventually from a state of
disjunction with truth to one of conjunction. In formal terms:

126

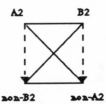

Y(W)—> [(W ∧D ∨ T)—> (W ∨ D∨ T)—>(W∨ D ∧ T)].

This performance, as well as the logical square, provides a new angle for the analysis of the overall trajectory and performance, but there are further relevant perspectives.

States A, non-A, A1 and (non-A1), have been characterized by the status of the subject (Israel/Judah or the nations) in its relation with YHWH, namely, the subject is about to be punished by YHWH or is not about to be punished by YHWH, is indicted by YHWH or is not. Obviously, these stages can also be described from the perspective of the manifestation of YHWH's attitude to Israel/Judah or the nations. YHWH's attitude towards Judah/Israel, as expressed in past or future events, moves therefore, from a status (A2) of hostility (punishment, anger, etc.) to a status (non-A2) of non-hostility and eventually to reconciliation (B2).[127] Accordingly one may write YHWH's performance as follows:

Y(Y)—> [(Y ∧ H ∨ R)—> (Y∨ H∨ R)—>(Y∨ H ∧ R)].

However, it is noteworthy that this expression of the performance reflects the text only in a partial form. YHWH's conjunction or disjunction of objects like hostility to Israel (or the nations) and reconciliation with them is not independent of the actions of Israel or the nations. Misbehavior on their side is mutually exclusive with YHWH's conjunction with reconciliation. Thus, the change of the manifestation of YHWH's attitude from hostility to reconciliation is only one aspect of a comprehensive change from A* (A, A1, A2, A3) to B* (B, B1, B2, B3) that may be approached from different angles as "monodimensional" trajectories (e.g.,

---

[127] Thus one may draw the logical square:

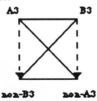

The relationships between A2, non-A2, B2 and non-B2 will be those defined by their places in the square and see above.

A——> non-A——> B), but each of them is a partial (and dependent) representation of a multidimensional movement from A* to B*. In A*, Israel and the nations misbehave, and therefore are indicted and about to be punished; the manifestation of YHWH's attitude towards Israel and the nations is hostility, and at that time the message of the world does not reflect YHWH's real attitude to Israel and the nations. In B* there is no one in Israel who will do wrong (Zeph 3:13), the nations will serve YHWH (Zeph 3:9), and the manifestation of YHWH's attitude is reconciliation.

Does this manifestation reflect the real attitude of YHWH, the long term will of YHWH concerning Israel and the nations? The answer is: Yes. Clearly, any different position would either contradict the logical sense of the announcements of judgment and the OAN section (see above) or lead to a sadistic image of YHWH (one who wishes for human beings to sin in order to punish them) or at very least to an impassible (and amoral ?) image of YHWH (one who punishes or blesses according to the human actions but who does not care what humans are doing and therefore leaves them alone without any guidance; in other words something like: do whatever you want but pay the bill). The text of Zephaniah, as well as the other prophetic books, renders the two latter alternatives entirely impossible. How does it accomplish this endeavor?

According to the text, there is a clear difference between the action of YHWH from A* to non-A* and the action of YHWH from non-A* to B*. The first action is described as provoked by the deeds of human beings (Israel and the nations). One should assume therefore, that had the peoples behaved in an appropriate way no judgment would have taken place. In clear contrast, the second action of YHWH (from non-A* to B*) is not described as provoked by the deeds of the peoples. To be sure, this second action is conditioned by their deeds, i.e., it could not take place if the peoples were behaving wickedly, but YHWH is not described as compelled to bring the peoples to the ideal status because of the actions of the peoples. YHWH will do so because this is YHWH's will. This will is, obviously, one the major attributes of YHWH. Moreover, since the text claims to make known the secret knowledge that YHWH gave to the prophet and this knowledge makes clear what is YHWH's real will, then the secret conveys an image of YHWH. This image is based on predicates like "longs for reconciliation with Israel and the nations," "is capable of bringing Israel and the nations to the ideal status, "and the like, and has the legitimacy of YHWH's own disclosure.[128] One may say that the text moves from a situation in which YHWH's true attributes (e.g., "longing for reconciliation with Israel and the nations," "capable of bringing Israel and the nations to the ideal status") are not known to Israel and the nations to a state in which these predicates of YHWH are publicly known. One may call these states A4 and B4, and since A4 and B4 are logical contraries, one may draw the logical square and describe a performance in which YHWH is the agent who causes Israel and the nations to move from a state of disjunction with the knowledge of the true image of YHWH to a state of conjunction, i.e., $Y(I+N) \longrightarrow [(I+N \lor K) \longrightarrow (I+N \land K)]$. Nevertheless, it should be noticed that something highly meaningful happens in the axis of time. The community reading the book is the only one that receives the knowledge in a historical present. Thus, the difference between Israel, represented by the community of readers, and the nations (along with those of Israel who reject the message of the book) becomes clear: The community of readers now knows the true attributes of YHWH, the latter do not. The latter will know that only in stage B.* It is worth noting that this difference is rooted in nothing but YHWH's free disclosure, i.e., in a facet of his/her true image.

The case against the impassible, or sadist, YHWH can be approached from a different (but converging) perspective. The tripartite structure of the book of Zephaniah, as well as the the text itself, makes clear that status A* is not a final status. Is B* a final status? Since there is no mention of a status C, one can safely say that anything beyond B* is beyond the horizon of the book, and perhaps of its audience. But what about a reversal? A* is an unstable status; it leads to non-A* (see above) and eventually may

---

[128] It is noteworthy that predicates explicitly assigned to YHWH in the text (e.g., Zeph 3:5) converge to this image of YHWH but they do not have the legitimacy of the divine revelation. (YHWH is mentioned in third person).

lead, and certainly leads in the book to B*. Is B* an unstable status that
leads to non-B* and eventually may lead to A*? If that is the case, and
taking into account that in the text the agent of all the trajectories is
YHWH, one would have to conclude that YHWH shows no preference.
A* may and will turn to B* but also B* to A*. Is that the case? What is
the message that the book of Zephaniah conveys in this respect?

According to the logic of the book of Zephaniah, the root of the nations'
misbehavior was that they did not recognize YHWH; yet in the ideal status
B* they will recognize YHWH (Zeph 3:9). Israel/Judah "knew" YHWH,
but in spite of this it had forsaken YHWH. Thus, in another example of
differences against the background of similarities, the composition of
Israel/Judah is to be drastically changed. Thus, concerning the nations it
is said that YHWH will cause them to speak a "pure language" (Zeph 3:9)
but concerning Israel/Judah (and only concerning Israel/Judah) it is said
that YHWH's action will destroy all the haughty people and will leave
only a humble and poor folk.[129] Moreover, the waw connecting the sentence "I [YHWH] will leave within you a poor and humble people" (Zeph
3:12a) and "they [this poor and humble people] will find refuge in the
name of YHWH" (Zeph 3:12b) points to both a temporal and a logical relationship.[130] Furthermore, in verse 13 it is explicitly said that the remnant of Israel (i.e., the poor and humble people) will do no wrong, that it
will speak no false language. Therefore, YHWH's actions are aimed to
preempt the possibility of a pendular movement from B* to A*. The Book
of Zephaniah conveys, therefore, a clear message: YHWH has preferences, and for the ideal situation, B*.

The ideal situation reflects the real will of YHWH. Any difference between Israel/Judah and the nations, if it is to exist in the ideal situation,
should be anchored in a difference between the relationships YHWH-na-
tions and YHWH-Israel/Judah that will exist at the ideal time. At that

---

[129] Haughty, non-poor, and non-humble come closer to a common denominator of the
features of the wrongdoers of Judah/Israel mentioned in the book. For humble and poor
see our previous analysis.

[130] Cf. GK 112 s.

time, all the peoples will be serving YHWH and doing the divine will. Also at that time, all the peoples will have true knowledge about the true attributes of YHWH (they will be publicly known because the manifestation of YHWH's will be consistent with YHWH's long term will). Thus, while before YHWH moves the world to the status B*, the particular (secret) knowledge of the divine attributes claimed by communities of readers, and interpreters, of the tripartite prophetic books (see above) certainly unifies and identifies these communities, the same will not hold true once the world reaches the B* status. In other words, either the book provides the communities with a conceptual self-definition that will withstand the realization of the ideal or, if it fails to do so, the book leads the communities to the notion that there will be no difference.

The book of Zephaniah provides a clear response: הר קדשי ("my holy mountain," Zeph 3:10; cf. Zeph 3:14-15, 16-17). YHWH has, and will have in the ideal time, a special relationship with Zion and with the people who live there. Thus, the choseness of Israel and the choseness of Zion become one. This recalls the theme of the Zion tradition. But what kind of Zion tradition? This is not the Zion tradition that emphasizes that Zion is inviolable because YHWH will fight on its behalf and that proved to be false in 586 BCE. In the book of Zephaniah, Zion will be certainly a peaceful place in a peaceful human world in which all the peoples will serve YHWH. Among them, Zion and the people living there, i.e., Judah/Israel, will have a special role (see Zeph 3:10-13). This line of thought comes to the forefront in the subsequent units. In Zeph 3:14 one finds the parallel Fair (בת) Zion, Israel, Fair (בת) Jerusalem; according to Zeph 3:15, YHWH, king of Israel, is (and will be) in the midst of Fair Jerusalem, and in v. 17 YHWH will be in the midst of Zion (paralleled in v. 16 with Jerusalem). Zion, Jerusalem turns out to be equivalent to Israel in the ideal situation B,* but obviously not equivalent to the nations. The difference will exist even in the ideal future.

The present analysis of the structure of the book of Zephaniah and its message has been developed against the background of the existence of a common tripartite structure in certain prophetic books. As mentioned

above, the existence of this structure does not obliterate their differences in
style and content; nor the fact that each of them underwent a separate
redactional process; nor that there are units that do not entirely conform to
the patter in each of the books. However, the fact that despite all these differences, four different books, in their final form, show a similar structure
leads to the unavoidable conclusion that this form addressed itself to the
kind of questions that troubled the communities in which these books received their final form, i.e., questions concerning their self-understanding,
their understanding of the world and of YHWH's will, and their longing
for an ideal future. One should also conclude that the message conveyed
by the book of Zephaniah is to be grasped as a dialogue between the general structure of the book along with its logical implications and the text (or
any subsequent redactional level of the text) or between the general structure of the book along with its logical implications and the thoughts, the
beliefs and the hopes of the communities behind the text.[131]

---

[131] It is likely that the same holds for the other prophetic books with the tripartite structure.
An analysis of these books is beyond the scope of this work.

5. Conclusions

The commentary section has demonstrated that there are at least three levels of development reflected in the Book of Zephaniah. There is a compositional level, several units that reflect pre-compositional material, and a few additions that are likely to be post-compositional. In other words, the compositional level did not produce the Book of Zephaniah out of nothing, but there was no Book of Zephaniah before the compositional level.

One may assume that at a certain point in the production of the book, an individual person, a "compositor," or author, was responsible for the writing of main parts of the book. But the book does not claim to be the work of its author; neither does the author claim to have a special word from YHWH. The individuality of the author is simply ignored, for it was considered irrelevant to the communicative value of the text.

Moreover, the compositional level cannot be equated with the work of a single author, for none of the criteria used in the determination of this level (e.g., cross references, language, stylistic devices, ongoing elaboration of message, the specific contents of the message of the book, etc.) necessarily imply single authorship.[1] There is coherence at the compositional level, but this coherence is not necessarily due to the work of a single author.

Furthermore, pre-compositional materials reflected in the compositional level were not considered a "frozen" text by the community in which the compositional activity took place, even if it certainly appreciated these received materials. (If it were the case, these materials would have never been included in the compositional level.) This being the case, it is highly

---

[1] See chapter 3.1.

unlikely that a new-born text such as the compositional level text or a version of it was considered by the community a "frozen" text. (The existence of post-compositional material proves the point beyond any doubt). Thus, the audience addressed by the ongoing compositional level text, or by a version of it, included at least some privileged readers who were entitled to legitimately interpret, redact, edit, or further develop this text. Since the still "open" text was a communicative message developing within the community and for the community, one has to conclude that at the very least these privileged readers/interpreters were able to understand this message. In other words, one cannot but assume that there was an audience able to understand the "code" of the text at its compositional level. Consequently, the following two premises are unreasonable, and should be rejected: (a) these interpreters always failed to understand the coherence of the ongoing work (and therefore always missed the point of the ongoing text); and (b) these interpreters always felt compelled to write their own additions to the work in a such a way that disturbs the coherence of the text that helped their own reading. The rejection of both (a) and (b) leads to a clear conclusion: not only that the coherence that characterizes the compositional level—functionally defined by the criteria mentioned above—does not necessarily imply a single individual author, but the claim that it may reflect the work of several privileged readers, interpreters, redactors, and the like is a very reasonable one.

To sum up, to emphasize the individuality of the author is neither methodologically possible nor advisable for the understanding of the text as a communicative message in historical-critical terms.

The alternative to the flesh and blood author is an abstract subject defined by the predicates that characterize the horizon of the compositional level, for the compositional level points to a horizon of concepts, of religious questions, of images (including self-image), of knowledge and of social claims for authority. Further references in this section to the author of the compositional level, i.e., the author of the Book of Zephaniah, will refer only to this abstract subject.

The author does not claim to be a prophet. He or she wrote a book about the word of YHWH that came to a prophet in the past, and writing a book about the prophecies putatively delivered by a prophet at a certain time in the past is clearly a different activity than prophesying.

This author engaged in a well attested activity in the post-monarchic period. There is almost no dispute among scholars that the the Book of Isaiah (i.e., Isaiah 1-66), the Book of Jeremiah, the Book of Ezekiel, the Book of Obadiah, the Book of Jonah, the Book of Haggai, the Book of Zechariah, and the Book of Malachi are all post-monarchic. Moreover, most scholars would probably agree that the Book of Joel, the Book of Amos and the Book of Micah are post-monarchic in their present form. The present study of the Book of Zephaniah has pointed out that also this book is post-monarchic.[2]

It is worth noting that while at least twelve out of fifteen prophetic books are post-monarchic, it is significant that the superscriptions of the prophetic books relate only two prophets (Haggai and Zechariah) to the post-monarchic period. Is this accidental? Most likely not. If this is the case, then important historical-critical conclusions follow, such as that the social group that carried out the writing, the transmission, and the reading for instruction of the prophetic books, tended to reject or minimize the authority of its contemporaneous prophets.[3] Such conclusion implies that the authors of the books that shaped our understanding of classical

---

[2] That is, the date of only three out of fifteen prophetic books remains open for further consideration; namely, the Book of Hosea, the Book of Nahum and the Book of Habakkuk.

[3] Cf. notes and commentary on Zeph 3:16-17.
This tendency is hardly surprising. When the "authors" of the Book of Deuteronomy wrote a book containing the putative saying of Moses they certainly did not assume that one of their contemporaries could rightly claim the same authority that they claimed for Moses, for if it were the case what kind of authority would Deuteronomy enjoy? Taking a non-biblical example those who composed the Code/s of Handsome Lake did not compose the Code while thinking that another equally authoritative person is living in their days and teaching in contradiction to the Code (if a holy person is supposed to teach in accordance to the Code this will imply a dependent role). On Handsome Lake, see Fenton, 1968; Wallace, 1970.

prophecy were written by people who probably tended to minimize the authority of the prophets of their own days.[4]

One may wonder to what extent this tendency shaped the images of the prophets in the prophetic books. In any case, if this tendency was active its more likely influence would be to stress the difference between the two groups of prophets. Significantly, Zephaniah, the prophet, never stands at the center of the Book of Zephaniah; the word of YHWH is at the center of the book. Zephaniah is mentioned only insofar as he is necessary for the interpretation of the text, i.e., as the word of YHWH that came at a certain historical period (and to a Judean, see Zeph 1:1). If despite the fact that not only the author but also the prophet is secondary to the message of the book, one attempts to reconstruct a picture of the prophet from the text, one immediately notices that Zephaniah is depicted neither as a holy man (e.g., Elijah and Elisha) nor as an ecstatic prophet (e.g., Zech 13:6). He neither performs nor announces miracles nor claims that his prayers may influence or even change the expected course of events (e.g., 2 Kgs 20:1-11; Jer 7:16), he does not perform any symbolic acts (e.g., Jer 19:1-2, 10), neither is he related to the Temple (cf. Lam 2:20). Instead he is described as a speaker who delivered a quite sophisticated speech or speeches concerning the future and called for repentance (Zeph 2:1-3). Perhaps in one case he even introduced his saying with a title (Zeph 2:5). This is certainly not the image of a prophet as it emerges from anthropological studies, or from the prophetic legends. Instead, this is the image of an idealized prophet, who most likely did not resemble the prophets, flesh and blood, of the monarchic period nor those of the days of the author.

Did this image resemble the self-image of the author of the book? To a certain extent this seems to be the case. Both present themselves as secondary to the message they are conveying to their public. The prophet is described as providing knowledge concerning the future and preaching repentance; the author wrote a book in order to be read by the community so

---

4   Although the issue of the "end of the classical prophecy" stands beyond the scope of this work, the above and below considerations are relevant to the discussion.

it may know the future God will bring, and how to behave in the present. That is, both are "teachers," educational figures. Moreover, the message conveyed by the "prophet" is presented by the author as authoritative (of divine origin); similarly the author presents his/her book as authoritative. Furthermore, the book describes the prophet as one delivering sophisticated speech or speeches (see below), this would be unimaginable if there was no sophisticated audience that could understand these cross references, tensions, ambiguities and the like at the time of the composition of the book. Thus, the author and his/her audience on the one hand and the image of the prophet and his audience, on the other, tend to converge on this point.

To sum up, to some extent one may describe the image of the prophet in the book as shaped in the author's likeness. Nonetheless, likeness is not sameness. While the prophet is described as receiving the divine word; the author tells the audience about someone else who received the divine word. While the authority and legitimacy of the prophet depend on direct divine intervention, the authority and legitimacy of the author depend on faithful transmission (and interpretation) of the divine word received by someone else (cf. "a deceitful language will not be found in their mouths" in Zeph 3:13; see 3.4.11 and cf. 3.4.13).

There are further differences. The prophet is described as prophesying about the future, from his standpoint his prophecies are yet unfulfilled; from the standpoint of the author and his or her community the prophecies concerning judgment have been fulfilled, those concerning salvation are still unfulfilled. Thus, from the standpoint of the author and his/her community the fulfillment of the announcements of judgment is an "empiric" argument supporting the legitimacy of the prophetic message, this cannot be the claim of the described prophet.

The prophet is clearly anchored in a certain set of "historical" circumstances; the author is not. The validity of the "empiric" argument mentioned above depends on the description of a prophet as living and prophesying in a specific historical situation. The author, on the other hand, had no reason to explicitly anchored him/herself in time.[5] Moreover, given the completely self-effacing character of the author, and the atemporal message of the book concerning the long term will of YHWH (see 4.5) such a temporal reference would be very unlikely. In fact neither the author of the Book of Zephaniah nor the author of any prophetic book contain a direct temporal reference to the time of the author.

To sum up, the image of the prophet provided by the Book of Zephaniah stands in sharp contrast with the most likely image of prophets, flesh and blood, of the author's days, of the post-monarchic period. By describing the ancient prophet as a kind of forerunner of him/herself, the author stresses his/her authority in the community, probably against alternative claims for divine authority made by prophets who were similar to the actual monarchic prophets. Significantly, the author of the book points to a pattern of communal acquisition of imparted divine knowledge as an action of reading (/learning) the sayings of an ancient prophet as they were written down (and interpreted) by the author of the book (cf. Hos 14:10). Were any alternative ways to this pattern of communal learning of the divine message? One may assume that there were. Probably, one of the most important alternatives was listening to contemporaneous prophets whose actions (and character) may have led the community, or members of the community, to believe that the "Word of God" has come to them.[6] In this respect, it is worth noting that while individual character and deeds of a living prophet play a role in the communal acceptance of the prophet as such, the author of the Book of Zephaniah clearly claims that not only writer of the book is secondary to the divine message, but also the ancient prophet. Thus, the book tends to de-legitimize the very grounds on which a living prophet may have convinced a contemporaneous audience of his or her authority.

---

[5] There are additional reasons for anchoring the prophet to historical circumstances. See Tucker, 1977.

[6] The existence of prophets in the so-called post-exilic period is beyond doubt.

To sum up, the Book of Zephaniah—as many other prophetic and non prophetic books— reflects and takes sides in struggles about religious and social authority in post-monarchic Israel.

The most probable image of the author that one can reconstruct from the available data in the text points to a person who lived in the post-monarchic period, after the early post-monarchic period (see below) and before the Hellenistic period (for there is no detectable Hellenistic influence in the Book). The author was influenced by other prophetic traditions, by wisdom literature, and whose work shows influences of the *anwim* Psalms, the *malak* Psalms and congregational Psalms.

The author is a very sophisticated writer, and since the book was written as communicative object, one has to assume a very sophisticated audience; i.e., one able to understand the system of cross references, ambiguities, puns on words, ongoing heightening of messages through consecutive versets and the like. Of course, these considerations point to a high level of literacy. Thus, unless one assumes that all Israelites including the poorest peasant achieved the same high level of literacy (which, of course, is highly unlikely), one has to conclude that certain social locations are more likely than others. The analysis of Zeph 3:13, which clearly belongs to the compositional level (see 4.4.2.1) pointed to one possible social role, that of a communal teacher (see 3.4.11).[7] In a more general level, it seems that a social location related to the "service" sector of society is more likely than alternative proposals. It is worth noting that when references to actual economic activities such as "pasturing" occur in pre-compositional material, the text is re-interpreted in the compositional level in such a way that the economic activities are certainly de-emphasized (cf. Zeph 2:6-7 and Zeph 3:12-13; see esp. 4.3.3.1).[8]

---

[7] It is worth noting that the analysis of certain pre-compositional units in the book pointed to a social and conceptual horizon that is more likely to be found in people working in the "service sector" and in an city environment than in other social groups (see 4.2.2; 3.4.3).

[8] Some pre-compositional material also suggest that a social location related to the "service" sector is more likely than any other alternative. See 3.4.3.

In which community did the author live? One cannot know for sure. But the description of the ideal community in the Book of Zephaniah clearly resembles the requirements for being a legitimate member of post-monarchic communities such as those whose requirements are expressed in Ps 15. The self image of the ideal community of the pious in the Book of Zephaniah resembles the self image of the community in the *anwim* Psalms, i.e., a community that considers itself oppressed by wicked, wealthy, proud, impious enemies, and hopes for their destruction by means of a divine action. Of course, these communities had to cope with the question why the wicked prevail, at least from their own perspective, and therefore they faced the problem of theodicy.

The author of the Book of Zephaniah was troubled not only because the wicked at home seem to prevail but also because of the relative situation of Israel among the nations. How could this relative situation be compatible with a special relationship between YHWH and Israel that exists because both of them (YHWH and Israel) are related to Jerusalem/Zion? Significantly, Israel is not supposed to include the "wicked" ruling elite, but only those "humble and poor" that meet the criteria for being members of the ideal community.

Concrete political and military crises are referred to as past events. There is no expectation of a near political and military upheaval. Rather, the text conveys a clear message: The world as it stands will not hold, it will be changed, judgment will be executed, and only thereafter will the world be ready for the ideal future. The agent of these changes will be YHWH; the community, which is not described as politically or militarily active (see esp. Zeph 3:12-13), is asked to wait patiently for this day (Zeph 3:8).

Since the audience of the book, i.e., the historical community, is asked to be actively involved in the reading of the book, and to identify with or relate itself to different characters in the book, an analysis of these characters may suggest some features of the actual community of readers.[9]

---

9 The request to be involved is clearly conveyed by the recurrent use of vocatives and of the address in the second person. Cf. Whitelam, 1984.

Some of these potential characters are related to the described past, some to the described future. The former include YHWH, the prophet, the monarchic society, and the pious group in Zeph 2:3; the latter YHWH, the pious ideal community of the future, and, perhaps, the voice reflected in Zeph 3:16-17—though it may well be an addition, it does not seem to reflect an audience substantially different from the audience of the compositional level. It is self-evident that the sinful monarchic society, and especially its elite ,is not a character playing a positive role model. To the contrary, it points to what ought not to be imitated. The partial identification of the audience with this society fulfills a sense of historical continuity which is rhetorically used to reinforce the already forceful warning conveyed to the post-monarchic audience. Against the background of the disaster brought by YHWH (and only by YHWH) upon the ancestors of the audience, the text claims again and again that YHWH was "innocent" of wrongdoing, that the divine punishment was justified —of course, the logic of this stance leads to a clear stress on the sinful character of the described monarchic society and its elite. The prophet, the main human positive character of his time, is described as the key provider of true knowledge to the monarchic society of his time. A knowledge that could have helped his society to understand the world and change its fate. Regretfully, this society rejected this divine knowledge and brought disaster upon itself. The actual audience of the book had no comparable living figure (the image of Zephaniah in the book is not like the image of its contemporary prophets). But this audience can receive the necessary divine knowledge. Of course, from the standpoint of the readers of the Book of Zephaniah, the author of the book is the key provider of the divine true knowledge, and this author resembles to a certain extent the ancient prophet (see above).

One may assume that among the described groups of the past, the audience could identify itself with the one mentioned in Zeph 2:3. This group is characterized in terms of the ideal society. Cross references link this group and the ideal one who stands in the future (see 3.3.3; 4.3.1). It is described as "humble," and as not having social or political power. The audience is certainly asked to identify itself with the ideal society in Zeph 3:11-13,14-15. Significantly, in this society, not only that the old social-political monarchical elite will have no place, but no other and just social-political elite is mentioned as replacing it. No human (or messianic) just and pious king, officer or judge is referred to; there is no expectation of their coming in the book. None in the audience is called or expected to identify with such social or political roles. The only King in the ideal society will YHWH; the only social group, those humble and poor people who rely only on YHWH and speak no lies. Since the book was written for a certain audience, and assumes that this audience could actually identify itself with this ideal society, then it is reasonable to assume that this audience could understand itself as a post-monarchic group whose horizon and focus is not that of creating (or recreating) a political center of power, a new and just bureaucracy, and the like. Instead, this group centers on set of communally accepted religious attitudes such as total reliance on YHWH, humbleness, truthful speech, and on its "knowledge" that YHWH is just, that will redeem, and will bring the ideal world that the community knows about it by reading the prophetic book.[10]

The present analysis of the Book of Zephaniah does not provide enough evidence for a precise dating of the post-monarchic community in which and for which the Book of Zephaniah was written. The most likely (but very broad) limits are later than the early post-monarchic period and earlier than the Hellenistic period. Further studies on other biblical texts that seem to reflect similar communities (e.g., the *anwim* Psalms, the *malak* Psalms and congregational Psalms), as well as comparative studies with other prophetic books, may shed additional light on this issue.

---

[10] It is worth noting that, the only "particular" voice of the ideal time mentioned in the book is not that of the prophet, or of any prophet, but a self-effacing one. The voice in Zeph 3:16-17 is presented only as reference to and as a reinterpretation of the message of the "original" prophet, the communal source of true knowledge concerning YHWH and the world (see 4.5). Of course, a source that is brought to the community in the form of the book written by the "author" of the compositional level, and later edited and reinterpreted by other "authors."

As the commentary has shown, the existence of the Book of Zephaniah suggests the existence of certain corpora of traditions commonly accepted as Zephanic prior to the compositional level. Moreover, it seems that if the book were to be accepted by a community that was aware of these traditions it had to include at the very least elements of some of them.[11] In other words, the authority of the text relies, partially, on the fact that it is composite, or better, on the fact that it contains or reflects received elements.[12] Of course, from the "fact" that pre-compositional traditions or texts were accepted by a post-monarchic community as Zephanic does not necessarily follow that they actually contained the words, the message of historical "original" prophet, or that they present a historically faithful description of the role of the monarchic prophet.

The analysis of some of the units (e.g., Zeph 1:4-6, 10-11, 3:3-4) shows that to a certain extent one can discern elements of the religious thought and social circumstances of the pre-compositional traditions. It is worth stressing that the analysis has also shown that the pre-compositional traditions are not likely to have come from one single written source,[13] or even reflect a certain set of religious and cultural ideas, or one shared social perspective. To the contrary, the opposite seems true.[14] This study has also pointed out that the hypothesis that the units reflecting pre-compositional material, or some of them, constitute one single Zephanic source is to be rejected (4.2.11). This being the case, the quest for the "original" teaching (or even simple "sayings") of the prophet Zephaniah is an impossible endeavor. The most one may say with any critically convincing weight is that through time certain traditions were attached to the figure of

---

[11] The only alternative is to assume that these traditions were the esoteric knowledge of a closed "Zephanic group." There is no support in the biblical text for such a proposal.

[12] Cf. the synagogal liturgical examples presented in the preliminary remarks of the commentary.

[13] Especially see commentary on chapter 1 but the conclusion expressed in the text is based on the whole notes and commentary sections.

[14] For instance, compare Zeph 3:3-4 with Zeph 1:4-6.

Zephaniah son of Cushi, a prophet who probably lived in the days of
Josiah.

Some of the pre-compositional material underwent some kind of redactional activity before it was integrated into the compositional level of the
Book of Zephaniah. For instance, the criteria for inclusion and exclusion
from the list of nations mentioned in the "Oracles against the Nations"
(OAN) section points to the early post-monarchic period. This date is
consistent with the pattern of occurrence of expressions closely related to
שארית בית יהודה in the announcement against Philistia. The present
analysis has pointed out that שארית בית יהודה points to pre-
compositional material whose contents and language are different from
those that characterize the compositional level, which can be dated,
therefore, as later than the early post-monarchic period.

The present Book of Zephaniah contains not only pre-compositional
material but also post-compositional material.[15] In two cases the latter
concerns the ethical image of YHWH (Zeph 1:3,17) and in one case is related to the issue of theodicy (Zeph 3:5).[16] It seems that these two interrelated questions continued to be the focus of the religious thinking that was
carried out on the basis of the text of the Book of Zephaniah before the text
was completely fixed. Later, exegetical approaches ceased to affect the
Hebrew text, but certainly not its interpretation. The present work is a
contribution to this interpretative endeavor that spans more than two millennia, from the specific perspective of the historical-critical method as described in the methodological guidelines.

---

[15] See, for instance, the notes and commentary on Zeph 1:17 and Zeph 3:5. See also chapter
3.4.13, esp. footnote 251.

[16] See notes and commentary on these verses.

6. Bibliography

Abrabanel, I.

1960   *Prophets and Writings. Perush* [Heb.]. Jerusalem: Elisha.

Allegro, J. M.

1968   *Discoveries in the Judean Desert of Jordan* V. *DJD* V.
        Oxford: Clarendon Press.

Alonso Schökel, L.

1988   *A Manual of Hebrew Poetics.* Subsidia Biblica 11. Roma:
        Editrice Pontificio Istituto Biblico.

Alter, R.

1985   *The Art of Biblical Poetry.* New York: Basic Books.

Altschuler, D. and Altschuler J. H.

1959   *Mezudat David. Mezudat Zion.* According to *Miqraot
        Gedolot.* New York: Tanach Publishing Co.

Amit, Y.

1989   "The Multi-Purpose "Leading Word" and the Problems of its
        Usage." *Prooftexts* 9: 99-114.

Andersen, F. I. and A. D. Forbes

1986   *Spelling in the Hebrew Bible.* BibOr 41. Rome: Biblical
        Institute Press.

Anderson, A. A.

1981   *The Book of Psalms.* 2 vols. NCB. Grand Rapids: Eerdmans/
        London: Marshall, Morgan & Scott.

Anderson, G. A.

1977/78 "The Idea of Remnant in the Book of Zephaniah."*ASTI* 11:
        11-14

Asurmendi, J. M.

1981   "Sofonías y Jerusalén. Análisis estilístico." Pp. 153-69 in R.
Aguirre and F. García Lopez (ed.) *Escritos de Biblia y Oriente*.
Bibliotheca Salamanticensis, Estudios 38. Salamanca: Kadmos.

Aufrecht, W. E.

1988   "Genealogy and History in Ancient Israel." Pp. 205-35 in L.
Eslinger and G. Taylor (ed.) *Ascribed to the Lord. Biblical &
other Studies in Memory of P.C. Craigie*. JSOTSup 67.
Sheffield: JSOT Press.

Avigad, N.

1967   "A group of Hebrew Seals." *Eretz Israel* 9: 1-9 [Heb.].

1978   "Baruch the scribe and Jerahmeel the king's son." *IEJ* 28: 52-56

1981   "New names in Hebrew Seals." *Eretz Israel* 15: 303-6 [Heb.].

1886   *Hebrew Bulae from the time of Jeremiah*. Jerusalem: Israel
Exploration Society.

Ball, I. J.

1972   *A Rhetorical Study of Zephaniah*. Th.D diss., Graduate
Theological Union, Berkeley, CA. Ann Arbor: University
Microfilms.

1988   *A Rhetorical Study of Zephaniah*. Berkely, CA: Bibal Press.

Barr, J.

1961   *The Semantics of Biblical Language*. Oxford: Oxford University
Press.

1968   *Comparative Philology and the Text of the Old Testament*.
Oxford: Clarendon Press.

Barthélemy, D.

1955   *Discoveries in the Judean Desert I. DJD I*. Oxford: Clarendon
Press.

1963   *Les Devanciers d'Aquila*. VTSup10. Leiden: E. J. Brill.

1980   *Preliminary and Interim Report on the Hebrew Old Testament
Project*. Vol 5. *Prophetical Books II. Ezekiel, Daniel, Twelve
Minor Prophets*. New York: United Bible Societies.

Bartlett, J. R.

1989   *Edom and the Edomites*. JSOTSup 77. Sheffield: JSOT Press.

Barton, J.

1984   *Reading the Old Testament. Method in Biblical Study.*
        Philadelphia: Westminster.

Begg, C.

1987   "The Non-mention of Zephaniah, Nahum and Habakkuk in the
        Deuteronomistic History." *BN* 38/9: 19-25.

Bennet, C. M.

1983   "Excavations at Buseirah (Biblical Bozrah)." Pp. 9-17 in J. F.
        A. Sawyer and J. A. Clines (ed) *Midian, Moab, and Edom*.
        JSOTSup 24, Sheffield: JSOT Press.

1984   "Excavations at Tawilan in Southern Jordan, 1982." *Levant* 16:
        1-23.

Bennet, W. H.

1918/9 "Sir J.G.Frazer on 'those that leap over (or on) the threshold."
        Exp. T. 30: 379-380.

Bentzen, A.

1950   "The Ritual Background of Amos i 2- ii 16." *OTS* 8: 85-99.

1961   *Introduction to the Old Testament* . 2 vols. Reprint of the 2nd ed.
        (1952). Copenhagen: G. E. C. Gad.

Benoit, Pierre, J. T. Milik, and R. de Vaux

1961   *Les grottes de Murabba'at*. DJD II. Texts. Oxford: Clarendon.

Ben Zvi, E.

1987   *Judah in the days of the Assyrian Hegemony: History and
        Historiography*. [Heb.] M.A. diss., Tel Aviv University.

1990   "Who Wrote the Speech of Rabshakeh and When?" *JBL* 109:
        79-92.

1991   "Isaiah 1,4-9, Isaiah, and the Events of 701 BCE in Judah. A
        Question of Premise and Evidence." *SJOT* 1: 95-111.

Berlin, A.

1985   *The Dynamics of Biblical Parallelism*. Bloomington: Indiana
        University Press.

Betlyon, J. W.

1986   "The Provincial Goverment of Persian Period Judea and the Yehud Coins." *JBL* 105: 633-42.

Beyerlin, Walter, (ed.)

1978   *Near Eastern Religious Texts Relating to the O.T.* (ET from 1975 ed.) OTL. Philadelphia: Westminster.

Bic, M.

1968   *Trois prophètes dans un temps de ténèbres. Sophonie. Nahum. Habaquq.* LD 48. Paris: Éditions du Cerf.

Blau, J.

1956   "Über homonyme und angeblich homonyme Wurzeln." *VT* 6: 242-48.

Blenkinsopp, J.

1983   *A History of Prophecy in Israel.* Philadelphia: Westminster.

Boadt, L.

1978   "Textual Problems in Ezekiel and Poetic Analysis of Pair Words."*JBL* 97: 489-99.

1982   *Jeremiah 26-52, Habakkuk, Zephaniah, Nahum.* Wilmington, Delaware: M. Glazier.

Borger, R.

1954   "Zu.'ית/שבו שוב.'" *ZAW* 66: 315-16.

Borowski, O.

1987   *Agriculture in Iron Age Israel.* Winona Lake, IN: Eisenbrauns.

Boudreil, P. and A. Lemaire

1979   "Noveau groupe de sceaux hebreux arameens et ammonites." *Semitica* 29: 71-84.

Bowman, S.

1984   "The Meaning of the name Qumran." *RevQ* 11: 543-47.

Bracke, J. M.

1985   "Sub sᵉbut: A Reappraisal." *ZAW* 97: 233-44.

Bright, J

1965   *Jeremiah.* AB 21. Garden City, New York: Doubleday.

1972   *A History of Israel.* Second edition. Philadelphia: Westminster.

Brin, G.

1967 "On the title 'בן המלך'." *Leshonenu* 31: 5-20, 85-96, [Heb.].
(ET *AION* 29 (1969):433 ff.)

Brockington, L. H.

1973 *The Hebrew Text of the Old Testament. The Readings adopted
by the Translators of the New English Bible.* Oxford University
Press/Cambridge University Press.

Broshi, M.

1975 "La population de l'anciennne Jerusalem." *RB* 82: 5-14.

1978 "Estimating the Population of Ancient Jerusalem."*BAR* 4 : 10-15

Bula, M.

1970 "The Book of Zephaniah," in *The Twelve (Trei 'asar).*Jerusalem:
Mosad haRav Kuk [Heb.].

Burns, J. B.

1989 "Hôles(h) 'al in Isaiah 14: 12: A New Proposal," *ZAH* II: 199-
204.

Buss, M. J.

1969 *The Prophetic Word of Hosea. A Morphological Study* BZAW
111. Berlin: Töpelmann.

1978 "The Idea of Sitz im Leben—History and Critique." *ZAW* 90:
157-70.

1981 "An Anthropological Perspective Upon Prophetic Call
Narratives." *Semeia* 21: 9-30.

1981a "On Social and Individual Aspects of Prophecy." *Semeia* 21:
121-24.

Butcher, J. D.

1972 *The Significance of Zephaniah 3: 8-13 for Narrative
Composition in the Early Chapters of the Book of Acts.* Ph. D.
diss. Case Western Reserve University. Ann Arbor, Mich.:
University Microfilms.

CADIR

1976-78 "Rudiments d'analyse narrative I." *Sémiotique et Bible* 1:2-5.
"Rudiments d'analyse narrative II." *Sémiotique et Bible* 2: 2-5.

"Rudiments d'analyse narrative III." *Sémiotique et Bible 3:* 2-3.

"Rudiments d'analyse narrative IV." *Sémiotique et Bible* 4: 3-8.

"Rudiments d'analyse narrative V." *Sémiotique et Bible* 5: 1-6.

"Rudiments d'analyse VI." *Sémiotique et Bible* 6: 1-4.

"Rudiments d'analyse VII." *Sémiotique et Bible* 7: 1-6.

"Rudiments d'analyse VIII ." *Sémiotique et Bible* 8: 1-6.

"Rudiments d'analyse IX." *Sémiotique et Bible* 9: 2-9.

"Rudiments d'analyse X." *Sémiotique et Bible* 10: 1-26

"Rudiments d'analyse XI." *Sémiotique et Bible* 11: 1-6.

"Rudiments d'analyse XII." *Sémiotique et Bible* 12: 1-4.

"Rudiments d'analyse XIII." *Sémiotique et Bible* 13: 2-8.

1977   "Prophétie et manipulation ou le catastrophism optimiste. Analyse sémiotique de livre de Joël." *Sémiotique et Bible* 7:7-29.

Calloud, J.

1979   "A Few Comments on Structural Semiotics. A Brief Review of a Method and Some Explanation of Procedures."*Semeia* 15: 51-83

Calvin, J.

1950   *Commentaries on the Twelve Minor Prophets*, vol. 4, ET J. Owen. Grand Rapids, Michigan: Eerdmans.

Carroll, R. P.

1979   *When Prophecy Failed. Cognitive dissonance in the Prophetic Traditions of the Old Testament*. New York.: The Seabury Press.

1986   *Jeremiah*. OTL. Philadelphia: Westminster.

Cathcart, K. J.

1984   "'Boset' in Zephaniah 3:5." *JNSL* 12: 35-39.

Cazelles, H.

1967   "Sophonie, Jérémie et les Scythes en Palestine." *RB* 74: 24-44.

Cerny, L.

1948   *The Day of Yahweh and Some Relevant Problems*. Prace z vedeckych Ustavu 53. Praze: Nákladem Filosofické Fakulty University Karlovy.

Chang, Y.

1987   *The Theme of Oppression in the Psalms in relation to its occurrence in Prophecy and Ritual.* Ph.D. dissertation, Emory University.

Cheyne, T. C.

1903   "Zephaniah." *Encyclopaedia Biblica* vol. 5: 5402-07. New York: Macmillan.

Childs, B.

1979   *Introduction to the Old Testament as Scripture.* Philadelphia: Fortress.

Christensen, D. L.

1975   *Transformations of the War Oracle in the Old Testament Prophecy: Studies in the Oracles against the Nations.* Missoula, Montana: Scholars Press.

1984   "Zephaniah 2:4-15: A Theological Basis for Josiah's Program of Political Expansion." *CBQ* 46: 669-82.

Clark, D. J.

1981   "Wine on the lees (Zeph 1.12 and Jer 48.11)." *BT* 32: 241-43.

1983   "Of birds and beasts: Zephaniah 2.14." *BT* 34: 243-46.

Clark, D. R.

1984   *The Citations in the Book of Ezekiel: An investigation nto method, audience, and message.* Ph.D. diss. Vanderbilt Univ. Ann Harbor: University Microfilms.

Clark, W. M.

1968   "The Animal Series in the Primeval History." *VT* 18: 433-439.

Clements, R. E.

1982   *Isaiah 1-39.* 2nd ed. NCB. Grand Rapids: Eerdmans/ London: Marshall, Morgan & Scott.

1983   *A Century of Old Testament Study.* Guildford, Surrey: Lutterworth Press.

1985   "Beyond tradition-history. Deutero Isaianic Development of First Isaiah's Themes." *JSOT* 31: 95-113.

Coellin, D. A.

1818   *Spicilegium. Observationum Exegetico-Criticarum ad Zephaniae Vaticinia*. Vratislaviae: Barthii Academics.

Cogan, M.

1974   *Imperialism and Religion: Assyria, Judah and Israel in the Eighth and Seventh Centuries B.C.E.* SBLMS 19. Missoula: Scholars Press.

Cooke, G. A.

1937   *The Book of Ezekiel*. 2 vols. ICC. New York: Scribner's.

Cowley, A.

1923   *Aramaic Papyri of the Fifth Century BC*. Oxford: Clarendon.

Crüseman, F.

1969   *Studien zur Formgeschichte von Hymnus und Danklied in Israel.* WMANT 32. Neukirchener-Vluyn: Neukirchener Verlag.

Daniels, D. R.

1987   "Is there a 'Prophetic Lawsuit' Genre?" *ZAW* 99: 339-60.

Dahood, M.

1957   "Some Northwest Semitic words in Job." *Bib*. 38: 306-320.

1965   *Ugaritic-Hebrew Philology*. BibOr 17. Rome: Pontifical Biblical Institute.

1965-70 *Psalms*. 3 vols. AB 16, 17, 17a. Garden City, NY: Doubleday.

1972   "Hebrew-Ugaritic Lexicography. X" *Bib* 53: 386-403.

Davidson, A. B.

1905   *The Books of Nahum, Habakkuk and Zephaniah*. Cambridge: Cambridge University Press.

Delcor, M.

1978   "Les Kerethim et les Cretois." *VT* 28: 409-22.

Delekat, L.

1964   "Zum hebräischen Wörterbuch." *VT* 14: 7-66.

1964 a   "Probleme der Psalmenüberschriften." *ZAW* 76: 280-97.

Dietrich, E. L.

1925   שוב שבות. *Die endzeitliche Wiederherstellung bei den Propheten*. BZAW 40. Giessen: Töpelmann.

Donner, H.

1970 "Die Schwellenhüpfer. Beobachtungen zu Zeph 1,8f." *JSS* 15: 42-55.

Doran, R.

1986 "Narrative Literature." Pp. 287-310 in R.A. Kraft and W.E. Nickelsburg (ed.), *Early Judaism and its Modern Interpreters.* Atlanta: Scholars Press.

Driver, G. R.

1960 "Abbreviations in the Massoretic Text." *Textus* 1: 112-31.

1964 "Once again Abbreviations." *Textus* 4: 76-94.

Driver, S. R.

1897 *An Introduction to the Literature of the Old Testament.* Edinburgh: T. & T. Clark.

Duhm, B.

1910 *Die zwölf Propheten.* Tübingen: J. C. B. Mohr.

Eco, U.

1986 *La estructura ausente. Introducción a la semiótica.* (tercera edición). Barcelona: Lumen.

Edens, A.

1954 *A Study of the Book of Zephaniah as to the Date, Extent and Significance of the Genuine Writings.* PhD Diss. Vanderbilt University. Ann Arbor, Michigan: University Microfilms.

Edler, R.

1984 *Das Kerygma des Propheten Zefanja.* Freiburg Theologische Studien 116. Breisgau: Herder.

Ehrlich, A. B.

1969 *Miqrâ ki Pheschutô.* Vol. III. (First. Pub. 1901). New York: Ktav [Heb.].

Eichrodt, W.

1979 *Ezekiel.* OTL. London: SCM Press.

Eiselen, F. C.

1907 *The Minor Prophets.* Commentary on the Old Testament vol. IX. New York: Eaton & Mains/ Cincinnati: Jennings & Graham.

Eissfeldt, O.

1965   *The Old Testament. An Introduction.* ET P. Ackroyd. New York
        and Evanston: Harper & Row.

Elliger, K.

1950   "Das Ende der 'Abendwölfe' Zeph 3,3 Hab 1,8." Pp. 158-75 in
        W. Baumgartner, O. Eissfeldt, K. Elliger and L.Rost (ed.) *FS
        A. Bertholet,* Tübingen: J. C. B. Mohr.

1951   *Das Buch der zwölf Kleinen Propheten.* ATD 25/ II. Göttingen:
        Vandenhoeck and Ruprecht.

Everson, A. J.

1974   "The Days of Yahweh." *JBL* 93: 329-37.

Fensham, F. C.

1967   "A Possible Origin of the Day of the Lord." *OTWSA* 2: 90-97.
        "The Poetic Form of the Hymn of the Day of the Lord in
        Zephaniah." *OTWSA* 13/14: 9-14.

Fenton, W. N. (ed.)

1968   *Parker on the Iroquois.* Syracuse, NY: Syracuse Univ. Press.

Fishbane, M.

1988   *Biblical Interpretation in Ancient Israel.* Oxford: Clarendon.

Fitzmayer, J. A. and D. J. Harrington

1978   *A Manual of Palestinian Aramaic Texts.* Rome: Biblical Institute
        Press.

Florit, D. E.

1934   "Sofonia, Geremia e la cronaca di Gadd." *Bib* 15: 8- 31.

Fohrer, G.

1970   *Introduction to the Old Testament.* (ET from 10th ed.[1965]).
        London: SPCK.

1982   "Der Tag Jhwhs." *EI* 16: 43*-50*.

Frazer, J. G.

1923   *Folk Lore in the Old Testament.* London : Mc Millan.

Fredericks, D. C.

1988   *Qohelet's Language. Re-evaluating its Nature and Date*. Ancient
        Near Eastern Texts and Studies 3. Lewiston/Queenston, Ontario:
        The Edwin Mellen Press.

Freedy, K. S. and D. B. Redford

1970   "The Dates in Ezekiel in relation to Biblical, Babylonian and
        Egyptian Sources." *JAOS* 90: 462-85.

Fritz, V.

1980   "The Meaning of the word 'HAMMAN/HMN'." *Folia Orientalia*
        21: 103-115.

Garscha, J.

1974   *Studiem zum Ezechielbuch*. Bern/Frankfurt: H. Lang/P. Lang.

Gaster, T. H.

1966/7 "Zephaniah iii.17." *ExpTim* 78: 267.

1969   *Myth, Legend and Custom in the Old Testament. A comparative
        study with chapters of Sir James G. Frazer's Folklore in the Old
        Testament*. New York and Evanston: Harper & Row.

Gelston, A.

1980 (ed.)*The Old Testament in Syriac. According to the Peshitta.
        Dodekapropheton*. The Peshitta Institute. Leiden: E. J. Brill.

1987   *The Peshitta of the Twelve Prophets*. Oxford: Clarendon.

George, A.

1958   *Michée, Sophonie, Nahum*. La Sainte Bible. Paris: du Cerf.

Gerleman, G.

1942   *Zephanja. Textkritisch und literary Untersucht*. Lund: Gleerup.

1973   "Review, L. Sabottka, Zephanja." *VT* 23: 252-3.

Gerstenberger, E. S.

1962   "The Woe-Oracles of the Prophets" *JBL* 81 :249-63.

1985   "The Lyrical Literature." Pp. 409-44 in Knight D.A. and G.M.
        Tucker (ed.), *The Hebrew Bible and its Modern Interpreters*,
        Philadelphia: Fortress/ Chico, California: Scholars Press.

1988   *Psalms. Part I*. FOTL 14. Grand Rapids, Michigan: Eerdmans.

Gese, H.

1962   "Zephanjabuch." *RGG³*, 1901-2.

Gevirtz, S.

1963   "Jericho and Shechem: A Religio-Literary Aspect of City
Destruction." *VT* 13: 52-62.

1972   "On Canaanite Rhetoric. The Evidence of the Amarna Letters
from Tyre." *Or* 42: 162-77.

Geyer, J. B.

1986   "Mythology and Culture in the Oracles Against the Nations." *VT*
36: 129-45.

Gibson, J. C. L.

1971   *Textbook of Syrian Semitic Inscriptions. Vol 1. Hebrew and
Moabite Inscriptions.* Oxford: Clarendon.

Ginsberg, H. L

1950   "Some Emendations in Isaiah." *JBL* 69: 51-60.

1953   "Gleanings in First Isaiah." Pp 245-59 in *Mordecai M. Kaplan
Jubilee Volume on the occasion of his seventieth birthday.*
English section. New York: JTS.

Gitin, S.

1987   "Urban Growth and Decline at Ekron in the Iron II Period." *BA*
50: 206-22.

Gordis, R.

1987   "A Rising Tide of Misery: A Note on a Note on Zephaniah II 4."
VT 37: 487-90.

Gozzo, S. M.

1977   "Il propheta Sofonia e la dottrina teologica del suo libro." *Anton*
52: 3-37.

Gray, J.

1953   "A Metaphor from Building in Zephaniah II:1." *VT* 3: 404-407.

1970   *I and II Kings.* 2nd ed. OTL. Philadelphia: Westminster.

Greenberg, M.

1983   *Ezekiel 1-20.* AB 22. Garden City, NY: Doubleday.

van Grol, H. W. M.

1988   "Classical Hebrew Metrics and Zephaniah 2-3." Pp. 186-206 in
        W. van der Meer & J.C. de Moor (ed.) *The Structural Analysis
        of Biblical and Canaanite Poetry*. JSOTSup 74. Sheffield: JSOT
        Press.

Hacket, J. A.

1984   *The Balaam Text from Deir 'Alla*. Chico, California: Scholars
        Press.

Halpern, B.

1988   *The First Historians. The Hebrew Bible and History*. San
        Francisco: Harper & Row.

Hamborg, G. R.

1981   "Reasons for Judgment in the Oracles against the Nations of the
        Prophet Isaiah." *VT* 31: 145-59.

Hare, D. R. A.

1985   "The Lives of the Prophets." Pp. 379-99 in J. H.
        Charlesworth, *The Old Testament Pseudepigrapha.*. Vol II,
        Garden City, NY: Doubleday.

Hayes, J. H.

1968   "The Usage of Oracles Against Foreign Nations in Ancient
        Israel." *JBL* 87: 81-92.

1973   "A History of the Form-Critical Study of Prophecy." *SBLSP* 1:
        60-99.

1988   *Amos, the eighth-century prophet, his time and his preaching*.
        Nashville: Abingdon.

Hayes, J. H. and P. K. Hooker

1988   *A New Chronology for the Kings of Israel and Judah and its
        implications for Biblical History and Literature*. Atlanta: Knox.

Hayes, J. H. and S. A. Irvine

1987   *Isaiah, his time, and his preaching*. Nashville: Abingdon.

Heller, J.

1971   "Zephanjas Ahnenreihe, Eine redaktionsgeschichliche
        Bemerkung zu Zeph I,1." *VT* 21: 102-4.

Heider, G. C.

1985   *The Cult of Molek.* JSOTSup. 43. Sheffield: JSOT Press.

Herbrechtsmeier, W.

1987   *The Biblical Legacy of Religious Violence: The Evolution of Deuteronomic Law and Israelite Religious Culture.* Ph.D. Diss. Columbia Univ.. Ann Arbor, Michigan: University Microfilms.

Hillers, D. R.

1983   "Hôy and Hôy-Oracles: A Neglected Syntactic Aspect." Pp. 185-88 in C. L. Meyers and M. O'Connor (ed), *The Word of the Lord Shall Go Forth. Essays in Honor of David Noel Freedman in Celebration of His Sixtieth Birthday.* Winona Lake, Indiana: Eisenbrauns.

1984   *Micah.* Hermeneia. Philadelphia: Fortress.

Histrin, R. and D. Mendels

1978   *Hebrew, Ammonite, Moabite, Phoenician Seals from the First Temple Period.* Jerusalem: Museum Israel.

Hoffmann, Y.

1981   "The Day of the Lord as a Concept and a Term in the Prophetic Literature." *ZAW* 93: 37-50.

1982   "The Root QRB as a Legal Term." *JNSL* 10: 67-73.

1982 a "From Oracle to Prophecy: The Growth, Crystallization and Disintegration of a Biblical Gattung." *JNSL* 10: 75-81

Holladay, W. L.

1958   *The Root Subh in the Old Testament with Particular References to its Usages in Covenantal Contexts.* Leiden: Brill.

1986   *Jeremiah 1.* Hermeneia. Philadelphia: Fortress.

Hollenstein, H.

1977   "Literarkritische Erwägungen zum Bericht über die Reformmassnahmen Josias 2 Kön. xxiii.4ff." *VT* 27: 321-36.

Horgan, M. P.

1979   *Pesharim: Qumran Interpretations of Biblical Books.* CBQMS 8. Washington, DC: The Catholic Biblical Association of America.

1986 "The Bible Explained (Prophecies)." Pp. 247-53 in R. A. Kraft and G.W.E. Nickelsburg (ed.), *Early Judaism and its Modern Interpreters*. Atlanta: Scholars Press.

House, P. R.

1988 *Zephaniah. A Prophetic Drama*. JSOTSup 69. Sheffield: Almond

Hrushovski, B.

1971 "Prosody, Hebrew. Some Principles of Biblical Verse." *Encyclopaedia Judaica* 13: 1200-1202.

Hunter, A.V.

1982 *Seek the Lord! A Study of the Meaning and Function of the Exhortations in Amos, Isaiah, Micah, and Zephaniah*. Diss. Basel. Baltimore, Maryland: J. D. Lucas Printing Co.

Hurvitz, A.

1988 "Wisdom Vocabulary in the Hebrew Psalter." *VT*: 41-51.

Hyatt, J. P.

1948 "The Date and Background of Zephaniah." *JNES* 7: 25-29.

Ibn Ezra, A.

1959 *Commentary*. According to *Miqraot Gedolot*. New York: Tanach Publishing Co.

Irohmi,

1983 "Die Häufung der Verben des Jublens in Zephanja III14 f., 16-18." *VT* 33: 106-109.

Irsigler, H.

1977 *Gottesgericht und Jahwetag. Die Komposition Zef 1,1-2,3, untersucht auf der Grundlage der Literarkritik des Zefanjabuches*. ATSAT 3. St. Ottilien.

1977 a "Äquivalenz in Poesie. Die kontextuellen Synonyme sa'qa-yalala-sibr gadu(w)l in Zef 1,10c.d.e." *BZ* 22: 221-35.

Jeppesen, K.

1981 "Zephaniah i 5b. *VT* 31: 372-73.

Jolles, A.

1958 *Einfache Formen*. Zweite Auflage. Darmstadt: Wissenschaftliche Buchgesellschaft.

Jones, D.

1955   "The Traditio of the Oracles of Isaiah of Jerusalem." *ZAW* 67:
        226-246.

Jones, G. H.

1984   *I and II Kings*. NBC. Grand Rapids, Michigan: Eedermans/
        London: Marshall, Morgan & Scott.

Jongeling, B.

1971   "Jeux de mots en Sophonie III 1 et 3?" *VT* 21: 541- 47.

Kaiser, O.

1983   *Isaiah 1-12*. (Rev. ed.) OTL. Philadelphia: Westminster.

Kang, S.

1989   *Divine War in the Old Testament and in the Ancient Near East*.
        BZAW 177. Berlin/New York: Walter de Gruyter.

Kapelrud, A. S.

1975   *The message of the prophet Zephaniah. Morphologie and Ideas*.
        Oslo: Universitetsforlaget.

1984   "The Traditio-Historical Study of the Prophets." Pp. 53-66 in
        Jeppesen K. and B. Otzen, *The Productions of Time. Tradition
        History in Old Testament Scholarship*. Sheffield: Almond Press.

Kara, J.

1964   *Commentary*. According to *Miqraot Gedolot* with Malbim's
        Commentary (ed. by R. J. and A. Buch). Jerusalem: Re'em.

Kauffmann, Y.

1938-56 *Toldot haEmunah haIsraelit*. 4 vols. Tel Aviv: Debir [Heb.].

1960   *The Religion of Israel: From its Beginnings to the Babylonian
        Exile*. Trans. and abridged by M. Greenberg. New York: Schocken.

Keller, C. A.

1971   *Nahoum, Habacuc, Sophonie*. CAT 11/b. Neuchâtel: Delachaux
        et Niestle.

Knierim, R.

1985   "Criticism of Literary Features, Form, Tradition, and
        Redaction." Pp. 123-65 in Knight D.A. and G.M.Tucker (ed.),

The Hebrew Bible and its Modern Interpreters, Phildadelphia:
Fortress/Chico, California: Scholars Press.

Knight, D.A.

1975 *Rediscovering the Traditions of Israel*. Rev. ed. SBLDS 9.
Missoula, MT: Scholars Press.

Krasovec, J.

1977 *Der Merismus im Biblisch-Hebräischen und
Nordwestsemitischen*. BibOr 33. Rome: Biblical Institute Press.

1983 "Merism - Polar Expression in Biblical Hebrew." *Bib* 64:
231-39.

Kraus, H. J.

1978 *Psalmen*. (5th. ed.) BKAT 15/1-2. Neukirchen- Vluyn:
Neukirchener Verlag.

Krinetzki, G.

1977 *Zefanjastudien. Motiv- und Traditionskritik +Kompositions-und
Redaktionskritik*. Regensburger Studien zu Theologie 7. Bern:
Herbert Lang.

Koch, K.

1982 *The Prophets. The Assyrian Period*. Philadelphia: Fortress.

Köhler, L

1940/41 "Hebräische Vokabeln III." *ZAW* 58: 228-34.

Koenen, L.

1970 "The Prophecies of a Potter: A Prophecy of World
Renewal becomes an Apocalypse." *Proceedings of the XII
International Congress of Papyrology*: 249-254.

Kselman, J. S.

1970 "A Note on Jer 49,20 and Ze 2,6-7." *CBQ* 32: 579-81.

Kugel, J. L.

1981 *The Idea of Biblical Poetry. Parallelism and its History*. New
Haven/London: Yale University Press.

Kühner, H.

1943 *Zephanja*. Zürich: Zwingli Verlag.

Kutler, L.

1984   "A 'Strong' case for the Hebrew 'MAR'." *UF* 16: 111-18.

Kutscher, R.

1982   *A History of the Hebrew Language*. Jerusalem: Magnes/ Leiden:
         E. J. Brill.

Lande, I.

1949   *Formelhafte Wendungen der Umgangssprache im Alten
         Testament*. Leiden: E. J. Brill.

Langhor, G.

1976   "Le livre Sophonie et la critique d'authenticité." *ETL* 52: 1-27.

1976 a   "Rédaction and composition du livre Sopohonie." *Le Muséon*
         89:51-73

Lawton, R.

1984   "Israelite Personal Names on pre-exilic Hebrew inscriptions."
         Bib 65: 330-346.

Leeuwen, C. van

1974   "The Prophecy of the YOM YHWH in Amos V 18- 20." *OTS*
         19: 113-34.

Lemaire, A.

1979   "Note sur le titre "BN HMLK" dans l'Ancient Israel." *Semitica*
         29: 59-65.

1985   "Fragments from the Book of Balaam found at Deir Alla." *BAR*
         11.5: 27-39.

Levenson, J. D.

1975   "Who inserted the Book of Torah?" *HTR* 68: 203-33.

Lipínski, E.

1975   "Review, A. S. Kapelrud, The message of the prophet
         Zephaniah." *VT* 25: 688-690.

Lods, A.

1937   *The Prophets and the Rise of Judaism*. ET S. H. Hooke. New
         York: E. P. Dutton.

Lohfink, N.

1984   "Zephanja und das Israel der Armen." *BK* 39: 100-08.

1986 "Von der 'Anawim-Partei' zur 'Kirche der Armen'." *Bib* 67: 153-75

1987 *Option for the Poor. The Basic Principle of Liberation Theology in the Light of the Bible.* Berkeley, California: Bibal Press.

Long, B.

1981 "Social Dimensions of Prophetic Conflict." *Semeia* 21: 31-54.

1981 a "Perils General and Particular." *Semeia* 21: 125-28.

Longman, T.

1982 "A Critique of Two Recent Metrical Systems." *Bib*: 63: 230-45.

Loretz, O.

1959 "Kleinere Beiträge." *BZ* 3: 290-94.

1973 "Textologie des Zephanja-Buches." *UF* 5: 219-28.

1979 *Die Psalmen.* AOAT 207. Neukirchen-Vluyn: Neukirchener Verlag.

Loewenstamm, S. E.

1959 "The Hebrew root חרשׁ in the light of the Ugarit texts." *JJS* 10: 63-65.

Luther, M.

1975 *Luther's Works. Vol. 18. Lectures on the Minor Prophets I.* Saint Louis: Concordia Publishing House.

Martin-Achard, R.

1965 "Yahwé et les 'anawim." *ThZ* 21: 349-57.

1976 "ענה 'nh II" *THAT* II: 341-50.

Martin, F.

1985 "Le Livre de Sophonie." *Sémiotique et Bible* 39: 1-22; 40: 5-20.

Mayes, A.D.H.

1978 "King and Covenant: a study of 2 Kings chs 22-23." *Hermathena* 125: 34-47.

1981 *Deuteronomy.* NCB. Grand Rapids: Eerdmans/ London: Marshall, Morgan & Scott.

Mays, J. L.

1969 *Amos.* OTL. London: SCM Press.

1969 a *Hosea.* OTL. London: SCM Press.

1976   *Micah*. OTL. Philadelphia: Westminster Press.

Mc Carter, P. Kyle Jr.

1980   "The Balaam Texts from Deir 'Alla: The First Combination."
           BASOR 239: 49-60.

Mc Gregor, L. J.

1985   *The Greek Text of Ezekiel*. SBLSCS 18. Atlanta: Scholars Press

Mc Kane, W.

1967   "The Interpretation of Isaiah VII 14-25." VT 17: 208-19.

1986   *Jeremiah I. Introduction and Commentary on Jer I-*
           XXV. ICC. Edinburgh: T. & T. Clark.

Meek, T. J.

1955   "Result and Purpose Clauses in Hebrew." *JQR* 46: 40-43.

Melammed, E. Z.

1961   "Break-up of Stereotype Phrases as an Artistic Device in Biblical
           Poetry." Pp. 115-153 in *Scripta Hierosolymitana* 8, Jerusalem:
           Magness Press.

1978   *Bible Commentators*. 2 vols. [Heb.]. Jerusalem: Magnes Press.

Meyer, R.

1966-72 *Hebräische Grammatik*. 4 vols. Berlin: W. de Gruyter.

Meyerhoff, H. (ed.)

1959   *The Philosophy of History in Our Time*. Garden City, NY:
           Doubleday.

Michaeli, F.

1967   *Les livres des Chroniques, d'Esdras et de Nehemie*. CAT 16.
           Neuchâtel: Delachaux et Niestle.

Milgrom, J.

1976   "Sanctification." *IDBSup*: 782-84.

1976a   "Prophane Slaughter and a Formulaic Key to the Composition of
           Deuteronomy." *HUCA* 47: 1-17.

Miller, J. M.

1976   *The Old Testament and the Historian*. Philadelphia: Fortress.

Miller, J. M. and J. H. Hayes
1986   *A History of Ancient Israel and Judah.* Philadelphia:
        Westminster.
Miller, P. D.
1973   *The Divine Warrior in Early Israel.* Cambridge: Harvard
        University Press.
Montgomery, J. A. and H. S. Gehman
1951   *The Books of Kings.* ICC. Edinburgh: T. & T. Clark.
Mowinckel, S.
1946   *Prophecy and Tradition.* Oslo: A.W. Brøggers Boktrykkeri.
Muilenburg, J.
1961   "The Linguistic and Rhetorical Usages of the Particle כי in the
        Old Testament. *HUCA* 32: 135-60.
Myers, J. M.
1965   *Ezra, Nehemiah.* AB 14. Garden City, NY: Doubleday.
Na'aman, N.
1986   "The Negev in the Last Days of the Kingdom of Judah."
        Cathedra 41: 4-15 (Heb.).
Naveh, J.
1962   "The excavations at Mesad Hashavyahu. Preliminary Report."
        IEJ 12: 89-113.
Nickelsburg, G. W. E.
1981   *Jewish Literature Between the Bible and the Mishnah.*
        Philadelphia: Fortress.
Nicolsky, N. M.
1927   "Pascha im Kulte des jerusalemischen Tempels." *ZAW* 45: 174-
        90, 241-53.
O'Connor, M.
1980   *Hebrew Verse Structure.* Winona Lake, Indiana: Eisenbrauns.
Oeming, M.
1987   "Gericht Gottes und Geschicke der Völker nach Zef 3, 1-13."
        TQ 167: 289-300.

Oesterley, W. O. E.

1904   "Notes and Studies. The Old Latin Texts of the Minor Prophets."
        JTS 5: 76-88, 242-53, 378-86, 570-79.

Ogden, G. S.

1982   "Prophetic Oracles Against Foreign Nations and Psalms of
        Communal Lament: The Relationship of Psalm 137 to Jeremiah
        49: 7-22 and Obadiah." *JSOT* 24: 89-97.

Olivier, J. P. J.

1980   "A Possible Interpretation of the Word 'syya' in Zeph. 2. 13."
        JNSL 8: 95-97.

Olmo Lete, G. del

1973   "El libro de Sofonías y la filología semítica nor-occidental."
        EstBib 32: 291-303.

Overholt, T. W.

1981   "Prophecy: The Problem of Cross-Cultural Comparison."
        Semeia 21: 55-78.

1981a   "Model, Meaning and Necessity." *Semeia* 21: 129-30.

1988   "The End of Prophecy: No Players without a Program." *JSOT*
        42: 103-15.

Pardee, D.

1974   "Review. Zephanja: Versuch einer Neuübersetzung mit
        philologischen Kommentar, by L. Sabottka." *JAOS* 94: 506-09.

Parker, R. A. and W. H. Dubberstein

1956   *Babylonian Chronology: 626 BC-AD 75*. Providence: Brown
        University Press.

Petersen, D. L.

1977   *Late Israelite Prophecy: Studies in Deutero-Prophetic Literature
        and in Chronicles*. SBLMS 23.Missoula, Montana: Scholars
        Press.

1981   *The Role of Israel's Prophets*. JSOTSup. 17. Sheffield: JSOT
        Press.

Petersen, J. E.

1970   *The use of the Divine Name in the Greek Version of the Minor
        Prophets with comparison of the readings in the Aramaic
        Targum.* Ph.D. diss. New York Univ. Ann Arbor, Michigan:
        University Microfilms.

Pfeiffer, R. H.

1948   *Introduction to the Old Testament.* New York: Harper.

Polzin, R.

1976   *Late Biblical Hebrew: Toward an Historical Typology of
        Biblical Hebrew Prose.* HSM 12. Missoula, MT: Scholars
        Press.

Pope, M.

1965   *Job.* AB 15. Garden City, NY: Doubleday.

Porten, B.

1981   "The identity of King Adon." *BA* 44: 36-52.

Rabin, Ch.

1961   "Etymological Miscellanea." Pp. 384-400 in *Scripta
        Hierosolymitana* 8, Jerusalem: Magness Press.

von Rad, G.

1959   "The Origin of the Concept of the Day of Yahweh." *JSS* 4: 97-
        108.

Radak

1959   *Commentary.* According to *Miqraot Gedolot.* New York:
        Tanach Publishing Co.

Rainey, A.

1975   "The Prince and the Pauper." *UF* 7 : 427-432.

Raitt, T. M.

1971   "The Prophetic Summons to Repetance." *ZAW* 83: 30-49.

1977   *A Theology of Exile.* Philadelphia: Fortress.

Ramsey, G. W.

1977   "Speech-Forms in Hebrew Law and Prophetic Oracles." *JBL* 96:
        45-58.

Rashi

1959   *Commentary*. According to *Miqraot Gedolot*. New York:
         Tanach Publishing Co.

Reade, J.

1970   "The Accession of Sinsharishkun." *JCS* 23: 1-9.

Redford, D. B.

1970   *A Study of the Biblical Story of Joseph*. SVT 20. Leiden: Brill.

Reid, S.

1985   "The End of the Prophecy in the Light of Contemporary Social
         Theory: A Draft." *SBLSP* 24: 515-23.

Reiner, E.

1958   *Surpu. A Collection of Sumerian and Akkadian Incantations*.
         AfO 11. Graz: Selbstverlage des Herausgebers.

Renaud, B.

1977   *La formation du livre de Michée*. Paris: J. Gabalda.

1986   "Le livre de Sophonie. Le jour de YHWH thème structurant de a
         synthèse rédactionelle." *RevScRel* 60:1-33.

Rendtorff, R.

1954   "Zum Gebrauch der Formel ne'um Jahweh in Jeremiabuch."
         ZAW 66: 27-37.

1986   *The Old Testament*. An Introduction. Philadelphia: Fortress.

Ribera Florit, J.

1982   "La versión aramaica del Profeta Sofonías." *EstBib* 40: 127-58.

Rice, G.

1979   "The African Roots of the Prophet Zephaniah." *JRT* 36: 21-31.

Richter, W.

1971   *Exegese als Literaturswissenschaft*. Göttingen: Vandenhoeck &
         Ruprecht.

Rimbach, J. A.

1972   *Animal Imagery in the Old Testament: Some Aspects of Hebrew
         Poetics*. Ph. D. diss. John Hopkins University. Ann Arbor,
         Michigan: University Microfilms.

1980 "Those Lively Prophets- Zephanjah Ben-Cushi." *CurTM* 7: 239-42.

Robbins, V. K.

(forthcoming) "The Social Location of the Implied Author of Luke-Acts." In J. H. Neyrey (ed.), *The Social World of Luke-Acts: Models of Interpretation*. Peabody, MA: Hendrickson.

Roberts, J. J. M.

1982 "Form, Syntax, and Redaction in Isaiah I: 2-20." *Princeton Seminary Bulletin* 3: 293-306.

Roche, M. de

1980 "Zephaniah I 2-3: The 'Sweeping' of the Creation." *VT* 30: 104-09.

1980 a "Contra Creation, Covenant and Conquest (Jer. viii 13)." *VT* 30: 280-90.

Rofé, A.

1979 *The Belief in Angels in Israel*. Jerusalem: Makor [Heb.].

1982 *Introduction to Deuteronomy. Further Chapters*. Jerusalem: Academon Publishing House [Heb.].

1982 a *The Prophetical Stories*. Jerusalem: Magnes [Heb.]

1988 "The Vineyard of Naboth: The origin and message of the story." *VT* 38: 89-104.

1988 a *The Prophetical Stories: The Narratives about the Prophets in the Hebrew Bible. Their Literary Types and History*. Jerusalem: Magnes.

Rose, M.

1977 "Bemerkungen zum historischen Fundament des Josia-Bildes in II Reg 22f." *ZAW* 89: 50-63.

1981 " 'Atheismus' als Wohlstandserscheinung? (Zephanja1,12)." *TZ* 37: 193-208.

Rudolph, W.

1949 *Esra und Nehemia*. HAT 20. Tübingen: Mohr.

1971 *Joel-Amos-Obadja-Jona*. KAT 13/2. Gütersloh: Gütersloher Verlaghaus Gerd Mohn.

1975   *Micha-Nahum-Habakuk-Zephanja.* KAT 13/4. Neukirchen-
        Vluyn: Neukirchener Verlag.

Sabottka, L.

1972   *Zephanja, Versuch einer Neuübersetzung mit philogischem*
        Kommentar. BibOr 25. Rome: Pontificial Biblical Institute.

Sandmel, S.

1963   *The Hebrew Scriptures. An Introduction to their Literature and*
        Religious Ideas. New York: A. Knopf.

Scharbert, J.

1982   "Zefanja und die Reform des Joschija." Pp 237-53 in *Künder*
        des Vortes. Beiträge zur der Theologie der Propheten (FS J.
        Schreiner), Wurzburg: Echter.

Schneider, D. A.

1979   *The Unity of the Book of Twelve.* Ph. D. diss. Yale, Ann
        Arbor, Mich.: University Microfilms.

Sellin, E.

1922   *Das Zwölfprophetenbuch übersetz und erklärt.* KAT 12/2.
        Leipzig: Deichertsche Verlagsbuchhandlung Dr. Werner Scholl.

Seybold, K.

1984   "Text und Textauslegung in Zef 2,1-3." *BN* 25: 49-54.

1985   *Satirische Prophetie. Studien zum Buch Zefanja.* SBS 120.
        Stuttgart: Verlag Katolisches Bibelwerk GmbH.

1985 a "Die Verwendung der Bildmotive in der Prophetie Zefanjas," in
        Weippert H., Seybold K. and Weippert M., *Beiträge zur*
        Bildsprache in Israel und Assyrien, OBO 64,Freiburg/
        Göttingen: Universitätsverlag/ Vandenhoeck & Ruprecht.

Shilo, Y.

1980   "The Population of Iron Age Palestine in the Light of a Sample
        Analysis of Urban Plans, Areas and Population Density."
        BASOR 239: 25-35.

Sivan, D.

1984   *Grammatical Analysis and Glossary of the Northwest Semitic*
        Vocables in Akk. texts of the 15th-13th Century BC. AOAT

214. Kevelaer: Butzon u. Berger-Neukirchen-Vluyn:
Neukirchener Verlag.

Smith, G. A.

1929   *The Book of Twelve.* Vol 2. Garden City, NY: Doubleday,
Doran and Co.

Smith, J. M. P.

1911   "Zephaniah." Pp. 159-263 in *Micah, Zephaniah, Nahum,
Habakkuk, Obadiah and Joel.* ICC. New York: Charles
Schribner's Sons.

Smith, L. P. and E. R. Lacheman

1950   "The Authorship of the Book of Zephaniah." *JNES* 9: 137-142.

Smith, R. L.

1984   *Micah-Malachi.* WBC 32. Waco, Texas:Word.

Snaith, N. H.

1964   "The Meaning of the Hebrew אַף." *VT* 14: 221-25.

Soggin, A.

1976   "Sub-שׁוּב zurückkehren." *THAT* II: 886-92.

1980   *Introduction to the Old Testament.* (ET from 3rd Italian ed.)
OTL. Philadelphia: Westminster Press.

Spalinger, A. J.

1973   "The Year 712 B.C. and its Implications for Egyptian History."
JARCE 10: 95-101.

1974   "Assurbanipal and Egypt: A Source Study." *JAOS* 94: 316-28.

1974 a   "Esarhaddon and Egypt: An analysis of the First Invasion of
Egypt." *Or* 43: 295-326.

1976   "Psammetichus, King of Egypt: I." *JARCE* 13: 133-47.

1977   "Egypt and Babylonia: A Survey (c. 620 B.C. - 550 B.C.)
SAK 5: 228-44.

1978   "Psammetichus, King of Egypt: II." *JARCE* 15: 49-57.

1978 a   "The Date of the Death of Gyges and its Historical Implications."
JAOS 98: 400-09.

1978 c   "The Concept of the Monarchy during the Saite Epoche—an
Essay of Synthesis." *Or* 47: 12-36.

Sperber, A.

1966   *A Historical Grammar of Biblical Hebrew.* Leiden: E. J. Brill.

Spieckerman, H.

1982   *Juda unter Assur in der Sargonidzeit.* Frlant 129. Göttingen:
        Vanderhoeck & Ruprecht.

Stenzel, M.

1951   "Zum Verständnis von Zeph. III 3B." *VT* 1:303-305.

Strugnell, J.

1970   "Notes in marge du volume V, DJD." *RevQ* 7: 153-276.

Stuhlmacher, C

1986   "Justice toward the Poor." *TBT* 24: 385-90.

Sweeney, M. A.

1988   *Isaiah 1-4 and the Post-exilic Understanding of the Isaianic
        Tradition.* BZAW 171. Berlin/New York: de Gruyter.

Talmon, S.

1960   "Double Readings in the Masoretic Text." *Textus* 1: 144-   84.

1976   "Conflate Readings (OT)." *IDBSup*: 170-73.

Taylor, C. L.

1956   "The Book of Zephaniah." Pp. 1007-34 in *IB* Vol 6.

Thomas, D. W.

1962-63 "A Pun on the Name Ashdod in Zephaniah ii.4." *ExpT* 74: 63.

Thompson, J. A.

1974   "The Date of Joel." Pp. 453-64 in H. N. Bream, R. D. Heim
        and C. A. Moore (ed.), *A Light unto My Path. Old Testament
        Studies in Honor of Jacob M. Myers.* Philadelphia: Temple
        University Press.

Thompson, M. E. W.

1982   *Situation and Theology. Old Testament Interpretations of the
        Syro-Ephraimite War.* Sheffield: Almond Press.

Tigay, J. H

1985   "Conflation as a Redactional Technique." Pp. 53-95 in J. H.
        Tigay (ed.) *Empirical Models for Biblical Criticism.*
        Philadelphia: Univ. of Pennsylvania Press.

1986 *You Shall Have No Oher Gods: Israelite Religion in the Light of Hebrew Inscriptions.* HSS 31. Atlanta: Scholars Press.

van der Toorn, K.

1988 "Ordeal Procedures in the Psalms and the Passover Meal." *VT* 38: 427-45.

Torrey, C. C.

1946 *The Lives of the Prophets. Greek Text and Translation.* SBLMS 1, Philadelphia: SBL.

Tucker, G. M.

1971 *Form Criticism of the Old Testament.* Philadelphia: Fortress.

1977 "Prophetic superscriptions and the growth of a canon." Pp. 56-70 in B.O.Long and G. W. Coats (ed.), *Canon and Authority: Essay in Old Testament Religion and Theology.* Philadelphia: Fortress

1978 "Prophetic Speech" *Int* 32: 31-45.

1985 "Prophecy and Prophetic Literature." Pp. 325-368 in D.A. Knight and G.M. Tucker (ed.), *The Hebrew Bible and its Modern Interpreters.* Philadelphia: Fortress/Chico:Scholars Press

de Vaux, R.

1965 *Ancient Israel.* 2 vols. (2nd ed.). New York: Mc Graw-Hill.

Vermeylen, J.

1977-78 *Du Prophète Isaïe a l'Apocalyptique* Vols I- II Ebib. Paris: Librairie LeCoffre.

Wagner, M.

1966 *Die lexikalischen und grammatikalischen Aramaismen m alttestamentliche Hebräisch.* BZAW 96. Berlin: de Gruyter.

Wallace, A. F. C.

1970 *The Death and Rebirth of the Seneca.* New York: A. A. Knopf.

Watson, W. G. E.

1976 "Review. L. Sabottka, Zephanja." *Bib* 53: 270-71.

1988 "Some Additional Word Pairs." Pp. 179-201 in L. Eslinger and G. Taylor (ed.) *Ascribed to the Lord. Biblical & other Studies in Memory of P.C. Craigie.* JSOTSup 67. Sheffield: JSOT Press.

Watts, J. D. W.

1965   "Yahweh Malak Psalms". *ThZ* 21: 341-48

1975   *The Books of Joel, Obadiah, Jonah, Nahum,Habakkuk, and
        Zephaniah.* CBC. Cambridge: Cambridge Press.

Weinfeld, M

1977   "Judge and Officer in Ancient Israel and in the Ancient Near
        East." *IOS* 7: 65-88.

Weiss, M.

1966   "The Origin of the Day of the Lord – Reconsidered." *HUCA* 37:
        29-60.

Wellhausen, J.

1892   *Skizzen und Vorarbeiten, V: Die kleinen Propheten..* Berlin:
        Reimer.

Wernberg-Møller, P.

1957   "Pronouns and Suffixes in the Scrolls and the Masoretic Text."
        JBL 76: 44-49.

Westerman, C.

1967   *Basic Forms of Prophetic Speech.* ET H. Clayton. Philadelphia:
        Westminster.

1984   *Genesis 1-11.* ET. Minneapolis: Augsburg.

1987   *Prophetische Heilsworte im Alten Testament.* Göttingen:
        Vandenhoeck & Ruprecht

Whitelam, K. W.

1984   "The Defence of David." *JSOT* 29: 61-87.

Whybray, R.N.

1974   *The Intellectual Tradition in the Old Testament.* BZAW 135.
        Berlin and New York: de Gruyter.

Widengren, G.

1984   "Yahweh's Gathering of the Dispersed." Pp. 227-245 in
        W.B.Barrick and J.R.Spencer (ed.) *In the Shelter of Elyon.
        Essays on Ancient Palestinian Life and Literature* in Honor of
        G.W. Ahlström. JSOTSup 31. Sheffield: JSOT Press.

Wifall, W.

1981   "The Foreign Nations: Israel's Nine Bows." *BES* 3: 113- 24.

Wilderberg, H.

1972/78/81 *Jesaja* I-II-III. BKAT 10, 10/1, 10/2. Neukirchen-Vluyn:
            Neukirchener Verlag.

Willi, T.

1972   *Die Chronik als Auslegung.* FRLANT 106. Götingen:
        Vandenhoeck & Ruprecht

Williams, D. L.

1961   *Zephaniah: A Re-Interpretation.* PhD diss. Duke   University.

1963   "The Date of Zephaniah." *JBL* 82: 77-88.

Williams, R. J.

1976   *Hebrew Syntax. An Outline.* (2nd ed.) Toronto: University of
        Toronto Press.

Wilson, R. R.

1973   "Form Critical Investigation of the Prophetic Literature. The
        Present Situation." *SBLSP* 1: 100-121.

1977   *Genealogy and History in the Biblical World.* New Haven and
        London: Yale University Press.

1980   *Prophecy and Society in Ancient Israel.* Philadelphia: Fortress.

Wintermute, O. S.

1983   "Apocalypse of Zephaniah." Pp. 497-515 in J. H.Charlesworth
        (ed.), *The Old Testament Pseudepigrapha.* Vol. I. Garden City,
        NY: Doubleday.

Wiseman, D. A.

1985   *Nebuchadrezzar and Babylon.* Gloucester: Oxford Univ. Press.

Wolfe, E.

1935   "The Editing of the Book of the Twelve." *ZAW* 53: 90-129.

Wolff, H. W.

1974   *Hosea.* Hermeneia, (ET BKAT 14/1,1965 ed.) Philadelphia:
        Fortress.

1975   *Joel and Amos.* Hermeneia, (ET BKAT 14/2,1969 ed.)
        Philadelphia: Fortress.

van der Woude, A. S.

1965   "Predikte Zephanja een Wereldgericht?" *NTT* 20: 16-21.

Whybray, R. N.

1981   *Isaiah 40-66.* NCB. Grand Rapids/London: Eerdmans/ Marshall, Morgan & Scott.

Zadok, R.

1978   "Phoenicians, Philistines, and Moabites in Mesopotamia." *BASOR* 230: 57-64.

Zalcman, L.

1986   "Ambiguity and Assonance at Zephaniah II 4." *VT* 36: 365-71.

Zakovitz, Y.

1983   "Story versus History." *Proceeding of the eighth World. Congress of Jewish Studies* (Aug. 1981). Bible Studies and Hebrew Language. Panel Sessions. Jerusalem: World Union of Jewish Studies/ Magnes.

Ziegler, J.

1944   "Studien zur Verwertung der Septuginta im Zwölfprophetenbuch." *ZAW NF* 19: 107-31.

1967 (ed.)   *Septuginta. vol XIII. Duodecim prophetae.* Göttingen: Vandenhoeck & Ruprecht.

Zimmerli, W.

1979   *Ezekiel* vol. 1. Hermeneia, (ET BKAT 13/1,1969 ed.) Philadelphia: Fortress.

1979 a   "Vom Prophetenwort zum Prophetenbuch." *TLZ* 104: 481-496.

1983   *Ezekiel* vol. 2. Hermeneia, (ET BKAT 13/2,1969 ed.) Philadelphia: Fortress.

HERAUSGEGEBEN IM AUFTRAG DER
KIRCHENVÄTER-KOMMISSION DER
PREUSSISCHEN AKADEMIE DER
WISSENSCHAFTEN

Athanasius Werke

In kartonierter Ausgabe sind folgende Lieferungen
(im Quartformat)
zum Preis von je DM 19,50 zu beziehen:

II. Band, 1. Teil
(1935–41 herausgegeben von Hans-Georg Opitz)

Lieferung 1 (De decretis Nicaenae synodi 1,5 – 40,24).
Seiten 1–40. Best.-Nr. 3-10-320635-3

Lieferung 2 (De decretis Nicaenae synodi 40,24 – Apologia de fuga
sua 18,3).
Seiten 41–80. Best.-Nr. 3-10-320635-4

Lieferung 3 (Apologia de fuga sua 18,3 – Apologia secunda 43,4).
Seiten 81–120. Best.-Nr. 3-10-320635-5

Lieferung 4 (Apologia secunda 43,5 – Apologia secunda 80,3).
Seiten 121–160. Best.-Nr. 3-10-320635-6

Walter de Gruyter Berlin · New York

Lieferung 5 (Apologia secunda 80,3 – Historia Arianorum 32,2)
Seiten 161–200. Best.-Nr. 3-10-320635-7

Lieferung 6 (Historia Arianorum 32,2 – De synodis 13,2)
Seiten 201–240. Best.-Nr. 3-10-320635-8

Lieferung 7 (De synodis 13,3 – Apologia ad Constantinum 3,4)
Seiten 241–280. Best.-Nr. 3-10-320635-9

III. Band, 1. Teil
Urkunden zur Geschichte des Arianischen Streites 318–328
(1934– 35 herausgegeben von Hans-Georg Opitz)

Lieferung 1 (Brief des Arius an Euseb von Nikomedien und dessen
Anwort – Das Schreiben der Synode von Antiochien 325)
Seiten 1–40. Best.-Nr. 3-10-320634-1

Lieferung 2 (Kaiser Konstantins Schreiben zur Einberufung der
nicänischen Synode – Brief Kaiser Konstantins an Arius und
Genossen)
Seiten 41–78. Best.-Nr. 3-10-320634-2

ISBN für alle noch greifbaren Lieferungen: 3-11-012986-8

Lexicon Athanasianum

Digessit et illustravit Guido Müller S. J.

Quart. VIII Seiten, 1664 Spalten. 1952. Halbleder DM 405,–
ISBN 3-11-003150-7

Walter de Gruyter Berlin · New York